LIVING ABROAD
PARIS

AURELIA D'ANDREA

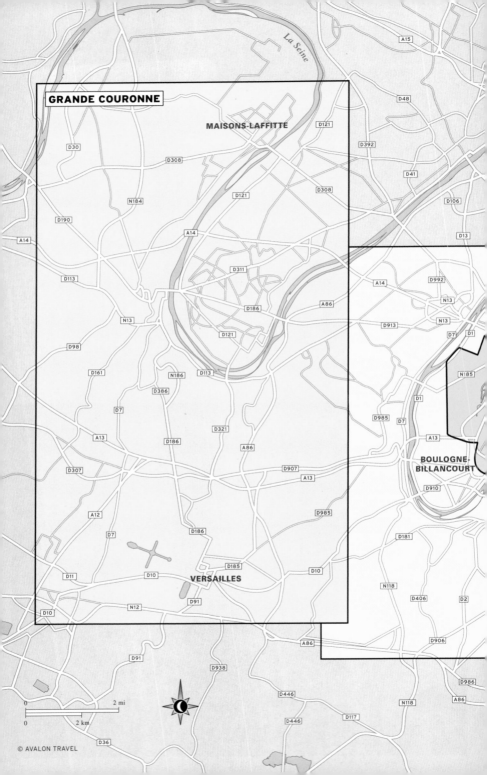

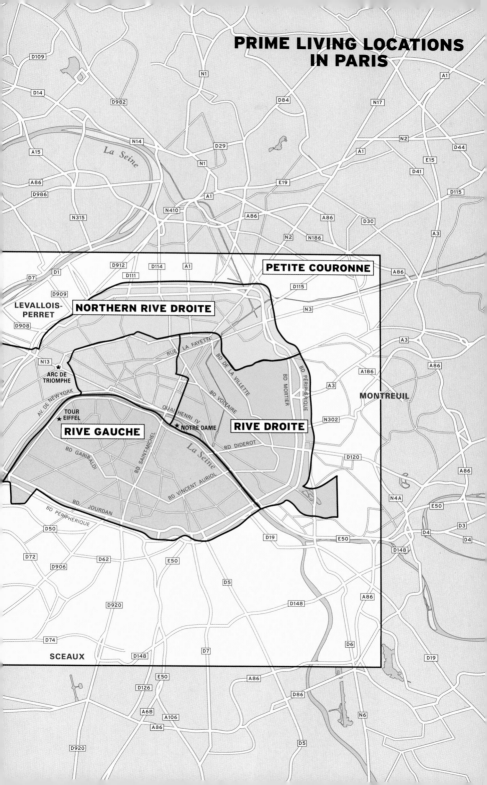

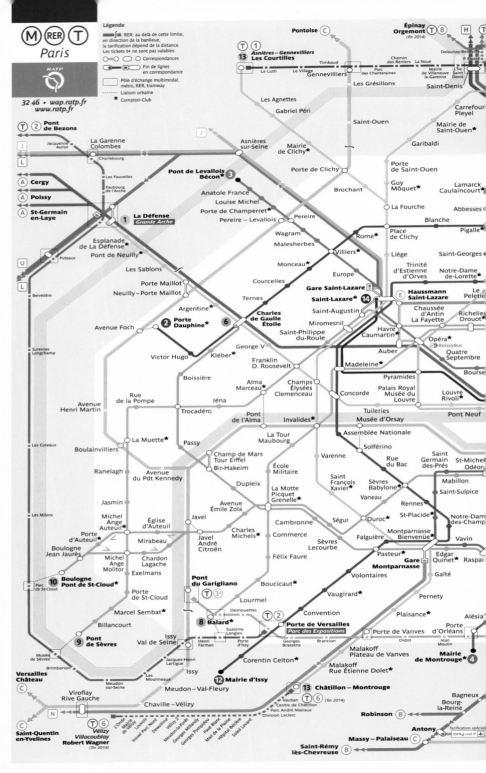

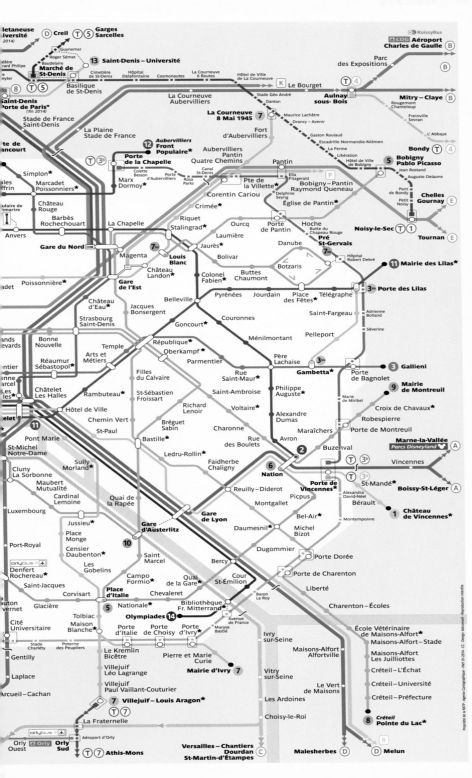

Contents

At Home in **Paris**

It was celebrated expatriate writer Gertrude Stein who wrote, "America is my country, and Paris is my hometown." After five years in the French capital, I've adopted Stein's perspective. Paris really *is* home—but it was a long, bumpy, and occasionally confusing settling-in process.

The qualities that drew me to *La Ville Lumière* are the same ones that have lured dreamers and romantics here for centuries: the unabashed beauty of the city's urban landscape; the sense of history that beckons from every cobbled corner; the respect bestowed upon artists, writers, and musicians, no matter their educational background; and the lively multiculturalism that gives Paris not only its energy, but its metaphorical and literal flavor.

But there's no beating around the bush: Paris isn't an easy city to get to know. Beyond the language barriers are endless cultural idiosyncrasies known to propel less sturdy types into apoplectic meltdowns. Customer service? Forget about it. Those two words haven't even entered the local lexicon yet! Don't have a *dossier?* Then don't even bother paying a visit to your insurance agent, doctor, tax office, *préfecture de police*, or banking institution. And we might as well address the weather: It's not great. And how about Parisian traffic? It's brutal at best, save Sundays, holidays, and the month of August. But what hometown doesn't have its share of minor detractors?

If you've got stamina and a willingness to learn some French, rich rewards are yours to be reaped in the French capital. The simplest acts

here can border on the sublime—something every flâneur knows a bit about. Merely stepping outside brings into focus a multilayered sensory pastiche: the changing sky that beguiled the Impressionist painters, meshed with the seductive aroma of baking bread, atop the distinctly French sound of a distant accordion playing a familiar melody. Closer to earth are the stately reminders of architectural history, recalling epochs of royalty and revolution, and the quintessential city snapshot of a silver-haired woman walking her dog down a picture-perfect Parisian street. This is everyday life in the French capital—if you choose to see it this way.

As you settle in and attune to the rhythms of life in this eclectic city of 2.3 million, you'll discover those charms—some of them bordering on cliché—that keep the expat community thriving. Discovering that perfect neighborhood café to call your own takes on a deeper meaning when the proprietor greets you with a *bisou* on each cheek and a simple *"ça va bien?"* This is the signal that you have arrived. You have found your home.

▶ WHAT I LOVE ABOUT PARIS

- Those first glorious, sunshiny days of spring, when Parisians can't help but smile as they bask in the sun at terrace cafés across the city.

- *Brocantes* (antiques markets), *marchés aux puces* (flea markets), and *vide-greniers* (rummage sales), where scoring second-hand treasures is a popular weekend sport.

- Mid-November, when Parisian streets get gussied up with twinkling lights, decorated trees, and *marchés de Noël* that usher in the holiday season.

- Mastering the myriad meanings of the beloved expression *"oh là là."*

- Watching strangers helping strangers lug suitcases, *poussettes* (baby strollers), and grocery bags up and down those seemingly endless Métro stairs.

- The outdoor produce market in autumn, when summer's ripe peaches and cherries give way to earthy mushrooms, fresh hazelnuts, and crisp Normandy apples.

- The way Velib' has transformed the city into a cyclist's . . . well, not paradise, exactly, but something close!

- Sharing conversation with friends over perfectly quaffable €3 glasses of côtes du rhône at a local *bar à vins*.

- Hopping an early morning TGV from Gare de Lyon beneath gray skies, and arriving in warm, sunny Nice just in time for a prix fixe lunch en plein air.

- The way my neighborhood *boulanger* reaches for the *tradition graine* baguette as soon as I walk in the door.

- The unabashed topless septuagenarians sunbathing at the public swimming pool.

- The simple act of filling my empty wine bottles from one of the enormous wood casks at my favorite *caviste*'s.

- Community gardens, where growing kale isn't just an activity for transplanted Californians.

WELCOME TO PARIS

INTRODUCTION

There are many ways to describe the French capital in the 21st century, but the most fitting might be "traditional." Parisians, like their provincial counterparts, cling to their customs with an unrivaled tenacity for reasons as mysterious to foreigners as they are to the locals themselves. Ask why something is the way it is, and you're very likely to be met with a rote "that's the way we've always done it, or *"C'est comme ça"*—that's just the way it is. Progress can wait, they seem to be saying. What's the big hurry?

Change tends to make the French feel a bit uneasy, so forward motion takes place at an *opération escargot* pace. Yet it's those same timeless, traditional values attract many foreigners to Paris in the first place.

The French have earned a global reputation for having mastered the art of living, and they are worthy of it. In a manner that elicits envious sighs around the world, they continue to show us that balancing work and home life isn't just an impossible dream. Here, the motto seems to be "work to live, and live *la belle vie.*" In Paris, this is particularly evident at lunchtime, when construction crews and suited-up office workers from Porte de Clichy to Place d'Italie file into homey brasseries to relish their perfectly quotidian three-course lunches—*with* wine. You also see it in the healthcare safety net that guarantees 90 percent of the population is covered by comprehensive medical insurance. And you feel it during the month of August, when the entire local

population evacuates en masse, heading to the seashore, mountains, and vast country-side, leaving the city to the tourists. In French, *relaxation* is definitely not a dirty word.

In so many ways, Parisians exemplify the good-life ideal, but certainly not in *every way*. In Paris and elsewhere throughout l'Hexagone, the bureaucrats in charge could stand to learn a thing or two from their New World brethren. Why, for example, does one need to lug a small forest-worth of paperwork to every appointment? Even the most mundane tasks—opening a bank account, getting your electricity connected—are often an exercise in frustration that will test the patience of the most laid-back émigré. Parisians are also a guarded bunch, with a very distinct line separating public and private life. Many an American expat laments never getting invited into a French friend or colleague's home. This is the norm, not the exception, and it's not worth getting offended about. Give your new French friend time—five or six years, perhaps—and you just might just find yourself on the receiving end of that most mysterious, coveted dinner invite.

What seems to matter most here is family, and that's reflected in the social system. Even before a child is born, the social benefits kick in: Parents-to-be are entitled to special grants for having a child through biological means or adoption. From 11 days' *congé de paternité* for new fathers (new moms get 16 weeks to bond with their offspring) and subsidized childcare for preschool-age kids, adding to the population is rewarded rather than punished. France consistently ranks at the top of the global charts when it comes to the scope and standard of healthcare, and a government-subsidized "family allowance" is given to all families with two or more children, regardless of income. Equally, housing benefits are doled out to all families with children under the age of 20. To the uninitiated, these social benefits might seem excessive, but voters consistently say "yes" to the established welfare system.

In spite of France's deeply held traditional values, there is a sense of transition in the air. Traditionally valued institutions such as marriage are waning, but civil unions—including same-sex unions—are on the rise. English is more widely spoken than ever before, and multiculturalism has reached unprecedented levels. Immigrants from North and West Africa, Eastern Europe, and Asia continue to alter the look, feel, and flavor of France, taking the edge off the homogeneity that has long defined the French ethos.

As private, traditional, family-oriented France slowly adapts to its changing landscape, it continues to attract an expatriate community that fortifies itself on those timeless, easily accessible attributes that have stood the test of time: dazzling architecture, towering snowcapped mountains and picture-perfect seashores, unrivaled cuisine, a fascinating history, and an unsurpassed quality of life. There's never been a time as prime as now for letting this seductive country make its everlasting imprint on the adventurous Francophile.

Lay of the Land

Metropolitan France, or what the locals refer to as La Métropole, is carved into 22 culturally distinct regions, including the island of Corsica. Each of these regions is further divided into 96 *départements,* and, in the manner of Russian dolls, each department contains *arrondissements, cantons,* and *communes.* For the day-to-day practical purposes of the expat, knowing your regions and departments is what matters most.

Departments are numbered alphabetically, beginning with Ain (01) and ending with Val d'Oise (95). Corsica is the one anomaly, with two departmental codes—2A and 2B, representing Corse du Sud and Haute Corse—standing in for 20. In the same way that all French phone numbers begin with a two-digit sequence that indicates the region, French license plates bear the two-digit departmental number at the end of the seven-character alphanumeric sequence. This indicates where that car was registered and makes for a great game during long-haul road trips.

Each department has its own elected officials and an administrative capital known as a *préfecture.* The *préfectures*—the places to go to register a birth, report a death, acquire a driver's or a marriage license, or register a new address—are responsible for carrying out national law on a local level. This system, first instituted under Napoléon I, allows local administrative hubs to function with a certain degree of autonomy within the centralized French government. *Préfectures* are also the primary public administration zone most foreign nationals get to know on an intimate level; expect to spend hours here waiting in line, having your dossier scrutinized, and ultimately registering your legal status as a temporary resident in France.

PARIS AND THE ARRONDISSEMENTS

The first thing a newcomer learns when arriving in Paris is that it is carved into 20 distinct regions called arrondissements, each an administrative unit with its own mayor and town hall. These districts spiral out clockwise from the geographic center of the city, ending in the northwestern quadrant. La Tour Eiffel and the Musée d'Orsay can be found in the 7th; the Louvre is just across the river in the 1st. Sacré-Coeur is in the 18th, and the Quartier Latin is in the 5th. Studying a map of the city—or, better still, picking up the very handy pocket-size Michelin map atlas of Paris—will facilitate your orientation within each of the various districts.

While there are legions of commuters who live outside the city and drive or take public transport in each day, many more Parisians live and work within a short distance of their homes. For those who do traverse the city for work, the efficient, relatively fast public transportation network means no point within the *périphérique* is more than 45 minutes away.

Rive Gauche and Rive Droite

Each of the two sides of Paris, *la rive gauche* and *la rive droite,* has its own special flavor, and locals feel passionate about the benefits of their side of the Seine. The Left Bank (Rive Gauche) is where you'll find the Sorbonne, the Eiffel Tower, the Catacombs, and those cafés and brasseries made famous by centuries of writers and philosophers: Brasserie Lipp, Les Deux Magots, Café de Flore. Today, it seems that more tourists

PARIS TODAY

Ask around and Parisians will tell you that change is afoot in the French capital. Superficially, the changes are visible in its urban topography; the skyline's familiar landmarks are interspersed with cranes and scaffolding as new construction expands urban housing options, shopping districts, and transportation. In neighborhoods on both sides of the Seine, American-style hamburger joints and skateboards squeeze in beside the ubiquitous cafés and *trotinettes* (kick scooters); and new laws are bridging the gap between the old guard and an evolving society in ways that are palpable on the streets. These subtle shifts take the form of a welcome mat for newcomers. Like the belle époque of more than a century ago, Paris is experiencing a renaissance that gives fertility to new ideas, allowing them to flourish in a way we've not seen here in decades.

In 2014, Paris elected its first female mayor, and she has inherited all of the exciting changes set into motion by outgoing mayor Bertrand Delanoë: improvement and expansion of the public transportation system, beautification projects, creating more bike-friendly streets, and making the arts accessible to all. With an annual budget of €1.4 billion, it's all do-able, and every Paris resident gets to reap the benefits.

than locals are pulling up chairs at those revered sidewalk terraces, but if you move just south of Saint-Germain-des-Prés, you'll discover homey neighborhoods and a safe, child-friendly atmosphere. The Left Bank feels more sedate, more residential, and slightly less *populaire,* or working-class crowded. If it weren't for the tourists, you might not know you were in Paris.

On the other side of the river, you'll find the Champs-Elysées, the Marais, the Bastille, and Sacré Coeur. The Right Bank (Rive Droite) feels hipper, younger, and edgier, particularly in up-and-coming neighborhoods like Belleville and La Villette. Paris's gay hub is here, in the old streets of the Marais; and just north of the Bastille, on rue de la Roquette and rue Oberkampf, you'll find the highest concentration of pierced and tattooed locals.

La Défense

Paris doesn't have a typical "downtown" in the way that, say, New York City has Lower Manhattan or San Francisco has its financial district. But what it does have is La Défense, a cluster of skyscrapers on the southwest edge of the city where more than 150,000 workers migrate seven days a week. As well as being home to high-tech corporations, government offices, and state-run businesses, La Défense also houses the region's largest shopping mall, Les Quatre Temps (open on Sundays), and a handful of residential complexes.

ÎLE-DE-FRANCE

The expansive cluster of cities, villages, and wide-open green spaces that form the greater Paris region is known collectively as Île-de-France. It is one of 22 regions that make up Metropolitan France, which nearly 12 million people—or roughly 20 percent of the country's population—call home. The Parisian suburbs—la *banlieue*—are varied and interesting, and attract people for different reasons: family-friendliness, affordability, and access to nature, among them. For this book, the *banlieues* are divided into two categories: the Petite Couronne, which sits just on the other side of Paris's *périphérique,* or ring road, and is accessible from Paris by Métro, and the Grande Couronne, which sits further afield from the city center and requires regional trains, buses, or personal transportation to reach.

Relocating to the Paris suburbs allows newcomers to ease into French living without the added strain of population density, extreme traffic, and pollution. The four inner suburbs featured—Sceaux, Boulogne-Billancourt, Levallois-Perret, and Montreuil—were chosen for their accessibility, quality of life, and eclectic, interesting personalities. Ditto for those distant suburbs of Maisons-Laffitte and Versailles. Each offers a similar climate to that of Paris, as well as access to shops, *boulangeries,* restaurants, and parks

POPULATION DENSITY

More than 85 percent of the population resides in urban areas, with Paris topping the charts as the most dense, accounting for a full 3.5 percent of the country's population. With approximately 65.2 million inhabitants, France is the fourth-largest country in Europe, falling behind Germany (81 million) and just ahead of the United Kingdom (63 million). In only a few major cities—Paris, Marseille, and Lyon in particular—and their suburbs will you feel the suffocating glut of overcrowding, and often during rush hour or during one of the many annual public festivals.

France differs from North America in that its suburbs, or *banlieues,* are often as densely populated as the urban centers they skirt. This is a symptom of poor urban planning; to meet the needs of a growing immigrant population in the '70s and '80s, enormous concrete housing developments called *cités* were hastily erected, intended as

© PAUL PRESCOTT

Parks, squares, and gardens elevate the standard of living in the French capital.

temporary dwellings to house a population that was expected to return "home" at some point. Some of these *banlieues,* most notably to the north of Paris but also on the periphery of Marseille, have been the sites of police clashes and rioting. In 2005, a notorious week of riots in the northern Paris suburbs, replete with burning cars and Molotov cocktails, made international headlines and drew attention to the racial issues that had previously been ignored by the mainstream media. Marginalized populations—often discontent second-generation immigrant youth caught between two cultures—are credited as the source of the suburban "problem," but humanizing the structure of suburban communities through better urban planning is seen by many as one possible solution.

Parisian streets, on the whole tend to feel lively and functional rather than clogged. Every arrondissement offers a similar range of amenities, including a post office, café, *boulangeries,* supermarkets of varying sizes, coin laundries, and other services. Most neighborhoods are also equipped with user-friendly squares or parks with benches, picnic tables, and children's play areas. Whatever the season and the weather conditions, you're bound to see silver-haired grandmothers out buying bread, fathers ushering their children to school, working women cycling to their offices, and people of all ages out walking their dogs.

After a long spell of declining birthrates, the numbers have charted a steady increase over the past decade, so much so that France now boasts the highest birthrates in Europe, with roughly two children per woman of childbearing age. This increase is due in large part to family-friendly social policies and financial incentives, though recent reforms in these areas by Socialist president François Hollande's government may end up bursting the population-growth bubble. Lifespans in France tend to be on par with the rest of Western Europe: 78.5 years for men, and 84.9 years for women—not bad, considering the number of cigarettes inhaled by the general population. (One quarter of all French women smoke, and a full third of men, but the e-cigarette and tobacco taxes are helping shrink those numbers.)

WEATHER

Like the rest of the country, Paris is a four-season city, but the winter you get in the French capital is definitely not the same one you'll experience in Nice. Winter in the Île-de-France region is guaranteed to be considerably colder and a few shades grayer than in its southern cousin.

The north of France holds the honor of that oft-touted temperate climate, with cool springtime temperatures, warm summers, cold and wet winters, and a mild autumn. You can also expect year-round rain showers—summer in the capital may mean dramatic thunderstorms and spirited downpours often followed by explosive bursts of sunshine and rainbows over the Seine.

Savvy Parisians carry an umbrella with them all year round, and keep their *impermeable* at the ready.

FLORA AND FAUNA

Before the industrial revolution in the mid-19th century, when forests and woodlands were razed to lay the foundation for industrial agriculture and an emerging city-centric way of life, France teemed with diverse wildlife and plant species. Now untamed wilderness has given way to structured farming, formal parks and gardens, and concentrated urbanism, but within the man-made order you can still find natural pockets of biodiversity.

Plane trees dominate the picturesque Parisian streetscape, lining up majestically along the avenue des Champs-Élysées and every other major thoroughfare in the French capital. But oak, beech, poplar, and chestnut trees are the scene-stealers throughout the rest of France. To get a good grasp of regional plant life, a visit to either the Bois de Vincennes or the Bois de Boulogne (or both) is recommended. These two forests straddle Paris to the east and west, respectively, and give nature-starved city dwellers a chance to commune with local species. Mushrooms, wild irises and violets, berries, and chestnuts are just a few of the flora-spotting possibilities.

Dozens of daily outdoor markets offer opportunities to experience the country's edible bounty without venturing outside of Paris. *Champignons*—from the legendary black truffles to woodsy morels and bright yellow girolles—grow wild in every corner of the country and are a point of culinary pride. But don't think about harvesting any you stumble upon without seeking permission. French law dictates that mushrooms belong to the owner of the land they grow on, so getting the all-clear before harvesting will help circumvent any unnecessary visits to the *préfecture de police.*

The most beloved crop grown in France is surely the grape, with dozens of varieties produced for both *la table* (table grapes) and for that bottle of *vin rouge* you'll be sipping with your next meal. Grape-growing has been part of the Parisian agriculture movement since the Gallo-Roman times, but fell out of favor in the 18th century when competition from across the country increased. However, a renaissance of sorts erupted in the 1990s, when three new vineyards were planted across the city—in the Parc de Belleville (20th), Parc de Bercy (12th), and on a sloping swath of terrain in the 19th known as the Vigne de la Butte-Bergeyre. Paris's oldest vines, the Vigne de Montmartre, still produce grapes that are transformed into wine, which makes its annual debut each autumn at the festival known as la Fête de Vendanges de Montmartre. When shopping for grapes at your local market, it's customary to sample the wares before buying; just ask for *un petit goût*—especially if the heavenly purple muscat grapes are on offer.

Apples are the most popular fruit consumed in France, and, like grapes, they are also transformed into beverages; in this case, cider and that potent elixir Calvados, both of which have been produced in Normandy for nearly 500 years.

Despite a long tradition of hunting in the countryside, wild boar and deer still manage to survive in French forests, but the wildlife you're most liable to stumble upon throughout the country is the ubiquitous *lapin.* Rabbits have proven to be particularly adaptable creatures, burrowing holes along the runways at Charles de Gaulle airport and proliferating with healthy vigor in urban parks from coast to coast. The farther you move away from urban centers, the more likely you are to spot the foxes, badgers, and martens that also make their home here.

Many species of birds make temporary pit stops in Paris along their migratory routes, and pheasant, partridge, and gulls linger as year-round residents. Although the bird-watching *observatoire* in the Bois de Vincennes was destroyed by fire in 2011, amateur ornithologists can spot kingfishers, woodpeckers, owls, robins, and other birds throughout the forested spaces.

Social Climate

President François Hollande surprised more than one compatriot recently when he proclaimed that the Eurozone economic crisis was effectively over. Despite his ambitious assertion, unemployment remains high (10.5 percent throughout France and 8.9 percent in Paris) and petty crime is on the rise.

Even though union membership is waning, the tradition of the nonviolent *grève* (strike) lives on in Paris and throughout the country. The masses—young and old, male and female—take to the streets several times a year to protest the rising retirement age and other threats to the French lifestyle. To the untrained eye, it sometimes looks as if France's social order is spiraling out of control, but it's really just par for the course in a country with a long history of social action and galvanizing for a cause.

Thankfully, it's not all doom and gloom in the land of the Gauls. In spite of a sluggish economy, free enterprise is finally catching on here, and newly relaxed tax laws for small businesses have spawned a wave of entrepreneurship. As foreign immigration continues to change the face of France, it is also reshaping ideas inside contemporary art, politics, and social policy, building onto an already impressive foundation. Could the collective chokehold on the past be slowly loosening its grip? Time will tell for certain, but all the elements are in place for a modern French renaissance.

When president Nicolas Sarkozy passed the torch to newly elected Socialist rival François Hollande in May of 2012, France's political agenda shifted from curbing crime and stemming the tide of immigration to developing affordable public housing and reducing public spending. It's too early yet to see what kind of legacy the 24th president of the Republic will leave, but between the current infidelity crisis and plummeting approval ratings, odds are good that Hollande will be a one-term president. The next presidential election takes place in France in 2017, and two contenders—François Fillon and Xavier Bertrand—have already announced their candidacy. Perhaps outgoing Paris mayor Bertrand Delanoë will throw his hat in the ring, as did one-time mayor and multi-term president Jacques Chirac.

PARIS AND FOREIGNERS

For centuries, foreigners by the boatload have flocked to France in search of political liberty, freedom of artistic expression, and unfettered adventure. Writers from Ernest Hemingway to Adam Gopnik have parlayed their fabled expatriate experience into a literary canon that continues to enthrall and entice new generations of immigrants, but it's easy to focus on the fantasy and forget the reality of moving abroad. In France, the success of your individual experience hinges greatly on whether or not you make an effort to assimilate quietly into the local culture.

Most French men and women will tell you that their country is a place where tolerance is exercised—if you play by the rules. Tune into the local frequency, and you'll feel the sense of "sameness" that permeates French society, from the standardized education model to the way public parks are designed to the uniform manner in which people dress. Uniqueness isn't a prized quality here in the same way it is in North America; here, upholding the status quo means maintaining order, and that's the way

© AURELIA D'ANDREA

Beautiful and tasty baguettes beckon from *boulangeries* in every arrondissement.

the French like it. This commitment to homogeneity is palpable on many levels, and it sometimes comes cloaked in the separation-of-church-and-state veil. In a notable example, the 2004 ban on headscarves in French public schools stirred heated public debate, prompting some pundits to call it an act of "neocolonialism."

Since the early 20th century, France has developed repatriation schemes loaded with seductive promises of all-expenses-paid travel and cash bonuses to those willing to commit to quitting the country for good. The truth is that most of these programs target specific populations—unskilled workers, illegal migrants, and other candidates perceived as taking advantage of a generous public welfare system—while immigrants from the United States and other developed nations aren't generally regarded as part of the "problem."

Politically, the French public view of the United States shifted with the departure of George W. Bush back in 2009 and the election of Barack Obama, who is held in high esteem among many Parisians. With the new American Democratic regime came an updated take on foreign policy, which heralded a newfound sense of solidarity between the two countries. Culturally, France has long resisted the Americanization effect inherent in globalization, but there's no denying the presence of Starbucks, "McDo's," and more recently, Burger King, which opened its first branch at Paris's Saint-Lazare train station in December 2013 and was so mobbed that a security team was called in. And American television programs, dubbed into French, of course, are popular here, including *The Simpsons, Friends,* and *House.*

Since the French are purveyors of public politesse, you probably won't sense it if they *aren't* in the mood to welcome foreigners. If you swagger into town with a purple mohawk, tattoos, and a face full of piercings, you're likely to garner some down-the-nose looks (this is especially true in Paris)—but for the most part, your new neighbors will keep their thoughts about your appearance to themselves. The key to ingratiating yourself with the locals is as easy as learning a few key words of the language and always remembering to say *"merci"* (thank you) and *"s'il vous plaît"* (please). If you adopt the unifying national characteristic of formal politeness, the French will warm up to you in no time and will help ease the shock of transitioning to a country that is, indeed, very different from your own.

A MATTER OF MANNERS

Snobby. Rude. Elitist. These are some of the nicer adjectives folks who haven't even visited France will casually bandy about to describe an entire nation and its inhabitants. Maybe even a person or two who *has* set foot on French soil will substantiate the pejorative name-calling with an anecdote, likely based on a hurried weekend trip to Paris armed with little more than a loud American accent. Give the country's 64 million people half a chance, however, and they'll show you that the negative stereotypes are unfounded.

What many mistake for snootiness is actually an ingrained social formality that, from an outsider's perspective, can feel very old-fashioned. People still greet their neighbors with a cordial *"Bonjour, madame,"* never forget to say *"Au revoir, monsieur"* at the pharmacy, wine shop, and post office, and always hold the door for the person behind them, regardless of gender. A certain attention to dress—nice shoes, for instance—is almost universal in French cities, and only recently has the casual sartorial approach (sweatpants, white gym shoes) inched its way into the fashion sphere. If you want to make a good first impression and feel like a local *tout de suite* (immediately), commit these phrases to memory and employ them liberally.

What to Say	What It Means
Bonjour, madame/monsieur.	Hello, madam/sir.

When to Say It: When entering any shop, restaurant, or business during the day.

Bonne journée, madame/monsieur.	Have a nice day, madam/sir.

When to Say It: When leaving any shop, restaurant, or business.

Bonsoir, Madame/Monsieur.	Good evening, madam/sir.

When to Say It: When greeting shopkeepers and others after dark.

Bon soirée, madame/monsieur.	Have a nice evening, madam/sir.

When to Say It: When saying goodbye to shopkeepers and others after dark.

Au revoir, madame/monsieur.	Goodbye, madam/sir.

When to Say It: When leaving any shop, restaurant, or business (often combined with *bonne journée* or *bonne soirée*).

S'il vous plaît	Please

When to Say It: Before approaching strangers for help, before placing your order at a restaurant, and when trying to get someone's attention.

Merci bien, madame/monsieur.	Thank you very much, madam/sir.

When to Say It: At the close of any transaction

Excusez-moi, s'il vous plait.	Pardon me, please.

When to Say It: When asking strangers for directions or other information.

Je suis désolé(e) de vous déranger, mais…	I'm so sorry to bother you, but…

When to Say It: When you want to lay it on thick in the gratitude department.

Merci, c'est très gentil.	Thank you, that's nice of you.

When to Say It: When you're especially grateful for something.

Je suis très désolé(e), mais je n'ai pas compris.	I'm so sorry, but I didn't understand that.

When to Say It: When you want to elicit sympathy and possibly an English-language response.

HISTORY, GOVERNMENT, AND ECONOMY

Wherever you are in France, you are never more than a few paces from some landmark that recalls the rich and illustrious France of antiquity. Majestic arches conjure memories of great battles and conquests, majestic cathedrals recall the legends of martyred saints, and those turreted châteaux stand as reminders of the rise and fall of the French monarchy. Signs of more recent history are evident at every turn, too. It's hard to step across a rough patch of road that reveals a cluster of cobblestones without remembering the student uprising of 1968 and its famous freedom cry, "Beneath the cobblestones, the beach!" Plaques commemorating World War II feature prominently in most provincial towns. In other words, finding a corner of the country that doesn't overflow with profound historical significance is next to impossible.

Tucked among the symbolic remnants of yore are emblems of modern France that hint at what sort of potential the future holds. In multicultural metropolises, thriving art scenes driven by the younger generations continue to propel France to the forefront of the avant-garde movement. Daring culinary experimentation is staking its claim amid the old-guard, *très* traditional *cuisine française* in cutting-edge restaurants, and

© AURELIA D'ANDREA

France continues to surprise the rest of the world with its realization of novel ideas that raise the quality of living, from public bicycle networks to public art.

Above all, the French themselves represent the spectacular convergence of old and new. Immigrants in traditional West African boubous and dashikis mingle at the markets with men in djellabas and women in hijabs, modern-day reminders of France's colonial past. A population in flux means more diversity: gay, straight, Muslim, Jewish, old, young, conservative, liberal. Active participation in politics, as evidenced by high voter turnout—the 2012 presidential election drew 80 percent of eligible voters, versus 57 percent in the U.S.—reflects an empowered population with a vested interest in creating a 21st-century society that meets the basic needs (and quite often the wants) of every citizen.

History

PREHISTORIC FRANCE

In 1940, four teenage boys spelunking in the bucolic town of Montignac, in the Dordogne Valley, accidentally discovered an ancient treasure trove that put France on the map as an important source of prehistoric riches. The cave paintings of Lascaux, dating back nearly 20,000 years to the upper Paleolithic period, feature larger-than-life-size renderings of horses, bison, bears, and other animals, hinting at the hunter-gatherer civilization's two preoccupations: sourcing an adequate food supply and avoiding becoming someone else's *déjeuner*.

Beyond providing clues about the eating habits of early humans, these vivid murals support the theory that Cro-Magnons were not just modern humankind's closest ancestors but possibly the earliest French aesthetes; decorative objets d'art ranging from primitive statuettes to more ornate pottery have been discovered in many French cave dwellings. Fashion before function? Indeed. Damage from human traffic prompted officials to close the Lascaux caves in the early 1960s, but an artificially re-created Lascaux II, complete with reproduction murals, opened 20 years later. It now welcomes thousands of visitors each year.

The early hunter-gatherer civilization that thrived throughout southern France, from the Dordogne to the Mediterranean, fed on the abundant plant and animal life that flourished along the waterways. Homo sapiens mastered the art of tool-making for hunting and ultimately evolved their tools to adapt to a more sedentary agricultural society that followed the hunter-gatherer epoch. It was during this period that *Canis familiaris*—hunter, protector, and friend—was domesticated in France, solidifying its status within the French family structure.

THE CELTS AND THE ROMANS

On the outskirts of the tiny seaside village of Carnac, in the far west region of Brittany, rows upon rows of lichen-covered stones rise up from the grassy fields, looking very much like an army of frozen soldiers standing sentinel over the windswept terrain. These Celtic megaliths, known as menhirs, date from the Neolithic period. They are not as well known as their celebrated neighbors at Stonehenge, but their historical significance in France is on par with that of their British counterparts. How the heavy stones, each of which weighs tons, got there is an unsolved mystery—but the historical consensus is that they were arranged here by the early Celts, who settled in France beginning as early as 8000 BC. Debate continues about the stones' original purpose, but it was most likely related to astrological forecasting or religious worship.

Mysterious origins aside, modern France has embraced its ancient Celtic roots through music festivals, literature, and efforts to keep the Breton language alive. Even the fictional character Obélix, from the beloved comic book series *Asterix,* is a menhir sculptor by trade, often depicted lugging around one of the giant stones on his enormous back.

Skip forward a few millennia from the Neolithic period to the 1st century BC, when Julius Caesar and his massive army of 65,000 men marched into France with an eye on transforming the country into the newest corner of the Roman empire. In 49 BC, after nine years of near-constant battle, their conquest was complete. Their legacy was sealed with the introduction of a newly revamped centralized political system, the introduction of the Latin language, and an art-and-architecture overhaul that gave France a distinctly Roman aesthetic. In the southern city of Nîmes, the "Rome of France," a well-preserved amphitheater hosts gladiator reenactments for enthralled crowds of tourists, and other relics—aqueducts, arches, forums—remind the contemporary population of the lasting influence of the Roman reign.

STORMING OF THE BASTILLE AND THE REVOLUTION

Long before a mob of angry men marched toward the Bastille prison on the infamous gray and dreary afternoon of July 14, 1789, discontent had been brewing among the French common classes. While the First Estate (nobility) and Second Estate (clergy) were essentially exempted from taxation, the Third Estate—the bulk of the population, made up of middle-class merchants and farming peasants—was left to pay the price for an overindulgent parade of kings, beginning with Louis XIV and ending with Louis XVI and his queen, Marie Antoinette.

As the country sank into bankruptcy, the commoners of the Third Estate felt the sting the sharpest. The price of bread, their primary food staple, had risen so high that the average family spent 80 percent of its income just to feed itself. Unemployment had reached frightening highs of nearly 50 percent, and the burden of heavy taxation showed no signs of ebbing. Meanwhile, Madame Deficit, as the spendthrift queen was nicknamed, continued to indulge in her excessive shopping habits while her king struggled to keep all the segments of French society in a state of relative calm.

When the alienated public learned that they would be denied voting privileges at a representational meeting of the Estates General, social discontent reached a fever pitch. Instead of sulking, the people formed a new national assembly and, when the king saw he had no hope of wielding his absolute power against the growing legions of disgruntled citizens, he struck a deal: We'll make it formal, he suggested, with a newly established National Assembly, wherein each Estate will have equal representation. Sovereignty of the people in, absolute monarchy out. This was the first revolutionary act. The storming of the part-prison, part-munitions warehouse known as the Bastille was next.

While the events of July 14 were more symbolic than truly revolutionary—there were only seven prisoners being held at the Bastille at the time, and the amount of arms collected was negligible—it is recognized as such because it returned power to the people after a long spell of rather tyrannical rule. Not long afterward, King Louis XVI relinquished his governing power, though he was left with the honorary title of King of the French. He held this new post until being tried and convicted of treason, then guillotined in front of a public audience in Paris's Place de la Révolution (now Place de la Concorde) in January 1793. His wife of 23 years, the reviled Marie Antoinette, was beheaded on the same spot nine months later.

Less than a month after the Bastille drama unfolded, a 17-point blueprint for a new constitution was drafted. The Declaration of the Rights of Man—a pastiche of ideas borrowed from the Declaration of Independence and the English Bill of Rights—proclaimed that the law exists to support and carry out the idea that every French citizen is born equal and with inalienable rights; that man is entitled to freedom of speech and freedom of religion; and that he is innocent until proven guilty. The 10-year revolutionary period was marked by brief changes in control, juggled in turns by the middle-class liberals, the radical revolutionaries, and the counterrevolutionaries whose champion, Napoléon Bonaparte, helped cement France's future as a global powerhouse. On September 21, 1792, the French royalty was abolished and, amid much celebration by the people, the First Republic, founded on the principles of *liberté, égalité,* and *fraternité,* was born.

NAPOLÉON BONAPARTE AND THE FIRST REPUBLIC

Even before he became emperor of France, in 1804, Napoléon Bonaparte reigned as a well-respected military leader in the French Revolution whose ambition for power matched his skill at war. Throughout his adventurous life, he earned a reputation as both a misogynist and a genius, but there's no debating the petite corporal's legacy as a reformer in the areas of education, religion, and government.

Before the monarchy was dissolved, education was a privilege extended primarily to the wealthy. Napoléon believed that developing a strong, unified population began with education—for boys in particular—and under his leadership, a uniform system of post-elementary schools called *lycées* was established. Through these education hubs, which most closely resemble North American high schools, a unified body of thought could be transmitted to generations of moldable minds. This is still the basis for today's highly centralized French public school system, which continues to preach loyalty to the republic and dictates which path a young student will follow later in life.

Subverting the dominant role of the Catholic church became an obsession for Napoléon I, who kickstarted this project at his coronation, which was completely devoid of any religious pomp and circumstance. He bucked tradition by denying Pope Pius VII the honor of crowning him the new emperor, but he wasn't anti-church. Napoléon saw the power that religion wielded in the lives of French citizens, and he merely wanted to seize control of that. With the signing of the Concordat, Napoléon got his wish, gaining the right to choose bishops and control land once belonging to the church.

Not long after being crowned emperor, Napoléon made one major restructuring move: The constitution, known as the Rights of Man, was transformed into the Napoleonic Code. For some, this presented a distinct advantage: Special privileges for the wealthy were effectively abolished, which was good for the 99 percent of the population that fell into the common class. Religious freedom was also guaranteed, as was the right to a trial before being sentenced for a crime. At the same time, the changes weakened status for others. Women and children were essentially deemed the property of their husbands and fathers, and women were stripped of the right to buy or sell property. The freedom of the press suffered, too, with Napoléon famously proclaiming that "if the press is not controlled, I shall not remain in power three days." But it's probably safe to say that Napoléon's good deeds outweighed the bad. The public works projects he commissioned—wide boulevards, shipping canals, and the famous Arc de Triomphe—are the modern-day symbolic reminders of the diminutive leader's vision of France.

FIRST AND SECOND WORLD WARS

When Archduke Franz Ferdinand was shot and killed by a Serbian assassin in Sarajevo on June 28, 1914, the Austro-Hungarian government didn't waste any time before declaring war on Serbia. Soon, one country after another was at war with its enemy, but World War I wasn't *officially* called until Austria's strongest ally, Germany, declared war on Russia.

As a Serbian ally, France was pulled into the fray, but there was no widespread public support for this war. Speaking on behalf of the pacifist community, French Socialist Party leader and lefty newspaper publisher Jean Jaurès called for peace, but he was silenced by a bullet fired by an overzealous pro-war French nationalist on July 31, just a month after war was declared. Four years later, on November 11, 1918, the signing of an armistice agreement put an end to the long, catastrophic conflict.

The final tally of France's dead reached nearly 1.4 million, and the number of wounded a staggering three million. Birthrates dropped, the national debt exploded, and a third French Republic was declared. It took years for France to recover, and when it did, it didn't get much of a breather before being thrust back into the cold embrace of another devastating world war.

No event in modern history has had as profound an effect on the French national psyche as World War II, especially in the way it has shaped French identity and solidified the necessity of social unity. In 1939, after Germany invaded Poland, France (a Polish ally) and Great Britain jointly declared war on Germany. By 1940, France had surrendered to the Germans, who began a humiliating occupation of France lasting four years.

On October 24, 1940, after the French had already surrendered to German forces, a new regime took control of the country, collaborating with the Nazis but still retaining some small level of autonomy. The Vichy Government, led by Marshall Philippe Pétain, was merely a French extension of the Nazi establishment, and the effects of this collaboration spawned its own post-traumatic stress disorder: the Vichy Syndrome.

Through the hardship of occupation and war, a sense of solidarity grew among the greater French community. Thousands of men and women joined together to form the French Resistance, and volunteer armies from North and West Africa sprang up to fight alongside the French army. Mini-armies began to sprout, too. The most significant of these independent brigades were the maquis, small groups of men and women who worked in concert with the resistance movement against German forces. Rather than be conscripted into the German workforce, they took to the hills with their guns and ammunition, battling long and hard in their signature Basque berets.

In 1944—the same year French women earned the right to vote—the Allied Forces liberated France from Germany's iron grip. After a triumphant promenade down the Champs-Élysées, General Charles de Gaulle addressed his fellow citizens in a celebrated speech thanking them for their concerted efforts, closing with a fervent *"Vive la France!"*

The memory of occupation is never far from the modern French person's consciousness, yet there isn't a palpable sense of melancholy rooted in those memories either. *C'est la vie,* say the French, but let us not forget completely *les années noires.*

MODERN FRANCE

The Fourth Republic sprung up on the heels of World War II, with de Gaulle, France's trusted and revered wartime chief, serving a brief stint as head of the provisional postwar government. He stepped down not long after his appointment but was elected president of France more than 10 years later, in 1958, marking the beginning of the fifth and current republic.

After a successful first term, he was reelected to the country's top post, which he served until retiring from politics in 1968, when his viewpoints were falling out of favor with the young postwar generation. The end of his political career was punctuated by a wave of social unrest throughout France, beginning at the universities and ending at the heart of the industrial sector: the factory.

In the spring of 1968, what started as a couple of small student protests against comingling of the sexes in student housing at the University of Nanterre and Paris's Sorbonne quickly morphed into something out of a fictional police drama: students and armed riot police going toe-to-toe on the streets; hundreds of young men and women being thrown to the ground and arrested; tear gas shot from cannons, the air so thick with haze that it felt like a battlefield in winter. Three days later, on May 6, more than 20,000 students, professors, and supporters marched through the streets of the capital to call attention to an overzealous police response to a simple, nonviolent campus protest—and again were met with baton-wielding riot police, tear gas, and aggressive arrests.

The great *manifestations* (political demonstrations) lasted for days, virtually halting all normal activity in Paris and its close suburbs. Brick throwing and Molotov cocktail tossing brought the city to a standstill. Students, borrowing ideas from anarchist ideology and using language tinged with Marxist rhetoric, demanded social change to benefit the people rather than the powers in charge.

Events took a turn for the worse when a 17-year-old high school student was killed by riot police in Paris's Latin Quarter on June 10; reverberations were felt acutely during the following weeks. Simultaneously, discontent that had been percolating in France's automobile factories reached a boiling point, prompting a frustrated labor force to engage in both sit-ins and walkouts. Workers at Renault, Citroën, and Peugeot voiced their own demands for a set minimum wage, salary increases, and reduced work hours. At one Peugeot factory, two workers were killed by police, prompting another wave of dissatisfaction to ripple through the country. Walkouts at banks, public transportation centers, department stores, and even hospitals paralyzed France. An estimated 10 million *grévists* (strikers) from Toulouse to Saint-Nazaire took to the streets in protest throughout May 1968, and made their thoughts about France's old-school, outdated political direction known in their cry: "Adieu, de Gaulle!"

The government reacted with tough-guy posturing, threatening an official state of emergency if things didn't simmer down. They finally did. The government met the

© AURELIA D'ANDREA

Demonstrations can (and do) happen all year in Paris.

demands of the automobile unions, offering a shorter work week, increased salaries, and an increased minimum wage, which the unions accepted, and students returned to their university lecture halls. Yet as daily life settled back into a state of normalcy, the days were numbered for de Gaulle's government. The aftereffects on French society were still being registered decades later, with political analysts referring to the period as "a revolution" with many of the same attributes of revolutions past. A body of rebel artwork—graffiti, protest posters—produced during the era survives in archival galleries as testament to the social upheaval.

In the decades that followed, France underwent several presidential shifts: Georges Pompidou ('69-'74), Valéry Giscard-d'Estaing ('74-'81), socialist François Mitterrand ('81-'95), and former prime minister and Paris mayor Jacques Chirac ('95-'07). Mitterrand's presidency marked the first time a leader on the political left had taken that office, and during his tenure he abolished the death penalty and initiated a moratorium on nuclear testing.

Chirac, who founded the center-right RPR (Rally for the Republic) party, led France with a more conservative vision, but he will probably always be remembered in North America for taking an active stand against the U.S. invasion of Iraq. (Remember "Freedom Fries?") The French supported his opposition to the war, but his domestic policies left much to be desired among French voters, who ranked him the least popular president of the Fifth Republic in 2007.

Chirac's successor, former minister of the interior Nicolas Sarkozy, was voted in as the sixth president of the Fifth Republic on May 7, 2007. The son of a Greek-Jewish mother and a French-Hungarian father, the former lawyer promised to give France a good kick in the pants to bolster the economy, get tough on immigration, and reform the social welfare system. Part of his reform agenda included tightening access to foreign student visas, which he saw as an easy ticket for potential ne'er-do-wells to obtain residency status. At the end of his first and final term, faced with dismal popularity figures and an underperforming economy, Sarkozy was still able to count a handful of accomplishments, including passing a referendum that whittled down presidential term limits from a limitless quantity to two, easing taxation to encourage entrepreneurship, and extending the imposed 35-hour workweek to allow workers to put in as many as 48 hours each week without employers having to pay overtime benefits.

François Hollande, a member of the Parti Socialiste, was sworn in as the 24th president of the Republic on May 15, 2012. Two years into his first term, Holland has heard the deafening roar of enthusiasm that ushered him into the Palais de l'Élysée dwindle to a chirp, with just 19 percent of the population who voted for him happy with his performance after his first year in office. During his campaign, Hollande promised to bring "normalcy" to the country's highest post after too many years of President Bling-Bling's arrogance and flash, and there's still time. Despite the tabloid drama plaguing him midway through his first term, he is making strides to cut public spending and trim social benefits for the wealthiest French populations; time will tell if he'll yank the country out of its financial crisis before the 2017 elections.

Government

As a representative democracy, the Republic of France is ruled by a president who is voted in by the public and eligible for a maximum of two five-year terms (reduced from seven in 2000). The president appoints a prime minister and a cabinet to help run the show, but there's no question who holds the top spot—and with it the larger burden of responsibility. In addition to ensuring that the constitution is upheld, the president enacts French laws, oversees the military, and has the ability to dissolve the French parliament. The president must also solicit the signature of his prime minister for every official document he signs, with the exception of dissolving parliament.

On the legislative end, parliament is made up of a 577-member lower house called the National Assembly, whose representatives, called deputies, are elected directly by the public to five-year terms. The 321-member upper parliament, or senate, is voted in by an electoral college representing each of the 92 departments, overseas territories, and French citizens living abroad; each member serves six-year terms. Together, the two houses meet for nine-month sessions that begin in October and end in June, voting on issues as varied and contentious as gay marriage (which finally received a *"oui"* vote in May 2013) and voluntary euthanasia (which still hasn't passed).

France has a multiparty system that spans the spectrum from the extreme right to the extreme left, but a few parties dominate, including Hollande's Parti Socialiste and Sarkozy's UMP (Union pour un Mouvement Populaire). The far-right Front National, and Communists and Greens pick up the remaining seats in parliament. Regional elections are held every four years, departmental representatives and city council members are elected every six, and elections are always held on Sundays, which helps ensure a solid voter turnout. The French take the voting process quite seriously, and the rules

© AURELIA D'ANDREA

You might see Francois Hollande's scooter zipping out of the presidential palace.

governing campaign advertising and the prognostication of results on the day of the election are tightly controlled.

If no candidate wins more than 50 percent of the vote in a presidential election, a runoff election is held. The 2012 election pitted Socialist Party candidate François Hollande against the UMP's Sarkozy, with Hollande ultimately winning with 51.06 percent of the vote.

Though President Hollande will be eligible for re-election in 2017, his future looks a little iffy. In late 2013, polls put his approval rating at an all-time low of 15 percent, though the subsequent revelation by a French tabloid magazine that the president was having an illicit affair actually worked to improve his popularity ratings, which crept up to 31 percent in January 2014. While infidelity seems of little concern to the public, what does matter is whether or not the president can stem the ebbing tide of unemployment and realize the creation of new jobs.

PARIS POLITICS

Politically, Paris marches to the beat of its own oft-confusing drummer. It is a city with not just a revered and effective mayor, but 20 sub-mayors, each of whom govern their own mini villages known as *arrondissements* from their headquarters known as the office of the *mairie*. These sub-mayors, in turn, govern their districts with the help of *conseillers* or councilors elected by their arrondissement's constituents. Together, they decided which mayoral candidate would succeed Bertrand Delanoë, Paris's first openly gay leader, who stepped down in March 2014 to pursue other interests rather than run for a third term. Parti Socialiste member Anne Hidalgo was sworn in on April 5, 2014. Municipal officials can serve multiple six-year terms, and always undergo two rounds of voting before the winning candidate is called. To take the mayoral seat, the candidate must obtain absolute majority vote in both rounds. In the rare instance that a candidate doesn't earn more than 50 percent of the vote on the second round, a third voting round will be instituted.

Economy

After World War II, France boomeranged back into shape with unrivaled optimism and vitality. Those three fruitful decades even earned a special moniker: les Trente Glorieuses, or the Glorious Thirty. Under de Gaulle's leadership, an initial five-year

LADIES FIRST

When beloved mayor Bertrand Delanoë announced that he wouldn't run for a third term, the collective sigh of disappointment could be heard from Porte Maillot all the way to Porte de Montreuil. Since 2001, the Parti Socialist member has upped Paris's cool quotient with countless maverick initiatives, from Paris Plages to Velib'. He also earned the respect of his constituents for his progressive agenda and sense of humor–a true rarity among French politicians. Yet the news of Delanoë's impending departure was tempered by the exciting news that his replacement would be a woman–a first for the city of Paris.

Monsieur le Mayor himself supported fellow Socialist Anne Hidalgo, who had served as his deputy mayor since he took office in 2001. Hidalgo's rival was the media-savvy Nathalie Kosciusko-Morizet, a member of the center-right UMP and a former environmental minister under the Sarkozy administration, who suggested that Paris adopt a seven-days-a-week commerce economy. Hidalgo was against the open-on-Sundays idea, saying that everyone deserves a day off of work.

On April 5, 2014, Hidalgo was sworn into office as Paris' first female Mayor. Like Delanoë, her political focus is on making Paris a more livable city. Plans include pedestrianizing more streets, adding to the city's tree population, and creating more affordable housing.

plan was instituted, launching public-works projects and creating a climate ripe for new industries. French factories were overhauled, churning out products for a postwar population that skyrocketed to numbers not seen for more than 100 years. This baby boom sparked a cycle of production and consumption that helped keep the economy moving. New motorways were built to keep up with the number of new cars on the roads, and by 1960, the French owned more automobiles than refrigerators.

The big shift from rural to urban that took place in the 1960s and '70s translated to overcrowding in the major cities. To meet the needs of this expanding population, giant housing developments mushroomed outside the clogged metropolises, and the *banlieue* was born. The sense of France in transition was palpable from Paris to Perpignan.

With the establishment of the European Union and the introduction of a single currency, trade barriers were torn down and competition increased, generating new revenue streams that flowed throughout Europe. But the latest global economic crisis has done a lot to destabilize the French economy and the faith of the French people with regard to their future economic security. The Sarkozy government passed a number of stimulus packages, but France under Hollande still faces high unemployment (10.5 percent) and public debt (for which the government is trying to compensate by curtailing politicians' wine-fueled, expenses-paid lunches).

Among the most critical issues facing French voters today is coming to terms with the idea that the social safety net that has supported them for so long may sink under its own weight. Throughout September 2010, *grévists* again took to the streets of cities and towns throughout France to protest Sarkozy's proposed revamp of the country's cushy pension plan. Without a workforce to pay for the system, said Sarkozy, there will be no money left in the coffers for retirees to pull from. The public didn't buy it, and over the course of several weeks, students, unionists, and office workers alike waved banners of protest in the streets, halting commuter traffic, disrupting fuel deliveries,

© AURELIA D'ANDREA

Your local office of the *mairie* is guaranteed to become a frequent haunt.

and causing delays at airports and train stations nationwide. On October 23, 2010, much to the public's dismay, parliament passed Sarkozy's pension reform bill, raising the minimum retirement age to 62 and the full pension age to 67.

François Hollande has made a few ripples in the political pool since taking office, mostly in the area of taxation; during his presidential campaign he earned notoriety for proposing 75 percent taxation on Paris's wealthiest citizens. Those whose feathers were most visibly ruffled by the idea included actor Gérard Depardieu, who vowed to quit France for good if this promise was made real. It wasn't long before the stocky thespian was offered Russian citizenship directly from Vladimir Putin, who delivered on his proposal. (Depardieu currently holds a Russian passport even though he's chosen to live in Belgium.) But reaction to the tax increase hasn't been so dramatic across the board. Everyday citizens understand that putting the tax burden on the rich to support needier citizens is a core Socialist value, and one of the reasons the disenfranchised masses elected Hollande in the first place. His promises to increase corporate taxes, lower the retirement age for those who've paid taxes for a minimum of 41 years, and introduce thousands of new jobs into the French fold are still a work in progress.

PEOPLE AND CULTURE

France is fertile ground for cultural stereotyping. Those tenacious mental renderings of a beret-clad, baguette-hugging, bicycle-riding population have been etched into our collective unconscious via film, fashion magazines, and yes, even holiday snapshots. More than anything, perhaps, the French are known 'round the world for their way of life, which focuses on maximizing sensual pleasures. The truth is, they do love their wining, dining, and song, but surprisingly, not a whole lot more than their European neighbors. Over the years, the French have abandoned some of their legendary habits in favor of newer, healthier ones (*le jogging*, anyone?).

Per capita wine consumption has plummeted by more than 50 percent since 1970, when the average Jacques quaffed 103.6 liters all on his own each year. The French do guzzle more booze than the Poles, the Dutch, or even tipplers in the UK, but Jacques still throws back fewer drinks than his Irish counterpart. The amount of bread consumed per day by the French has steadily dwindled over the last century (though you'd hardly know it from the number of *boulangeries*), but the amount of yogurt, brie, and crème fraîche consumed has nearly doubled since the 1970s. Stroll down the dairy aisle at the nearest *hypermarché,* and you'll get a solid sense of how important the role of dairy is in the French diet. But an entire culture can't be distilled into a food-and-wine caricature.

© AURELIA D'ANDREA

Like the country they inhabit, the French are complex, idiosyncratic, and a tad mysterious, which makes them all the more interesting. "French" has come to mean something different in the 21st century than in previous eras: It now means Algerian, Tunisian, Malian, Moroccan, Senegalese, and even American. Each of these immigrant populations has left its mark on the established culture, producing something of a multicultural patchwork that gives France its special flavor.

Ethnicity and Class

One of the ideas propelling the French Revolution was that the social playing field could—and should—be leveled. Members of the proletariat, mostly working-class farmers and peasants, were fed up with being taxed while their upper-class comrades were exempt, and the clergy had had enough of the royals' having access to all the wealth. These issues germinated and sprouted into a rebellion, and subsequently the class system was abolished as members of the National Assembly renounced their class privileges.

No longer would the middle and lower classes be held liable for taxes that they could ill afford while the nobility and clergy skirted by without paying a centime. The revolution gave birth to a new constitution, the cornerstone of which was the Declaration of the Rights of Man. This critical rulebook defined the future of the Republic, setting forth the novel idea that all men are created equal. In subsequent decades, the leadership grappled with the inconsistencies of that basic assertion, particularly in light of the fact that slave ownership was alive and well in the French colonies and the role of women remained subordinate to that of men. The declaration has been rewritten over the years (and renamed the Constitution), but its fundamental assertion remains a critical component of what it means to be French.

Today, the issue of national identity remains a hot topic throughout France, especially around election time. The right-wing, anti-immigrant political party, Front National (FN) is led by Marine Le Pen. Le Pen inherited her father and FN founder Jean-Marie's passion for a very, well, "French" version of France, and she has put the issue at the front and center of her party's platform ever since assuming leadership in 2011. The FN promulgates the idea that a more homogenous France can be restored with measures that include expulsion of certain populations—primarily Arab Muslims—and shoring up immigration laws to prevent what the party believes to be unbridled waves of unworthy immigrants. The Front National motto "France for the French!" says it all.

In , ethnicity and class aren't dinner-table conversation topics, but they are a palpable component of life in the capital. The arrondissement in which you live—and, more specifically, the Métro stop you're closest to—give others a preliminary indication of your socioeconomic status and hint at your level of hipness. Tell someone, for example, that you live near Métro stop Victor Hugo in the 16th, and they might assume you're a work transfer from a multinational pharmaceutical company and your children attend private school. Mention you live in Belleville, however, and you earn a bit of street cred, possibly coupled with the question, "So, do you work in the arts?" Generally, where you live doesn't make or break your ability to integrate. Just don't expect your new friends from Maisons-Laffitte to be too excited about meeting up at your neighborhood café in the outer reaches of the 20th. They'll likely prefer the perceived sense of safety that comes with a night out in Saint-Germain-des-Prés or the Marais.

Customs and Etiquette

One of the first things you'll notice about living in Paris is the formal *politesse* that pervades daily interactions. Neighbors greet each other with a cordial *bonjour* and *au revoir*, sales clerks will always refer to you as *madame, mademoiselle,* or *monsieur,* and most of the time, drivers will actually slow their Citroëns and Renaults down to a stop at crosswalks for pedestrians—which may or may not be a direct result of the Ministry of Transportation's efforts to establish a Day of Courtesy. More important than mimicking the French version of Emily Post is to simply treat everyone you encounter with respect. Do as the locals do and be liberal with your pleases and thank-yous. When boarding the Métro or bus, step aside from the doorway to allow others to exit first. Offer your seat to the elderly, pregnant women, and parents juggling one or more children. The warm smile and gratitude you'll get in return are worth it, and you'll feel good about contributing to the social order.

LINE JUMPING

One annoying exception to the standard trend toward politeness is line jumping. It happens each and every day at Disneyland Paris, the local post office, and *hypermarchés:* A silver-haired granny or twentysomething hipster will glide in ahead of you, occasionally with cash in hand to announce the guaranteed swiftness of the impending transaction, with nary a glance in your direction, lest eye contact be made and guilt established. Fussing about this is rarely worth the effort, though many expats dare to speak up once they've mastered the language, and find the act of defending one's territory to be a confidence builder!

PDAS (PUBLIC DISPLAYS OF ANGER)

The French are quirky, so it follows they would have quirky customs, many of which foreigners find simultaneously befuddling and charming. The tradition of the *bisou*—kissing on each cheek as a form of greeting—is so ingrained that kids in diapers are practically pros by the time they reach the Terrible Twos. The French are not entirely immune to the urge to flip out in horn-honking traffic—as you'll discover any day during rush hour in Paris—but road rage isn't practiced here the way it is in other countries. If you want to react in a manner befitting the locals, you'll learn to puff out your cheeks, throw up your hands, and say *"Oh la la la la"* like the rest, while leaving the shouting and aggressive driving maneuvers to the uncivilized world.

TIPPING

Many North Americans are pleased to discover that tipping is not mandatory or even expected in France. Restaurant work is a profession with a modicum of prestige attached to it, and because waitstaff earn a living wage and are entitled to full benefits, they aren't motivated to perform any better in expectation of a monetary

FRENCH KISSING FOR BEGINNERS

Everyone's heard of a French kiss, but the voracious tongues-and-all method isn't the standardized variety carried out in *la belle France*. From the moment you step off the plane or alight from your train, you'll see what French kissing is really all about (and, perhaps, what it *isn't* about: tongues). The art of the *bisou* begins with identifying who's on the receiving end: If you're of the female persuasion, you'll dole out kisses to everyone. Ditto if you're a child. (They start 'em young here.) Men are typically exempted from kissing other men, unless they're family or extremely close friends. Step two is all about the action: Lean in toward your intended with your right cheek, allowing your respective cheeks to touch gently and momentarily while you make a kissing sound. Step three involves pulling back slightly and repeating the gesture on the left cheek. One or both hands can rest gently on the kissee's shoulders or an arm, or simply keep your mitts to yourself. In some parts of France, this act can be repeated for a total of four kisses; let the Frenchie take the lead if you're uncertain about local protocol. So what about that other French kiss practiced the world over? Yes, they do it in France, too, but here they call it *un bisou avec la langue*—a kiss with the tongue.

bonus. However, at cafés, it's customary to leave any small coins floating around in your pocket on the table or counter, and many diners—if they feel like it—will leave a euro or two after a restaurant or brasserie meal. These little acts of generosity are entirely voluntary, and you shouldn't feel obligated to leave anything beyond what's tallied up on your *addition*.

INVITATION ETIQUETTE

Here are a few rules of thumb to commit to memory, just in case you are lucky enough to earn a coveted invitation to a French person's home. Many expats report never having received a party invitation, let alone a dinner invite, even after years of working with someone or decades of daily chats with the next-door neighbor. This is less about you and more about the separation of public and private life—a cultural idiosyncrasy that is sacrosanct to the French. But when that elusive invitation comes, arrive at your host's home 15 minutes late, bring flowers instead of wine (they've already selected the wine to drink that evening), and don't be afraid of "awkward" silences; think of them as food-enjoyment pauses instead.

Food

Some tourists come to France almost exclusively for the food, and no wonder: They really know what they're doing here when it comes to creating culinary magic. Standard, everyday French fare tends to fall into the "honest" category—what you see is what you get, with the unique selling point of being exceptionally well prepared and made with good-quality ingredients. Fancy, no; delicious, yes. From humble brasseries to revered Michelin-starred restaurants, menus tend to reflect seasonal produce while adhering to a perennial list of *plats principals* (main courses): *poulet rôti* (roast chicken), *steak frites* (steak and french fries), *steak tartare* (raw minced beef, sometimes mixed with egg and onion), *porc rôti* (pork roast), *salade de chèvre chaud* (green salad with slices of warm goat cheese), and a variety of pasta dishes.

A lot of the meats served in France fall into categories many North Americans would file under politically incorrect. If eating baby animals is your thing, you're going to love dining in France. Veal is a popular meat, as is lamb. Foie gras, which translates as "fatty liver," is a specialty of the southwestern region; it's created by forcing a tube down a duck's or a goose's throat and pumping in an excessive quantity of grain. This causes the liver to inflate at an artificially induced rate. Expect to see lots of foie gras around the winter holidays, when it is marketed as a celebratory treat. Horse meat can still be found on restaurant menus, and butchers who sell it can be identified by the horse head mounted above the door, but its overall appeal is waning, particularly in light of the 2013 horsemeat scandal whereby horses from research labs who'd been

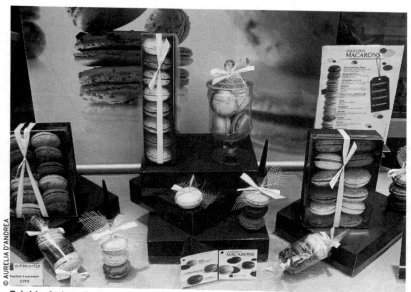

© AURELIA D'ANDREA

Bright window displays featuring traditional French treats beckon from every corner.

EXPAT EXPERIENCE: LET THEM EAT KALE

In 2011, Kristen Beddard picked up her life in New York City and moved to Paris. With very little knowledge of the French language, Kristen was not able to find a job and had a lot of time on her hands. So what's a smart girl with a longing for comfort foods from home to do with her spare time? Launch The Kale Project (www.thekaleproject.com), an online movement credited with bringing the Holy Grail of Greens to l'Hexagone. Here, Kristen explains how she did it.

Name: Kristen Beddard
Age: 29
Profession: Founder, The Kale Project
Hometown: Pittsburgh, PA
Current City: Paris, 17e

How did you picture your new life in Paris?
Before actually arriving in Paris, but looking ahead, my plan was to arrive, find our new apartment, settle in, and take French lessons for a few months. Since my husband is a German citizen, I was legally allowed to work, but due to the language issue, I was not able to find a job at any advertising agencies without fluent French. Working in the communications industry is great until you are not able to communicate! So all of a sudden, I was without a job, which was very difficult for me and while I enjoyed my French lessons, it was not fulfilling enough. I knew that teaching English was not for me and would have loved to volunteer but again, I was not able to hold a conversation. The Kale Project was a way for me to continue working in marketing and working with something I am very passionate about.

What were the initial reactions you were met with in France after launching The Kale Project?
When I first started The Kale Project, my immediate "target" was expatriates and the goal was to find just one local, French producer to grow the vegetable. As time went on and more farmers grew the vegetable, more people became aware and excited to try it. Overall, feedback has been positive because, after all, it is just a *légume oublié* (lost/forgotten vegetable) and has ancient, European origins.

The Anglos loved the Project, and while the majority of French did, I definitely received negative feedback. The best way to get through it was—and still is—reminding myself why I started the project in the first place and that my passion for leafy-greens is not necessarily someone else's passion.

dosed with experimental drugs were later sold as meat to unsuspecting French consumers. That old culinary cliché, escargots, is alive and well, but oysters and mussels are more popular among French diners.

French fast food resembles its North American counterpart, though McDonald's offers wireless Internet, table service, and made-to-order burgers. A more traditional fast food is the crêpe. In big cities and small towns, look for stands, both permanent and mobile, where you can order sweet crêpes topped with everything from sugar and lemon juice to a thick slather of Nutella, or savory versions topped with *un oeuf* (an egg), *fromage* (cheese), *jambon* (ham), or any combination thereof.

Vegetarians, vegans, and people with food allergies won't have trouble sourcing comestibles for home-cooked meals in Paris, but eating out can occasionally pose a

What were some of the challenges that you faced while launching this enterprise?

The biggest challenge is always the language. Over time, my French has dramatically improved but I know that if my language skills were better, I would have tried to do things differently or perhaps tried to work with different people to advance the project. And in France there are always bureaucratic hoops to jump through and starting your own endeavor is no different. It's impossible to avoid but you just have to keep trying and persevering to accomplish your goals.

The Kale Project is an international success story, but surely the process wasn't entirely smooth. Any wise words for others who want to embark on their own novel projects?

Network. The expat community is made up of so many smart, interesting and creative people—many of whom also have started new things in Paris. I found that while networking takes a lot of time, it has been invaluable to me and the project's success. And by surrounding myself with these people, I am always learning something new about France and the culture.

Wear a lot of hats. There are a lot of things that I have to do with the project that aren't my specialty or that I have a lot

of interest in, but starting any individual endeavor means having many roles which are all equally important. Embrace them all. Stay true. Be honest with yourself and with your audience. People can tell if you are being honest and will respect you and what you do even more.

© GRANT PARKER

Kristen Beddard

challenge. Most restaurant staff don't understand nonreligious dietary modifications or restrictions, and it's almost not worth explaining. Making food substitutions isn't part of the French dining-out style, so if you have a wheat allergy, you're better off ordering things you know to be wheat-free. Vegans will need to master *"sans fromage, s'il vous plaît"* (no cheese, please) when ordering pizza and sandwiches. Better still, seek out Paris's veg restaurants, of which there are dozens, ranging from macrobiotic to Indian and beyond.

Gender Roles

As quick as the leaders of the French Revolution and the authors of the Declaration of the Rights of Man were to espouse *liberté, égalité,* and *fraternité* as the founding principles of the new republic, they kind of forgot a big hunk of the population: women. Women's rights and the ideas supporting them didn't really enter mainstream French discourse until relatively recently. The country's earliest outspoken feminists and women's rights advocates—such as Olympe de Gouges, who also advocated on behalf of minorities—were simply silenced by the guillotine for their uppity ideas about equality. Those early rabble-rousers brought the idea of gender equality to the forefront in the 18th century, but women were not given the right to vote until 1944.

World War II altered the male-female dynamic in profound ways, for better and for worse. During wartime, traditional gender roles took a back seat as women and men crawled through the trenches side by side in the resistance effort, bearing arms with equal strength and commitment to both personal survival and the protection of their country. When the war ended, society fell into recovery mode, followed by a slow and steady rebuilding of the economy. The shift from rural to urban and from agriculture to industrialization fostered a new middle class. After decades of declining birthrates, the postwar message broadcast toward women from the church, the government, and the media echoed loud and clear: Stay home and have babies. Women listened; between 1943 and 1965, there were 14 million new additions to the French population. Thus began a return to the traditional family structure, with men re-engaging in the burgeoning industrial workforce and women staying home, dutifully raising children, cooking meals in their shiny new kitchens, and otherwise presiding over the domestic realm.

In 1949, five years after women were given the right to vote, writer-philosopher Simone de Beauvoir penned *the* manifesto on French gender equality theory, *The Second Sex,* which is often credited for kick-starting the modern feminist movement in France. Her writing encouraged women to examine their role in society, to consider themselves as autonomous agents rather than merely inferior sidekicks to the dominant male power, and to "aspire to full membership of the human race." De Beauvoir's work heralded a new way of thinking that laid the groundwork for significant improvements for women's equality. In 1967, birth control was finally legalized in France, and the roaring baby boom slowed down considerably, beginning to rise again only in the early 21st century. This allowed women to consider their work potential outside the home.

France has sort of made up for its female-unfriendly past by bestowing specific social benefits on women for doing the one thing their male counterparts can't do: Bear children. Women are entitled to everything from a four-month federally mandated maternity leave (in contrast, employers in the U.S. are not required by law to offer any leave) to postnatal "vaginal rejuvenation therapy." (Really.) Those perks aside, women in France still have a long way to go before they reach true equality. Most medical school graduates are female but the majority of hospital heads are male, and women still earn 75 cents for every euro a man earns. Though they invest as many hours working outside the home as men do, women carry the heavier burden in the domestic sphere.

EXPAT EXPERIENCE: GAY PAREE

What's it like being gay in Paris? A lot like being gay in other cities around the world: not without its challenges, but overall, pretty fabulous. Here, American expat Steve Kocheran-Letrouit shares his perspective on life in Gay Paree.

Name: Steve Kocheran-Letrouit
Age: 63
Occupation: History teacher at a private international high school
Hometown: San Diego, California
Current city: Paris, 3rd

In 2004, I had reached the point where teaching was no longer fun and, so I decided to take an early retirement to live my dream of residing in Paris. That same year I met my husband, Eric, which added an extra incentive to make the move. We were PACSed in 2008, which helped with my paperwork and allowing me to work at any kind of job in France. No limits. It also gave me access to social security. We were married in the U.S. in 2013.

I have never experienced homophobia personally, either in Paris or in the small villages we have visited throughout France. Acceptance and validation are the norm. Once same-sex marriage was approved here, the religious extremists, who came out of the woodwork, returned to their homes and have been quiet ever since. This differs from the United States because every day there is some bigoted politician or religious leader spewing hatred against the LGBT community.

Being gay is really a non-issue for me. Our friends here, as well as Eric's family, have accepted and validated our marriage. Congratulations arrived in abundance and love. It was such a great feeling. Even at my favorite café, the staff and owner know I'm gay and celebrated my marriage. I truly wish I could say the same thing about being gay in the United States.

The gay scene is pretty much the same no matter where you are. There are specific bars for whatever your interests are. There are cliques just as there are in the United States. It is just as difficult to meet someone for a long-term relationship. This is based on conversations with my single, gay friends. Eric and I are not into the "gay scene," so to speak. We love to go the Marais for dinner and drinks, but really avoid the bars. We've been there, done that.

I firmly believe that when you live your dream, the universe blesses you with abundance. I did just that. The moment I knew it was time, everything fell into place. It has been and continues to be a fulfilling, abundant life. Contentment. I love that word because is describes me and my life with my husband.

a wedding officiated by the deputy mayor of Boulogne-Billancourt

© AURELIA D'ANDREA

Women are still the primary caregivers for children and devote a larger chunk of time to housekeeping, grocery shopping, and other household chores.

GAY AND LESBIAN CULTURE

Paris in the early years of the 20th century attracted a wild and woolly lot of characters who defined themselves as "artists." Many of them also called themselves "gay." Even though the Assemblée Nationale didn't vote to decriminalize homosexuality until 1982, the closet door swung wide open throughout those heady Lost Generation years, and artists, intellectuals, and everyday folk resisted the urge to hide their sexuality from the judgmental eyes of the world. Gertrude Stein and her longtime partner, Alice B. Toklas, lived out and proud in Paris's Left Bank, as did Sylvia Beach, the respected proprietor of landmark bookstore Shakespeare & Company. Oscar Wilde, the great Irish writer entombed beneath a majestic headstone in Paris's touristy Père-Lachaise Cemetery, sought sanctuary in France after a horrible episode in which he was imprisoned in England for the crime of being gay. World War II was a dark era for gays and lesbians, who were shipped off with Jews, gypsies, and other "deviants" to concentration camps. Thankfully, a lot has changed since then.

In 1999, the Assemblée Nationale passed a law to protect individuals in civil unions and extended this coverage to gay men and lesbians. PACS (Pacte Civile de Solidarité) allows gays and straights alike to register their partnerships and share in some of the social benefits and protections extended to married heterosexual couples. The PACS union is so popular that it's well on its way to eclipsing traditional marriage as the bond uniting most straight couples. In 2009, more than 170,000 French couples were "PACSed." In that same year, 200,000 couples married. In theory, based on the French

In 2013, gay marriage became legal in France.

constitution, France only recognizes *citoyens;* special rights are not accorded to these citizens with relation to their gender, sexual orientation, and religious preference.

For gays and lesbians who believe in the old-fashioned tradition of marriage, there's good news: In May 2013, President Hollande kept one of his campaign promises and signed into a law a measure making it legal for same-sex couples to not just marry, but adopt children together, too. Believers in true *egalité* cheered the long-overdue gesture, while French conservatives did everything they could to halt the law's passage, with legal maneuvering and noisy nationwide protests. Still, polls report that 60 percent of the population stands in support of gay marriage, and in the first six months after the law was signed, more than 7,000 same-sex couples tied the knot throughout l'Hexagone.

Each June, gay pride festivals throughout France draw hundreds of thousands of participants and spectators. In Paris, former mayor Bertrand Delanoë usually makes an appearance at the rainbow-heavy funfest as it weaves through the city, blasting techno music to enthusiastic crowds; and the city's homosexual hub, the Marais, begins to resemble a gay Disneyland in all the best ways. One way to get a sense of French ideas on homosexuality is by watching films with gay themes. Some of the most interesting, entertaining, and popular among the international crowd are *Côte d'Azur, Défense d'Aimer, Donne-moi la Main, Drôle de Félix, Entre Nous, French Twist, Je t'aime . . . moi non plus, Ma Vie en Rose, Naissance des Pieuvres, Presque Rien, Les Témoins,* and *La Vie d'Adèle.*

Religion

When the Romans conquered Gaul, in 58 BC, they claimed their territory using an age-old approach: religious conversion. The tactic worked. More than 2,000 years later, Roman Catholicism is still the most widely claimed religious group in France, though it's difficult to say for sure; in 1872, the government banned the gathering of both religion- and ethnicity-related statistics. All information collected today is via voluntary polls. Recent figures point to the not-so-surprising fact that Roman Catholics are the reigning religious group claiming 85 percent of the population, though most are largely thought to be non-practicing, with a mere 12 percent attending mass on a regular basis. Muslims, Protestants, and Jews split the remaining 15 percent, and for the most part, everyone coexists peacefully.

THE JEWISH COMMUNITY

France is currently home to the largest Jewish population in all of Europe, with 600,000 members. Nearly two-thirds of those live in Paris, and smaller Jewish communities thrive in Marseille, Lyon, Toulouse, and Strasbourg. During the 1950 and '60s, the population grew when more than 200,000 Sephardic Jews from North Africa abandoned their homes in an extended exodus kickstarted by the Six-Day War. Settling primarily in the French capital, where a solid Jewish infrastructure including synagogues, *cacher* (kosher) restaurants, and Hebrew schools was already in place, they formed new communities and assimilated into existing ones. Jewish artists Amedeo Modigliani and Marc Chagall came to France to work and live, and their creations are celebrated in art institutions nationwide, such as the Musée d'Orsay and the Paris Musée d'Art Moderne.

The Marais is one of the oldest Jewish neighborhoods in France.

In Paris, Jewish neighborhoods tend to spring up around synagogues, of which there are more than a dozen in Paris. Besides the well-known Jewish quarter in the Marais and its multiple synagogues, there are also sizeable communities around the Grande Synagogue in the 9th, Beth Yacov in the 19th, and Kehilat Gesher in the 17th. In these neighborhoods you'll find kosher restaurants, delis, bakeries, and even kosher chocolatiers. On Saturdays, expect to see bearded men in tall black hats and starched white shirts and plenty of men of all ages sporting yarmulkes.

THE MUSLIM COMMUNITY

France also houses Europe's largest population of Muslims—more than six million, a full 10 percent of the population. In big cities such as Paris, Marseille, and Lyon, the distinctive, throaty chatter of Arabic fills the air, and street scenes are alive with women in hijabs, bustling halal butcher shops, and kebab joints. Fast-food chains—notably Quick Burger, the French equivalent of Burger King—offer halal hamburgers to observant Muslims, to the chagrin of some political groups who see expanding menus as "preferential kowtowing." This is one of the selling points used by the Front National to promote its anti-immigration platform, suggesting that specialized menus create a sort of divide that isn't in line with "French values," in particular the separation of church and state, known in France as *laïcité*. Despite these challenges, hundreds of mosques throughout the country help solidify a sense of community, and they often serve as all-in-one centers with hammams, daycare, and meals.

As with Paris's Jewish communities, Muslim communities also congregate around places of worship. More than a dozen mosques, masjids, and Islamic cultural centers can be found within the city limits, but the most popular are the Grande Mosquée

©PAUL PRESCOTT

Though France is home to Europe's largest Muslim population, there are more Catholics than all the other religions combined.

in the 5th, the Mosquée Al-Fath in the 18th, and Mosquée Abou Ayou al Ansari in the 11th. You'll find halal restaurants, Islamic bookstores, and Arab-style *salons du thé* in these areas, as well as men and women dressed in traditional Islamic clothing.

THE ROMAN-CATHOLIC TRADITION

At major Christian holidays, such as Christmas and Easter, you'll be reminded that this country is still Roman Catholic at heart, at least superficially. Christmas is celebrated with an endless parade of fanfare: Town halls are kitted out with giant sapins de Noël; the *rues* and boulevards are strung with colorful lights; shops bust out the bows, balls, and flocking spray and go to town. Best of all, the *boulangeries* and pâtisseries churn out seasonal treats that people of all religious persuasions enjoy. The *bûche de Noël,* a cake baked in the shape of a log, is often decorated with tiny wintertime scenes, and the *galette des rois,* a frangipane-filled pastry eaten in celebration of Epiphany, comes with a hidden trinket and a paper crown that lets one lucky indulger be king or queen for the day.

The Arts

The earliest creative expression in France can be found in the now famous caves in the verdant river valleys of southern France. The art of the Homo sapiens zeroed in on the important issues of the day: food, shelter, and threats to safety. Rendered in rudimentary paints and chalks, these primitive pictures offer a glimpse of the more refined art to come. Millennia later, France has transformed into a cultural nirvana, and Paris is its artistic epicenter. Fine arts, architecture, music, sculpture, and literature are just some of the arenas in which France boasts a disarming number of highly skilled denizens. So beloved are these contributors to the artistic canon that streets, hospitals, and schools throughout the country bear their names: Voltaire, Balzac, Renoir, and even Gainsbourg among them.

To say that the French place an extremely high value on the arts would be an understatement. In this country of 65.2 million, 30,000 are registered "dramatic artists" and dancers, and an equal number are registered musicians. The country boasts 1,200 museums, 288 yearly arts-related festivals, and an annual arts-and-culture budget that tops 7 billion euros. This investment clearly pays off: Every year, millions of visitors

KING OF CAKES

It happens every year after the Christmas holiday, just as it has since the 15th century: *Boulangeries* throughout France set up their homogenous display of circular tarts, the shiny brown crusts topped with a golden crown signaling to passersby that Epiphany is just around the corner. For Christians, these *galettes des rois*, or kings' cakes, are symbolic reminders of the visit of the Magi to the infant Jesus. For the rest of us, they're just a delicious wintertime treat.

What makes these sweet confections so special isn't necessarily their decadently creamy frangipane interiors redolent of butter and almonds, but the other pleasant surprise they hold: the *fève*. Baked inside every *galette* is a tiny porcelain figurine—in the old days, they used a dried fava bean—that entitles you to wear the paper crown for a day should you be lucky enough to find it in your slice.

Something about that *fève* brings out the cheating impulse in people, and many Frenchies admit they've sought out the slice with the most noticeable bump as a shortcut to earning the royal headpiece. (A well-prepared *galette*, any baker will tell you, will reveal no such telltale signs.) Holiday rule makers have found a way to encourage fair play: The youngest child at the Epiphany soirée decides who gets which slice of cake.

The frangipane-filled variety gets the most play, but the Provençal version of the *galette des rois* is worth a mention (and a taste). The crown-shaped ring of brioche is studded with candied fruit and coarse sugar, and, like its flat counterpart, also contains a *fève*. Besides the calories involved, there's only one downside to indulging in this annual tradition: Whoever earns that crown has to buy the next cake.

come to Paris to ogle the Mona Lisa, peer up at la Tour Eiffel, and take in a feathers-and-sequins show at the Moulin Rouge, pumping in billions of dollars to the local economy. The government has even created a special dole just to support the new generation of artists, who are guaranteed a living wage should they find themselves unable to find work in their craft.

IMPRESSIONISM

France has given birth to numerous art movements, but none whose global impact has been as profound as Impressionism. It began with Édouard Manet. After being turned away from the great Paris salons sponsored by the government-run École des Beaux Arts in the late 19th century for expressing ideas on canvas that were too avant-garde and nonconformist, Manet rallied together a few other rejected painters eager to show their work to an interested audience. Together, Manet and his artistic consorts developed an alternative salon featuring work focused on everyday life, much as their Cro-Magnon predecessors had: on the streets, in the home, at lively cafés, at work in the fields, and at play on the *plage*. The movement began in Paris and spread south to Provence, where Auguste Renoir and Paul Cézanne lived and painted.

The work of Renoir, Camille Pissarro, Edgar Degas, and Cézanne evoke a specific vision of France, one where distinctive brushstrokes and reflected light conspire to dazzle the eye. Considering the era, the movement was very progressive—and it was also short-lived, petering out in just 10 years—paving the way for the post-Impressionists. Always in high demand, Impressionist paintings from the great French museums are often loaned to art institutions outside of France, but the Musée d'Orsay's permanent exhibit is a perennial go-to for a broad cross section of art lovers.

ARCHITECTURE

Walk down any street in France, and you'll undoubtedly encounter the past. In Paris, it's said, you're never more than 10 paces from a view onto that iconic monolith, la Tour Eiffel, but it's the broad avenues hemmed by manicured trees and tidy apartment buildings that your gaze will surely settle on time and again. The City of Light wasn't always the bright and airy *ville* it is today; those beautiful sand-colored buildings, with their giant, wooden double doors and ornate metal balconies festooned with potted geraniums, are the work of baron Georges-Eugène Haussmann, a 19th-century architect and urban planner commissioned by Napoléon III to revamp Paris's cramped, unsanitary alleyways and transform them into broad, beautiful boulevards.

Beginning in 1852, Haussmann took to his task of modernizing Paris and making it easier for the bourgeois class to partake in their preferred pastime: strolling. In Haussmann's distinctive style, which made great use of straight lines, the streets were widened, groomed parks were constructed, functional squares were designed and built, and those sometimes confusing star-shaped roundabouts were put in place. This regimented style was fraught with design restrictions that defined the height, width, pitch, and color of all new construction. In 1870, Haussmann completed his work of transforming the Paris of the past into the Paris of the future. Today, the architects behind the design are acknowledged for their work by an engraved stamp on the front of many private and public buildings throughout the capital.

Charles-Édouard Jeanneret, better known as Le Corbusier, is Swiss by birth, but he is easily France's second-best-known architect. Like Haussmann, he was engaged by the government to design aesthetically pleasing urban housing that would offer function and design at once. Many of his ideas didn't make the cut—there are, for instance, no 60-story tower blocks in central Paris, as he proposed—but the structures that did come to life have stood the test of time, including the boxy, beehive-like Maison du Fada in Marseille and the Notre-Dame-du-Haut chapel in Ronchamp. Simultaneously loved and loathed for his modern, hard-edged style, Le Corbusier is credited with ushering in the prevailing aesthetic of contemporary French design.

Today, Paris is receiving attention from the global urban-planning crowd for daring to create modern public housing with a green focus. With solar panels, common gardens, flora-as-insulation, and design that maximizes access to natural light, these aesthetically pleasing subsidized communities soften the rough image of public housing and entice families from different social strata.

LITERATURE

Their reputations are so heady and their work so iconic they need only one name to be recognized: Balzac, Camus, Colette, Flaubert, Molière, Proust, Zola. France's premier contribution to the arts might very well be its body of literature, even if the majority of Americans have never read from it. The heyday of French literature peaked in the 19th century, when Jules Verne pumped out his sci-fi body of work and Flaubert titillated readers (and irked early censors) with *Madame Bovary*. French students begin studying the great writers in elementary school and have read many of the classics by the time they finish *lycée.*

French literature has had an interesting cultural impact on the rest of the world as well: Alexandre Dumas's stories have been made into ballets—*The Nutcracker,* for starters—and his *Trois Mousquetaires* was co-opted by Disney (and morphed into Mousketeers, if you recall), as was Victor Hugo's famous *Hunchback of Notre-Dame.* Hugo is also responsible for one of Broadway's longest-running musicals, *Les Misérables,* which was made into an Academy Award-winning feature film in 2012.

Jean-Paul Sartre won the Nobel Prize in Literature in 1964 but famously declined the honor, saying that were he to accept it, he would be in some sense beholden to the awarding institution and thus compromising his artistic integrity—a risk that he believed no writer should feel compelled to experience. Writers who have happily accepted the award include Algeria-born Albert Camus, who won the prize in 1957 for his contributions to the field of modern literature.

Modern French writers who have also cracked the global literary scene include Faïza Guène, whose 2006 book *Kiffe Kiffe Demain* (*Kiffe Kiffe Tomorrow*), about life in a contemporary suburban housing project, has been translated into more than 20 languages, and Catherine Millet with her saucy 2002 memoir *The Sexual Life of Catherine M.,* which details the between-the-sheets (and open-air) exploits of a liberated, middle-aged Frenchwoman.

FASHION

For the past 100 years, France and fashion have been synonymous. Blame Gabrielle "Coco" Chanel, who began her career as a milliner; she put Paris on the fashion map with her signature tweed jacket that combined a masculine edge with a ribbon-trimmed feminine sensibility. A century later, the Chanel brand—and the cut of that jacket—is still a coveted symbol of high style. In the 1950s, Christian Dior reigned over the glamorous world of couture party dresses, ball gowns, and stylish prêt-à-porter suits, giving French women a fashion prototype to emulate (or at least to admire on the pages of fashion magazines). In the 1960s, the house of Courrèges altered the fashion landscape with an ultramod aesthetic that married bright white dress suits with shiny patent boots that hinted at fashion's space-age potential.

When revered couturier Christian Dior died in 1957, a very young Yves Saint Laurent took over as head designer at the fashion house, giving the brand a modern makeover. In the '70s, the bespectacled designer revolutionized the sartorial scene with Le Smoking—a structured, menswear-inspired jacket that became one of the harbingers of the gender-neutral fashions of later decades. Saint Laurent's designs have been showcased in popular exhibitions in both French and American museums, and several years after his death, he remains one of France's most beloved fashion icons.

Chanel, Dior, Céline, and Chloé still attract the world's deep-pocketed pretty people to high-end boutiques on Paris's avenue Montaigne and beyond. But as if the incessant television commercials don't give it away, designer perfumes are reeling in the most cash for French fashion houses, to the tune of billions of dollars each year. Also making a comeback after a long lull in inspiration is Jean Paul Gaultier, whose glam Spring 2014 couture shows sparkled with a femininity inspired by butterflies. The hottest name in contemporary French fashion, however, is Isabel Marant. Marant's chic,

ESCAPE ARTISTS

For more than a century, North Americans have migrated to Paris in search of creative freedom, heady inspiration, adventure tinged with a seductive accent, and a slice of that celebrated *joie de vivre*. It's no wonder that writers, musicians, actors, and especially painters are drawn to this country where the arts are seen as a right rather than a privilege. From the Lost Generation to Gen X, meet some of the daring dreamers who shipped off across the pond to hone their craft in *la Ville Lumière*.

- Josephine Baker
- James Baldwin
- Art Buchwald
- Belinda Carlisle
- Sofia Coppola
- R. Crumb
- Johnny Depp
- John Dos Passos
- Feist
- F. Scott Fitzgerald
- Adam Gopnik
- Ernest Hemingway
- Langston Hughes
- Washington Irving
- Henry James
- Scarlett Johansson
- Diane Johnson
- Aline Kominsky
- Carson McCullers
- Henry Miller
- Jim Morrison
- Charlie Parker
- Cole Porter
- Natalie Portman
- Ezra Pound
- Molly Ringwald
- Jean Seberg
- David Sedaris
- Nina Simone
- Gertrude Stein
- Alice B. Toklas
- Tina Turner
- Edith Wharton

urban, gender-neutral garments are coveted by Parisian women of all ages, and spawn knock-offs (remember the colorful wedge-heeled sneaker?) each season.

Sports

When France lost to Mexico 0-2 in the first team match of the 2010 World Cup in South Africa, the mood among French sports fans turned somber. Instead of screaming in anger at the television or sharing conciliatory slaps on the back with fellow sports fans packed inside cafés and brasseries, the French sulked in silence before the big screens, staring into their pints of Pelforth with a mixture of shame and denial.

Some analysts called the sporty comedown a metaphor for the social problems plaguing French society: Both, they say, are mired in ego, strained relations among minorities, and the refusal to accept blame for failure. To others, football—what Americans refer to as soccer—is just a game. Everyone in France, however, has some sort of opinion on the country's most popular sport. Football is played in minor and major

Fashion shows, art, and swanky parties are what you'll find at the Grand Palais.

leagues throughout the country, packing stadiums and luring multiple generations of fans. When the home team wins, packed stadiums vibrate with the stomping of feet, waving of flags, and the chanting of thousands of vociferous spectators.

Paris's Parc des Princes and Saint-Denis's Stade de Paris—with more than 100,000 seats between them—play host to the most international football games. If there's one place you don't want to be stuck, it's in your car anywhere near the choked arteries around these arenas, especially if the home team has lost. For an authentic local experience, regional stadiums in smaller cities and towns are the places to be to see a match. Expect up-close views of the action that allow you to see the subtle nuances of the game and to feel part of the local community every weekend, year-round (or almost year-round—like the rest of the country, football takes a two-month summer holiday).

Like football, France's cycling culture reaches back to the 1800s, when velodromes drew crowds (Ernest Hemingway was a fan) for dizzying races that sometimes lasted six days, ending for some fatigued riders in a bloody pile on the wooden racetrack. (The historic La Cipale velodrome in Paris's Bois de Vincennes is still open to the public.) It's the sexy Tour de France, though, that has earned the most international attention when it comes to the two-wheeled sport. Every July since 1903, racers from around the world have pedaled a circuit that takes them up and over some of the country's tallest peaks, down through picturesque medieval villages, and finally up the Champs-Élysées for a final lap before hundreds of thousands of whistling, cheering, clapping fans.

PLANNING YOUR FACT-FINDING TRIP

It's easy to fall in love with the surface image of France, but there's only one way to find out whether the Parisian personality meshes with yours and whether there's hope for a long-term relationship, and that's to come visit and stay awhile. You'll want to not only explore the celebrated corners of the city, but also the less flashy residential neighborhoods in arrondissements or suburbs where you might settle down. This will enable you to attune yourself to the rhythms of your potential new home before making a commitment.

The most important part of your reconnaissance mission is to veer off the tourist trail: Skip the hotel directly beside the Eiffel Tower and park yourself at a neighborhood *auberge* in a less touristy arrondissement. In the suburbs, you'll benefit by skipping the budget chain hotels near the freeway and looking for accommodations (independent or otherwise) in the center of each town you're considering. Give yourself at least a few days to *really* get to a know a place: When and where the nearest outdoor market is held, which of the cafés feels most like home and which *boulangerie* bakes the best baguettes, and who your future neighbors will be.

Bring your sense of adventure, your best manners, and your French phrasebook, and

don't be afraid to ask questions—even if you don't always understand the responses. Reaching out will let the locals know you've got nothing to hide, and will give you the opportunity to see what the regional mores and attitudes are toward foreigners. Eat out, take public transport, visit the post office, shop at the local grocery store, and imagine what life will be like in your adopted hometown.

Preparing to Leave

Your fact-finding mission is different from a standard vacation because you're looking not just to enjoy yourself and see the sights, but to make an assessment that has the potential to alter the course of your life for the better. The important thing to remember, besides to have fun, is to carry your critical eye with you on your journey. Consider each place you visit with a dash of realism. How close are amenities? Are there parks nearby for walking the dog? What about schools and libraries? Where is the closest transportation stop, and will you mind the walk to the bus or Métro when it's January and snow blankets the cobblestones?

The Internet is a traveler's best friend and can support you on your living-abroad adventure before you've even hopped the plane for Paris. Begin by seeking out blogs written by locals to get an insider's perspective that's tailored to your situation. Are you moving with kids? With a major food allergy? With your four cats? Odds are good that someone before you has done it already, and has survived long enough to write about it. Find them online and get acquainted—you might even strike up a friendship if you take the initiative and send a note of introduction. Also use the Internet to check the pre-departure weather forecast so you know whether to pack an *imperméable* in addition to your *parapluie*. And if you're ready to practice your French, it couldn't hurt to see if any transit strikes are in the cards. The website www.francegreve.com will keep you up to date.

Guidebooks are indispensable travel companions that will point you in the direction of a dependable hotel, restaurant, or sightseeing spot without your having to weed through the never-ending possibilities that the Internet is so good at providing. If traveling light is a major concern, pack your e-reader and buy the digital version of your favorite guide. Having maps, language guides, and tourist information in one handy place can simplify the travel process and offer a sense of security.

As you narrow down areas to explore and consider your needs, wants, and dreams, you might find it helpful to rank your list in terms of importance. What comes first: career, school, play, or family? If you're moving without a job and need to find work right away, Paris proper is the obvious choice for the sheer variety and number of employment opportunities. Ditto for rental housing. Crave access to wide-open green spaces and cringe at the thought of tourists asking you for directions? The suburbs might be more to your liking. And if you're a retiree on a limited budget, you'll want to consider neighborhoods where housing is affordable but where you'll still have access to cultural amenities—and a decent *boulangerie*. Be realistic as you begin your search, but don't deny your dreams. A happy medium does exist!

WHAT TO BRING
Passport

Before you book your travel plans, make sure your passport is up-to-date, and ideally valid for six months beyond your expected return date. Make two copies of the first few pages of your passport, then leave one with a trusted friend or relative back home and stick the other in your travel bag. If your passport is lost or stolen, you'll be able to take a copy to the American embassy in Paris and have a new passport issued, usually within 24 hours. While you definitely need to carry your passport with you, if you're staying in France for less than 90 days, you won't need a long-stay visa. Keep in mind that many travelers bend the rules and stay longer than 90 days without any problems, but it's always best to err on the side of the law and play by the rules, lest you are sent home with a mysterious red mark scribbled into your passport.

Money and Credit Cards

Credit and ATM cards are widely accepted in France; a sticker system, usually posted on the doors or windows of businesses, indicates exactly which cards you can use at a specific establishment. Some shops—most often small grocery stores and many restaurants—have minimum-purchase requirements that hover around €10 or €15, in which case a notice of some sort will be posted at the register or another easily visible spot. There is one major difference between U.S. credit cards and French ones, and that's the *puce*. Embedded inside French cards (and most European credit cards) is a tiny microchip encrypted with a variety of data. These cards are known within the banking industry as EMV (short for Europay, MasterCard, and Visa) cards and they generally require a pin code. Unlike American cards that are fitted with a magnetic strip, the EMV cards are much more fraud-proof. Some companies, including American Express and Discover, are already rolling out EMV cards in the U.S., and most banks and credit unions will have introduced them by 2015. It's worth checking with your bank to see if a *puce* card is possible; if you'll be traveling with a non-EMV credit card, you may not be able to purchase Métro tickets from every station's vending machines or rent a Vélib' bike from a kiosk (though you can still do this online before you leave). But as long as the credit card reader is equipped with a swipe feature (you may need to assist the person behind the counter with this—it's not every day they see a non-European card), your card will be readable and therefore usable. Keep in mind that *boulangeries* and small mom-and-pop shops still aren't outfitted with any kind of sophisticated apparatus, so it's wise to always carry at least €10 in change at all times for those little necessities like your morning *café* and croissant.

Before you ship off, check in with the banks that issue your credit and debit cards to let them know you'll be traveling and to expect foreign transactions to appear in their computer systems. If you forget to do this, you may find your account suspended after the first foreign purchase, and undoing this damage from a continent away can be a frustrating challenge. If you forget to make the call in advance of your trip, do so the moment your memory is jogged. Some banks and credit card companies charge a commission or a one-time transaction fee for every foreign purchase or cash withdrawal. These 2- and 3-percent charges on purchases and as much as $10 in fees for each withdrawal are annoying and can definitely add up, so your best bet is to withdraw the maximum amount of cash possible from an ATM to use for your purchases or carry cards that don't penalize you for foreign purchases. If your bank account has a per-day withdrawal limit, ask about increasing it before you leave.

ATMs, known as *distributeurs* in French, are ubiquitous throughout Paris and in suburban city centers. Cash-back on purchases isn't really commonplace here, but you will nearly always find a cash machine at the post office, when all else fails and cards aren't accepted at those rare exceptional destinations.

Driver's Permits

International driver's permits are not required by car-rental agencies in France, but it can't hurt to have one just in case you need an extra piece of ID, or if the rules suddenly change overnight (which is altogether possible), or if you're stopped by the *police routière* and want to show what a good citizen you are by having an "official" document translated into French. International permits are valid for one year can be purchased by licensed drivers at AAA offices, where they cost $15. The forms are available online at www.aaa.com. Another option is to secure your permit through one of many private companies acting as intermediary agents, and that generally charge twice as much at AAA. You'll need two passport-size photos and your U.S. driver's license to complete the transaction, either way.

Communications

The value of a French phrasebook cannot be underestimated. If you're polite and apologetic, it is very likely that the person you're trying to communicate with will break into English (don't ruin your chances by immediately asking, "Do you speak English?"), but attempting to speak the language—even if you're reading straight from a guidebook and sound like an uneducated automaton—will make the French more inclined to help you when you need it most. Foreign phrasebook applications are available to smartphone users, so for the light traveler, this may be the way to go. Many people who aren't yet conversational in French find making telephone calls nearly impossible. Still, if you can't live without your phone for the duration of your stay, check with your carrier to see if your mobile roaming privileges extend to France. If not—or if the costs are prohibitively exorbitant—you have other options.

If you own a late-model mobile phone and it has been unblocked, you can buy a France-friendly SIM card to temporarily replace your American SIM card. If you want to take care of those details before you leave, purchase one online through a company such as www.lefrenchmobile.com, www.lebara.co.uk, or www.cellularabroad.com. Some *tabacs* also sell SIM cards, but this might require a bit of advanced French to navigate. A better bet would be to visit a store in Paris such as Phone House, where many of the staff are bilingual and can fit your phone with the correct card while you wait. Cell phone rentals are not necessarily cheap, but they do exist; look for kiosks at Charles de Gaulle Airport or rent one at home before you leave. You might also consider purchasing a pay-as-you-go phone once you arrive; they usually cost between €30 and €50. Recharging the phones is easy: You simply visit the nearest *tabac* and ask for *une carte recharge*. You might be asked whether you want the more cost-effective SMS (texting) option, and you'll certainly be asked how much credit you want, usually a minimum of €5 and increasing in increments of €5 or €10. Keep in mind that phone credit has an expiration date—usually one or two weeks from the date of purchase.

Electronics

The power animating all those electric hair dryers, microwave ovens, televisions, and other appliances in France courses through the wires at 220 volts—double the U.S. and Canada's 110 volts. Some machines—laptop computers, digital camera battery chargers, cell phone chargers—are designed to run on both voltages, so they simply need a cheap and easy-to-find outlet adapter. Radio Shack and Best Buy are reliable places to buy these adapters. If you can't live without your iPod docking station or your electric razor, you'll need to source a transformer. They come in different shapes, sizes, and degrees of reliability. For a dependable experience, invest in one or two of those rather industrial-looking step-up/step-down transformers. They aren't worth the extra weight or investment for a short trip, but you'll definitely want to consider them if and when you make the big move. A good one will allow you to use your stereo, lamps, or food processor if you've shipped them from the U.S.

Even if you don't see one in your room, hair dryers are available at most hotels in France. Ask about availability when you check in, or send an email inquiry in advance. Online language converters such as www.freetranslation.com and www.translate.google.com can help you get your question across in a way the recipient will understand.

Medication and Personal Items

One of the hardest things to get used to in France is learning which products are and are not available at the supermarket or drugstore. Everyday items like multipurpose contact-lens solutions and good ol' Advil are only found in pharmacies, and often they're stashed behind the counter, requiring you to practice your French yet again to get relief from that headache or dry-eye spell. Prices are comparable to those you'd find in the U.S., though some items are noticeably cheaper, including homeopathic remedies and many prescription medications. For the most part, you'll find that discount-price goods are hard to come by. Expect to pay around €10 for a bottle of contact-lens solution, €3 for a box—yes, a box—of ibuprofen or acetaminophen (which is called paracétamol in France), and €3 or €4 for sore-throat lozenges.

The French are known as the world's leading consumers of prescription drugs, so tracking down your prescription medication at the pharmacy shouldn't pose a problem. But for convenience's sake, you're still better off carrying your prescriptions from home. If you must get a refill while you're here, make sure to bring the brand name, generic name, and dosage, along with your doctor's prescription.

Clothing and Accessories

If you want to look like a local, then it helps to dress like a local—and in France, that means black, black, and more black. Women, men, and children tend to take a formal approach to dressing, and the style is easy to mimic with a monochromatic ensemble and a few nice accessories. Parisians in particular tend to shy away from too much color, sticking to black from their berets right down to their stiletto boots. Wearing your nice shoes might not be the most comfortable route, but if possible, leave the bright white running shoes at home and opt for something with a lower, darker profile. And flip-flops? Well, save those for summer on the Riviera, if you must. Men might find it difficult to trade in their baseball caps for an empty head, but if you want to blend in, leave the sportswear at home.

Paris is a four-season city, so you'll want to pack gloves, scarves, and hats for wintertime travel, and they'll come in handy during early spring and late fall, too. These items are easy to find at chains like Monoprix and in little shops throughout the country, but if you have them already, stuff them in your suitcase, just to be safe (and warm). The most indispensable year-round item to carry with you is an umbrella. Showers can and do erupt without warning in any season. Umbrellas are easily acquired once you're here, but even the cheapest models aren't that inexpensive by American standards. Expect to pay €15 for a small travel umbrella at a department store or pharmacy. If you're lucky, you might bump into the clever salesmen who congregate outside some Métro stations on rainy days selling cheap Chinese models for about €5.

Until recently, the French really didn't do sunglasses. They're becoming more common with each passing year, but people still rarely wear them in winter or on overcast days. If you're a sunglasses devotee, consider bringing an extra pair, as they aren't as easy to find as they are in the United States and Canada. In a pinch, head to the Marché aux Puces Saint-Ouen and comb the African-run stalls outside the main market. You can find trendy designer doppelgangers for around €10.

WHEN TO GO

You'll find France a welcoming destination at any time, but there are seasonal idiosyncrasies to keep in mind when planning your trip. Weather can certainly impede travel—as it did in late winter of 2013, when flights in and out of the country were cancelled because of snowstorms and trains were delayed by as long as several days. And if you plan to travel to smaller towns and villages, be warned that some virtually shut down for the entire winter season, making it a challenge to find accommodations. (In Paris and the suburbs, you'll be fine.) During the month of August, when the entire country goes on vacation, you will also find signs affixed to the doors and windows of many Parisian businesses announcing closures for *"congés annuels"* or *"fermé pour les vacances,"* often accompanied by a very apologetic note explaining where in the neighborhood you'll be able to find similar baguettes/chocolate/shoe repair services/haircuts, as well as the business's reopening date. During the winter and spring school breaks, you'll find that many tourist hubs—especially the ski and seaside resorts—are full of Parisians, who often grab the best deals on accommodations months in advance. If you plan to escape the Île-de-France region and head for one of the French resort towns at these peak times, it's a good idea to book in advance, too.

Aside from requiring you to bundle up to ward off the cold, winter can be a festive time of year to make your investigative visit. Paris kicks up the visual charm with yuletide displays befitting a world-class city: Christmas lights, markets, and roasted chestnuts for sale on street corners are all part of the allure. Getting a reservation at the hotel and restaurant of your choice is usually easier this time of year, too. If you're focusing your search on Paris, expect most everything to be open for business. Depending on the neighborhood, more businesses are actually open on Christmas than on New Year's Day, so you won't go hungry or thirsty just because it's a major holiday. (This is especially true in Jewish and Muslim neighborhoods.) In the suburbs, however, you'll be lucky if the *boulangerie* is open for a couple of hours in the morning, if at all.

Spring and autumn offer the mildest temperatures and possibly the best glimpses of "real France," without the vacationing hordes to impede your view. (If you want the

Côte d'Azur all to yourself, head south in late September.) Pack layers—shirt, jacket, trench coat, scarf, hat—and be sure your umbrella makes its way inside your suitcase.

Summer has the most predictable temperatures, which tend to fall into the warm range. But it can get scorching hot, and some of us have been known to turn on the heater on oddly nippy July mornings. Remember that late July and the entire month of August are national holiday periods, as well as the standard vacation time for much of the rest of Europe, so some destinations can feel quite crowded with a mix of international and local tourists. Men: If you foresee wanting to make use of Paris's affordable and accessible public swimming pools, pack your Speedo—they're mandatory. For everyone: If you've got a swimming cap, bring it along. Otherwise, you can purchase suits and the requisite caps in special vending machines inside the lobbies of public pools.

WHAT TO DO

The French value face-to-face interactions, so you'll have more success arranging things like real-estate viewings and mortgage inquiries if you wait until you arrive in France and do it in person. After you've settled in the hotel or short-term rental apartment, set off and explore. This is Phase One of your neighborhood assessment. As you stroll, keep your eyes peeled for banks, real estate agencies (*immobliers*), and neighborhood associations offering courses in French and other activities.

The Neighborhood Assessment

Quality of life is at the top of my neighborhood wish-list. That translates into an ideal dwelling situated within a five-minute walk of a Métro or Vélib' station in a lively *quartier;* a produce market and *boulangerie* within a few blocks' walk; and a quiet street without the incessant honking of car horns or scream of police sirens. (I lost out on the last one, but there's always a compromise.) What does your wish-list look like? You'll need a few items at the ready to outline your dream, including the following:

- pen
- notebook
- French phrasebook
- list of deal-breakers
- digital camera or smartphone camera
- a local phone number for people to contact
- an open mind

With these tools, you'll be able to communicate with locals, jot down addresses of businesses and telephone numbers printed on *à louer* (for rent) and *à vendre* (for sale) signs, and photograph any housing contenders. If you plan to enroll your child(ren) in local schools, find the nearest park and introduce yourself to *nounous* and parents, and ask questions about the quality of schools and amenities for children. A trip to the weekly outdoor market is another good method of reading a neighborhood and seeing who lives there.

Rendezvous with Realtors

Throughout Paris and the suburbs, you'll discover real estate offices with for sale and

© AURELIA D'ANDREA

Visit real estate agencies in the neighborhoods you're interested in to learn about housing availability and costs.

for rent signs in the window, complete with photos and details of each property. Once you've surveyed the outside, head inside and ask to speak with a realtor. You'll be invited to sit (and maybe even offered a cup of coffee) and explain your situation. Are you looking to rent or buy? What is your budget? Do you have a *garant?* (See more on this in the *Housing Considerations* section in the *Daily Life* chapter.) Finding a friendly, motivated realtor will support your quest to make a home in Paris.

Suss out Financial Institutions

In some ways, it's better to set up a bank account after you've established a permanent address. The branch where you opened the account becomes your "home" bank, and it's here that you create a relationship with the bankers and handle important matters relating to your account, including picking up new cards, applying for a mortgage, or modifying your account in any way. (See more in the *Finance* section of the *Daily Life* chapter.) Still, scoping out the banking situation and inquiring about documents for your dossier are good first steps. Popular banks in the Paris area include BNP Paribas, Caisse d'Épargne, and Société Générale.

Mingle with Locals

This is your opportunity to meet some of the people you've established relationships with before you ever set foot on the airplane bound for Paris. Bloggers, friends of friends, or even host families from your high-school trip abroad; hopefully, you've sought them out in advance and are using this visit to (re)establish those contacts and glean valuable insider information. Joining a local Meetup (www.meetup.com) group event is one of the smartest and most fun modes for connecting with locals. Events span the spectrum from outdoor adventure to book clubs and even spicy dining groups. Find one that appeals to your interests, then plan to meet and mingle.

Mosey over to the *Mairie*

Scope out the *mairie* and have a peek inside. This is an important hub, especially if you want to get married, have a child, or take city-subsidized French classes while you're here. Help yourself to the free local newspapers and cultural calendars available in the lobby; these make good reading at the café. Talk to the person behind the desk to find out about upcoming events, and to inquire about anything else with a municipal focus—schools, libraries, and public markets, for example. Armed with these resources, you'll be better informed to assess your preferred neighborhoods.

Arriving in Paris

If you're flying into Paris from North America, you'll mostly likely land at Charles de Gaulle, the country's primary international airport that sits roughly 27 kilometers northeast of Paris. The airport is connected to bus, train, taxi, and private-car services that can ferry you to central Paris and beyond.

VISAS AND PASSPORTS

The customs experience is generally a no-fuss exercise requiring little more than standing in line for 10 minutes, followed by a friendly *bonjour* as you hand over your passport for stamping. In France, appearances do matter, so to make sure your experience runs as smoothly as possible, trade in your comfy sweats for dark jeans and a nice jacket, tuck your green mohawk inside your beret, give your shoes a shine, and be prepared to offer a friendly *bonjour* and *merci* in French. There is always a chance you'll be pulled aside to have your luggage unceremoniously rifled through. Officials are looking for contraband items, so it's best not to pique their curiosity by smuggling in your favorite fresh fruit or your beloved Venus flytrap. If you're flying with a pet, have your travel documents ready, but don't expect anyone to actually ask to see them. (In years of back-and-forth travel with a small dog in a carrier, I've never once been asked to show officials my doggy's dossier, though it's a given that were I to travel without the proper paperwork, I'd certainly be asked to cough it up.) Once you've cleared customs, the real Parisian adventure begins.

A pet passport will help you and your four-footed friend better navigate the immigration process.

TRANSPORTATION

There are multiple options for escaping the airport frenzy and getting to your final destination; the one you choose depends on where you're headed, your budget, and your time constraints. Want to address your jetlag by going to sleep immediately? Consider taking a shuttle bus to a nearby airport hotel and starting fresh in the morning after a little shut-eye. Shuttles are free, and there are many bargains to be found within 10 minutes of the airport, from budget-friendly chains to cushy five-star digs.

If you're headed to Paris, the possibilities abound. One of the simplest is

Prepare for your voyage solo or with the help of an agency.

RoissyBus (wah-see-BOOS, which runs every 15 to 20 minutes, depending upon the time of day. The extra-long bus—two cars with an accordion-style middle section—costs €10 per trip and drops you off in the heart of Paris, behind the Opéra Métro station. You can pay with cash or a credit card once you're on the bus, and there are pickup locations at every airport terminal. During rush hour, the journey can take more than an hour; on a good (no-traffic) day, the trip takes about 35 minutes.

The RER B is a regional train line that connects all three airport terminals to Paris and its suburbs. For roughly the same price and same time commitment you'd invest in RoissyBus, you can hop aboard a train and arrive at one of three central Paris train stations: Gare du Nord, Saint-Michel, and Denfert-Rochereau. If you're staying in Paris's popular Latin Quarter, the Saint-Michel station is your stop. Tickets can be purchased from the agents staffing the station kiosks (ideal if paying with a non-*puce* card), or you can use an automated vending machine (best if using cash). Tickets are €9.50 and the trip takes 30 minutes from the airport to Gare du Nord.

Air France offers a deluxe bus service into the city, stopping at the Porte de Maillot Métro/RER Station in northeast Paris, as well as Gare Montparnasse via Gare de Lyon. Tickets are available for purchase online (www.lescarsairfrance.com) for €16.10 (Porte de Maillot) or €16.60 (Montparnasse), and roughly a euro more when you purchase tickets from the driver or the airport kiosks.

Shuttle buses are a newly emerging alternative to RoissyBus, the RER, and the Air France bus, but they're slightly more expensive and offer a somewhat clunkier experience, since you have to call the company—albeit on a toll-free number accessible from an airport pay phone—to let them know you've arrived. To get the best deals, it's imperative you book your pickup in advance. Try www.bluvan.fr, www.supershuttle.fr, or www. parishuttle.com, each of which offers English-language options on its website.

If money is no object, or if you just want to get to your hotel or apartment with a minimum of hassle, taxis are the way to go. Expect to pay between €45 (early-morning or late-night light traffic) and €100 (rush-hour traffic) to ride from the airport to your front door. Though tipping isn't standard in France, there is an exception for taxis. An extra 5 percent on top of the fare is standard, or 10 percent if your driver is extra helpful with your baggage or doesn't make a fuss about your dog or cat in its carrier.

Sample Itineraries

Even if you only have a week, you can pack a lot of exploration into your fact-finding experience, thanks to France's marvelous public transportation system. Two weeks will provide you with a cursory sense of what to expect when you lay down more permanent roots. If you have a month to spare, consider yourself an honorary local. Before you leave, you'll want to get familiar with the regional transit system website, www. transilien.fr for planning local excursions, day trips, and overnight adventures. Once you're here, try to imagine yourself as a resident. Hit the neighborhood cafés, visit the cinema or the theater, take in a musical performance, picnic in the neighborhood parks, and above all, sample the wares at the local *boulangeries;* there's no underestimating the importance of a good baguette.

ONE WEEK: MORE THAN THE MARAIS

Besides la Tour Eiffel, the **Marais** is probably the biggest tourist magnet in all of Paris, and with good reason: It's lively, fun, and crammed with history and visual interest. Make this your home base for a week and you might not even need to rely on public transport; just be sure to pack your (stylish) walking shoes, because some of Paris's most exciting neighborhoods are within a 45-minute promenade of that shopper's thoroughfare that slices through the Marais, the rue de Rivoli.

Squeezing in some social time is a great way to have fun and make contacts with locals in Paris. Check the events webpages of both the American Library and the legendary bookstore Shakespeare and Company; both institutions hold English-speaking events that, besides sharing bookish themes, usually include wine and snacks, which can help lubricate conversation.

Day 1

Once you've settled into your temporary **Paris** digs, you need to get out there and explore. Use your first day to orient yourself to the city and its major landmarks as you shake your jet lag. Pick up a free city map at the tourist office next to Notre-Dame, and use it to set your course for the week. If you're not quite ready to dive into the serious business of assessing your future home, consider popping into **Berthillon** on Île Saint-Louis for a scoop or two of dark chocolate sorbet, and devour your icy treat as you walk to the **Hôtel de Ville**, where rotating art exhibits are always free and, more often than not, extremely interesting.

© VENIAMIN KRASKOV /123RF

Exploring Paris's neighborhoods is part of the fun.

Days 2-3

Once you've got your bearings, you'll be able to settle on a neighborhood to explore on foot. Heading north toward **République**—where the revamped plaza hums with the energetic buzz of skateboards, bikes, and flâneurs—you'll pass several neighborhood attractions, including streets lined with boutiques offering clothing in varying degrees of affordability, art galleries, and several museums. Just beyond Place de la République, you can continue walking north toward **Belleville**, or lean left and explore **Canal Saint-Martin**. Either direction you follow will lead you to enchanting corners brimming with cafés, food shops, and street art. Wine bars like **La Verre Volé** (67, rue de Lancry, tel. 01/48 03 17 34) and hipster cafés like Ten Belles (10, rue de la Grange aux Belles, tel. 01/42 40 90 78) or **Holybelly** (19, rue Lucien Sampaix, tel. 09/73 60 13 64) offer great opportunities to refuel with your tipple of choice and a nibble before your exploration recommences.

Day 4

If your legs haven't turned to Silly Putty, spend today exploring east Paris and the young, hip neighborhoods around Bastille. At the every-day-except-Monday **Marché d'Aligre** (place d'Aligre) open-air market, you can pick up all kinds of goodies for an afternoon picnic and get a feel for the daily shopping rituals that take place in neighborhoods across Paris. Follow the nearby multi-use path known as the Promenade Plantée toward the Bois de Vincennes, and veer off to visit the **Musée de l'Histoire de l'Immigration** (293, avenue Daumesnil, tel. 01/53 59 58 60), which charts migratory trajectories and personal narratives of the many hundreds of thousands of newcomers before you who have made this city the multicultural oasis it is today.

Days 5-6

Days 5 and 6 ought to strike a balance between work and play. Visit an *immobilier* (realty office), inquire about opening a bank account, then take a Seine cruise from the **bateaux mouches** at Pont Neuf and see the city from a new perspective. Boats traverse the waterway in both directions, ferrying passengers up to Bercy, and back down to the twinkling Tour Eiffel.

Day 7

Spend your final day in Paris parked at a café, taking notes and logging impressions of your experience. Did any neighborhoods call out to you? Did you make any contacts you'll want to reconnect with by email or Skype when you get home? Are you able to rule out places to live and narrow the search down to a quartier or two? When you get home, log onto FUSAC (www.fusac.fr) and bookmark the *les annonces* page; you'll want to check back frequently to see if any apartments have become available in your preferred neighborhoods, and whether any dream jobs in your area of experience and expertise have opened.

TWO WEEKS: SUBURBAN EXPLORATION

Two weeks is a luxurious amount of time for getting acquainted with the Île-de-France region. In 14 days, you can become familiar with multiple arrondissements on both sides of the Seine, branch out into the Petite Couronne with trips to La Défense and Montreuil, and stay overnight in Versailles and Maisons-Laffitte.

Day 1

After you've settled into your digs, set off to secure your travel passes. If you plan to use a combination of public transportation and walking, spend €13.70 on a *carnet* of 10 tickets good for the Métro and city buses that will last the duration of your stay—if you rely primarily on walking, and use the Métro or bus to dodge the rain or whisk you across town. For a little more than €20 per week, you can splash out on an un-limited Navigo pass that'll get you to and from the airports on the RER, as well as the suburbs of Maisons-Laffitte, Sceaux, and Versailles. Less expensive Navigo options are also available, including those for students, and can be purchased from kiosk vendors in train stations, some Métro stations, and many *tabacs*. Another possibility is simply to buy tickets as you go; 2014 Paris transit tickets cost €1.70 when purchased indi-vidually. The RER train to both Versailles and Maisons-Laffitte is currently €4.20, whereas the 45-minute trip to Sceaux costs €2.65 each way.

Days 2-5

If you haven't yet had the chance to explore more far-flung arrondissements, now is the time. In northwest Paris, the **Sacré-Coeur** stands like a bright white beacon, drawing tourists and those in the know to one of the coolest neighborhoods in *la Ville Lumière* at the foot of **Montmartre**. Wander rue des Abbesses, stopping for a glass of wine and a nibble at **La Cave des Abbesses** (43, rue des Abbesses, tel. 01/42 52 81 54) to get you into the local spirit. Climb one of the vertiginous staircases to the top of the hill for amazing views over the city, then set off back down and mosey toward Gare du Nord and Little Jaffna, where South Asian restaurants, sari shops, and Bollywood music stores sit cheek-by-jowl for several blocks. If you've worked up a hankering for a spicy curry or dosa, pop into **Chettinadu Mess** (15, rue Cail, tel. 01/40 34 49 17), where a filling, flavorsome thali will set you back €7.50 and fuel the rest of the adventures that lie ahead.

Days 6-8

La Villette is where joggers, cyclists, and parents pushing strollers make good use of the open green spaces. If it's a Saturday morning, mosey over to the lively **Batignolles** neighborhood, where a weekly *bio* (organic) market is in full swing. While you're here, stop into every *immobilier* (real estate office) you pass and pick up a copy of its latest listings.

From here, hop on the Métro and migrate south toward the **Parc de Saint-Cloud**, where you can look back at Paris and admire the view, as Marie Antoinette and Napoleon III once did, while getting a taste of what suburban Paris has to offer. Crossing the *périphérique* back into Paris proper, head toward the **Alésia** neighborhood in the 14th, visit the cool (and kind of creepy) catacombs, then pick up a copy of *Particulier à Particulier* at the nearest *la presse* kiosk, tote it to an inviting terrace café, and enjoy the last rays of the sun while perusing your collection of apartment-rental listings.

Days 9-10

If you're moving to Paris with children, use one of these days to visit schools you're considering enrolling your wee one(s) in. In Paris and its suburbs, private school options range from traditional Catholic schools to Montessori, Waldorf, and beyond. (Read more in the *Language and Education* section of the *Daily Life* chapter). School administrative officials are available to answer your questions in person with a bit of advance warning, so get in touch as soon as you land and schedule those all-important rendezvous.

You can use another day to scope out the Wednesday entertainment opportunities for your kids. In France, Wednesdays are a no-school day (or a half-day), and one hallowed tradition is the afternoon *atelier*. These workshops are geared to children between the ages of 3 and 15, and vary between one- and four-hours long. Often hosted by museums, including the Louvre, d'Orsay, and Rodin, the classes might include art history, jewelry making, cooking, sculpture, or painting. Classes cost between €5 and €25. Information on dozens of workshops can be found at www.atelierenfant.com/paris, as well as on websites for individual museums.

Days 11-12

After immersing yourself in urban culture for more than a week, you might be ready for a getaway that combines research with relaxation. First stop: Versailles. The RER C takes approximately 40 minutes to ferry you the 20 kilometers to the Versailles Rive Gauche station. From here, you can make the five-minute walk to the **Hôtel des Roys** (14, avenue de Paris, tel. 01/57 32 34 61), conveniently located right around the corner from the train station and practically next door to the flag-flanked *mairie*. Once you've settled in, you can take the 10-minute walk to the château and stroll its legendary grounds. Between your hotel and the palace's entry, you'll find the **Office de Tourism** (2, avenue de Paris, tel. 01/39 24 88 88), where the nice people behind the

© AURELIA D'ANDREA

Signs point the way to some interesting destinations.

counter will answer your questions and load you up with enough maps and brochures to see you through to next year. Several dining opportunities exist inside the royal grounds; try one of the terrace restaurants where pizza and wine will set you back less than €20.

Tuesdays, Fridays, and Sundays are market days in Versailles. If your visit falls on one of these mornings, grab your *chariot* (or recyclable shopping bag) and make a beeline for the **Place Notre-Dame.** Here, your wheely-bag will converge with those of locals, who will load them with edible goodies, while giving you a sense of the type of neighbors you might end up with if you relocate to this corner of Île-de-France. The Saturday morning organic market at **Place de la Cathédral Saint-Louis** is also worth a visit. Before lunch, pop over to the office of the *mairie* for a new-arrivals package, with details on schools, local events, places of worship, and civic life in the city. You might also consider renting a bike from **Phébus** (place Raymond Poincaré, tel. 01/39 20 16 60), a municipal bike-rental agency that offers electric and standard issue two-wheelers by the hour, day, month, or even year. A €20 per day electric bike rental allows you to cover a lot of territory, including neighboring villages like **Le Chesnay**, home to a sizeable community of fellow expats.

Day 13

Squeeze in a trip to **Sceaux**, whose sprawling, manicured park is without question its allure. Like Versailles, it boasts a château—albeit much more humble than its royal equivalent to the west. A day trip to discover the charms of the *centre-ville* followed by an excursion to this historic green space feels a lot like a mini-vacation all on its own. At the *mairie,* you can ask about local French courses and solicit recommendations for things to see and do during your visit.

Day 14

Following a diagonally northwest trajectory from Sceaux, you'll end up in **Maisons-Laffite**, home of the Paris-Brest pastry (and yes, tasting one while you're here is compulsory) and a famous horse-racing track that bears its name. The town's bilingual international school is one of the reasons so many Anglophones settle here, and if you attend one of the city-sponsored cultural events on the subject of literature, art, and history, you'll likely meet a few of them. You might also want to connect with the folks at ASTI, an acronym for *Association de Solidarité aux Travailleurs Immigrés de Maisons-Laffitte* (www.asti-maisons-laffitte.com). As its name implies, this nonprofit, volunteer-run organization exists to support foreign workings who live here, and services include French-language courses and academic support for non-French-speaking school-age children.

Practicalities

ACCOMMODATIONS

One of France's best-kept secrets is its value-for-money lodgings. Who needs a fancy €3,000-per-night suite at the Plaza Athénée when, for a fraction of the price, you can relax for a night or two in a comfortable room with free wireless Internet *and* a view of the Eiffel Tower? Bargains aren't limited to Paris or to hotels—you'll also discover great deals on bed-and-breakfasts, *gîtes,* and short-term apartment and villa stays throughout the Île-de-France offering clean comfort for the night. France holds the distinction of having a counterintuitive cheaper-on-the-weekends hotel policy, so if you're flying in on a Friday, Saturday, or Sunday, you'll likely get your room for an even better rate than you would midweek.

If you're going the good old-fashioned hotel route, it's helpful to know what those stars posted at the hotel entryway mean. The French government has instituted a rating system that the majority of establishments adhere to, with the number of stars clearly visible outside, usually affixed to a blue sign on the wall adjacent to the front door. The number of stars doesn't reflect quality per se, but it does correspond to the amenities available to guests, which may act as an indicator of quality. A hotel with five stars might have a swimming pool and a refrigerator full of booze and bottled water, but that doesn't mean it's immune from the dreaded cockroach. What you *can* expect at the bottom level is a no-frills room with a bed, a TV, and a bathroom equipped with a tiny shower stall. There may or may not be an *ascenseur* (elevator) to take you to your fourth-floor room. Budget chains include Kyriad, Ibis, and Formule 1, which offer a uniform aesthetic with predictable, midlevel quality and comfort. Further up the starry ladder are the Novotel and Mercure chains, which fall into the three- and four-star range. Only a handful of French hotels reach five-star status.

So what can you expect to pay, and what do you get for your euro? In Paris, you could find a chic little boutique hotel with a cut-rate room priced at €100, with a Métro stop a two-minute walk out the lobby door and a *boulangerie* on the corner where all of your brioche-for-breakfast dreams can come true. In the Petite Couronne, chain hotels are ubiquitous, particularly so right near the freeway off-ramps. You can get a simple room for €45, with the sound of highway traffic lulling you to sleep. In the Grande Couronne, Maisons-Laffitte and Versailles offer a combination of chain hotels (particularly the popular Accor group establishments: Ibis, Kyriad, etc.) and small independent hotels with rooms that start around €60 per night for two people. In other words, there's a lot of variety, and the prices aren't bad either.

If you're securing a place to stay on the spot rather than booking in advance, ask to see a room before committing. In France, you always pay at checkout and you'll be asked for your passport at check-in, at which time they might decide to hold on to your passport for the duration of your stay. Accommodations run the gamut from thrifty to fancy, and while the room you get may not exactly match the description precisely, you can be sure of quality, safety, and a good night's sleep.

Dogs are generally welcomed at hotels throughout France. You may have to pay a per-day fee of €5 or so, but more often than not, furry friends get to tag along for free.

Paris

The French capital is loaded with options for accommodations, from short-stay apartment rentals and niche B&Bs to swanky upscale hotels and family-run one-star dives. Subletting is a common practice throughout France, and if you plan to stay for a month or more, Craigslist is a great place to start your search for a temporary apartment rental, especially during school vacation periods. Beware of anyone who asks you to wire money in advance (though if they accept PayPal, you're safe). For added security, Airbnb is a reliable and interesting option, with accommodations in virtually every price range and style, from campgrounds to châteaux. Veering off the tourist path will lead you to more bargain digs than you could ever hope to find near the Champs-Élysées and will give you the chance discover neighborhoods worth considering as your new home.

On a quiet but interesting street in the Batignolles neighborhood, **Hotel El Dorado** (18, rue des Dames, tel. 01/45 22 35 21) offers arty comfort at a bargain price. A tidy, slightly bohemian room overlooking a lovely garden costs €98 (shave off €10 for a room overlooking the street), and the downstairs bistro serves afternoon drinks and tasty meals to guests and non-guests alike. Not far away, in the hipster SoPi (South of Pigalle) neighborhood is the beloved-by-many **Hotel L'Amour** (8, rue de Navarin, tel. 01/48 78 31 80). As the name implies, this is a dreamy spot to rest your head for the night, and because it was designed with lovers in mind, you won't find TVs or other distractions to impede romance. You will find cozy, arty rooms, some of which overlook the darling courtyard café. Double rooms start at €170 per night.

Sceaux

What Sceaux lacks in accommodations, it more than makes up for in down-to-earth charm. Directly in front of the town's suburban train station is **B & B by Isa** (1, rue Raymond Gachelin, tel. 01/49 73 14 52), a pleasant *maison d'hôtes* run by Isabelle Guillamet, a friendly, bilingual Frenchwoman. She'll make you feel right at home, and offer ideas for getting-to-know Sceaux itineraries.

The town's only hotel isn't a bad option. **Hôtel Colbert** (20, avenue de Camberwell, tel. 01/46 60 02 21) sits smack in the center of everything, and offers 37 rooms—three of which are handicap-accessible, a true rarity in France. Doubles start at €99, and dogs are an extra €5.

Boulogne-Billancourt

In pleasant, Seine-side Boulogne-Billancourt, a vivacious Hungarian expat offers simple accommodations in her modern and private **apartment** (21, quai Alphonse le Gallo, tel. 01/41 31 01 49). The price is right at €40/55 (single/double), with homemade breakfast included. Nature lovers will appreciate easy access to the verdant and historic Parc de Saint-Cloud, a five-minute walk out the front door and across the river.

Levallois-Perret

Just over the *périphérique* in Levallois-Perret, the chain hotel **Ibis** (24, rue Trébois, tel. 01/47 57 43 99) sits right in the town's homey, welcoming commercial center, within a two-minute walk of the covered market, cute cafés, and boutiques. Modern rooms outfitted with flat-screen TVs and free Wi-Fi average around €75, and dogs are welcome.

Montreuil

In eastern Paris, not far from Montreuil and the bois de Vincennes, hipster hideaway **Mama Shelter** (109, rue de Bagnolet, tel. 01/43 48 48 48) welcomes guests for a stylish stay. Luxe doubles begin at €89, and include free movies and Wi-Fi, and easy access to the on-site restaurant that makes some of the best pizza in the city.

Versailles

There's no question that Versailles is a tourist magnet, but most folks who find their way here are merely day-trippers from Paris coming to ogle the magnificent château and steep themselves in history. Staying for a day or three gives you the advantage of seeing the town from a local's perspective, and the options for making yourself at home here are plentiful.

One of the most delightful places to overnight is at **l'Orangerie White-Palacio** (37, avenue de Paris, tel. 09/53 61 07 57). Tucked into a gorgeous garden just a hop, skip, and a jump from the château gates, l'Orangerie offers two bright, cheerful rooms and one studio garden apartment. Patricia, the Spanish proprietor, opened her boutique establishment in 2008, and offers a warm welcome to all who cross her threshold. Room rates begin at €110.

Another charming possibility at a slightly lower price point is **Hôtel des Roys** (14, avenue de Paris, tel. 01/57 32 34 61), conveniently located next door to the *mairie*. Double rooms, which start at €90, are simple and comfortable, and the English-speaking staff are friendly and helpful. Modern conveniences include flat-screen TVs and all the free Wi-Fi you can handle.

Maisons-Laffitte

Even though it's a mere 20 kilometers outside of Paris, Maisons-Laffitte feels a world away from the hyperkinetic city clamor. The bucolic ambiance is cultivated in large part by the equestrian community that flourishes here (it's not called "the city of horses" for nothing). In fitting with the horsey theme, accommodations here tend to be nestled in verdant spaces.

Villa Carioca (15, avenue Vergniaud, tel. 01/57 32 49 46) is as beautiful *maison d'hôtes* that sits in the former gardens of the local château. New arrivals will find exquisite rooms decorated in colorful 19th-century style. Double rooms begin at about €160, and bikes are available for guests to explore the city.

Another option, within a very short walk of the train station, is **Cerise Maisons-Laffitte** (16-18, rue de Paris, tel. 01/39 62 11 91). Each room in this '80s modern establishment is a self-contained studio with a mini-kitchen, making it convenient to prepare money-saving meals *chez vous*. Flat-screen TVs, free Wi-Fi, and complimentary newspapers are added perks.

FOOD

If Parisians aren't the dining-out champions of the world, then who could possibly claim that title? In even the quietest neighborhood, every street seems to have at least two restaurants, one of which is guaranteed to be hopping with happy patrons. Do as 62 percent of Parisians do, and eat in the quartier you call home. Don't know which restaurant on your block to try? Start menus are almost always posted outside the restaurant, which lets you explore your options before committing. Eating is one of the great joys of living in Paris.

Paris

Paris is experiencing a wine-bar trend; they've always existed here, but they haven't always served natural wines and fabulous selections of small plates in the way they do now. For a traditional experience near the Bastille that's festive and affordable, visit **Le Baron Rouge** (1, rue Théophile Roussel, tel. 01/43 43 14 32). The wonderful wine list is the main draw, but the cheese and charcuterie plates are popular, as are the seasonal oyster platters. Not far away is **Septime** (80, rue de Charonne, tel. 01/43 67 38 29), a trendy spot that's both restaurant and wine bar. Head to the restaurant for a sit-down experience, or go around the corner for a casual glass of wine and nibbles.

For something less traditional, Paris offers oodles of options. For a taste of Africa, go to Batignolles in Paris's far northwest corner, where the scent of roasting coffee beans signals your proximity to **Menelik** (4, rue Sauffroy, tel. 01/46 27 00 82). At this lively Ethiopian eatery, every guest is greeted with a complimentary glass of *kir,* and everyone leaves utterly sated and happy. Closer to Gare du Nord, you'll discover blocks and blocks of South Asian restaurants, some better than others, but most offering flavorsome meals at excellent prices. At **Saravanaa Bhavan** (170, rue du Faubourg Saint-Denis, tel. 01/40 05 01 01), everything is prepared fresh, and the service is fast and efficient. Try the dosas or the uthappam, and make use of the coconut chutney served with them.

Sceaux

Sceaux lacks pretention. Friendly service, a warm welcome, and down-to-earth food is what you can expect to find. One of the best places to experience this is at **Plaisirs du Thé** (96, rue Houdan). This cozy teahouse serves tea *(bien sûr),* as well as traditional hot chocolate, simple but tasty sandwiches, and scrumptious desserts. Across the street is chain creperie **L'île O' Crêpes** (93, rue Houdan), a sort of International House of Pancakes for the Francophile set. Savory galettes are served with a side salad and include intriguing varieties such as the Jersey (smoked salmon, crème fraîche) and the Ibiza (tuna and olives). Sweet crepes follow a similar geographic theme, with the Hawaii (dark chocolate and salted butter) and the Antigua (caramel and whipped cream). Sophisticated adults might prefer **La Table de Catherine** (30, rue des Écoles), where you can start with oysters in shallot vinaigrette, move on to roasted fish with tender spring greens, and finish with a chestnut-pistachio crème brûlée.

Boulogne-Billancourt

One of the benefits of living in Boulogne is that you don't have to make the jaunt into Paris to experience a tasty meal. Options run the gustatory gamut, from kebab-frites to top-tier gastronomy. If your tastes fall somewhere in between, you might like **Volfoni** (14-16, bvd de la République, www.restaurant-volfoni.fr), a popular spot serving modern interpretations of Italian classics. Generous antipasti plates, gorgeous pizzas baked in a wood-fired oven (€11.50-18.50), and delectable salads are just a few of the choices. Cocktails, Italian wines, and desserts—including the quirky Nutella pizza—have helped win over locals, as has the festive Sunday brunch (€28).

For something more deluxe, the **Table de Cybele** (38, rue de Meudon, www.latabledecybele.com) is worth the effort to make a reservation. Very French in feel (but run by American expats), the restaurant/wine bar's menu focuses on seasonal, local produce prepared with great care and presented in chic, modern surroundings. Try the daily formule (€24-29), which allows you to sample several courses in one fell swoop.

For a taste of *ailleurs* (another place) without having to board a plane, **La Medina** (110, ave du Général Leclerc, www.lamedina-boulogne.com) is the local culinary escape. From your terrace table, you can enjoy traditional plates, including the savory-sweet pastry known as *pastilla*, vegetarian and meat-based couscous and *tajines*, and delicately spiced desserts served with mint tea or the house specialty, pine-nut tea. Wine, beer, and cocktails are also on tap.

Levallois-Perret

The narrow streets that flank Levallois' covered market are filled with dining possibilities. Whether cobbling together a DIY lunch from treats at various market stands or sitting down to a relaxed three-course meal, you'll discover a solid variety to suit most palates. One cheap, tasty, and filling spot for a mid-day meal is **Beity** (17, rue Gabriel Péri), a Lebanese café where everything is house-made and fresh. From hummus and moussaka (€4.50) to falafel and *fatayers* (€4.50/4), an authentic taste of Beirut is guaranteed. Lunch specials (€9.50-11.50) are a veritable bargain. **L'Amethystos** (81, rue Chaptal) is the best spot in town for Greek cuisine. Excellent service, big portions, and bright flavors are its hallmarks; locals rave about the artisanal ice cream on the dessert menu. For a more typical taste of France, **Je l'M** (4, rue Henri Barbusse) is a stellar option. The meat-and-fish oriented menu offers entrées that hover around €12, and main dishes that top out at €24. The ambiance can be described as "cozy" and the service is flawless. Don't miss the Tarte Tatin (€8) served with crème fraîche for dessert.

Montreuil

Montreuil's dining options match the town's funky, artistic sensibilities and multiculturalism. New culinary ideas have flourished here, including food trucks and tapas bars—both of which have been slow to arrive in other parts of the Île-de-France region. For a unique dining experience that reflects community eclecticism, pop into **Casa Poblano** (15, rue Lavoisier, www.casa-poblano.fr). In this convivial dining space and cultural center, you can chow down on pizzas (€8-11), vegetarian daily specials (€7), and simple but tasty desserts. Wash it down with an icy cold beer, glass of fruit juice, or *verre de vin* (€2-2.50). To get into the local groove, head over to the marché de la Croix de Chavaux (place de la Croix de Chavaux) and look for **The Caravane d'Orée** (www.caravane-doree.com), a food truck serving Vietnamese style *bo bun* noodle bowls (€8), *banh mi* and bagel sandwiches (€6), drinks, and desserts. Spanish tapas are becoming a thing in Montreuil. If you want to see what it's all about, your best bet is **El Pincho**

(43, rue de Paris). A stone's throw from the marché de la Croix de Chavaux, El Pincho serves up good sangria (€4), salsa music, and a Spanish tortilla (€2.50). You'll also find burgers, club sandwiches, and even risotto on the eclectic menu.

Versailles

The dining options in Versailles veer toward the traditional. Cafés serving crepes, homey old-school brasseries, and chic bistros dominate the culinary scene, though there are more than a few Indian restaurants for those who prefer something with a bit more spice. One of the best Indian spots in town is **Le Shandrani** (12, rue Saint-Simon, www.shandrani.fr). Inside, it's homey-chic; outside, it's typical French terrace dining. Menu standouts include the spiced birianis (€13.50-14.50) and garlic naan. Set menus (€13-22) allow you to sample several dishes in one memorable meal. On the more traditional end of the spectrum is **Le Valmont** (20, rue au Pain, www.levalmont. com), where French food is king. Expect food fit for royals: Oysters, veal, foie gras, and mains served with creamy sauces. The price for a fixed-price gastronomic menu is €35, which is downright reasonable when compared to the queen of all Versailles restaurants, **Gordon Ramsay au Trianon** (1, blvd de la Reine, www.trianonpalace. com). Located on the grounds of the famous chateau, you'll be swept into haute-cuisine heaven with every spendy bite. Book far in advance to secure a reservation, and set aside about €250 per person to revel in the full experience.

Maisons-Laffitte

Avenue de Longueil, Maisons-Laffitte's main thoroughfare, is where you'll find some of the best dining possibilities. A neighborhood favorite—easily identifiable by the red telephone booth out front—is **Le Cosy** (37, ave de Longueil, www.lecosy.fr), which, as its name implies, is a warm and welcoming place to dine. The bilingual menu veers toward traditional French dishes, and includes such favorites as Tartare de Boeuf (€16), steamed mussels (€16), and cheese plates for dessert. Across the street is the uber-popular Italian spot **Caffe e Cucina** (36, ave de Longueil, www.pizzeria-restaurant-cucina. fr). Marinated-vegetable antipasti, risotto, and too-good pizzas beckon from the vast menu. A great wine selection and friendly waitstaff make you want to linger. Slightly off the beaten path, but within five minutes of ave de Longueil, is **La Maison de Tokyo** (17, rue des Plantes, www.lamaisondetokyo.com), where sushi-lovers unite over creative maki rolls (€5.80-8), sashimi (€10.50), and saki.

DAILY LIFE

MAKING THE MOVE

No more postponing the dream. You've decided to make the move to the world's most beautiful metropolis and integrate baguettes, berets, and cafés into your everyday life. Yes! What's more, you've already made a reconnaissance trip or two, decided where you want to live, and begun researching the area for schools, employment opportunities, and housing. Now comes the tricky part: how to make it all happen. Visas, *cartes de séjour,* residency permits—what do they all mean, and what exactly do you need to make this big leap a success? There's a lot to consider, but with a bit more planning and a lot of moxie, the transition can be practically pain-free. Stumbling blocks are bound to appear, but don't let the bureaucratic sludge drag you down. Follow the rules and somehow, thankfully, it all comes together. Excited? You ought to be! Just a few more hurdles and you're on your way.

Immigration and Visas

As a citizen of Canada or the United States, you don't need a visa for stays of fewer than 90 days. France is a signatory of the Schengen Agreement, which means it shares a flexible internal border-control system with fellow Schengen countries and a stronger border-crossing process with non-Schengen countries, such as the United Kingdom. Passport checks are rare between, say, France and Belgium, but they're a given if you're traveling to the UK. Your free 90-day visa is valid throughout the Schengen zone, but don't mistakenly believe that to extend your stay you just need to Chunnel on over to England, get your passport stamped, and resume another 90-day sojourn in France. Unfortunately, it doesn't work like that. If you want to stay legal, you can make only one 90-day visit within any six-month period. When in doubt, apply for a long-stay visa or accept the risks involved in overstaying your welcome.

The first step in determining what kind of visa to apply for is to ask yourself how long you plan to be in France. If you're subletting your flat back in Minneapolis and just want to try a three-month trial run, that's considered a "short stay"—as is any stay shorter than 90 days—and a valid passport is all you need. But if you're planning on a year (a school year or an actual calendar year), you'll need to begin the visa application process *tout de suite* (right away). Even though it probably won't take this long, give yourself a good two months to make it all come together.

Step two is figuring out what you're going to do when you get here, to help you zero in on which long-stay visa to apply for. Maybe you've always fantasized about living in France and just want an extended vacation to relax, study independently, or meet a handsome Frenchman or -woman and see where the relationship takes you. If so, you'll need money in the bank to show you can support yourself for the duration of your stay. Do you have a brilliant idea for a new business that *has* to be launched in France? There's a visa for that. It also requires evidence of your means of support, plus detailed information on how you plan to carry out the project, and you must prove that the idea itself fills a void in France to be eligible for approval. Maybe you're a college student who wants to study abroad for the semester or a nanny (or manny) who just landed an au pair job through an agency. Whether you're an artist, an entrepreneur, an intern, or a student, there's a long-stay visa with your name on it. Now getting that visa will take a bit of elbow grease and perseverance, but armed with willpower and solid resolve, you can make it happen.

WHERE AND HOW TO APPLY

Submitting your visa application must be done in person, but not every state or province in the United States and Canada has a French consulate. If your region does not, you'll have to make the trip for a scheduled appointment. One appointment is all you need: Follow-up requests for documentation can be mailed or faxed in, and your passport—with or without a shiny new visa inside—can be mailed back to you in the pre-stamped express-mail envelope you provide at the time of your appointment. To find the consulate closest to you, visit www.ambafrance-us.org (United States) or www.ambafrance-ca.org (Canada).

DOSSIER OR DIE

Dossier. OK, let's try saying that out loud the French way: "dohs-YAY." You'll want to practice this a few times to get the hang of it, because you're going to use it a lot. You'll need a dossier every step of the way on your move to France, beginning at the consulate, and ending with –well, it never ends in France. You'll create a dossier for the *préfecture*, the bank, the real-estate company, the movers, your university, your children's school, the gas company, the veterinarian, the doctor, and just about everything else you can think of.

The dossier is simply a file containing documents relating to whatever business is at hand. The foundation of nearly every dossier includes the following:

- a copy of your passport, *carte de séjour*, or other ID

- your EDF bill or another proof of residence (often an *attestation* written by the person hosting you, including *her* gas bill and copy of her *carte d'identité*

- two or three passport-sized photos, which you're expected to have taken in the automated photo booths found in administrative buildings and train stations, among other places.

Then, like a bureaucratic buffet, each agency adds on a series of extra must-haves that give your dossier its special flavor. Though most expats find the dossier system tiresome, each pile of paperwork you create makes building the next one that much easier.

LONG-STAY VISA

Visa laws have relaxed in the past few years, so most long-stay visa holders don't need to visit the *préfecture* on arrival, as had long been standard protocol. (An exception to this rule is the *carte compétences et talents*, which still necessitates a visit to your local *préfecture*.) Instead of schlepping yourself and your dossier full of paperwork to endless appointments, the streamlined system allows you to register with the French Office of Immigration and Integration (OFII) by mail within three months of your arrival.

Registration involves submitting copies of your passport pages that show your photo and expiration date; the entry stamp for your arrival in France; and the visa issued to you by the French Consulate. You'll also need to include a completed Demande d'Attestation OFII form, which you'll receive from consular officials when your passport is returned to you with your new visa. (If you don't automatically receive this form, ask for one or visit the OFII website to download a copy: www.ofii.fr.)

These items must be sent via *lettre recommandé*, which is essentially a registered letter that the recipient must sign for. Once your documents are received, you'll receive a notice of receipt from the OFII, which serves as temporary proof of your legal right to reside in France. Within three months, you'll be called in for the requisite medical exam, which includes lung X-rays and blood-sugar analysis, at which time you'll also pay for your *timbres* (tax stamps)—which, depending on your status, will vary between €58 and €260. Once this process has been completed, you'll receive the final passport stamp in the visa-acquisition process: a *vignette* stamp alongside your French visa.

STUDENT VISA

Probably the most popular of all move-to-France visas is the student visa. French universities are open to anyone of any age who has earned his or her high school diploma or equivalent. Because it's a relatively straightforward point of entry into France that also gives the holder the right to work part-time, this is an attractive option for getting your foot through the French front door.

Students used to have to apply for a visa even if they intended to stay for fewer than 90 days, but that's no longer the case: Your American or Canadian passport is sufficient if you'll be living and studying in France for less than three months—say, a summer study-abroad course. However, because students who hold a *carte de séjour* are entitled to work part-time during their residency, you might consider jumping through those more challenging hoops to get the long-stay visa even if you don't plan to reside in France for the entire duration, just for the added perk of being allowed to work legally.

It may take quite a few prefecture visits to sort out your *carte de séjour*.

If you'll be studying for more than three months, you'll need to apply for a long-stay student visa, which first requires you to register online with Campus France, an intermediary agency that handles the initial phase of your visa formalities. Here, you'll create the first of many *dossiers,* so consider it a necessary evil. Whether you're a Canadian or an American citizen, you will be expected to have your Campus France ID number at the time of your appointment at the consulate, as well as a long-stay visa application, travel itinerary, and proof of financial means of support while you're away. You may also be asked for several other documents, making for a multi-visit experience before you've even left the country. (If you live out of state or out of the area, you'll be allowed to fax or send in supplemental documents.) You'll need several passport-size photos throughout the process, so have a set made and carry them with you to each appointment in your home country as well as in France.

With most types of visa, once you arrive in France you'll need to follow the OFII registration procedure outlined in the long-stay visa section above. If, after your first year in France, you'd like to renew your residency permit, you'll have to do so at the prefecture two months before your current residency permit expires.

WORK VISA

If you're one of the lucky ones who has already received a job offer in France, you'll have to apply for a visa before you can receive your work permit. But before *that* happens, the company sponsoring you must file all the necessary paperwork on its end with the

French labor department (DDTEFP). (The exception to this is the work contract for 90 days or fewer; no visa is needed for short-term workers, but your employer must still file paperwork on your behalf to make the arrangement legal.) Once it's approved, you can start cultivating your own paper trail.

Don't have a job offer yet? Start scouring the employment opportunities on sites like FUSAC (www.fusac.org), Craigslist, the UN, OECD, and UNESCO. A wise idea is to investigate all the American-owned companies in Paris, of which there are scads, including restaurants, boutiques, hotels, and tourism-related enterprises. Note that high-level, well-paid positions are in high demand among future expats, and the pool of qualified applicants will be full and competition stiff. Be honest with yourself when submitting your résumé: If you don't have a college degree, the likelihood you'll land one of the coveted positions with an international NGO or multinational with offices in Paris or La Défense is slim. The odds aren't impossible, but they're not great. The more advanced your educational qualifications, the better your chances of getting a sponsored gig. Ditto for your language skills. If you aren't equipped with at least conversational French, you may have a tough time securing your dream job with a company that will sponsor your visa. (See more about working in France in the *Employment* chapter.)

If you work at a company in the United States or Canada with offices in France, explore transfer opportunities. Many banks, high-tech companies, and fashion-related organizations have set up shop here and offer first-consideration privileges to those who have been on their employment rosters for at least three months. As a final option, you can hit up your French friends to "hire" you to work for them. If a good friend or family member is willing to climb the bureaucratic Mont Blanc on your behalf, this could be your ticket. As with any endeavor that attempts to skirt the standard procedure, there are inherent risks involved; still, this sort of creative problem-solving is not unheard of. Approached with a modicum of professionalism, it can be a successful way to move to France and secure legal permission to work.

CARTE DE SÉJOUR COMPÉTENCES ET TALENTS

In theory, this "skill and talents" card is a dream made real for independent, creative types who want to live in France but don't fit into any of the other visa categories. The idea is that you come up with a project you'd like to work on in France that fits within your professional and educational experience. The tricky part is that it must in some way function as a means of bridging the cultural relationship between France and your home country. Perhaps you own a bicycle shop in Portland and teach mountain-biking clinics on the weekend; you may want to parlay your experience into a business that teaches children how to ride downhill in the Alps. Or maybe you're finishing up your PhD in 20th-century American literature and want to start a tourism business that takes travelers on a journey along the path of the Lost Generation in Paris and beyond. There are countless ideas, but this visa is still in the experimental phase. There are no exact parameters on what the powers-that-be are looking for, and therefore no guarantees that they'll accept your proposal. To boost your chances of getting the green light, invest time in creating a solid business plan before presenting it to French consular officials. Get creative with your powers of persuasion, pull out all your credentials (letters of recommendation, diplomas, and certificates), and really sell yourself and the lasting contribution your project will have on the French public.

When applying for a *carte de séjour compétences et talents,* you'll need to prepare yourself for the number of trees that will be sacrificed to meet the demands of consular officials: long-stay visa forms, letters from your bank, a police record release or FBI clearance form, résumé, proof of insurance, proof that you have a place to live in France, flight itineraries—all in duplicate.

If you are granted this visa, you are entitled—again, in theory—to a renewable three-year *carte de séjour* that allows you to work in your chosen profession. If you are married, your spouse will receive a *vie privée et familiale* card that entitles him or her to work as well. But don't get too excited just yet. Even if you're granted this visa, you can still expect to jump through a lot of hoops to get your *carte* once you arrive in France. Expect to spend many hours over several days, weeks, and even months at the *préfecture.* You will be asked to produce supplemental material—notarized translations of specific documents, French-language copies of your rental agreement, proof of address, copies of your passport, photographs—and even then you may be told that they're only going to give you a one-year *carte* "to see how it goes" before allowing you to renew.

FOREIGN TRADER'S CARD

Some people are born with an entrepreneurial spirit. If you want to start a business in France, it will help to be equipped with both that spirit *and* the patience of a saint. You've heard a bit about French bureaucracy, right? Well, it hits its zenith at the business-launching phase. The good news is that tax laws have been relaxed in the last few years, making it easier for startups than ever before. But before you start thinking about applying for this special *carte,* be sure to do your research and have a solid business plan ready. In addition to your long-stay visa application, you'll be asked to provide budgets, proof of funding, and other documents that support your assertion that you know what you're doing and have the backing to carry out the project. Pull out all the stops: Got an aunt in Brittany you haven't seen in 20 years? Call her up and ask if she'll act as a *garante* (financial guarantor). If you have a bank account established in France already, ask the bank to write a letter attesting to your solid financial history and line of credit. Most of all, pitch your idea by touting all the wonderful ways in which it will benefit France, fill a major void, and better serve the community. Your education, experience, connections within France, and ability to communicate in French will all be taken into consideration by the consulate.

VISAS FOR ACCOMPANYING SPOUSES AND CHILDREN

Depending on the type of visa you've applied for, your children and spouse will likely be authorized to join you, provided you've all filled out the necessary forms and provided the required paperwork. Before you begin the process, make sure you have copies of your marriage license, spouse's birth certificate, and birth certificates of your children. If you or your spouse has children from a previous relationship, a notarized letter from the other parent granting permission to move to France will also be required.

For holders of the *carte de séjour compétences et talents,* your spouse also receives permission to work—one of the many reasons this carte is such an alluring possibility. Workers that are sponsored by an employer and who want to bring their families with them to France need to ensure that the "accompanying family member" paperwork is being taken care of by said employer. Be sure to follow up to thwart unwelcome surprises.

OTHER VISAS

Visas for nannies, researchers, interns, and retirees also exist, and the steps for applying for each are similar to the aforementioned visa application processes. And if you've met a French national and want to marry and move to France, there's a visa for you, too. If the visa you are applying for is likely to be denied for some reason, you will probably be notified of this at the time of your consular appointment. There's a chance that your visa request will be outright refused, in which case you have the right to reapply. If you don't hear back from the consulate within two months, this means the rejection is firm.

Beyond the Visa

When asked to sign formal documents at the *préfecture,* you will often be required to ink your John Hancock into a little rectangular box. Note that this box has very specific boundaries, and if your signature extends beyond any of the four sides of said box, you have effectively ruined the entire document and will have to start over from scratch. So remember to write between the lines—seriously.

Before you are granted any kind of official *carte,* you will be given a temporary Récépissé de Demande de Carte de Séjour, a small rectangle of paper with your photo attached and an official seal and expiration date stamped on it. Before you trade in the interim paper for the official pink laminated version, you'll be required to undergo a quick health screening at a public clinic. The government foots the bill for this—which seems appropriate considering that you'll have the un-fun task of getting naked from the waist up while a stranger photographs your lungs to ensure they're free of tuberculosis.

Depending on where you settle, your experience can vary vastly. Expats report shorter waits at *préfectures* outside Paris city limits, and less muss and fuss in general when it comes to the bureaucratic processes. You can expect long lines—sometimes to the tune of a five-hour wait—and even then, you might not get in the building before they close for lunch or, worse, for the day. Inside, you'll need to pull a numbered ticket from the little machine and wait your turn. Expect line-jumping—lots of it. It's annoying, and you can choose whether or not to pitch a fit. But whatever you do, do not lose your cool with a staff member. Even if you feel as if your brain will explode with frustration after a daylong wait and ruthless line-jumpers, you must keep a calm and composed demeanor when face to face with the people behind the desk if you want a successful experience.

Though it may seem superficial, it helps to take extra care with your personal appearance on the day of your *préfecture* visit. Wearing chic, stylish clothing—don't forget to polish your shoes and groom your hair—and having your dossier neatly organized in a professional-looking attaché case will convey to the authorities that you've got your act together, even if that's the furthest thing from the truth. Some people report getting to bypass certain steps, such as providing proof of funds, and credit the fact that they dressed the part of the professional, upstanding citizen.

RESIDENCY

Visas and *cartes de séjour* have temporary residency periods built into them. Your visa buys you a finite amount of time, and your *carte* gives specific time parameters with renewable options. After three continuous years of residency, holders of the *visiteur, salarié, étudiant, vie privée, commerçante, scientifique,* or *artistique carte* visas are eligible to apply for a 10-year residency permit, which gives you the luxury of returning to the *préfecture* only once a decade. Everyone else must have established five years of residency before they can apply for the 10-year *carte*.

French immigration laws are prone to change with disarming regularity. Keep reviewing the consular websites for new updates and changes, and keep a flexible attitude if at all possible.

Moving with Children

Getting your children to France with you is fairly straightforward, and once you're settled, you'll discover that France is an extraordinarily kid-friendly country—hardly surprising, considering the central role that the family plays here. The first stop in your children's move-abroad adventure is securing your own visa; if you're in, they're in. Like you, they'll need specific documents for the consular appointment: two photos, a long-stay visa application, a copy of their birth certificate and passport. If you are a single father or mother traveling without your child's second parent, you'll also need to bring a notarized letter of authorization to travel signed by him or her.

SCHOOL-AGE CHILDREN

Parents of school-age children will need to begin thinking about enrolling them in some sort of academic institution, and your options are contingent in large part on where you live. *Écoles privées* (private schools)—from Montessori and Waldorf to good old-fashioned Catholic schools—exist throughout the Île-de-France, and like elsewhere, you'll have to pay tuition. The cost varies from school to school, but it's generally less expensive than private schools in the U.S. International schools, which are basically American in concept and function, are also available and provide a familiar academic structure at a premium price. Unlike other countries, where "state-run" anything has negative connotations, French *écoles publiques* (public schools) are of uniformly high quality and are a good way to begin your child's integration into French culture. Just like back home, schools want to see a child's academic records and inoculation history, so don't forget to bring copies of those.

CHILDCARE

If your child is younger and you want to consider daycare, it's helpful to register with your local *crèche* (state-run daycare center). These agencies follow the standard academic cycle and generally accept new wards only in September and occasionally in January, and the registration process begins months in advance, so it plays to plan ahead if you want to guarantee your child a spot. Children as young as three months are welcome, and the staff are highly trained and qualified. Throughout Paris, you will see brigades of nannies, often from former French colonies in West Africa, pushing

The international school in Maisons-Lafitte attracts many expat families.

prams full of infants. You too can find a nanny via word of mouth, Craigslist, FUSAC, an agency, or a referral from your *mairie* (city hall).

RESOURCES FOR FAMILIES

As with any major life change, there is bound to be an adjustment period for your child. Kids are often more adaptable than adults when it comes to new situations—and definitely have an edge up on older family members when it comes to the ability to learn new languages—French culture is different from North American culture, and all the unfamiliarity can be unsettling. Fortunately, there is a lot of support here for you and your family.

Families in the Paris area will want to check out MESSAGE (www.messageparis. org), a support network of fellow Anglophone parents and parents-to-be whose aim is to help you and your family integrate, adapt, and adjust to life in the City of Light. They produce a quarterly magazine with information about regional child- and family-friendly events and activities, host social events, and offer a slew of parenting resources. They charge annual membership dues, but you can find valuable information on their website without having to officially join, and if you want to join but find it economically unfeasible, the organization does offer subsidized memberships to those in need. Another website worth frequenting for information, forums, and articles on a wide range of topics is www.expatica.com, which is particularly comprehensive when it comes to children and family issues. Any question not answered on the site can be posed to the helpful audience in their various forums, and chances are you'll be received warmly and given plenty of helpful information from people who've been through it all already.

A CONVERGENCE OF *NOUNOUS*

Parc Monceau is one of Paris's most picturesque green spaces. Tucked amid fashionable townhomes in the chic 8th arrondissement, the well-groomed 20-acre park is hemmed in by towering wrought-iron gates and stately sycamore trees, and frequented by joggers and old ladies walking fluffy little dogs. But what's most visually striking about this park isn't its perfectly coiffed lawns nor its statues of Chopin and Maupassant. It's the sheer volume of children accompanied by their dutiful *nounous*.

Nounou is French for "nanny," and in this privileged corner of the city, most *nounous* wear the colorful dresses typically worn in West African countries, while their charges, strapped into prams or playing on the jungle gym, sport the distinct uniform of the French upper classes, including expensive shoes and designer jackets from Bonpoint or Tartine et Chocolat. The juxtaposition offers a striking visual insight to the class structure in Paris, where race, class, and privilege collide.

Moving with Pets

One of the most common complaints among expats who move to France with their companion animals is how they were allowed to just breeze right in with their pet after going through all the trouble and expense to secure health certificates and other travel documents. "But don't you want to see my paperwork?" is the common newcomer's cry, and "Not at all, madame! Welcome to France!" seems to be the official response.

This doesn't mean you should skip the pre-departure health check; your airline might request documentation confirming that your cat or dog is healthy and disease-free. For dogs and cats, a microchip is required, as well as current rabies vaccinations. Your vet back home will have the necessary animal-export forms to be stamped by the USDA, the agency that oversees domestic-animal import and export. France does not have an open-door policy for some breeds of dog categorized as "dangerous": pit bulls, rottweilers, and dogs in the mastiff family. If your dog falls into any one of these categories, you'll have to check with the consulate to confirm the import legalities.

FLYING WITH YOUR PET

Some airlines—United and Air France are just two—allow cats and dogs who meet certain weight restrictions to fly in the cabin with you, under your seat. This does not apply to flights coming in and out of the UK, where stringent anti-rabies policies are in place (complete with quarantine) and all animals must be flown in the plane's cargo hold. If you're traveling with your dog or cat, do your best to book a direct flight. The shorter the trip, the less stressful it'll be for your pet—and therefore for you.

It's not generally recommended to sedate your pet because the risks outweigh the benefits. If your four-footed friend reacts badly and looks sick on arrival, customs officials can hold the animal for observation and evaluation by a state-sanctioned veterinarian. Better to time your flight for the evening (or your pet's normal downtime), and if he or she is particularly prone to travel stress, consider a milder approach, such as Bach Flower Remedies' Rescue Remedy, which many pet people swear by. (It reportedly works for stressed-out humans, too.)

CARING FOR YOUR PET

Once you're here, you'll have many veterinarians to choose from, and it wouldn't be a bad idea to visit one and establish a dossier for your pet. This way, you can keep up on necessary vaccinations and have a place to go if your pet should ever fall sick. Don't be surprised if your vet writes you a prescription for Fluffy's antibiotics at the local human pharmacy; many pharmacies throughout France do double-duty vending veterinary and human medical supplies. Pet food is easy to get in France through a number of sources, including at grocery stores, natural-food stores, dedicated pet-supply stores, veterinarians' offices, and online. Depending on the type of food your pet eats, you may want to shop around to see who offers what and at what price. You'll find premium brands such as Science Diet and Eukanuba at veterinary offices, and if your pet happens to be a vegetarian, chains like Naturalia vend plant-based dry and canned food.

Though France is home to more than 18 million dogs and cats, suggesting a country of animal lovers, some antiquated attitudes toward their care still exist here. It's not uncommon to see dogs out "walking themselves," even in big cities like Paris, and when you find a lost or injured animal on the street, it can be a challenge finding an agency willing to accept responsibility for its care. In theory, you should be able to take the animal to the local *commissariat,* which acts as an intermediary between the public and the SPA (Société Protectrice des Animaux); but in practice, you'll most likely find yourself shouldering the responsibility of taking a found animal to the nearest animal protection agency, which might be in a distant suburb.

What to Bring

The three most stressful events in a person's life are said to be death, divorce, and moving. To take some of the stress out the already stressful shift from there to here, it's a good idea to begin planning at least six months in advance. This gives you enough time to decide whether to ship your stuff, store it, sell it, or leave it in a sublet. It also gives you enough time to decide what you really need, what you really want, and how to reconcile the two.

HOUSEHOLD ITEMS

With a few minor exceptions, everything you could hope to procure in North America is equally procurable here: furniture, clothing, knick-knacks and tchotchkes, appliances, automobiles, bicycles, jewelry and watches, houseplants, garden furniture, lawnmowers. While most of us don't want to add to the landfill problem by needlessly throwing away things we already have just to turn around and replace them, that's definitely one option. (And if you have a garage sale or sell your stuff on Craigslist, you might even earn enough money to cover the cost of replacement or the cost of shipping what's left.)

Many items for sale in French stores seem a lot pricier than they do back home, but often they're made better and therefore worth the investment. Tools, for example, can

SOS FOR ANIMALS

If wildlife rehabilitation agencies, animal shelters, and sanctuaries exist in the Île-de-France region (they do), it's a well-kept secret. Some of us learned this the hard way when we've found a stray dog wandering the boulevards of the French capital or discovered a baby bird on a busy *trottoir* (sidewalk). And while most Americans will sense right away that the French animal welfare is not up to modern standard, things are slowly changing and France is becoming a better place for animals.

Stray animals, in theory, can be brought to the local *commissariat*, where they promise the poor beast will be kept alone in a small cage for several days until they decide what to do with it. That leaves you with two options: Reconnect the critter with his or her human yourself, or pay a visit to the nearest animal adoption half-way house known as *fourrière*, the closest to Paris being the **Fourrière interdépartementale de Gennevilliers** (30, avenue du Général de Gaulle, Gennevilliers). To save a dog or a cat by adopting, or to volunteer to help animals, try these worthwhile organizations.

PARIS
Alerte SOS (30, rue du Poteau 18e, tel. 06/61 27 04 46, www.alertesos.com): This all volunteer-run animal shelter is on the backside of Montmartre.
Fondation Brigitte Bardot (28, rue Vineuse 16e, tel. 01/45 05 14 60): This nonprofit offers information on animal issues and referrals to adoption agencies.
SPA Société Protectrice des Aminaux (5, avenue Stéphane Mallarmé 17e, tel. 01/46 33 94 37): This agency offers low-cost spay, neuter, and vaccination services.
Association Stéphane Lamart (www.associationstephanelamart.com): A local animal welfare and animal rights organization.
Second Chance (www.secondechance.org): An online portal for would-be adopters.

LEVALLOIS-PERRET
Association AED (www.associationaed.com): Volunteer-run group that works to place dogs and cats into loving new homes.

MAISONS-LAFFITTE
AidoFélins (www.aidofelinsml.fr): Local cat rescue organization that hosts regular public adoption events.

MONTREUIL
Association Chats Indésirables (20, rue Coli, tel. 06/07 99 48 56): This organization with the saddest name ever finds homes for homeless felines.
Chats des Rues (1 rue Malot, www.chatsdesrues.fr): This organization rescues cats from the streets and finds them new homes.

be very expensive, so pack your wrenches, hammers, and screwdrivers if you can't live without them. Your teenage son (or inner teenager) might be disappointed to learn that video games tend to cost about twice as much as they do in the U.S., so if you're a grade-A vidiot, pack your games.

If you settle in Paris, you'll be within driving distance of (or a train-bus combo trip to) an IKEA, whose goods seem to fill half of all French homes these days. It's no wonder: The Swedish chain offers handsome, modern design at bargain-basement prices. In Paris, a city where people come and go like the seasons, you'll find Craigslist and FUSAC full of ads posted by folks looking to unload their things at great prices. You can easily furnish your entire apartment or *maison* with quality secondhand goods.

IKEA OR BUST

Parisian apartments from the posh Golden Triangle to the *populaire* northern neighborhoods all seem to have something in common: Ikea. The Swedish brand has definitely made its mark on the local interior design scene, and it's easy to see why. Stylish, affordable, AND they deliver--what's not to like? For expats, in particular, Ikea makes a smart, affordable alternative to shipping your furniture from home, which can cost between $5,000 and $10,000 each way. For many making the move to *La Ville Lumière*, it makes more sense to sell or store the contents of your home, especially because most housing geared toward the expat market is furnished--likely with Ikea. Those rare empty apartments, should you land one, can be filled on the cheap with the help of an Ikea catalog and a computer to place your order. There are seven outlets in the Île-de-France region to choose from; and if and when you decide to repatriate, do like the locals do and sell your furniture on Craigslist or FUSAC. Here is some vital terminology to help you navigate the Ikea experience:

Canapé	Couch
Coussins	Cushions
Fauteuil	Armchair
Lit	Bed
Matelas	Mattress
Oreillers	Pillows
Rangements	Storage units
Rideaux	Curtains
Tapis	Rug

For small household items, like washcloths, dish drainers, kitchen towels, and sewing supplies, try the Chinese and South Asian-owned markets. They're treasure troves for all those little knick-knacks you forgot to pack. At *marchés aux puces* (flea markets), you'll also find stalls selling new items—cutting boards, bars of soap—and wallet-friendly buys can be had if you keep your eyes open.

ELECTRONICS

When packing, consider whether or not to replace your electronic items. If you choose to bring them with you, you'll need a series of transformers and adapters to make them work in France, and you'll always run the risk of overloading your appliances' electrical circuits. As many of us have learned the hard way, all transformers are not created equally.

Electricity in Europe comes through the wires at 220 volts, double the amount of power that surges through standard U.S. and Canadian lines. In order to whittle the energy down to something your appliances can handle, you'll need a heavy-duty step-up/step-down transformer. This is not the kind you'll find in most travel shops—those are designed for appliances like electric razors and coffee makers—and should not be confused with the little adapters you'll be able to use to plug in your laptop, cell-phone charger, and camera-battery charger. A transformer is a solid, square, brick-size metal box that converts those 220 volts into 120. This is generally considered safe for things like televisions, DVD players, and small kitchen appliances.

Regional standards may also affect your decision on whether or not to pack your U.S.-configured electronics. You won't be able to play French DVDs in your American DVD player, for instance; you'll need a PAL (Phase Alternating Line)-compatible DVD player, which costs less than €50 new at electronics specialty stores like Darty, to watch all those straight-to-video releases.

Most new laptops come equipped with a DVD drive, making it easy to watch any old video, provided you've switched the region settings to the European standard. The only tricky part is that most computers have restrictions on how many times you can make this regional switch; five is the norm.

The big news for film fans is that Netflix is coming to France in 2014. After a long battle with pay-TV networks like Canal Plus, who didn't want the competition in their cozy marketplace, it's all systems go for the online video company. Before the end of 2014, you should be able to indulge in day-long video marathons from your Parisian living room, just like you used to back home.

If you've packed your PlayStation to play games and run Blu-ray Discs, be aware that there are three disc-playing zones—A, B, and C—and the European standard is Zone B. When renting or buying Blu-ray Discs, look for Zone A on the back of the box; changing the region settings on your machine isn't possible, so anything other than Zone A discs will be unreadable.

Considering that you'll need one of those bulky, expensive transformers to run most American electronic gadgets, on top of having to futz with regional codes and standards, it really makes more sense to sell your electronic goods before you leave and replace them with European versions once you get here, especially if you plan to live here for any length of time.

If you are particularly attached to your lamps, it is possible to convert them to the French standard by purchasing a European standard plug (and 220-volt light bulb to match), available at just about every *quincaillerie* (hardware store) in the country. If you're feeling DIY-ish, you can easily splice this new plug onto your existing electrical cord and, if you end up returning stateside, repeat the conversion process by splicing a 110-volt plug on the end when you get back home.

SHIPPING OPTIONS

If all this talk of electrical currents and step-up/step-down transformers hasn't scared you away from packing your life up and shipping it across the ocean, then it's time to consider your transport options. If you've decided to start fresh and just pack your clothes, toothbrush, and passport, good for you! You'll be more mobile that way and will have a lot more flexibility in terms of where you live. For most of us, paring life down is not so simple. It's hard to let go. If you're taking everything with you, your best bet is to send it by sea in a shipping container. Prices vary depending on where you're shipping from and to, how much space you'll need in a container (measured in cubic feet or meters), and whether or not you share your container with someone else. But the first step is finding a company with availability to help you make it all happen.

To find a qualified moving company, start with FIDI (www.fidi.com), the international nonprofit agency representing moving companies worldwide. Shipping companies who are part of the FIDI alliance have met a series of quality standards that put them in a league above the rest, but that doesn't mean that if you choose a non-FIDI mover, you'll have a lesser experience. Another place to look for moving-company references is at the consulate, which should be able to provide you with a

You may find it challenging to squeeze your furniture into a tiny, top-floor apartment.

handout with some good leads. Do your research, ask for testimonials or reviews, and give yourself enough time to shop around so you're not stuck with the only company that's available when you need to move.

Peak moving season in the northern hemisphere begins in mid-May and ends in September. It might not be possible for you to arrange your move at any other time, but you'll have more options if you can be flexible with the date. Though you'll want to start your research six months in advance, if you're trying to budget your move with care, you'll want to book your moving reservation no sooner than one month before departure. Why? Freight charges fluctuate—sometimes drastically—from month to month, based on a number of factors including the value of the dollar and the price of oil. So the figure you're quoted could change significantly, usually in the direction you don't want.

Moving companies offer a range of services, from we'll-do-it-all-for-you to we-just-ship-and-that's-it and everything in between. There are a couple of approaches you can take to sort out all of the details.

If you're lucky enough to be transferred by your company, chances are they'll be handling (read: paying for) all the details of your move, in which case you can just kick up your heels and start plotting the adventures you hope to see unfold in your new French life. For the rest of us, there's a bit of decision-making involved. Do you want to go the cheapest route possible? Then get a shared "groupage" container, but expect it to take anywhere from one to four months for your goods to arrive. The shipping company sends movers to pick up your stuff in a truck, deliver it to the loading docks, and either put it in a container that already has someone else's (or several someone else's) belongings in it—or put it in a container and wait around for another shared load to arrive to fill the container space. This costs about half—sometimes less than half—of what you'll pay for an exclusive container. To bring the cost down further, you can deliver the stuff to the container yourself.

The next cheapest option is direct shipping, meaning your stuff goes inside your own dedicated shipping container; no shared space. The shipping company will either send movers over to pick up your packed goods and deliver them to the shipping port, or they might actually bring your shipping container right to your front door and load it there, sealing the doors afterward with a plastic security band that you will later snip open when your container is delivered to you in France.

Armed with the basics, you'll want to visit FIDI online or use *bouche-à-oreille* (word-of-mouth) references and make a few calls. Shipping containers come in two sizes, 20-foot and 40-foot, so expect to be asked how many cubic meters' worth of goods you have. The shipping company should send a representative over to make an assessment. Once you've been given an estimate that works for you—and it's definitely worth shopping around, since prices can vary by thousands of dollars—you'll be asked to submit a down payment, with the rest payable upon delivery.

CUSTOMS

Customs is a relatively straightforward process, but you won't necessarily know that if your shipping company contact isn't well informed. You'll have to fill out a customs form that your shipping company will submit to the *douane* (customs) agents at the port of entry, but unless your cargo is made up of brand-new electric items that look like they might be ready for immediate resale in France, you won't have to pay an import fee. You will be asked to attest on paper to the fact that you have lived in your country of residence for the last 12 months and that the items you are shipping are older than six months. (Items purchased less than six months before your ship date are subject to import fees.) If you can solemnly swear that this is true, you won't need to pay any fees.

One important consideration is the storage fee. If your shipping dossier is not in order at the customs agency at the port of entry in France—this usually happens when you do your paperwork yourself or use an underqualified moving agency with little overseas shipping experience—your container may have to be "stored," with daily fees in the realm of €250. To avoid getting saddled with hefty fees, confirm with your shipping company that your paperwork is in order, and that there will be no hidden and unwarranted customs fees. You or your shipping agent should have collected in your dossier the following papers:

- a copy of your passport
- pay stubs or other proof that you have lived in the U.S. or Canada for at least six months
- a copy of your rental agreement and/or proof of current residence in France (an electricity bill works)
- a French customs inventory form
- a signed letter attesting that the purpose of importing your goods is not to resell them upon arrival
- a Représentation en Douanes form

HOUSING CONSIDERATIONS

From chic Left Bank flats furnished in fancy Louis XIV fashion to ultra-modern stand-alone houses complete with American-style driveways, housing runs the gamut in the Île-de-France region. Exactly where you decide to live is surely contingent on work, school, and budget, but once you've sorted out those fundamentals, you'll be ready to embark on your hunt for the perfect home. Finding a place to live is best reserved for when you actually arrive; as alluring as online ads can be, making a decision from afar isn't really practical. If you'll be spending more than six months in your new abode, you'll want to ensure that the neighborhood meets your standards, that the advertisement in square meters matches the spatial picture you had in mind (and that your antique dining-room table will fit in the *salle à manger*), and that you'll have access to transportation and other amenities. It's hard to judge this accurately without a visit. Once you're here, there's a lot to see, so bring your phrasebook, comfy walking shoes (but not the sporty white ones), and your sense of humor.

The Housing Market

© PAUL PRESCOTT

Not all housing options are of the vintage variety.

The French housing market finally rebounded in 2014 after a multi-year slump, making it more of a seller's than a buyer's market. Paris is the one exception, having remained virtually untouched by market fluctuations in other parts of the country. Buyer optimism is at last on the mend, thanks to a strengthening economy, and banks have begun lending again after a temporary dry spell related to the most recent economic crisis rattling through Europe and the rest of the world.

France has long been a popular place for foreign investors and second-home buyers; the British especially have done a number on the real-estate industry here, snapping up properties to fix up and rent out or fix up and live in, if only for part of the year. (In some pockets of France—particularly where access to the UK by ferry, Chunnel, and plane is quick and easy—Anglophones outnumber Francophones.) The economic parity that is now settling in between the two countries means there isn't a feverish race to the realty finish line, and there are more options for those interested in buying now.

Even with the dollar weak against the euro (the exchange rate is a dismal €1 = $1.36 at the time of writing), Americans can find some incredible bargains here, both within and outside of the French capital. On one end of the spectrum are the million-dollar Parisian apartments and chic garden villas in the *bobo* suburbs; on the other are options for those with more modest budgets. Fancy a homey little cottage in the suburbs, or perhaps a 19th-century walk-up with a balcony to fill with potted geraniums? For less than €200,000, these options can be yours with patience, flexibility, and a little help from your banking institution.

Renting

Renting has its advantages over buying, the most obvious being a much lighter initial investment. For the French, housing laws that favor the tenant over the landlord make renting a safe and secure option. Even if you don't pay your rent, a landlord can't give you the heave-ho in the thick of winter, for instance. But as a foreigner entering the rental market, you won't necessarily have all the same advantages extended to you—one reason why French homeowners seek out foreign tenants.

DAILY LIFE

Paris rental laws are particularly strict, and it's technically illegal for owners to rent to anyone—foreign or not—for periods of less than one year. To do so legally would require owners to change the status of their property from private to commercial, and securing the coveted commercial status is next to impossible. Theoretically, the law was intended to ease Paris's shortage of affordable housing; you'll often hear the story of the lifelong Parisian sent packing to the suburbs because he can no longer afford the city's astronomical rents. The law is easy to skirt, however, as evidenced by the number of ads offering short-term "furnished" accommodations. "Furnished" is a loose term that can mean anything from a bare room save a single chair or bed to a decked-out space with all the mod cons in place: microwave, television, sofa, etc. Short-term rentals bring in far more income for owners than long-term rentals, so flying under the radar and hoping not to get caught is a risk many landlords are willing to take.

French bureaucracy doesn't end at the front door of your new house or apartment, which can make finding a place to live a challenge, particularly if you are short on time or funds. If possible, rent a short-term place for a month while you look for your permanent housing, which will buy you enough time to find something that will feel like a true home and not force you into something less—or more—than you'd hoped for. You can find more affordable options for short-term and long-term rentals on Craigslist and FUSAC. More expensive possibilities are also available via dozens of short-term rental agencies (again, check out the FUSAC magazine online), but they will charge higher rents and also include a supplemental fee for finding you a place to live that could either be a percentage of the overall rental period or the equivalent of one month's rent. If you want to avoid the hassles of combing the want ads altogether, this is a viable option even for the long term, but note that nearly all rentals will come in varying degrees of "furnished." So if you're expecting a cargo container to arrive with all of your belongings, you'll need to make sure you have the room for it or risk paying hefty storage fees.

You're already familiar with the dossier, and you'll be needing one to rent a house or apartment from either an agency or a private party. Your dossier should contain the following:

- copies of your passport
- your last three bank statements
- your last three pay stubs (French or otherwise)
- proof of insurance (if you have it)
- an *attestation* from a *garant* or *cautionnaire* saying you'll be covered if you can't pay your rent
- personal letters of recommendation (translated into French, if possible)

Without these, it's unlikely you'll find any standard real-estate agency that will rent to you long-term. Even familiar North America-based companies like Century 21 have rigid policies that will exclude you based on missing documents in your dossier. The tricky part is that this rule doesn't always hold. If you have time and tenacity, 1 out of 20 agencies you visit or speak with by phone (or email) might be willing to look the other way on missing documents if they like you, or more likely, like your bank statement. If you make a breakthrough and actually get someone to show you an apartment (be forewarned that some agents won't even consider showing you a place until they've seen your paperwork), and you fall in love with the place, work those negotiating skills and see what happens. Some expats have reported that homemade brownies

If you want a cute French car to go with your cute French apartment, invest in a private parking space.

work as a form of bribery, but simply being personable and connecting genuinely with the person you're hoping to impress is probably the best route to take. Their bottom line is, "Will she be able to pay the rent?" If you can convey a sense of trust and reliability, you're halfway there.

FINDING THE RIGHT PLACE

When you launch your home search, it helps to put *all* your feelers out—all of them! This is not the time to be a wallflower. Check the bulletin board at your local chapter of the Alliance Française back home for possibilities, scour Craigslist and FUSAC to get a sense of the rental climate in the town you're moving to, ask everyone you know if they have friends-of-friends-of-friends who might have a place to rent in France, and visit sites like Se Loger (www.seloger.com) and Particulier à Particulier (www.pap.fr) to start getting a feel for French-language rental ads. The more familiar you are with the lingo and the more questions you formulate before you leave, the better prepared you'll be for your next challenge.

When you get here, get out there and start networking. Join expat groups, venture out to Meetups (www.meetup.com), and read every bulletin board you pass. As much as you want to integrate into French society, your best bet for finding a place to live is through word-of-mouth within the Anglophone community, so cast your net as wide as it will go.

It takes many North Americans some time to get used to the size of French dwellings. Unless you're looking at a château or a modern apartment, you'll find traditional French rooms to be a little on the small side (and often plastered with outdated

DAILY LIFE

CLASSIFIED INFORMATION

Scouring the want ads for the perfect place to call home can be a fun pastime that helps you better imagine yourself living your French dream. If your language skills aren't up to snuff, though, it can become frustrating drudgery. Don't know your *cuisine* from your *cave*? Bone up on the essential real-estate lingo before you hit the *immobilier* (real-estate agency) to know exactly what you'll be investing those hard-earned euros in.

à louer/location - for rent
ascenseur - elevator
à vendre - for sale
bail à ceder - for lease
cave - cellar
chambre - room, usually referring to a bedroom or main room in a studio
charges - supplemental charges for water, garbage, maintenance, and sometimes electricity
chauffage - heating
colocation - shared rental unit
couloir - hallway
cuisine - kitchen
dépot de garantie - security deposit

2ème étage - second floor
deux pièces - standard one-bedroom
disponible - available
équipée - furnished (usually describes a kitchen with refrigerator and stove)
escalier - staircase
gardien(ne) - onsite manager
honoraire - finder's fee to the real estate agency
hors charges - not including charges
immeuble - building
immeuble ancien/neuf - old/new building
jardin - garden
loué - already rented
meublée - furnished
mezzanine - elevated area, often a DIY loft space for sleeping that frees up floor space
pièce - room
une pièce/studio - studio
pierre/pierre de taille - stone
placard - closet
rénové - renovated
rez de chaussée - ground floor
salle d'eau - washroom
salle de bain - bathroom with tub or shower
sans vis à vis - an unobstructed view
séjour - living room
toilette - toilet

wallpaper, which can make a room feel even smaller). And that oversize sofa you packed? Good luck squeezing it into an elevator (which most building *syndicats* don't allow you to do anyway) or wrangling it around the twisty stairwell. You'll need to hire a special moving *élévateur* to lift it up and through the window.

Short-Term Rentals

If you don't have someone with very strong ties to France arranging your move for you, you're probably going to need to give up on the notion of finding an unfurnished rental. They do exist, but they're *very* hard to get your hands on as a solo-flying expat on a noncorporate executive's budget. For the short term, it's usually preferable to settle into a furnished place anyway, since you'll just need something in the interim until your cargo container arrives or while you investigate a permanent place to live. And if you're only staying for a brief period, a furnished rental unit makes a lot of sense.

Your options for short-term rentals are vast and varied. You can go through a big agency that will likely charge you a big fee or a mom-and-pop business offering the same service but charging less, or you can bypass surcharges altogether by working directly with a landlord, who might himself be a subtenant to another landlord. There is

T1/T2 - studio/one-bedroom apartment   *vendu* - already sold
tout compris, cc, or ttc - all-inclusive   *vide* - empty
vendeur/vendeuse - seller

© AURELIA D'ANDREA

Many Parisian apartment dreams begin with a wrought-iron balcony.

a bit of risk involved in the latter option on both the landlord's and the tenant's sides; you are being entrusted with someone else's property, and you're handing over your hard-earned cash to someone you hope is on the up and up. Odds are they will be, but always trust your instincts—if something doesn't feel right, don't feel obligated to follow through. In any situation, it is advisable to always leave a paper trail and to draft a lease, even if the person renting to you doesn't think it's necessary or, more likely, didn't think of it.

Within the law, short-term rentals of a year or less that don't come with a lease are supposed to be rented only to tenants who have a primary residence other than the one being rented. This would be a challenge for anyone to disprove, and rarely is it an issue in terms of the law cracking down on you, but the person renting to you may ask you to sign a paper stating as much to cover his or her tail.

For a nice cross section of short-term rentals throughout Paris, try www.perfectlyparis.com. The friendly Canadian owner, Gail Boisclair, is fluent in English and happy to use her years of expertise to help you find a place to call home, if only for a short while. Craigslist and Airbnb both offer a plethora of possibilities, and don't forget to check out the ads at fusac.org for referrals to other rental agencies eager for your business.

SHORT-TERM TIPS FROM THE TOP

You've booked you flight to Paris for your fact-finding adventure, but there's still one little detail that needs attending to: finding a short-term place to stay. Canadian expat Gail Boisclair is here to help. She's the owner of Perfectly Paris (www.perfectlyparis.com), a company offering short-term Paris apartment rentals, with a specific emphasis on Montmartre. *Condé Nast Traveler* has named Gail their Top Villa Rental Specialist for Paris each year since 2008, so you know you're in good hands. Here are her tips for finding that perfect place to call home—if only for a week or two.

· **Book early!** Paris is a year-round destination, so it's important to start looking at least six months in advance for your best choice. Other than January through March, November,

and early December, finding something at the last minute can be very difficult.

· **Think outside the arrondissement.** Size-wise, Paris is a small city with a very efficient transit system, so location may not be as important as you think. Pick a flat you would look forward to going home to at the end of your day and make sure it is close to a Métro station.

· **Avoid scams!** Definitely don't book if you are asked to pay by Western Union, Money Gram, etc., and confirm in advance that the agency you are renting from is reputable. Search the travel forums to find out what people have to say about the company.

If you're looking for a temporary sublet, summer is a great time to check out Paris and its suburbs while the locals flee to the sea and countryside for their multi-week escapes. You will have lots of room to negotiate, since people don't want to get stuck paying all their rent while they're away, and you'll get to experience what it could be like to live in a real French home (versus a sterile short-term rental unit).

Long-Term Rentals

A long-term rental has lots of advantages: It allows you to get to know a place before buying, lets you feel more integrated in a community knowing you won't have to pick up and leave in three months, and often is a lot less expensive than a short-term arrangement. The only problem is *finding* a long-term rental, though that isn't necessarily a problem if you have the luxury of time.

As with short-term rentals, it's possible to go through an agency whose specialty is expatriate rental services, but you will pay a premium, usually in the form of a "finder's fee" surcharge amounting to the equivalent of one month's rent or a percentage of the rent you'll pay over the months (or years) you'll be staying. It's also possible to go through an *immobilier,* a real estate agent who often deals in rental units as well as selling homes. The tricky part will always be to meet the *dossier* demands, which generally require three months' worth of French pay stubs proving that you earn several times the amount of the rent, a *garant's* attestation, and more.

It's no secret that French landlords like renting to North Americans. They know you'll be leaving Paris to return to your "real" home at some point, and therefore won't be taking advantage of the tenant-friendly laws that essentially guarantee you can't be forcibly evicted. This also allows many landlords to get around the law that says empty units must be rented with three-year leases; many North Americans are staying only for a year or two, so the landlord won't be locked into long-term situations. You're also generally considered more financially stable than your French counterparts, making you prime tenant material.

Renting directly from the owner gives you a lot of flexibility; you can negotiate the removal of existing furniture, open a discussion about filling voids—for example, if your "furnished" apartment doesn't come with a TV or washing machine, you may be able to persuade the *propriétaire* that these are necessities. (As always, ask nicely and be prepared to make a convincing argument if necessary.) Sometimes you can negotiate both the rent and the length of your stay. So there's a lot to be said for finding your home this way. Even though it's not as popular in France as in North America, Craigslist is a good place to start your housing search, especially if you'll be settling in Paris. Many real-estate agents use this online venue to showcase their available dwellings. You'll find a broad variety of possibilities for rent by individuals, and the people advertising are almost always Anglophones. One thing to be wary of is any deal that seems too good to be true. They almost always are! Warning signs include (1) impossibly cheap rent (such as a luxury apartment for €750 per month) and (2) a request for money transfers or wires before you've even seen the place. Don't sign anything, and *don't* hand over a euro until you've seen the place—and the person renting it—in person.

Particulier à Particulier (www.pap.fr) advertises apartments and houses directly from the owner, so if your French skills are up to snuff, you can probably circumvent the challenges inherent in working with an agency—namely, a rigid set of dossier requirements. In addition to the website, PAP publishes a thick, oversize journal every Thursday. Pick it up at newsstands for €2.95, and you'll have access to oodles of ads. Brush up on your French and be prepared to pick up the phone to get the best deals. If your French isn't that good but you have a friend who's fluent, have her make the call for you.

Shared Rentals

Finding a *colocation* (shared rental) situation in France is relatively simple, particularly in university towns with large student populations. The site to visit to find your next roommate situation is www.colocation.fr, but it will benefit you greatly if you speak French. You *do* want that €100 living situation, *don't* you? The downside to this otherwise wonderful site is that to access the contact information of your potential new roommate, you have to pay for the access number; usually the fee is less than €2, but if you're calling more than a handful of people, it adds up. A no-cost option is www.recherche-colocation.com—also in French, but at least membership is *gratuit* (free). If you're still most comfortable with an English-language publication, head straight for the old tried-and-true FUSAC and Craigslist.

RENTAL AGENTS AND LEASES

Before signing on the dotted line, you'll want to have some sort of contract in place, even if it's just a simple form you downloaded off the Internet 10 minutes before your hand-over-the-keys meeting. (You and your landlord wouldn't be the first.) What you sign and what kind of information it contains hinges on what you're renting and the landlord's level of professionalism. Let's say you're renting a furnished apartment

THE *GARANT(E)* AND WHY YOU MIGHT NEED ONE

If you've moved house in the last 10 years, you know the renter's drill: Arrive early to the showing to beat the crowds, have your credit report and application ready, and—if you're feeling spunky—bring a bribe in the form of fresh-baked cookies to really grab the real-estate agent's attention. Well, in France, it's going to take a bit more effort to land that perfect apartment, and we're not talking about swapping out the cookies for croissants. If you don't have a job contract and three months of pay stubs to demonstrate your fiscal stability, you can kiss that cute 18th-century walkup *au revoir*. Even a bank account loaded with euros won't help you here. Rules are rules, and what the folks renting to you require are those pay stubs, showing earnings equal to three times your monthly rent —or, if you can't pull that off, a *garant*'s attestation. *Garant? Attestation?* What's all this, you ask?

A *garant* is someone with income or assets greater than your own who acts as a financial guarantor in case you default on your rent. This person is expected to provide a dossier full of documents similar to those you're unable to provide: proof of residence, proof of monthly income equal to three times the amount of your rent, and copies of her own rental agreement or real-estate tax forms. Employers occasionally extend this perk to staff, but not always. If you're lucky enough to have a wealthy aunt in France who's willing to put three years' worth of rent into a "hold" at the bank, rental agencies will consider that in place of a *garant*.

Recently, public *garant* agencies have sprouted up, offering their services to desperate would-be renters, but not all rental agencies will accept this sort of arrangement. If all other options fail, there's still hope: Enroll in a university (students are usually exempt from the *garant* rule) or rent straight from the owner (try Craigslist and Particulier à Particulier), which usually allows for a more flexible negotiation process.

directly from an owner who takes the matter rather seriously and has taken steps to keep the transaction on the up and up. In this case, you can expect to be presented with a lease or rental contract (*bail à loyer* or *contrat de location*) containing the following information:

- name of the owner, contact information, and rental address
- a description of the rental: floor, door, dimension in square meters
- a mention of communal access and services: a courtyard, bike parking, elevator
- a definition of purpose: whether the space is for living or working
- the length of the contract and whether it's renewable or not
- an outline of the charges—rent, *taxe d'habitation*, electricity—and when they are made payable
- the amount of your security deposit
- an outline of any proposed work to be done on the dwelling, including dates and whether less or more rent will be charged as a result
- a statement indicating that the renter will leave the space in the same state it was rented out in to guarantee you get your deposit back

Rental signs dot the windows of many choice neighborhoods.

A short outline of the owner's obligations to the renter and the renter's obligation to the owner is also part of the contract, and often a *clause pénale* will be inserted declaring what will happen if the renter fails to pay his rent. But it's almost guaranteed that the contract you sign will be much simpler than the one outlined above, if you're actually offered a contact at all.

In keeping with the up-and-up theme: Even if you're not asked to provide a full-fledged dossier, you may be asked to provide proof of renter's insurance and income. Paying your last month's rent up front is not legally mandated, but landlords *are* legally entitled to ask for a deposit equal to one month's rent. They have two months to return it to you once you've moved out. You, on the other hand, can ask your landlord-to-be for a *certificat de ramonage,* which certifies they've had the chimney swept so you can have a cozy little fire roaring in the fireplace.

Buying

If you've never visited a real-estate website, consider yourself warned: They're deliciously addictive. There's nothing quite as tantalizing as poking around cyberspace and popping in and out of other people's *maisons*—homes that might soon be your own (if only in your fantasies). From a rural 17th-century cottage perched on the edge of a grassy glen in the southern Paris suburbs to a central Marais *pied-à-terre* equipped with a sunlit balcony built for two, a version of your French dream awaits you in the wonderful world of virtual real estate.

It takes a village to buy a home in France, and you can expect all kinds of seemingly superfluous individuals to become part of the transaction: *notaires,* the mayor, insurance agents, and even doctors. For some mortgages, you'll need to ensure that you'll live long enough to pay for your little piece of France—this is solved with the addition of a life-insurance policy, which you can't purchase until you've had a blood test and possibly an electrocardiogram, the results of which are supposed to indicate a life span beyond the terms of your mortgage. No, this is not a joke. If you want to bypass all that, you can always pay cash. (And plenty of people do—especially for those bargain properties.)

You're bound to find yourself looking at one or two "fixer uppers" throughout the process, and one thing you'll notice right away is that no two are alike. Some "fixer uppers" are veritable shells with sloping walls and a resident family of pigeons. If the ad describes the dwelling as *à rénover* (to renovate), be prepared for the worst, and maybe,

LOCATION, LOCATION, LOCATION

Realtor Charles Baumont, who has been practicing real estate since 2009, works for Century 21 in the Batignolles neighborhood of the 17th. He specializes in the *marché des particuliers* which is another way of saying he helps people find the perfect place to call home in Paris. If you're looking to buy an apartment, Charles is your guy. Here are his top five tips for would-be buyers to consider before making the leap into the Paris real-estate pool.

Define your priorities.
Before you start your search, determine what matters most: Is it location? A quiet neighborhood? A bright apartment? Your realtor can better assist you if these parameters are well-defined.

Establish your budget.
Knowing how much money you have to work with will help narrow down the ocean of possibilities and give a precise framework for your realtor to function within.

Compare and contrast.
Visiting as many apartments as possible helps build a more solid understanding of your options and keeps your expectations realistic.

Read the fine print.
Take the time to read all the documents concerning the building and the apartment before signing any contracts.

Go pro.
Find a real estate professional to give you advice. That's what they're there for!

Family-friendly neighborhoods aren't hard to find.

just maybe, it won't be that bad. The "to renovate" could simply mean they haven't yet installed the sunken bathtub in the master bath.

FINDING THE RIGHT PLACE

So where should you begin cultivating your French roots? Before sorting that out, you'll need to be firm about what sort of use you have planned for your place. Will it be strictly somewhere for you to live, or are you envisioning an income-generating rental property? Maybe you just want to let it sit empty until you come for your two months of vacation each summer, and let friends borrow it when you're not there. Buying into a retirement home where you can spend your golden years isn't a bad idea, what with the high quality of life here and the top-notch healthcare system. But don't make the mistake that many of your predecessors have: Buy a place and plan to rent it out without considering how many others have done the same thing. You will have a much more challenging time finding short-term tenants for your "vacation rental" if it doesn't stand out in a sea of similar offers. Proximity to restaurants, shops, and transportation are usually what people seek in a Paris-area vacation home—not a one-room cottage in a distant suburb where the only thing open on Sundays is the village church. Hold on to the dream, but don't let practicality fall by the wayside.

REAL-ESTATE AGENTS AND CONTRACTS

The most cursory Internet search points to an overwhelming reality: There are scads and scads of French real estate sites. The good news is that many of them cater to English-speaking shoppers. If your French is solid, even better. You'll be able to pop into any *immobilier* office during your information-gathering trip and inquire about that stately Haussmann-era apartment with the geranium-covered balcony and *à ven-dre* sign that caught your eye.

Like so much else in life, it's all about who you know in the French real-estate world. Ask around for references before settling on an agent. Some are nicer than others, and some charge heftier fees. You'll also need to engage the services of a *notaire* (more on that below) and a mortgage company. If you've got the resources, you can hire someone to see you through every step of the process and make the arrangements with notaries and bankers on your behalf. If you're flying solo—which is entirely possible to do, and definitely a money saver—and your language skills still aren't up to snuff, bring a good friend who speaks French to all your official rendezvous to help translate.

You'll need a French bank account, since most mortgage companies are going to want to debit the mortgage payments directly from that account. (To learn more about opening a bank account, see the *Finance* chapter.)

The French home-buying system is fraught with bureaucratic peculiarities, but the oddest of all is that bit about the blood test. If your mortgage is approved and you'll be borrowing more than €200,000, you'll be required to take out a life-insurance policy that will cover the remaining cost of your mortgage if you're, say, suddenly swept away by a tsunami while sunbathing on the Côte d'Azur. To qualify for that policy, you'll need a blood test and possibly a urine test. Oh, and we mustn't forget about the electrocardiogram.

PURCHASE FEES AND TAXES

One person you'll get to know well during the property-purchasing process is the *notaire*. This is an independent contractor who acts as the official hand representing the state in your home-buying transaction. The stamps, seals, and signatures the *notaire* applies to your *contrats* make a document official, and the buy/sell transaction cannot be completed without this authorizing signature. The *notaire*'s fees are not low, but they don't all go into her pocket. The bulk of what you pay to the *notaire* is actually local and national taxes, with the remaining fraction divided between the *notaire*'s actual employment fees (a fixed rate determined by the government) and expenditures for things like paperwork and travel. In terms of real estate transactions, *notaires* collect 5 percent of the sales fee for the first €45,735, and between 1 and 2 percent on the remainder, for an average total of between and 5 and 5.8 percent of the price of your home. That doesn't include VAT taxes, which add another 19.2 percent to the final price (based on

Living on a boat is one housing option.

the notaire's fees, not on the price of your home) It's worth budgeting in that extra expense as you determine what you can afford to spend in France. To find a *notaire,* try the word-of-mouth route or visit www.notaires.fr to search an online directory in English.

Once you've found a place you love and are ready to commit, you can set the process in motion by following these steps:

• Find a *notaire* and secure her services.

• Sign the *compromis de vente* that binds the seller to the transaction and pay a deposit of 10 percent of the purchase price.

• Mull it over and decide whether or not you have buyer's remorse within seven days (you can pull out without penalty before then).

• Apply for a mortgage. If you are rejected, try again and save the rejection notice. If you are unable to secure a mortgage, you can pull out of the agreement without penalty.

• Contact your *notaire* to say your mortgage has gone through and the transaction can be completed.

From start to finish, count on a good three months or more for the transaction to be completed.

French inheritance laws favor children over spouses, so if you want to ensure that any greedy offspring don't snatch up and sell your property after you die, leaving Pa or Ma out in the cold, bring this up to your *notaire,* who can use the right paperwork to help ensure that doesn't happen.

BUILDING AND RESTORING

As you know by now, no transaction involving the French bureaucracy is ever a cake walk. This holds true when it comes to rebuilding, renovation, and starting a housing project from scratch. Expect a long, dossier-encumbered process—but one that might be very much worth the effort if it means getting the house you've always wanted.

When scouring the real-estate ads, you'll often stumble upon land for sale. If there is a "permission to build" clause built into the sale deed, you're in luck: One major hurdle has been cleared. Otherwise you'll need to solicit permission to build on your own, starting at the *mairie* with a *certificat d'urbanisme.* This should be done *before* you make your land purchase. With permission to build in hand, you'll need to start beefing up that dossier with some more paperwork: architectural drawings from an officially recognized architect, building estimates, and construction contracts.

Your local *mairie* can help you along the way by directing you to free services that will ease the burden of DIY. The Conseil d'Architecture d'Urbanisme et de l'Environnement (CAUE) is one such valuable resource. To find a builder, good ol' word of mouth works best, but you can also ask for recommendations at the *mairie* or visit the website of the builder's union, Union Nationale des Constructeurs de Maisons Individuelles (UNCMI), for direction (www.uniondesmaisonsfrancaises.org).

French contractors do things at their own pace, so it helps to know who you're hiring before you hire them. You can expect long lunch breaks, regular vacations (just like everyone else), and a "What's the big rush?" attitude on the job, but it'll eventually get done. If you're a Mr. or Ms. Bricolage (handyperson), you might consider taking on some of the work yourself.

DAILY LIFE

Household Expenses

Once your new title of French homeowner is etched in *pierre* (stone), you'll want to start gussying up your new place and making it feel homey. But not so fast. First, you need to make sure there's running water, electricity, and—if you're way out in the suburban boondocks—a *fosse septique* (septic tank). Many houses are sold in deplorable states of as-is, and it's up to you to know what you've gotten yourself into before you take the plunge.

If your adorable old abode has a *fosse septique*, you may be required by your local *mairie* to convert to *mains drainage*, otherwise known as the municipal sewer system. This comes at a price, so be sure to factor that in before you buy. Electricity is not a given either; if you're not already hooked up, you'll have to put a call in to state-owned Électricité de France (EDF) to see what kind of magic they can make down on the farm. To get started, you'll need proof of sale of your home, called an *attestation;* ask your *notaire* for a copy.

There are three taxes you will be responsible for as a new French homeowner: *taxe d'habitation, taxe foncière,* and the TV tax called *redevance audiovisuelle.* The first is your residence tax, the second is your homeowner's tax, and the third is self-explanatory. If you lived in your home on January 1 of the given year, then you are responsible for *taxe d'habitation.* If someone else lived there, they are responsible for paying it—so if you moved in on January 2, you're off the hook. Landlords can also pass this fee on to their long-term tenants, but this should be outlined in a rental agreement first. The tax is determined by the powers-that-be in your community and varies from city to city. You will receive a *facture* (bill) in the mail from the local government when tax time draws near. If you are over 60, lucky you! You don't have to pay this one. Families with children are taxed at a reduced rate. You'll receive your €133 bill for the TV tax at the same time (and yes, you're off scot-free if you don't have a TV).

Taxe foncière, on the other hand, is a property owner's tax, and what you pay is again set by local authorities and relates to the value of your home as a rental property on the open market, minus cost-of-living fees. Like the other taxes, it hinges on a January 1 ownership date. Many types of properties are exempted from this tax, including homes remodeled for energy efficiency, and new construction, so you'll want to check with your local government to see if your property is exempted.

UTILITIES

The primary supplier of electricity, Électricité de France (EDF), offers notoriously expensive power for those who live on the grid. North Americans by the droves have stood slack-jawed over their first wintertime electricity bill, expecting a two-digit number like the ones they used to see back home.

The good news is that you can choose the kilowatt supply that comes to your home and effectively reduce the figure you write on that check every two months. First, though, you have to open an account at the EDF, which can be done in person or online at www.bleuciel.edf.com. As with most French bills, you can arrange to go paperless on this one and have the money debited directly from your bank account.

Getting water running through the pipes involves a similar process. If the previous tenant had water services engaged, you can have the billing information transferred to your name. If you're starting from scratch, you'll need to visit your local government to find out who your water supplier is before making contact. In Paris, the agency to contact is Eau de Paris (www.eaudeparis.fr).

One thing you can't help but notice is the quality of water throughout France; though quite potable, it is extremely calciferous, with telltale white flecks often visible in your glass after drinking. This may or may not explain the French love affair with bottled water, but it's perfectly OK to consume, though you might be interested in a filter system. The calcium build-up will affect the look of your water kettle, your dishwasher, and your coffee maker, but anti-calcium tablets that will dissolve the problem are readily available in supermarkets and hardware stores.

Telephone landline options are many and a veritable bargain, thanks to deregulation in the telecommunications sector. (Deregulation has not been good for everyone—restructuring and layoffs are said to be the culprit behind France Télécom's high rate of employee suicide: a frightening total of 60 since 2008.) Usually your phone fees are bundled together with your Internet and cable television fees. Companies including SFR (www.sfr.fr), Bouygues (www.bouyguestelecom.fr), and Orange (www.orange.fr) offer packages as low as €30 per month, and you can make all the arrangements for hookup online.

DAILY LIFE

LANGUAGE AND EDUCATION

It's a little-known fact is that approximately 99.9 percent of all French people know at least a word or two of English, and many are darn near fluent. You'd hardly know it, though, given the way you're often left struggling to puzzle together the simplest request (*Où est le WC, s'il vous plaît?*), only to be met with a remarkably accent-free response (The bathroom? In fact, it's right over there.).

It's certainly possible to get by in France without speaking French—many an expat before you has done it, sometimes getting by for years on end—but language restrictions will resign you to life in a bubble that only floats on the surface of a genuine French experience. At least part of what brought you here was your fondness for the rich culture, right? Language is the biggest cultural marker you'll find, so it makes sense to give it a shot and break free of the insular and—let's face it—superficial Anglophone-only experience. Plus, there's nothing quite as satisfying as ordering your meal at a restaurant in clearly enunciated French and having your request processed *without* quizzical looks and excessive head-scratching on the part of your waiter. Even more wonderful is the (relative) ease with which you'll glide through your *carte de séjour* experience and other official processes when armed with working French.

Regional dialects abound, but getting a grasp on the mother tongue—plain old French—is all you really need to assimilate into your new community and boost your own confidence along the way.

Learning the Language

If you were clever enough to have studied French in high school or college, lucky you! That foundation will give you the confidence you need to get started. One of the most difficult things for non-French speakers to get used to is the feeling of vulnerability that comes with not being able to communicate effectively. For some, those insecurities are compounded by the genuinely-trying-to-be-helpful French person who corrects your grammar (I promise they're not doing it to make you feel bad), often in public and loudly enough for others to hear. It's a challenge for us control freaks, but now is the time to let go and embrace the linguistic fumbling and stumbling. Relaxing a little will help you—and that ego of yours—move on to the experimental chatting phase that will ultimately benefit you immensely.

If you've seen the film *Paris, je t'aime,* you'll probably remember the vignette featuring Carol, an American postal clerk who takes her dream trip to the City of Light, narrating her experience in heavily American-accented French. She charms us with her earnestness—and an extraordinarily flat delivery where rolling *R*s ought to reside. When you start out, go the postal-clerk method and focus on just speaking, rather than speaking with a perfect accent. You'll have time for that later. Besides, when you have a good accent, people assume you speak fluently or at least conversationally and will begin yakking at you in rapid-fire French that you're not equipped to handle—yet.

DAILY LIFE

© AURELIA D'ANDREA

Sometimes learning a new language means starting small.

WORDY WISDOM

French and English have *beaucoup de* cognates in common—that is, words that share the same etymological roots—but don't jump to the conclusion that just because certain words look and sound similar, they have the same meaning in both languages. For instance, a tampon has a particular meaning in the U.S. (you're familiar with that one) and another in France—it's a stamp that makes documents official. Here is a list of common *faux amis* (false friends) and their unexpected meanings.

actuelle - current
assister - to attend
baskets - tennis shoes
car - because
chat - cat
coin - corner
collège - middle school

comédien - actor
crayon - pencil
culte - religion
demander - ask
douche - shower
entrée - appetizer
fantaisie - imagination
fart - ski wax
ignorer - to not know
gros - big
librairie - bookstore
magasin - store
raisin - grape
robe - dress
parole - song lyric
préservatif - condom
en retard - late
roman - novel
salé/sale - salty/dirty
sensible - sensitive
tube - hit song

BEFORE YOU LEAVE

Whether or not you've studied French before, as soon as you even begin *thinking* of moving, you should start thinking of enrolling in a language class. You'd be surprised how many resources exist. There really *is* something for everyone, no matter your budget or lack thereof. From Alabama to Winnipeg and everywhere in between, the nonprofit Alliance Française awaits your enrollment in one of its many classes, from structured beginner courses to more relaxed conversation groups. This isn't the most affordable option, but it might be the most fun: The AF also hosts events—art shows, film screenings, speaking engagements, mixers—with a French twist. One of the benefits of membership is access to the library of books, DVDs, and CDs, making for an all-in-one cultural immersion program minus mandatory exams and pesky report cards.

If you live near a community college, this is an excellent, budget-friendly option. For the cost of lunch at a French restaurant, you can take a semester's worth of classes in a structured environment with fellow beginners. The downside to college classes is that they tend to be heavily grammar-focused, and it often takes several semesters for you to work up to anything resembling a conversation level.

Private classes are another possibility. Look at the bulletin board at your local AF, troll the halls of the nearest university and look for the language department there, or ask the consulate for a list of references. Look for one-on-one lessons offered by French students at American universities or by Francophone expats looking to earn a bit of pocket money on the side. These personal sessions tend to emphasize conversation rather than grammar, and this approach can be a really great introduction to the colloquialisms and idioms you'll likely begin hearing as soon as you land.

Many people swear by the pricey audiovisual experiences offered by Rosetta Stone and Fluenz. For around $400, you can pick up one of these programs at the bookstore or online and study in the comfort of your own living room. The philosophy and approach to teaching languages differs significantly between the two (the former applies an immersion approach, while the latter feeds you morsels of the language one at a time), but both allow you to go to school whenever and as often as you like. For couples studying together or for those who don't have time to attend conventional classes, this option makes a lot of sense.

The most affordable of all your language-learning possibilities is the Meetup (www.meetup.com). While technically not classes, Meetups are social-networking groups that share a common interest, which, in this case, is the French language. Expect culture-oriented get-togethers—museum outings, gatherings at wine bars, French cinema rendezvous, cheese tastings—that all serve as fun vehicles for ameliorating your language skills *ensemble* (together). These sessions are often great networking zones where you'll meet not only other Anglophones but also honest-to-goodness French people. The casual ambience of most Meetups will relax you enough to loosen your chat mechanism and help fuel enthusiasm for your upcoming move.

LEARNING IN FRANCE

Not surprisingly, France is a hotbed of language-learning possibilities, so even if you arrive with French skills in the negative values, you'll be okay. A learning institution that meets your budget and experience will be available in your newly adopted country. Always begin by word of mouth—your friends, colleagues, and even the people standing in line at the *préfecture* will be able to weigh in on their experiences learning the language in France. In Paris, visit your local *mairie,* where the staff will gladly offer you a list of references for municipally run classes in your quartier. The government-sponsored Française Langue Étrangère (French as a Foreign Language or "FLE") classes are a veritable bargain at €41 per 180-hour, two-semester course, and when it's said and done, you'll have yourself a handy-dandy diploma or certificate to show for your hard work.

Expect a diverse student body, lots of structure, and a thorough introduction to the language. At the end of July, each office of the *mairie* in Paris offers the latest *livret de Cours Municipaux d'Adultes,* which lists all the courses available through the city at great prices, in multiple subjects. Another good place to learn about classes is www.fle.fr. This online portal offers an extensive list of schools and the information is available in English. You'll find public institutions as well as courses offered by nonprofits, such as the Alliance Française. Prices can vary dramatically from organization to organization; at the Sorbonne, you can expect to pay €600 for your summer semester French class, plus a €50 dossier fee. Private schools in Paris are a bit more expensive. For example, l'Atelier 9 offer a four-week, 80-hour session for €840, but there are never more than nine students in your class, which means plenty of attention from your professor.

As far as learning French goes, the best-kept secret in the Île-de-France region is that wonderful thing called the *association.* These are simply volunteer-run organizations that receive state funding for promoting the French language to the local non-French speaking community. Year-long courses are ridiculously inexpensive—€40 was the average in 2014, and that includes workbooks—and the student-teacher ratio is low.

Associations even subsidize the application fees for taking the standardized French exam known as DELF. (Having a DELF diploma in your dossier will likely impress the team surveying your file, so it's a good thing to have.) The nearest *association* may not be in your arrondissement, but to find the organization closest to you, check www. w35-associations.apps.paris.fr.

One of the best and perhaps most obvious ways to learn French is by getting out there, interacting with the locals, and trying your best to speak in their native tongue. At the supermarket, post office, and *bibliothèque* (library), you will find a surprisingly patient audience who will hear you out as you stumble along in elementary French, gently correcting you as you go. Don't miss these valuable learning opportunities by insisting that everyone speak English; you'll make friends and win hearts with a bit of earnest effort. Slightly more formal opportunities for interaction with Francophones can be found at local language-exchange groups, some of them cleverly disguised as English conversation groups. Don't be fooled: It's almost always a 50-50 French-English exchange, often over drinks with an eclectic international crowd. In Paris, the Big Ben Club (www.bigbenclub.eu) meets up every Thursday for French-English exchange at that Left Bank bibliophile's institution, Shakespeare & Co. Nominal dues will be solicited, but they resemble pocket change more than mortgage payments.

Education

Founded on the principles of *liberté, egalité,* and *fraternité,* the French education system is considered one of the better socialized-learning institutions in the world. Every child in France has access to a high-quality education, and between the ages of 6 and 16, they are required to attend school. Today, parents can choose between public, private, and home schooling, but it wasn't always this way.

During the Dark Ages, the importance of education in France fell by the wayside and didn't pick up again until the Enlightenment period, when Holy Roman Emperor Charlemagne introduced a centralized education model. Primarily religious in focus, the system was geared toward the elite and expanded through monasteries, later called "church schools." Catholic leaders, worried about losing their control to the professors at these schools, began hiring only those who were sanctioned by Catholic bishops to teach, thereby ensuring dogmatic, uniformly Catholic-oriented pedagogy.

Paris became the center for learning in the country in the 16th century, at which time Latin was supplanted by French as the lingua franca in universities and other learning institutions, but the Catholic church was still the controlling force behind the educational system. Reform continued throughout the 18th century with the development of *écoles centrales* and later *lycées*—a sort of middle-and-high-school amalgamation for the 11- to 18-year-old set. With a pedagogical model built on a well-balanced diet of math, science, literature, and the arts, each school was also decreed to have a library, garden, and natural history collection. During this period, teacher salaries were determined by the centralized government, but later this duty fell under the responsibility of the local departments, who still oversee regional educational institutions.

In the early 19th century, Napoléon overhauled the education system yet again, giving elementary schoolchildren a standardized education while 12-and-ups were given the choice between a civil servant's education or a military-bound secondary education. This blueprint is not too far off from today's model, wherein students are groomed for a specific career path that's usually determined by a test, the *diplôme national du brevet*, taken during a student's first year at *lycée*. The test is the deciding factor in whether a student pursues further studies and a subsequent career in science and math, economics, or the arts, or follows a trade-school path.

Under Napoléon's rule, women—long excluded from the education process—were finally admitted to study, but their education was limited to religious studies while a more rigorous academic training was the exclusive terrain of the men. That's changed a bit since Napoléon's time: Today, girls not only receive an equal education but outnumber boys in the *baccalauréat* path leading to careers in economics and the arts. They also attend institutes of higher learning at higher rates than their male counterparts.

EDUCATIONAL LEVELS

On the surface, the French education system looks a little more complicated than the North American one, but once you understand the naming convention, the stages begin to look a lot more familiar.

Children are eligible for *crèche* (subsidized daycare) when they are three months old and *maternelle* (preschool) at two years old. They don't enter *école primaire* (primary school) until the age of six. *École primaire* is the French equivalent of elementary school. Kids begin at roughly seven years old, working their way up through five years of classes focused on reading, writing, math, geography, history, and occasionally a foreign language, including English.

When American kids look forward to graduating to middle school, their counterparts

French public schools are identifiable by the flags flown out front.

in France move up to *collège,* four years of pre-high school academic training that begins with level six (*sixième*) and ends with level three (*troisième*). Here, they study more of the fundamentals, plus French literature, music, and up to two languages, including English, German, Spanish, or Italian. Students are taught in the same classroom all day, with a rotation of teachers coming in to instruct. Each year, two students from each class are nominated to act as liaisons between the students and the teachers, facilitating dialogue and helping make decisions that affect their fellow students, from scrutinizing academic performance to weighing in on disciplinary action.

A child's entrance into *lycée* marks the beginning of the French high-school equivalent, which some might be glad to know lasts only three years. Counterintuitively, the first year of *lycée* is the *seconde,* and the second is the *première.* The third and final year is known as *terminale.* The last two years are spent focusing on a specific track of academic training. Kids following the science path can expect to take plenty of math, physics, and chemistry classes; humanities students will focus on foreign languages, including the classics, plus literature, philosophy, and history; economics students will study social sciences and math.

ENROLLING IN FRENCH SCHOOLS

If you are planning to enroll your child in the French school system, it's important that he has a language foundation to help him through the rough world of being the new kid in school. For high-school students in particular, the ability to assimilate, make friends, and thrive in any new environment is contingent on a basic ability to communicate; the better her language skills, the more successful your child will be at adapting. The younger the child, the more adaptable to the new language she will be. But if you throw a *lycée*-age teen into an all-French class without any preparation, the outcome could be disastrous: depression, failing grades, and worse.

Before being placed in a class, your child will be given an entrance exam to determine which school level is best. Even for the brightest students, repeating a grade to compensate for language deficiencies could be a reality. A handful of public schools throughout the Paris area offer special "international" sections for North American students entering the system without a solid foundation in the language. These unique curricula differ from the standard education model; they are designed especially to facilitate the integration of foreign students into the French system. (They also work to prepare French students for living abroad in other countries). Students can expect an extra six hours per week of French study, as well as a lot of time spent with their noses embedded firmly in books.

PRIVATE EDUCATION

As in the United States and Canada, private schools can be found throughout France, including parochial schools, Waldorf and Montessori schools, and elite international schools with annual tuitions that rival the cost of a new car. Despite the generally high standard of public education throughout France, parents opt to enroll their children in private schools for the same reasons parents everywhere do, including higher teacher-to-student ratios, safety, religious purposes, proximity, or to give children the advantage of being instructed in their native tongue.

French private schools fall into two camps: *sous contrat* (under contract) and *hors contrat* (outside contract). Teachers at *sous contrat* schools are paid by the state, and tuition fees are generally on the low end of the spectrum. Curricula mirror those of public schools, and the academic calendar follows the same schedule. *Hors contrat* schools, because they aren't state-funded, are free to set their own curricula and tuition fees, and they run on an academic calendar of their own design.

The type of private education you choose for your children depends largely on your personal preferences, but your employer in France may affect your decision. Some employers offer new hires the option of enrolling their children in nearby international schools attended by the children of other international staffers. This may not provide the sort of enriching cultural exchange you'd envisaged for your child, but the assimilation process at an international *collège* or *lycée* will likely be smoother at an international school than at a French public school. To explore your options for French private schools, visit two online databases: www.enseignement-prive.info and www.fabert.com.

FRENCH UNIVERSITIES AND *GRANDES ÉCOLES*

There are two tiers within the French university system: the *université* and the *grande école*. The former are standard-issue universities that accept all who apply, as long as they meet the base criteria of having completed *lycée* (and survived the *baccalauréat*). Tuition fees are set annually and standardized throughout the country. In 2014, the annual tuition fees ranged from €183 to €606.

Grandes écoles are elite schools, not unlike American Ivy League colleges, which accept only the best of the best and charge tuition fees that run higher than the national average. Expect to pay as much as €10,000 per year if you or your child is accepted into one of these institutions, and also expect to earn a well-paying job at the end of your education. Whichever academic path you take, you can expect a long semester of it's-up-to-you-to-study independence, followed by a big make-it-or-break-it exam at semester's end. France has a relatively high university enrollment rate that's matched by a high dropout rate, due in large part to the stress of this virtually all-or-nothing system.

STUDY ABROAD

French universities roll out the welcome mat to 250,000 foreign university students every year, making France one of the most popular study-abroad destinations in the world. Coming into the French university system as an American college student is a significantly different experience than entering as a French *lycéen,* beginning with the fact that you won't have had to take the dreaded *baccalauréat* exam. Semester-abroad programs allow foreign university students to ease into the system; this is one of the most popular avenues for obtaining long-stay visas and *cartes de séjour,* which give students the right to work part-time. But first you must meet a few criteria.

To enroll without showing an *international baccalauréat,* you'll have to have two years of college under your belt already. Next, you'll have to decide if you want to study independently or through your university. The former is generally less expensive but requires more effort on your part.

You begin by contacting the school of your choice—a list can be found on the government-sponsored education portal www.enseignementsup-recherche.gouv.fr—then creating a dossier that you submit online directly at the university website. You will not be asked to show transcripts or grades; the onus will be on you to determine whether or not you're up to snuff, educationally speaking. Unless you are studying the French language exclusively, you will be asked to take a French-language proficiency exam or show a certificate attesting to your language skills.

Tuition at French universities is surprisingly affordable and varies slightly according to your academic goals. Here are the 2014 tuition costs: For a standard undergrad diploma, students pay €183 annually; for masters programs, the annual fees jump to €254; doctoral students pay €388 per year; and students pursuing a *diplôme d'ingénieur* pay €606 per semester. Certificate programs, including those that allow you to bypass the French-language proficiency tests, cost considerably more; expect to pay as much as €3,000 per four-month semester for the luxury of being instructed in English. Private school tuition is, not surprisingly, higher still. Don't be shocked if that exclusive private business school asks you to fork over more than €10,000 a year to earn your MBA. Still, it might be cheaper than the American equivalent, so if you're seriously considering this route, invest in some French classes and start your research *tout de suite*.

One final word of caution: A unique difference students will notice between the French and American university education is the level of responsibility that falls on the student's shoulders. Don't expect surprise quizzes, weekly assignments, or even midterms—but do expect cumulative exams at the end of the semester that will determine your final grade. To learn more about your options as an American or Canadian student studying in France, visit www.campusfrance.org or check with your university.

HEALTH

In the 2007 documentary *Sicko*, director Michael Moore used the French healthcare system to illustrate its American counterpart's many flaws. This cinematic tactic proved effective, earning the film an Academy Award nomination and prompting the viewing public to critically examine the issues that stirred such heated debate. But what stood out more than the U.S. healthcare system's startling deficiencies was that a humane, affordable, reliable government-run medical system is possible. In France, as it ought to be everywhere, medical treatment (and preventive care) is a right, not a privilege.

Consistently ranked the number-one healthcare system in the world, France's Assurance Maladie, part of the Sécurité Sociale system, is available to everyone who lives here legally and supports the system by paying taxes. People earning little or no income pay little or nothing. The rest of us pay according to our means. For the roughly 12 percent of the population that is self-employed, other forms of government-subsidized insurance is available. Even if you're not here legally, you won't be denied affordable healthcare: Low-cost public hospitals are at your disposal, and mobile doctors will even make house calls to those unable to get to a hospital at any time of day or night.

If you play by the rules, you will have confirmed that you are insured before you arrive in France, since this is a required component of most visa applications. You're asked to submit proof of insurance, but experience proves that consular officials don't

always fact-check the documents you provide, and you aren't likely to be asked to provide proof again once you get here. Maybe you went ahead and purchased a traveler's policy that covers you in case of catastrophic illness or injury or reimburses you for travel expenses should you need to fly home to see your own doctor. If you're a student, it's likely that your school provides coverage for study-abroad programs. Or maybe, just maybe, you came with nothing at all, and suddenly that tooth with the wonky old filling is starting to give you grief. If that's you, you don't have to suffer in silence.

Types of Insurance

There are several types of health insurance available to expats in France, the first being the aforementioned Assurance Maladie offered by the state. Supplemental insurance coverage, called *mutuelle,* is popular among the French, who use it to offset the already small (by American standards) deductibles, co-pays, and other types of care not covered by the regular system (cosmetic dentistry, for instance). Finally, there are private insurance options you can purchase in the U.S. or in France that provide different sorts of coverage—inpatient or outpatient or both, maternity, dental—at moderate prices. Which one you choose depends largely on your financial means and the kind of coverage you require for your own sense of security.

ASSURANCE MALADIE

The French public healthcare system is supported by the tax-paying public, which contributes approximately 20 percent of its income to prop up the system. It functions in a pay-as-you-can manner, which many tag as "socialist" because those who earn the most pay the most, and those with little pay less. (And those with no income pay nothing.) Even if you don't contribute taxes, you are entitled to Couverture Maladie Universelle (CMU) if you come from a country (like the U.S.) that doesn't offer universal coverage and will be residing France for more than three months, or if you are on a limited income. The system is stressed after years of seeing the contributor population dwindle. Retirees no longer contribute, and the birthrate has been low in France for decades—meaning there may not be enough new citizens to support the healthcare system in the future.

It's possible to come to France and sponge off healthcare, but this is not advisable. You don't want to be the

The American Hospital of Paris is actually just outside the city limits in Neuilly-sur-Seine.

proverbial straw that breaks the camel's back, nor the scapegoat for the failure of a generous, relatively smooth-running system. With public debt at an all-time high of 95 percent of GDP in 2014, it can't take much more stress, an issue that political leaders are struggling to address. Paying into the system will help keep it operating, and has the added benefit of looking good on paper for those nerve-wracking visits to the *préfecture*.

After applying for your CMU, you may need to wait a few months to get approval and, ultimately, your carte vitale. If you have to visit a doctor or pharmacy, save your receipts; the coverage is usually retroactive to the date on which you submitted your documents. The cost of your annual premium is determined by your income—expect to pay 8 percent of whatever income you declare—and is due in quarterly installments.

Once you have your bright green *carte vitale* in hand, you can rendezvous with your doctor of choice and visit hospitals, clinics, pharmacies, and laboratories. Produce your card when you pay for your goods and services up front, then submit your receipts to Assurance Maladie, which reimburses you a percentage: 70-100 percent of what you paid for services and 15-65 percent of what you paid for your prescription medicines. Reimbursement takes about two weeks and is deposited directly into your French bank account. Sound complicated? It might seem so at first, but like all things French (and therefore heavy on bureaucratic ritual), it gets easier the more you do it.

MUTUELLE

By American standards, the full cost of medical treatment at a French public hospital borders on a bargain; depending on the treatment you receive, an overnight stay with regular nursing care and medications at a public hospital could set you back just €100—a whole lot less than it would at any public or private hospital in the U.S. Most drug costs are lower here, too. These two factors combined have resulted in some expats scheduling full-fare medical procedures in France. But for regular folks who simply want basic coverage, Assurance Maladie is a good start. Next, you might consider *mutuelle,* the supplemental insurance coverage that most French families and individuals opt for. It covers the cost of deductibles and all the little things that add up when you need them: ambulance costs, private hospital-room fees, and cosmetic dentistry, for instance. You can choose from a number of configurations, depending on your needs, and the price will reflect what those needs are. Want to make sure your contact lenses are paid for in full by your insurance company? Identify that concern when making your *mutuelle* purchasing decision.

In addition to all the private agencies offering *mutuelles,* the government also offers this additional coverage to families and individuals of limited means through the CMU website (www.cmu.fr). The information is in French, so if your language skills are still at the work-in-progress phase, you'll want a French friend to help you with the technical translating. Some well-known *mutuelles* in France include France Mutuelle, MAAF, and Swiss Life.

PRIVATE INSURANCE

All you need to feel totally overwhelmed by the private insurance policy process is to type in "expatriate health insurance" into your favorite search engine. You'll be met with links to dozens of companies, each offering similar but different insurance options that span a frighteningly broad financial spectrum. So which do you choose? The best

DAILY LIFE

EXPAT EXPERIENCE: THE *CARTE VITALE*

Name: Elisabeth Lyman
Age: 39
Profession: French-to-English translator
Hometown: Minneapolis, Minnesota
Current City: Paris, 17th

Elisabeth moved to Paris in 2009 to expand her already-thriving independent translation business and meet new clients. In the intervening years, she's morphed into a fully-fledged Parisian, renting an apartment in the charming Batignolles district, establishing herself as an auto-entrepreneur, and developing an active social life in her new city. The transition was not without its hurdles and frustrations, however. It took Elisabeth more than two years to secure her *carte vitale*, the little green card that allows her to access the public healthcare system she's been paying into since 2011. Here, Elisabeth shares some of her experiences and suggestions to make the processes easier for newcomers.

What documents did you stuff into your dossier in anticipation of your first appointment at Assurance Maladie?
With my particular business type, I had to go through the RSI (Régime Social des Indépendants) to apply for my card. They asked for a *traduction assermentée* (cer-

tified translation) of my birth certificate as well as a photocopy of my residence permit, proof of residence, and copies of my business registration paperwork from URSSAF (a department within the French social security system that manages all aspects of *cotisation sociale*—otherwise known as the taxes that support the socialized medical system). I gathered all of this and mailed it in a large brown mailing envelope that would seem difficult to misplace. A couple of months later, after I had still not heard back from them, I called and was told my papers had never arrived. I realized later that this could have been avoided if I had only sent them *en recommandée avec avis de réception* (by registered mail with confirmation of receipt), as the chance of mail sent this way getting lost is far lower. By the time I learned they didn't have my documents, it was too late to apply again because my residence permit had expired in the meantime. Renewing it took an entire year, so I had to put the idea of getting the health card on the shelf for a while.

Two years and several months on, you finally have healthcare coverage. What was the most challenging aspect of the process, and was anything easier than expected?

bet is to go by word of mouth. Ask friends who've already made the move, post queries on expat forums, and check with the American Embassy in France, which offers a downloadable list of companies on its website (france.usembassy.gov). HCC Medical Insurance Services (www.hccmis.com) has earned high marks from some expats, with coverage in the US$700 to US$900 range annually. Also worth a gander are www.expat-medical-insurance.com and www.healthcareinternational.com.

UNINSURED

Nearly everyone who's lived in France for any amount of time has one healthcare story or another; it usually ends with "I couldn't believe how inexpensive the bill was/how short the wait was/how friendly the staff was." Even if you have no health insurance coverage, you will be treated respectfully and without palpable bias or hostility. You will not be asked to show proof of insurance before you are treated, and you will not be denied care in the emergency room because of lack of funds.

The most difficult parts were not knowing how much longer the process would take, and also the various frustrating dead-ends along the way. At one point, I received a letter from the RSI and opened it eagerly, imagining it held some kind of good news for me, or some information about progress made. Instead, it was a letter addressed to someone I'd never heard of but who was also apparently trying to get the *carte vitale*. My name and address were on the envelope and in the header at the top of the page, but someone else's name was in the salutation and the body of the letter made references to a situation entirely different from mine. I sent it back to them with an explanation and a renewed expression of my desire to get a card with my own name on it.

What words of wisdom would you share with others like you who are independent professionals hoping to secure their own healthcare coverage through Assurance Maladie?
Whenever possible, submit your paperwork in person and have them give you some kind of proof that you have done so. Also note down the name of the person who took your documents. If you mail any papers, do this only through registered mail with confirmation of receipt.

This way, you have proof of the steps you have taken so far in the process. Above all, no matter what happens, be friendly and show gratitude whenever dealing with the people responsible for getting you the card, whether over the phone or in person. A smile can sometimes go a long way.

© JON HELGE HESBY

Getting French health insurance wasn't easy, but Elisabeth Lyman didn't give up.

(You aren't even asked for a credit card or other payment during the course of your treatment; a bill will be mailed to you once your treatment is completed.) If you have no insurance and find yourself at the emergency room with a broken big toe or at the dentist's office with a faulty filling, be prepared to pay the bill when it arrives a week or two later, and expect the costs to be significantly less than if you were to have the same treatment back home. Remember to save your receipts, in case you sign up for Assurance Maladie; the program is retroactive and may cover a good portion of your out-of-pocket expenses.

PUBLIC HOSPITALS VS. PRIVATE CLINICS

Only one third of all French *hôpitaux* (hospitals) are privately run; the rest are non-profit public institutions run by the government, which sets fees for medical services rendered by any institution or individual medical professional on the government payroll. For example, on January 1, 2014, the fee for an office visit to a family physician

THE DOCTOR'S MODERN HOUSE CALL

It's 2am, and you haven't stopped coughing since 2pm. Your throat feels like a fiery furnace and your eyeballs are like dried raisins. Are you dying of some mysterious tropical disease, or is it a simple case of the 24-hour flu? If you don't have the strength to haul yourself to the nearest hospital, you're in luck. When you call SOS Médecins, an honest-to-goodness doctor will be knocking on your door within the hour, medical kit in hand, ready to diagnose what ails you and offer you a soothing balm –or at least an aspirin or two.

Assurance Maladie covers the cost of the home visit (€33), but even if you don't have insurance, there's no need to work up a sweat on top of your fever. You'll simply be charged the uninsured person's rate: €70 at the time of this writing. Don't have the strength to write out a check? Relax: They'll send you a bill.

SOS Médecins was founded in 1966 by a Parisian M.D. after one of his patients died on a Saturday –a day when doctors didn't regularly make house-calls. He figured that if you could get a plumber at home on a weekend, you should be able to get life-saving care, too. Today, SOS Médicins has been adopted by other Francophone countries, including Tahiti, Senegal, and Switzerland.

in France was set at €23, or €25 to visit with a specialist. Home doctor visits doctor ring in at €33.

Of the public institutions, many are *centres hospitaliers universitaires,* or research hospitals affiliated with a university. These are not the funky institutions that might come to mind when you hear "government-run facility." They are as warm and friendly as any hospital, and the care you'll receive is on par with private facilities. Expect the usual amenities in the rooms—toilets and televisions—and maybe even something more: Some hospitals post their menus online, so you can plan your overnight stay for a Saturday to benefit from the Sunday-morning croissants.

There are two different types of *cliniques* (private hospitals) in France—for profit and not-for-profit. The American Hospital of Paris, which is actually in the well-to-do suburb of Neuilly-sur-Seine, belongs to the latter category, and its foundation is supported in part by member and public donations. You'll pay more here, and Assurance Maladie won't be able to reimburse you in the same generous way it would if you'd gone to a public hospital. The benefit of private hospitals is that some specialize in specific types of services—maternity or oncology, for instance—and some also tout a bilingual staff, which can ease the stress of an already stressful situation for some.

In France, would-be doctors don't go into the medical field because they want to get rich; they do it because they were fast-tracked on a science route during their *lycée* years (and possibly because the wanted a career in which they could help people). Because medical school costs next to nothing to attend in France, many choose this path despite its dearth of economic advantages. You will find that there are two types of doctors here, just to add another layer of complexity onto the process: *conventionnée* and *non-conventionnée. Conventionnée* doctors have contracted with the state to provide their services at a set cost that's reimbursable by Assurance Maladie; *non-conventionnée* practitioners have no contract with the state and set their own fees. You'll find this disparity especially among dermatologists and cosmetic surgeons, where fees can vary widely depending on the doctor, the location, and the services being rendered.

Pharmacies and Prescriptions

You can't miss the pharmacy; just look for the flashing green cross, and *voilà!* You've arrived. French pharmacies are different from their North American counterparts in many ways. First, a doctor is always on staff and has the authority to prescribe or recommend treatment at her discretion, without consulting your primary physician. These pharmacy doctors are also authorized to administer first aid if you need it. Next, you'll notice that some over-the-counter drugs you take for granted back home—cough syrup, pain reliever, even sore-throat lozenges—are found behind the counter at the pharmacist's, and requesting them requires some basic working French. Need multipurpose solution for your contact lenses? Don't go looking for it at your local supermarket—you'll find it at the pharmacy, along with high-end face creams, diet pills and potions, homeopathic remedies, and multivitamins. (You'll also find contact-lens solution for sale at eyeglasses shops, where it is sometimes less expensive than at the pharmacy. It pays to compare.) Some pharmacies also vend veterinary medicines, so you can pick up Fluffy's heartworm medicine and your antibiotics in one fell swoop.

Picking up your prescription at the pharmacy works in a way you're probably familiar with: Bring your prescription to the counter, ask any questions, listen to the pharmacist explain how to take your medicine, pay for it (standard practice is to present your *carte vitale*, so you can be reimbursed), and save your receipts if you intend to seek reimbursement.

By law, every community must have a pharmacy that's open on weekends, holidays, and during off-hours; the information for the one closest to you can be found posted in the window or on the door of your neighborhood pharmacy.

VIVE LA VENDING MACHINE!

What do condoms, hypodermic needles, and wine have in common? If you guessed that they're all sold from vending machines in France, you're right. The French appreciate convenience as much as anyone, which is why you can also find espresso, razors, and Speedo bathing suits in automated machines here (yes, really).

As part of a nationwide campaign against HIV/AIDS, easy-access condom machines have been mounted outside nearly every pharmacy in the country, as well as inside most Métro stations. Syringe dispensers can be found in big cities like Marseille and Lyon, but unless you're trolling through the seedier parts of town, you probably won't even notice them. More eye-catching are the automated wine dispensers. At *hypermarchés* like Auchan, you can BYOB and fill 'er up, just like pumping gas at the gas station. Tend toward teetotalism? A few select Auchans have also begun dispensing raw milk by the liter.

Preventive Measures

No special inoculations are required to enter France, but it doesn't hurt to be in top health before your move. As part of the *carte de séjour* process, you'll have to have your lungs X-rayed for tuberculosis, but this is the only medical requirement you'll find here.

Like everywhere else, waves of viruses come crashing through the population every season, and many opt for flu vaccines as a prophylactic measure. If you didn't get that flu shot before you moved, you can still find one here. In France, the flu is called *"la grippe"* and often *"la grippe* H1N1," and pharmacies can direct you to health clinics where inoculations are administered or sell you the vaccine to take to your doctor to be injected.

ALTERNATIVE THERAPIES

The French love their medicine, whether it's the pharmaceutical kind or the kind created exclusively by Mother Nature. Homeopathy is particularly popular in France, and pharmacies everywhere sell homeopathic remedies behind the counter. Boiron, headquartered in Lyon, is the most popular brand, producing "remedies" for everything from bruises (arnica) to mental fatigue (nux vomica). The little blue vials run about €2, and many people swear by their efficacy. If you're one of the millions around the world who prefer to take the natural approach to healthcare, you'll find many opportunities to heal thyself in France. Flower essences, acupuncture, and massage are all on the menu. Herbal weight-loss formulations are in high demand in France, and you'll have dozens of varieties of liquids, pills, lozenges, and creams to choose from if you're looking to shed a kilo or two before bikini-and-Speedo season. Many healthcare services that fall under the "natural" umbrella are covered in part by Assurance Maladie, including homeopathy, which is reimbursed at 30 percent; be sure to inquire when seeking out your treatment.

© AURELIA D'ANDREA

Osteopaths, acupuncturists, and even herbalists can be found throughout Paris.

Environmental Factors

AIR QUALITY

Each year in France, 11 million tons of pollutants are pumped into the air from cars, factories, agriculture, and people living their day-to-day lives. This fact is particularly noticeable when you're stuck on your bicycle behind a two-stroke motorbike at a stoplight. In some ways, Paris looks like a developing nation when it comes to the color and quantities flowing out of auto exhaust pipes. Your health can be affected by all that pollution, both out in the streets and in your home. To see what the pollution levels are like in your town, visit www.airqualitynow.eu. In Paris and Bordeaux, the levels can look scary-high from time to time. Many city dwellers in France take the extra precautionary step of purchasing an air filter; try Darty (www.darty.fr) if you live on a particularly busy street or near a freeway on-ramp, where pollution levels are particularly high.

WATER QUALITY

The French are known for their love of bottled water, consuming 40 gallons of it per person per year. Stroll down the aisle at the nearest *hypermarché,* and you'll find yourself in a sea of drinking water. Do you like yours flat or still? Loaded with minerals or not? Are you on a diet? There's a bottled-water variety to help you through. Those who don't need fancy water (or who don't want to contribute more plastic to the wastestream) will be glad to know that tap water is safe throughout France, though it tends to have a very high lime content, which leaves a flaky white residue on glasses, in your sink, and in your tabletop water-filter pitcher. This necessitates the purchase of products that eliminate the funky buildup in your appliances, such as electric kettles and dishwashers. Public fountains are common throughout Paris—they're often green, and if it's a Wallace fountain, designed by 19th-century French sculptor Charles-Auguste Lebourg, it might even look like a piece of art. Potable water is available in public fountains, and numerous filter options are available for those who want to lessen the limestone content in their glasses. Around the Alps and Pyrénées, it's not uncommon to see cars pulled over on the side of the road, with a line of people bearing water bottles to be filled at natural springs.

SMOKING

Though the café smoking ban went into effect way back in 2008, France's addiction to "cancer sticks" still clings like tar to an old Gauloises fan's lungs. Where else will you find a pregnant mother-to-be puffing her hand-rolled cigarette, with nary a glance of disapproval from passersby? The good news is that the rates of stroke and heart attack have plummeted since the ban; the bad news is that it's still too late for too many. Lung cancer kills more people in France than any other type of cancer. Bad habits are hard to break, and that's particularly evident in the outdoor seating section of cafés, which tend to take on the air of a smoker's convention in wintertime when the heat lamps are activated and the plastic walls go up to keep the cold out. Smoking is no longer legal in public places, including office buildings, hospitals, museums, and school campuses, but that doesn't mean everyone adheres to the law. Enforcement has been

UP IN E-SMOKE

Smoking, that most beloved of French traditions, is on its way out. In its place? More smoking! E-smoking, that is. Touted as a harmless bridge between full-fledged addiction and absolute cessation, e-cigarettes offer the nicotine buzz without the toxic, lung-damaging smoke, according to the people selling them.

Seemingly overnight, e-cigarette shops by the dozens have hatched in every arrondissement of Paris, selling the hope of a life free from addiction, chronic coughs, emphysema, and worse for between €36 and €100. For France's 15 million smokers, this is a godsend. For your money, you get one battery-operated device in the color of your choice, plus a replaceable liquid-nicotine cartridge. *Vapoteuses* and *vapoteurs* throughout the capital swear by its efficacy, but French health experts are already issuing warnings about potentially detrimental long-term effects, and in more bad news, Health Minister Marisol Touraine wants the e-cigarette classified as a drug, which would mean a "smoking" ban similar to the one instituted in New York City that makes it illegal to puff away in indoor public places.

Electronic cigarettes are all the rage.

rather lax, and business owners are reluctant to ask clients to stub out their cigs if no one has lodged a complaint. If you're sensitive to cigarette smoke, avoid enclosed terraces at cafés and brasseries, and count your blessings that you didn't decide to move to France before 2008.

Disabled Access

Though disabled-access laws are now in place, France has a lot of catching up to do, beginning with ditching the word *handicappée,* which is the preferred term in France for people with any minor or major disability. This is not the most hospitable country for people with mobility issues. Despite a law passed in 2005 to make offices, businesses, and public spaces accessible to all, the changes are being implemented at an escargot's pace. The government agency that oversees laws relating to disabled citizens, the Ministère des Solidarités et de la Cohésion Sociale, launched a PR campaign to try and convince people that efforts are under way to make France more accessible, but those who have to navigate the cobbled streets, clogged sidewalks, centuries-old staircases and other public spaces will tell you it's just not happening fast enough.

The Métro is not worth the hassle: Not all stations are equipped with an elevator, and those that do have them can't ensure that they'll be functioning when you need to use them. Buses are more likely to have a wheelchair access. According to the law, by 2015 all public spaces are to be accessible to those with restricted mobility, but big projects rarely keep their schedules here so err on the side of caution and take extra care when planning your excursions.

Safety

There's no sugar-coating it: Crime is on the rise in France. Still, it isn't very likely you'll become a crime statistic if you live here. Strict gun-control laws do mean that you're more likely to get stabbed than shot, but the odds of either one are infinitesimally small. If you are the victim of a crime in France, it'll most likely be a pickpocketing or other petty theft. In Paris, Métro line 1 is notorious for pickpockets, who hunt for distracted tourists on their way to the Louvre, the Musée d'Orsay, and the Champs-Élysées.

Also growing in popularity among thieves previously resigned to wallets is smartphone theft, with iPhones being of particular interest. A recent spate of phone thefts in train stations and on the streets—generally the purloined items are snatched directly from the hands of their rightful owners—warrants extra care with your electronic doodads. Also be aware that when you're traveling by car, your license plate gives away your nonlocal status, and visitors in rental cars have reported break-ins at popular tourist sites. The key is not to leave anything of value in your car, and be sure to keep all the doors locked when you're driving.

One technique being employed to curb crime in public areas is the closed-circuit TV camera. A public surveillance system already in place expanded in 2013, when more than 1,000 new cameras were installed throughout the public streets of Paris, adding to the 935,000 cameras already in place throughout the rest of the country. If it feels like a futuristic police state, that's probably not too far off—but this system has proved effective in apprehending thieves in the Métro and otherwise identifying criminals in public places. In 2013, in the distant Paris suburb of Montereau-Fault-Yonne, closed-circuit cameras are being used to capture "criminals" of another stripe: locals who fail to do their civic duty and pick up after their dogs. A recent nationwide survey indicates that 75 percent of French citizens approve of public surveillance cameras.

POLICE

French police can help with matters as varied as finding a lost animal to giving you directions to helping you when your pocket is picked on the Paris Métro. There are several different types of police: *police nationale,* those legions of men and women who keep order and protect the public in metropolitan areas throughout France; *gendarmes,* who keep the peace in rural areas, provide military security, and stroll the welcome halls at airports; *police de la circulation,* who'll ticket you for breaking one of the rules of the road and issue you those pesky parking citations; and *douanes,* who enforce the law when it comes to customs and taxes. For basic issues, either go to the local *commissariat* of police in your arrondissement or town, or dial emergency number 17— it's the same throughout France—to speak with a law-enforcement agent equipped to help you. Note that French is the common language spoken, so be prepared to try and stumble through; if you get a nice person on the other end of the line, she may meet you halfway with some English.

EMERGENCIES

France is fully equipped to handle any emergency you may face, but you need to know where to call to get the care that you need. The fire department, or Sapeurs-Pompiers, is the go-to agency for most emergencies. The staff act as intermediaries to determine whether they should come to your aid themselves or send the police or a more urgent medical service. If they determine that you need a doctor at home right away, they'll direct you to SOS Médecins (or you can call them directly—in Paris, dial 01/47 07 77 77), who'll be at your home in less than an hour. Or they might send Urgences Médicales, who'll pay you a visit within 12 hours (tel. 01/53 94 94 94). Several times each year, cards with all the municipal emergency numbers are distributed to homes and apartments throughout France. Ask the *gardien(ne)* of your building for a card or request one at your local *mairie* if one hasn't been slipped under your front door in a while. The most common numbers you'll need in an emergency are:

15 - Ambulance (Service d'Aide Médicale d'Urgence/SAMU)
17 - Police (Police/Gendarmes)
18 - Fire (Sapeurs-Pompiers)

EMPLOYMENT

In 2011, as the nation ramped up for the presidential elections, then-president Nicolas Sarkozy reignited the heated debate over one of France's most controversial social issues by declaring, "The 35-hour workweek no longer exists." Threatening the status quo with that proclamation might be one of the reasons the French public elected François Hollande instead of re-electing Sarkozy in 2012, but Sarkozy was on to something: The 35-hour workweek is a bit of a myth; the national average is 39.5 hours of work-time each week, just behind the European average of 40.3 hours. But that's not to say there aren't perks galore for the employed populace. Americans are often left slack-jawed with a combination of disbelief and envy when they learn what their French counterparts are entitled to: free healthcare? A minimum of five weeks' paid vacation? Subsidized education? How can people gripe about a few increased work hours when they've got all that? Easy. The French work hard for their benefits and don't want to see them whittled away without a fight. Even if the 35-hour workweek works better in theory than in practice, at least the 218-day work year and five weeks of vacation are safe from the meddling hands of politicos, but it promises to be a frequent topic of conversation as the 2017 election inches closer.

For expatriates arriving in France with hopes of laying down roots and actually earning a living, there are numerous possibilities, some more feasible than others. In

a perfect situation, you'll be transferred here through your current job, settle into a cushy three-year contract complete with housing, travel, and food allowances. (This is a reality for many—your first social gathering in France with more than a handful of American expats will verify it.) American companies by the boatload have branched out with offices in France—American Express, Xerox, Hewlett-Packard, IBM, and many fashion and beauty brands—and if you've been employed with such a company for more than three months, you're eligible for an Employee on Assignment permit. Does your company have international offices? If so, it's worth checking with your HR department on the chances of an international transfer.

Teaching English has long been a popular way for Anglophone expats to earn a living in France, and it might be the one professional realm where Americans have an advantage over the French; employers often prefer native speakers and those with limited French because it reinforces the goal of the education process: Teaching (and learning) English. Private language schools and individual private lessons are the two paths of least resistance, and opportunities are plentiful if you establish yourself as a niche teacher of children, perhaps, or of legal English to traveling attorneys.

For the lucky arrivals armed with a law degree, finding employment in France and securing that all-important work-sponsored visa will be much easier. The nonprofit sector—the International Chamber of Commerce, OECD, and UNESCO—are good places to start your hunt for a legal job in France. Not an *avocat* (lawyer) and don't plan to become one? There's still hope, especially if you're in possession of a student visa, which allows you to work up to 20 hours per week (and more during the summer semester). With a long-stay visa, you can continue your freelancing gigs abroad without worrying about breaking any employment laws—though if you plan to stay more than three months and intend to sign up for Assurance Maladie, you'll need to file an income tax return so the French government can determine how much to charge you for healthcare coverage.

The unemployment rate is high in France, currently hovering just below 10 percent, and unemployment among foreigners is even higher, at 22 percent. When a position opens up, a French employer will first look to the pool of French applicants to find a qualified candidate. That's some stiff competition, considering that the natives are already equipped with a solid (and predictably uniform) educational foundation and, presumably, an extremely high level of French fluency. Bundled with the fact that they are citizens and you are not, they will most likely trump your qualifications unless you have some tricks up your sleeve. (Or if the jobs you're applying for aren't desirable, meaning the qualified locals may pass and take unemployment or job offer *numéro deux* instead.)

Another option for anyone not averse to a bit of risk-taking is under-the-table work. Though it's not discussed much in the open, there is a thriving underground economy in France, supported primarily by expats here on legal visas, as well as illegal immigrants who haven't taken the steps to get their visa situations sorted out. From restaurant work to teaching English to watching children and giving tours, there are endless opportunities to earn some euros by working *dans le noir* (under the table), but keep in mind that this option is neither ideal nor legal. Unsurprisingly, the big cities have the most opportunity, with Paris being the employment mecca of France. It's possible to tap into the diverse population and exploit it, if that's your thing. But be warned that getting caught could have dire consequences not just for you—including expulsion and being banned from returning for four years—but also for the person who hires you, who'll be slapped with a hefty fine.

Taxes run extremely high for employers in France; to cover your *cotisation,* or social benefits, they must pay the state an average of nearly a third of the wages they pay you, so the temptation is always there to add an extra undeclared body or two to the payroll. Surprisingly, even long-established companies, particularly those in the tourist trade whose day-to-day workings are limited mostly to foreign visitors, fly under the radar and employ people off the books. Either they have good lawyers, know the ropes, or are genuine roulette players willing to engage in the risks. Whatever the case may be, they're here, hiring people like you and me to our mutual advantage—but not without considerable hazards.

If all this talk of deportation, fines, and other risks have you reconsidering the illegal employment minefield, making your freelance status official or even starting your own business might be the solution. Be prepared to build a fat dossier of tax forms, *cotisation* papers, and endless copies of your *carte de séjour.* If your desire to make it work in France supersedes your fear of paperwork, prepare to investigate your moneymaking options.

Self-Employment

FREELANCING

Once you've been granted your visa and have either your *carte de séjour* or *recepisée* in hand, you'll need to register as an *auto-entrepreneur* with the Centre de Formalités des Entreprises des Autoentrepreneurs (www.lautoentrepreneur.fr). This allows you to go legit by declaring your activity and subsequent income, then paying the taxes that help support that generous healthcare system you're now entitled to take advantage of. You'll create an online dossier that describes the sort of work you'll be doing and answer all the nosy questions the government wants to ask about you to make your status official. Then hit the *envoyer* (send) button. (This process can also be done in person at the Centre de Formalités des Entreprises (CFE), Chambre de Commerce, or Chambre des Métiers). A month or two later, you'll receive a Notification d'Affiliation au Statut Auto-Entrepreneur, the form you'll use to declare any earnings. You'll also receive a chart that will help you determine the taxes or *cotisation* that you need to remit, which will fall somewhere between 13 and 23 percent of your declared earnings, contingent on the type of work you perform. You'll do this three times a year, and you'll be glad to know that if you've earned nothing, you owe nothing. However, if you declare no earnings or income for three consecutive trimesters, you'll lose your *auto-entrepreneur* status and be required to seek an alternative tax status.

STARTING A BUSINESS

Starting a business in France is a marvelous idea—if you have a solid plan, a healthy respect for paperwork, the patience of a saint, and, perhaps most importantly, a healthy bank account balance. Recent changes in French tax law have made it more feasible (and less expensive) for Average Jacques and Jacquelines to launch their moneymaking

EXPAT EXPERIENCE:
RECIPE FOR ENTREPRENEURSHIP

Name: Jennifer Eric
Age: 35
Profession: Owner, My Kitch'n
Hometown: Gothenburg, Sweden
Current City: Paris, 17th

Swedish entrepreneur Jennifer Eric settled in Paris in 2001 after a nomadic young adulthood with stints in Los Angeles, Ibiza, and Dubai. After earning her BA in Political Science and MBA in International Marketing, she put her skills and ideas to good use in 2013 when she opened My Kitch'n, a vegan restaurant in Paris's Batignolles neighborhood. The road to entrepreneurship was bumpy; along the way, she experienced sexism, ageism, and institutionalized resistance to new ideas. But with her moxie, tenacity, and above-par French skills, she made her dream a reality. Here, she shares her experience and offers tips for would-be business owners in the City of Light.

You launched My Kitch'n in 2013. How much time did you invest in your business plan before opening?
It took me about a year and a half to get all the paperwork in order. The business plan, financial previsions, and market study were not the hardest part; that all took me about three months, but I've had both theoretical and practical practice when it comes to that which most certainly helped speed up the process.

What component of the process required the most time and energy?
The hardest part was getting a space, as nobody believed in my idea. This took me over a year. "People don't eat like that," I was simply told. I'm sure they were rolling their eyes behind my back and calling me crazy-cat-lady, too. Finally, it was the City of Paris and the Ministry of Economic Development that gave me a shot at it by according me a space in the Marché Couvert des Batignolles, a public covered market.

What are some of the unexpected roadblocks you encountered as you embarked on opening your own business?
I didn't realize the extent of the gender gap when it comes to entrepreneurship. This is by far the most frustrating roadblock I've encountered. When trying to get the project off the ground, in meetings, I was first greeted by, "Maybe you should get some work experience after your studies before trying to do something like this." Then, after I'd set the record straight and pointed to my industry experience in addition to my education, I was told, "But aren't you looking to settle down any time soon?" You definitely have to work twice as hard as a woman, and earning respect takes much longer.

Was anything easier than expected?
Yes, actually, getting people to appreciate 100 percent plant-based cooking is

ventures here. But to get your foot through the self-employment door, it's wise to have it all worked out on paper for the consular officials before you even get here, meaning you must possess a student visa, *carte compétences et talents*, or other work-friendly visa.

If you can afford to hire a consultant before you get started, it's not a bad idea. She can help you with all the befuddling aspects of taxation, idiosyncrasies in labor law, and other formalities. The Agence Pour la Création d'Entreprises (www.apce.com) is a semiprivate organization—the government funds 60 percent of its budget—that helps entrepreneurs develop and launch their businesses in France. The APCE has devised a

DAILY LIFE

less of a struggle than I thought it would be, in the land of frog legs and *foie gras*. I know a lot of people who thought my project was a bit of a suicide mission, but people are adapting and adopting it quicker than I thought! And they are much less confrontational than I thought they would be, considering the traditional environment I'm in.

Did you make use of any small-business associations to assist you with your project?
Through the *Maison de l'Emploi et des Entreprises* and *Boutique de Gestion* I received technical assistance (such as lawyers and certified accountants) free of charge, validating my dossier according to French standards every step of the way. It was *Pôle-Emploi* that put me in touch with the *Maison de l'Emploi et des Entreprises,* and I was lucky to meet a woman there who was really on top of things and helped me out a lot, shortening the wait period between the stages of validation.

What three tips would you offer to expats thinking of launching a business in Paris, based on your own experience?
Never surrender. Everyone likes to tell you that building your dream project is impossible, here more than anywhere I've ever lived. Don't mind them.

Take your time to find a good accountant. Having an accountant is mandatory here, not a choice, when you put a business structure in place. (You are not required by law to have one as an auto-entrepreneur). You can be audited, so make

sure to keep all your papers in order from the get-go. Scan things and file everything on an external hard drive that you keep exclusively for accounting purposes.

Factor in one day of paperwork-only per week. Don't underestimate the time this will take you. France is very old-fashioned when it comes to business laws, and many things are still done the old-fashioned way. Government institutions make plenty of mistakes, so make sure you read everything thoroughly. And pay your bills and taxes on time!

PHOTO COURTESY OF JENNIFER ERIC

Jennifer Eric

helpful checklist for prospective *auto-entrepreneurs* to determine the viability of their ideas and help them pick which *statut juridique* they'll need to register under once they decide to give it a go.

Next, the process moves in much the same way as becoming an *auto-entrepreneur:* You create a dossier with the Centre de Formalités des Entreprises des Auto-Entrepreneurs (www.lautoentrepreneur.fr). You'll be prompted to determine which category your new business falls into: Artisan/Industriel/Commerçant or Profession Libéral. If you're a commercial agent, you'll need to register with the Registre Spécial des Agents Commerciaux (RSAC). As an artisan entrepreneur, you must follow up with the Chambre de Métiers. If you choose to start your own dog-walking business, private English school, or bicycle touring company, you will need to make your status as an Entrepreneur Individuel à Responsabilité Limitée (EIRL) formal at www.eirl.fr or www.guichet-entreprises.fr. Both of these agencies offer resources and services to aid you in your quest to become a successful entrepreneur in France.

Registering under some *statuts,* including the EIRL, allows you to defer the Contribution Foncière des Entreprises (CFE) tax for the first three years. However, if you don't report any earnings whatsoever within your first two years, your status will be reverted automatically to the not-so-budget-friendly *"entreprise individuelle"* designation, which means you'll be responsible for paying taxes on estimated revenue to the tune of €3,000 the first year. Investing in a tax accountant is a good idea if you want to avoid any potential financial surprises down the line.

If you move out of the country or decide to relinquish your self-employment status for another reason, it's important to declare the *cessation d'activité* on the URSSAF website (www.cfe.urssaf.fr).

TYPES OF BUSINESSES

The type of business you choose to undertake depends entirely on your skills, personal interests, demands, moneymaking potential, and location. Businesses that don't require retail space or office space are, from an economic perspective, easier than others. You might also consider buying an existing business—a *gîte,* a bed-and-breakfast, a retail shop, or perhaps a vineyard—and putting your own spin on it. But keep in mind that you'll inherit the previous owner's reputation, so if it wasn't a good one, you'll have some damage control to do. If you're a brazen risk-taker, it's a clear opportunity to take a good idea, improve on it, and integrate into your new community.

As you consider your options, make use of some of the free and very handy services that are there for the asking—as long as you're asking in French. The *maire* (mayor) of your arrondissement or town wants to see new business flourish in his or her district and is a wonderful resource. He or she can tell you what has worked or hasn't worked in the past, prognosticate on whether your business idea has potential for success in your chosen quartier, and direct you toward local resources to help your idea succeed. The *chambre de commerce* (www.cci-paris-idf.fr) serves a similar function; remember, it's in their interest for you to succeed, so it's worth taking advantage of the help and resources they offer.

The Job Hunt

EMPLOYERS

It's easy to get discouraged scouting the want ads on Craigslist or FUSAC: "Only those with working papers need apply." Well, don't take that at face value. Many companies publish similar phrasing in their ads to keep the government looking the other way, but when it comes down to interviewing and subsequently hiring, your lack of work permit may not be an issue at all. First and foremost, you'll find that you need to establish trust with your future employer. He doesn't want to offer you a job you're not legally entitled to take, only to get fined or, worse, forcibly ejected from France. If you do decide to take the below-board route, always be discreet and be honest with your employer, who is taking a risk to hire you. But don't be afraid to apply for that job, even if you're not 100 percent qualified. There may be an opportunity for a work sponsorship, or maybe your interviewer knows of another position at another company that needs someone with your skill set.

The job hunt in France begins much the same way it does in the U.S. or Canada. Start by talking to everyone you know—friends of friends of friends, distant cousins, elementary-school classmates—because it really is all about who you know. Don't know anyone? That's OK. But don't even think about hitting the pavement without fluffing up your dossier first. You'll need one, and it should include copies of every spelling bee award and talent-show ribbon you've ever earned, because that stuff matters here. Include copies of your college diploma—ideally translated into French—and

© AURELIA D'ANDREA

Visit an employment agency if you need assistance finding a job.

certificates of completion for any higher-education studies you've taken, including language courses. Have your letters of recommendation handy, too, and be prepared to tote them to your job interview along with the rest of your dossier documents.

Interviews

You've landed a coveted interview, and now you want to charm their socks off. How do you do it? Start by adhering to standard interview protocol—dress sharply, show up on time, and come prepared with a bit of background knowledge and questions for the person interviewing you—and end with a thank-you note. Take great care to tout your strengths and accomplishments without sounding like a braggart, and be prepared for questions that dip into

EXPAT EXPERIENCE: FAT TIRE BICYCLE TOURS

Young American David Mebane launched Fat Tire Bike Tours (FTBT) back in 1999 when he was just 22 years old. Today, his two-wheeled enterprise has expanded to include outposts in London, Berlin, Barcelona, and Washington, DC, but it's the Paris hub that remains the most popular with tourists—and with expats looking for paying work in a fun, dynamic environment. Here, David shares some tips on how to get hired for one of the most fun gigs in the City of Light.

Tell us about working at FTBT. What's the culture like?

I love going to the office each day. We're in the business of having fun, and that is a great place to be. Our customers are on vacation and ready to experience our beautiful city, and they're counting on us to show it to them in an informative, yet interesting and exciting manner. Our staff and guides are experts at customer service and group dynamics, along with a detailed knowledge of not only Parisian history, but also current events in the city.

Is there an ideal FTBT employee profile? In other words, what do you look for in new staff?

The ideal FTBT staff member comes to work with a smile on his or her face and is ready to have a good time, but is also professionally serious. While our job is wonderful in the fact that we get to have fun, our customers expect us to be organized, efficient, and prepared. We're not looking for someone who shows up for a paycheck, but instead someone that wants to participate in the business side of the tourism industry. We want people who do their jobs well so that the customers don't have to worry about anything.

Is it necessary to be bilingual to work at FTBT?

While it's not necessary to speak both French and English, it is favorably looked upon when we're hiring. All staff must speak virtually perfect English, though.

What about work visas—are they required?

They certainly are.

What are some mistakes people make when applying or interviewing for a job at FTBT?

I'm not sure if they can be categorized as a mistake, necessarily, but rather a

personal territory; it's not unusual to be asked about your hobbies and whether your plans include starting a family.

French employment laws make it difficult for you to be fired once you've been hired, so expect the interview process to extend the limits of thoroughness. This is so your future employer can get a full sense of what you're all about before she extends a potentially lifelong offer your way. You will be asked about your weaknesses and strengths and what you think makes you right for the job. Above all, you will be assessed for your French-speaking abilities—you must be conversational, at the very least, if you want to work for a French company. Don't expect special treatment as an *exotique* Anglophone, because you'll likely not get it.

Landing the Job

If you've been offered a job contract in France, it will fall into one of a few categories. The *contrat à durée déterminée* (CDD), a fixed-term contract good for 18 to 36 months, misconception. Some applicants believe this is an easy job and that a certain level of customer service and professionalism isn't required. That can be evident from our first meeting that they are not ready for the "big leagues" of what we do.

What are three things an interested candidate can do to increase his or her odds of a landing a job?
We want people that are customer-service driven, and just pleasant to be around. Much of what we look for cannot be taught, but instead is (or isn't) naturally there. We look hard at personalities, group dynamics, public speaking skills, and making sure their idea of the job fits that actuality of it.

What's the best thing about working at FTBT?
I love seeing happy customers tell us they had the best time visiting the City of Light with us. We know there are a thousand things that customers could do, but they have chosen to spend a few hours with us. And we know that while it might be the 500th tour, it is our customer's first tour and that they have a high expectation after reading about us or hearing about us from friends. The best part of my day is seeing the happy customers at the end of the tour—then having them ask which FTBT tours they can do tomorrow!

© FAT TIRE BIKE TOURS

Fat Tire Bike Tours is an American-owned company that regularly hires American expats.

DAILY LIFE

might be the most popular. This is the usual "starter" agreement between an employer and an employee; if the work relationship is to be extended, the CDD is transformed into a *contrat à durée indéterminée* (CDI). The CDI is an open-ended contract that implies permanency, though it usually comes with a two-month probationary period. It is also possible to work without any sort of contract, in which case it is implied that you will be hired on an ongoing, open-ended basis. When you sign your contract—whether it's a CDI, CDD, *contrat de travail temporaire* (CTT) or *contrat jeunes en entreprise* (CJE)—make sure it clearly states your salary, as well as any monetary perks to which you've agreed or are entitled. Many employers offer staff an annual bonus known as the "13th month" check, which is, ostensibly, a holiday bonus—check your contract to see if it includes one.

BENEFITS

As with most jobs, a contract position entitles you to social benefits ranging from family healthcare to retirement pensions. The onus is on you to learn what all the perks are and to maximize your access to the ones that may take a bit of sleuthing, such as restaurant meal vouchers or commuter compensation. Like everyone else, you will earn 2.5 days of vacation for every month worked. Both women and men are entitled to leave after the birth of a child (for women, it's 16 weeks; for men, it's just two; but both parents can take additional time off at a decreased salary). A few different forms of sabbatical are also available to *salariés* (employees), including up to a year off to study in a field that will enhance your work performance.

One significant difference between the U.S. and France is the frequency of paychecks. In the U.S., getting paid every two weeks—and sometimes every week—is the norm. In France, you'll likely get one paycheck on the first of each month. And if that paycheck looks small, it might be because it is; you contribute a share of your salary—up to 40 percent in the highest income brackets—to support the social benefits you and your colleagues are entitled to. But your company is also contributing on your behalf, usually considerably more than what you pay, to offset the financial burden.

Paris is home to a handful of English-language bookstores that may prove useful in your search for work.

© AURELIA D'ANDREA

Labor Laws

WORKERS' RIGHTS

France has such strong laws in favor of the employee that getting fired is practically impossible here—but that doesn't mean you should show up an hour late for work, take two-hour lunch breaks, and leave at 3 every afternoon. Plenty of people do this, but some actually get fired for it, as former Paris-based secretary Catherine Sanderson did back in 2006. Sanderson, who blogged under the nom de plume "La Petite Anglaise" until 2009, got the boot when her employers—an English law firm with offices in France—discovered she was blogging about her personal and professional life while on the job. She wound up winning a wrongful termination lawsuit, but you'll want to avoid that by simply showing up on time, taking the allotted hour-long break, focusing on your work, and leaving with the rest of your colleagues at the appointed hour. If you feel like you need a bit of support, you'll be able to find a trade union to advise you; though only 8 percent of French workers actually belong to a union (mostly those

SURVIVING THE *GRÈVE*

Type A people, prepare yourselves: You *will* have to wait in line at the grocery story as a slow-moving octogenarian counts change (those minutes feel like hours). You will *not* get "the customer is always right" service at the department store. And, at some point during your French sojourn, you will definitely experience the infamous *grève*.

A *grève*, otherwise known as a strike, is a part of the French political process that often precedes or immediately follows a legislative act. Like flu season, the *grève* makes an appearance every year—sometimes two or more of them. The key to surviving this inconvenience lies in planning. Because most strikes are coordinated in advance, it's very possible to create a Plan B that'll get you to work or to the airport on time.

Euphemistically called "disruptions," transportation strikes rarely last more than 24 hours. For commuters, this means exploring alternative ways of getting to work: public bike-sharing, *co-voiturage*, or walking are common solutions. Should you have bigger travel plans during a planned strike, check with the airline for up-to-the-minute changes; if you're traveling on the French national railway lines, chances are your ticket will be valid on any train heading in the right direction after the strike is over.

employed by multinational corporations), the unions still represent the entire workforce, so you can benefit from the strides they've made on your behalf without actually paying dues or participating in *grèves* during strike season.

By law, employers with more than 50 *salariés* on the payroll must create a *comité d'entreprise* (an employee's council), which acts as an intermediary between employees and staff on all issues affecting workers, and all companies with 11 or more employees must also have *délégués du personnel* (personnel representatives) that serve a similar function. Depending on the size of the company, there will be between one and nine elected *délégués*, each with an elected stand-in. Elections are held every two to four years, and *délégués* spend between 10 and 15 hours per month in their roles, which includes keeping employees abreast of changes in salaries, updated health and safety codes, modifications to the work code, and other changes in the workplace.

MINIMUM WAGE

If you're earning the French minimum wage in 2014, it will add up to €1,445.77 per month, which breaks down to €9.53 per hour. This wage increases when the cost of living index rises, ordinarily by 2 percent a year. Undocumented workers are clearly not protected by employment laws, adding extra risk to working under the table. Tipping for waitstaff and other service-industry jobs is not standard practice here, but it has come to be expected in heavily touristed areas. Don't feel obligated to leave a tip, and if you happen to find yourself employed in the service industry, don't expect to be tipped (but do expect a decent quality of life, even on your minimum-wage salary).

FINANCE

Whether you're a student, a work transfer, or a business entrepreneur, moving to France means getting intimately acquainted with your finances. Numbers not your thing? When all is said and done, they will be. From the moment you embark on this journey, you'll need to provide officials with financial data to prove your solvency in France; your visa application will ask for letters from your bank and proof of means of financial support. Once you arrive in France, you'll see how your previously prodigious peck of dollars morphs into a much smaller bundle of euros, which necessitates adjusting your way of thinking about your finances and your new currency.

France can feel expensive as a tourist, but as a resident, you won't have to worry about spending as much. You'll actually find some things to be a much better value for your money: Food (even if you eat more of it) and wine and medical care, for example. You'll also come face-to-face with the startling realization that some products and services are much more costly, including gasoline, electricity, and even manicures (don't expect to find the $10 equivalent anywhere in France, except at the local beauty academy). Sticker shock will happen, but not everywhere you go or with everything you buy.

You've probably heard of the VAT, or value-added tax. Conceptualized by Frenchman Maurice Laure and implemented in 1954, it has since been adopted by many European countries, where the tax rate reaches as high as 25 percent on consumable goods such

© AURELIA D'ANDREA

as clothing, electronic equipment, and wireless Internet and phone service. In France, the VAT rate was recently increased to 20 percent on most consumer goods; a smaller VAT tax is levied on the purchase of books, air and train travel, and food and drink. The tax is one of the key financial props holding France together, bringing in 45 percent of the country's tax revenue. The good news is that it is built into your purchases, so when you see something for sale for €20, that's exactly how much it will cost you.

THE EURO

France ushered in the euro era on January 1, 2002, and the monetary unit has proved to be a stabilizing force in the French economy. But 2002 wasn't the end of the franc; in some Parisian shops, you'll find prices still listed in that old relic of a currency, and bank receipts often include the franc rate, too. In the little town of Le Blanc, in the Centre region, they had a harder time than most letting go; 30 local businesses continued to trade in the franc right up until February 2012, when the currency was phased out for good.

Cost of Living

GROCERIES

Many a newcomer to *la belle France* is surprised to learn that the overall cost of living is less than in the United States. Locally produced fruits and vegetables are sold by the kilo (2.2 pounds), and when you break it down and compare it to the dollar, you'll see what a great deal you're getting. Carrots, potatoes, and onions run about €1.50 a kilo, tomatoes and peaches are about double that in peak season, and in wintertime, delicious little clementines from Spain and lychees imported from Madagascar will set you back about €2-3 per kilo. Much of the tastiest stuff (bread, wine) is subsidized or otherwise regulated by the government; a standard baguette costs about €1, and a perfectly quaffable bottle of Bordeaux supérieur can be had for less than €5. The key to shopping and saving is to do as the locals do: Patronize the outdoor markets for your produce, the *boucherie* for your meat, the *fromagerie* for your cheese, and the *caviste* for your wine. It's slightly more time intensive than hitting a *hypermarché* for an all-in-one experience, but when you factor in the travel time (Paris's biggest supermarkets are always situated on or near the *périphérique*), fuel prices, and quality, those one-stop shops begin to lose their appeal. Besides, French refrigerators and freezers are so small that it doesn't make sense to stock up; if you're lucky to have a little *balcon,* it can do double duty as a cold-storage unit in wintertime. But otherwise, you'll have some serious food shuffling to do.

If you're going to shop like a local, it's worth investing in a *chariot*—a shopping bag on wheels—or a reusable basket or bag. A ban on non-recyclable plastic bags has been in effect for several years in France (though not everyone adheres to it), and you'll have to buy a recyclable bag on the spot if you come to the market unprepared. At outdoor markets, you'll still be given small plastic bags for your fruits and veggies, but not a bigger bag to shove the lot of them into.

Grocery stores throughout Paris and the suburbs offer two kinds of customer perks, including online shopping options and free delivery service with a minimum purchase,

© AURELIA D'ANDREA

Many Paris newcomers find the cost of food less expensive than anticipated.

which is usually somewhere in the €50-75 range. Natural-food store giant Naturalia also offers delivery service and most stores also offer free *cartes de fidélité* that you scan each time you make a purchase to receive on-the-spot discounts and coupons for future purchases.

DINING OUT

Eating out in France is also good value for your money. Wine is usually affordable; expect to pay €3-4 a glass at most restaurants. (Coca-Cola and that bottle of bubbly water will almost always cost you more than wine or beer.) Plats du jour at lunchtime run anywhere from €8 to €14 and rise to €12-20 for dinner. Expect either an *entrée* (first course) and *plat* (main course) or *plat* and *dessert* for those prices; occasionally you'll be offered all three and a *café* or a *verre de vin* for that all-inclusive price. Meals are hearty and filling and usually include meat, a vegetable, and something starchy. Everyone in France takes advantage of these home-away-from-home-cooked meals at some point in their lives, so you might as well try it, too. Recently, it's become trendy on brasserie sandwich boards around Paris to chalk a slash through the "normal" price and put an "economic hardship" price beside it, so your €12 lunch now costs €10. Even recessions have their perks. Ask around to find where the best—and best-tasting—deals can be had.

HOUSING

Both renters and buyers will find good housing values in France; you'll probably spend about as much putting a roof over your head as you will putting food in your mouth. Students—French and foreign alike—are entitled to special housing allowances that

© AURELIA D'ANDREA

The cost of fuel, however, is more expensive.

can cut down the cost of living considerably. In Paris, the résidences du Crous (www.crous-paris.fr) offer government-subsidized studios or one- and two-bedroom apartments exclusively for students for about €380 per month. If you're here to study and are based in a university town, check with the *mairie* to find out which options may be available to you.

If you're a homeowner or plan to invest in real estate, it's worth looking into the government-sponsored rebates for using alternative energy methods. Going solar has its perks; if you generate surplus energy, it could mean you get a check *back* from EDF instead of having to send one. Other energy-saving efforts homeowners make to increase efficiency are rewarded by way of tax deductions and write-offs.

TRANSPORTATION

It's *très cher* (very expensive) to own a car in France, particularly in the big cities, where forking out €50,000 for a permanent parking spot is not unheard of—and that's in addition to insurance and maintenance costs. Fuel, sold by the liter at stations attached to big *hypermarchés* and at unassuming little curb-side stations in throughout Paris, is seriously spendy. Expect to pay €1.30-1.60 per liter depending on the type of fuel, or as much as €100 every time you fill up your tank. For the best fuel prices, skip the big service stations off the freeways and opt for fill-up stations attached to supermarkets, where it's significantly cheaper.

Depending on where you live in France, you'll want to budget around €70 per month for public transportation; less if you're a student purchasing a youth pass, more if you're a party-hopping Parisian who's used to the convenience of taxis. Public bike-share system Vélib' costs €29 per year plus any overtime fees (only the first half-hour is free), so buying your own bike will pay off over time if cycling is your primary means of transit. Beware, however, that bike theft is common in Paris, so a good lock—threaded through the rear tire for added security—is worth the added expense. The national train system, SNCF, offers discount cards for an annual fee of between €50 and €75 for those who travel regularly by long-distance train. The discounts—always a minimum of 25 percent off the standard fare, and as much as 65 percent off—can make the yearly investment worthwhile.

CLOTHING

Unless you shop exclusively at discount stores like H&M, Etam, or Tati (or Monoprix during the semiannual sales), you'll probably find the cost of clothing in France to be considerably higher than what you're used to. There are many reasons for this: the

© AURELIA D'ANDREA

A pair of French espadrilles may be the cheapest shoes you find.

VAT, which tacks nearly 20 percent on top of the base price; quality (French-made *everything* is built to last and priced accordingly); and salaries, which are higher here than in most countries even for minimum-wage workers, and therefore factored into the price of goods. You'll notice that at resale shops, called *depôt-ventes,* the sticker prices aren't all that discounted from what you'd pay for the same item brand-new in a department store or boutique. Eventually, you'll get used to paying more for things you used to take for granted, but in the meantime, let's set some reasonable expectations of average clothing prices:

- shoes (men and women): €100
- boots (men and women): €150
- dress (department store): €60-120
- dress (neighborhood boutique): €40-70
- coat (men and women, department store): €200
- jacket (men and women, neighborhood boutique): €80
- underwear (women): €10
- underwear (men): €7
- socks (men and women): €7

ELECTRONICS

Sticker shock is also bound to strike when you go computer shopping. When the time comes to invest in a new machine, you'll start asking yourself questions like, "I wonder if it's cheaper to buy a laptop on Amazon and spend $200 to have it shipped to me in France?" You'll grow accustomed to the steep prices, but if you have to get that *lave-linge* (washing machine) or *micro-onde* (microwave oven) right away, Darty, an electronics- and household-goods chain, is a good bet. From water-filter systems to American-style refrigerators, they can be found here—but it can't hurt to do a little comparison-shopping first. At www.prixmoinscher.com, you can compare goods by brand or product type and see who carries the most affordable version of the appliance you're looking for. A Sony 37-inch flat-screen television will set you back €279 (delivery included), a basic DVD player runs about €50, and you can nab your very own washing machine for around €175.

When you make an in-store purchase of a large electrical appliance such as a TV or an oven, don't expect to necessarily leave the store with your purchase in tow on that very day. Many items for sale in stores like Darty and Conforama aren't stocked on-site, but rather stored in warehouses in distant suburbs. You might have to wait as long as a week for your refrigerator to be delivered. (Sorry!)

Banking

Opening a bank account in France is another exercise in red-tape aerobics, but it's a very necessary evil. If you're planning a reconnaissance trip to scope things out before you move, pencil in a visit to a bank and open an account so you'll be ready to roll with your *carte bleue* (debit card), checkbook, and French banking history when you need them, which will be right away. You'll need a checkbook for your home hunt, setting up house, paying utilities through *prélèvement* (automatic debit), and receiving Assurance Maladie reimbursements.

CHOOSING YOUR BANK

Deciding which bank to work with is the first hurdle in the dizzying adventure of finding a new home for your money. There are so many banks, and who has time to check with each and every one to find out who has the most to offer? It's not just banks, either. Even La Poste—the post office—offers banking services. When making your choice, consider the minimum-balance requirements, English-language staff services (if you need them), and whether you need a savings or a checking account or both. Banks that can offer the services you need include Barclays France, BNP Paribas, Caisse d'Épargne, Crédit Agricole, Crédit Mutuel, HSBC France, La Banque Postale, and Société Générale. Note that you may be asked to have your *carte de séjour* in hand before you open an account; if you don't possess yours already, there are other options. At BNP Paribas, for example, you can open an international account at the Champs-Élysées branch without proof of residency, but you will need to meet their minimum bank-balance requirements.

You will end up developing a familiar relationship with your French banker, who, along with the rest of the staff, will greet you with a friendly *bonjour* and often by name. You can expect personalized service and a warm formality at your bank, especially if you have a good chunk of money stored there.

As a student—and especially as a student under the age of 26—you'll be entitled to all sorts of banking perks and incentives that make it easy for you to function in French society. Your school can help you find the right bank that offers the best student benefits, the lowest *carte bleue* fees, and the most advantageous interest rates.

France is idiosyncratic in a number of ways, including its approach to personal-finance management. The bank branch where you opened your account becomes your "home" office, and any changes to your account must be made at that branch, even if it's across town. If you move to another city, you'll have to arrange with your current bank branch to have your home office changed; be prepared for the time and paperwork involved, as it could take an hour or more of your life to complete this transaction. Ditto for adding names to your account: If you opened it under your own name but want to add your husband's name, it isn't as straightforward as you'd hope. Your spouse will have to provide additional financial information, including letters from "his" bank in the U.S. testifying to his banking history, plus an *attestation d'hébergement,* copies of his ID, and possibly quite a bit more.

BANK CARDS AND BANKING PROTOCOL

Generally, you'll be charged a fee for your card, which will be debited from your account. There are many types of *cartes bancaires*—commonly called *cartes bleues*—to choose from, and they all have a different price bracket. For €40 per year, you'll get a basic card that functions like most bank cards back home: withdrawals, basic traveler's insurance coverage, and supplemental car-rental insurance. For a little more—say, €130 per year—you could get a *carte* Visa Premier, with traveler's insurance that compensates you for late trains and canceled flights, as well as hospital stays in foreign countries. For €520 per year, you could get a fancy Carte Platinum American Express that earns you purchase points, covers legal fees in another country if you fall into trouble, and

© AURELIA D'ANDREA

To fully function in French society, you'll need an old-fashioned checkbook in addition to coins and bills.

CHECKS AND BALANCES

It's one of those things we all take for granted: writing a check. Easy as pie, right? But in France, sending your monthly rent check to your landlord is a tad more complicated than you might imagine. First, you have to figure out what goes where.

The first blank space on a standard French check reads *"Payez contre ce chèque non endossable"* ("Pay against this nonendorsable check"). Here, you'll write out the amount of the check –in French. It might look something like *"deux-cent euros"* (€200). You have two lines available for spelling out the amount.

Next up is the space where you write the name of the person or institution to whom the check is payable. This follows *"à"* ("to"). Just to the right of this, you'll find a little rectangular box. This is where you write the figure, using standard numbers. The French don't like it when you write outside the lines, so keep everything inside that little rectangle if you can.

Next are two short lines, one reading *à*–which in this case means "in," as in the city in which you are writing out the check –and the second reading *"le"* ("the"), which is prompting you for today's date. If you write the date in numeric format, be sure to do it the way the French do: date/month/year.

The last thing you'll need to do to make this check valid is sign it: Often there are no written prompts, only an empty space at the bottom. Go ahead and put your John Hancock there, but keep it contained! If your signature extends off the margins of the check, it may be rendered invalid.

covers you with a new pair of glasses if yours are lost or stolen while you travel. You can also choose special colors and designs for your card for an additional €12-24 per year.

Be warned that banks also like to charge you for things you wouldn't necessarily consider charge-worthy, such as phone calls to your banker, paper bank statements (rather than the digital option), additional cards, and, of course, checkbooks. Ask your banker to fill you in on all those little things, because they do add up.

When you open your bank account, it will be assigned an RIB (Relevé d'Identité Bancaire) number, which you'll need to memorize or have on hand when you want to transfer funds from your American or Canadian account to your French one, and to set up the *prélèvement* for automatic debits. RIBs also come in handy on the first of the month, when rent is due. *Propriétaires* and *locataires* alike appreciate the easy rent-paying potential inherent in direct deposit.

Depositing checks here isn't as straightforward as it is in American and Canadian banks. In France, you can deposit cash into *guichets automatiques* (ATMs), but you'll have to deposit checks by visiting the bank, filling out a form, handing it to the person behind the counter, and taking a receipt.

Fiscal responsibility and integrity are taken very seriously here. If you bounce a check, the consequences include a check-writing ban for as long as five years. If you lose your card (or have it stolen), you are responsible for the charges unless you report the loss or theft immediately and better still, file a police report. The latter is a no-fuss process that requires a visit to the nearest *commissariat* and filling out a single-page form in duplicate. Keeping a paper trail is important in France, so take the time for this if your wallet or cards go missing.

Banks won't charge you for using another bank's *guichet automatique* or *distributeur*

La Défense is the financial capital of the Île-de-France region.

for the first few withdrawals per month, but after the fourth, fifth, or sometimes sixth withdrawal, depending on the bank, they can—and often do—tack on a fee in the €1 range. If you're traveling outside the euro zone with your *carte bleue,* check with your bank beforehand to see which foreign banks it's partnered with. BNP Paribas, for instance, is partnered with Bank of the West in the U.S. and Westpac in Australia, and therefore doesn't charge a withdrawal fee if you use *guichets automatiques* at those banks.

CREDIT CARDS

Credit cards aren't used in quite the same manner in France as they are in the rest of the world. People tend to live within their means, and that means paying with good old-fashioned cash, or using your *carte bleue* or checkbook to debit funds directly from your account. If this feels kind of 1953ish to you (even if your parents weren't born then), learn to appreciate the old-timeyness of it, because it has its perks. At shops throughout Paris, proprietors may allow customers to take things home on credit. We're not talking brand-new Renaults here, but rather a baguette, newspaper, or bottle of *vin rouge* at those critical moments when you realize you've left your wallet at home.

French bank cards and credit cards are different from American ones in a very significant way: Instead of storing your information in a magnetic strip, the card houses it in a tiny embedded *puce* (literally "flea," but better known as a microchip). When inserted into an ATM, automatic ticket kiosk, or credit card reader at restaurants, the card transmits your information through radio frequencies; to complete the transaction, you need to input your PIN code. This protects you and your card from unauthorized transactions, which is the main reason Europe switched over to this credit card technology in 2004. As more and more countries switch to *puce* cards, the likelihood that North America will follow suit begins to increase.

It's important to have a card with a *puce* if you'll be spending a significant amount of time in France. For starters, many gas stations function at all hours without an attendant, and that's because you are expected to serve yourself and pay using a *puce* card. Most credit card machines can read American cards, but those cards aren't inserted into the machines the same way European *puce* cards are. If the person in charge of completing your transaction doesn't know how to do it, he is likely to tell you they don't accept those cards. (If your language skills permit, you can show him how it's done. Instead of inserting the card in the bottom of the machine, swipe it down a little trough on the right side.)

Taxes

FRENCH TAXES

It's been said that the only certain things in life are death and taxes, and that maxim doesn't lose any of its mojo just because you've moved to France. If you want to establish long-term residency, there's no way to make it more official than by declaring your earnings. For North Americans, this means double tax duty, since you'll still have to file taxes at home, too. In France, it means declaring all your income, regardless of where you earned it. Freelancers, now is the time to 'fess up, fully and completely. Don't know if you're obliged? If you've lived in France for more than 183 days out of the year, you're considered a resident in the eyes of the tax folks.

If you decide to go official with a small business and take advantage of Assurance Maladie, you'll need to begin paying French taxes. It's a complicated process that can be made a lot less confusing by enlisting the aid of a French tax specialist. (See the Resources section for referrals.) The investment may be many hundreds of dollars, but isn't peace of mind worth it? If your answer is "no," it's still possible to work things out yourself through trial and error—hopefully not too much of the latter.

As an *auto-entrepreneur,* you're responsible for paying taxes three times per year. You'll receive the paperwork in the mail; you simply have to report your earnings, calculate the amount due, and include a check if necessary when you mail it off. For employees, social charges (but not income tax) will be deducted from your paycheck, and the onus is on you to visit the local tax office each May to file your paperwork for the previous year's earnings (the exact cutoff date varies from year to year). Income tax is determined by the total earnings of your household, which includes your spouse and children, who are all parts of a taxable whole and subject to deductibles even if they don't work. For example, if you earned €6,011 or less in 2013, you'll owe nothing in 2014. Those who earned between €11,991 and €26,631 will owe 14 percent, and top earners who made more than €151,000 are taxed at 45 percent.

There are resources available online (and it's wise to check in a few times a year, since laws change with disconcerting regularity), but ultimately, the weight of figuring it all out falls on your shoulders. You can, however, share the burden with a professional tax advisor. Programs like Click Impôts (www.clickimpots.com)—the French equivalent of Turbo Tax software—can be very helpful *if* you understand the language. If not, find a tax specialist who speaks English until you get the hang of it on your own. The French tax year begins on January 1 and ends on December 31.

AMERICAN AND CANADIAN TAXES

Thank goodness for the Internet: Without it, we'd be cajoling our friends and family to send bulky IRS booklets to us overseas, and we'd be spending far too much time at La Poste mailing forms back when we could be relaxing beneath sunny skies at a terrace café. Because nearly everything is automated today, we get to benefit by filing taxes online from anywhere in the world. (You'll still need your W2 or 1099 forms, though, so have your employer send those to you at your French address.)

Even though you have to file your U.S. taxes as well as French taxes if you live in France, a treaty signed between the two countries means the taxes you pay in France

FISCAL RESPONSIBILITY À LA FRANÇAISE

If you've never examined the fine print at the back of your U.S. passport, now is a good time. There, under Article D, it reads, "All U.S. citizens working and residing abroad are required to file and report on their worldwide income." So, the bad news is that you still have to file American taxes even when you're living your dream life in France. The good news is, well, there's not a lot of good news when talking about taxes, but surviving the expat tax experience is something you can brag about once you've cleared the hurdle. These tips will help you survive the process with your nervous system intact.

File your taxes on time.
This is how you avoid a 10 percent penalty and stay on the government's good side. To get started, visit your arrondissement's tax office. Not sure where to find it? Plug your coordinates into the "contacts" section of the government's dedicated tax website (www.impots.gouv.fr.) and get an instant referral.

Extend your extension.
It's April 14 and you haven't even downloaded your U.S. tax forms yet. It's OK! You get an automatic two-month filing extension as an American living abroad. Need even more time to get your finances in order? Take advantage of form 4868, which stretches your filing deadline until October 15.

Don't forget the FBAR.
Is your French bank account cushioned with cash? If you've got the equivalent of US$10,000 racking up interest in any foreign account, you've got to declare it to the government with the FBAR (Foreign Bank Account Reports) form. The mandatory e- filing deadline is June 30. Hurry! The form is available online at http://bsaefiling.fincen.treas.gov/main.html.

are deductible on your U.S. tax forms. The IRS's online FreeFile program allows you to file online if your adjusted gross income (AGI) is less than $58,000. If you earned more than that, it's slightly more complicated: You'll need to purchase eFile software or go the old-fashioned paper route. Because of the potential hassles that filing at a distance can spawn, the nice folks at the IRS kindly extend a two-month filing extension to American taxpayers living abroad, so your paperwork isn't due until June 15. Tax experts will tell you that you actually have even more time—until October 15 as an American expat in France—but getting that extension requires that you fill out and include form 4868 when filing. Note that if you owe money, the IRS still wants it on or before April 15. Refunds can be direct-deposited into your existing U.S. account. Canadians can also Telefile from abroad as long as they do so before April 30, or face a 5 percent fine on whatever you owe.

Investing

France has embraced free-market economics, and with it a culture of personal investing has emerged. The best source of information for no- or low-risk investing opportunities is your banker, who will be happy to explain your options and set you up with an investment program. (Enlisting the help of an independent financial advisor is another good idea.) If you have €20,000 in the bank, that's considered a pretty hefty sum, and any banker worth her salt will offer suggestions for earning money on those funds even without a prompt from you. Forty percent of France's stock exchange value is held by foreign investors, so you'll be in good company if you decide to take this route.

If stocks, bonds, and mutual funds don't make your heart sing but you still want to invest in France, consider a business enterprise. The government-sponsored nonprofit agency Invest in France (www.invest-in-france.org, 01/44 87 17 27) has offices in the 14th arrondissement and offers free services and advice on setting up a corporation of 10 or more employees, tax preparation, employment laws, and all the hidden benefits of launching a large-scale business enterprise in France. With the second-largest consumer market in Europe and a very healthy tourist trade, France is ripe with opportunity for those with an entrepreneurial spirit and the extra money necessary to put an idea into action.

DAILY LIFE

INVESTING IN YOUR FRENCH FUTURE

Whether you plan to spend a year or a lifetime in l'Hexagone, it's prudent to enlist a professional to help you secure your financial future. After five years in New York City, independent financial advisor Philippe Jedar now helps both French- and English-speaking clients from his home base in the Dordogne Valley. Here are his tips for staying solvent and building economic security wherever you are in the world.

· **Tip #1: DO something!** Even if it is something as little as putting aside €50 every month! With time, it will put your mind in a different mode. It will force you naturally to catch a rhythm and little by little you will see your savings grow. If you don't do it, when you reach retirement age, you will be one of those who can apply Warren Buffet's quote: "After all, you only find out who is swimming naked when the tide goes out."

· **Tip #2 Seek the advice of a good financial advisor.** It's crucially important to have someone who is able to listen, and someone who is able to explain clearly why he or she chooses a particular investment solution for you. You have to understand what is proposed to you. You have to understand fully what you are investing your money in and be sure it fits your profile and goals. The responsibility of the advisor is to explain; yours is to understand.

· **Tip #3 Don't put all your eggs in the same basket.** It's a classic cautionary tale, but people often forget it. This is also a good way to weigh the "independence" of your financial advisor. If he or she absolutely wants to invest all your money in a particular area, he or she may have ulterior motives. A good advisor will propose a vast range of investment vehicles for safely investing your money, spreading the risk.

The one area where investing in France is still a little iffy is real estate. So many people find themselves seduced by the idea of buying a chic 19th-century pied-à-terre, decorating it with treasures unearthed from the *marché aux puces*, and earn a sustainable living from the rental income it generates, and this is where things go awry. Unless you're in a prime Paris arrondissement or another desirable city like Versailles with a year-round tourism base to pull from, you might be in for an unpleasant surprise. Furthermore, recent laws have affected the short-term residential housing market in Paris and other French cities, making it virtually illegal for owners to rent their properties for less than a year at a stretch. This doesn't affect owners of commercial property, but the taxes they pay are considerably higher. Think twice before investing in property as a moneymaking venture, and be sure to check with a tax consultant who can help you sort out the particulars if you decide to take this adventurous route.

COMMUNICATIONS

You don't have to look very hard in Paris to spot one of those familiar-looking relics from the past: the pay phone box. Some of them have been transformed into transparent mini-apartments by creative homeless folks, but otherwise, they're a rarely used but still prominent feature in the Parisian landscape. With a couple of minor exceptions, France has joined the 21st century communications revolution. From subscription-service smartphones and surprisingly affordable Internet service to ubiquitous cybercafés and print-media *kiosques,* staying connected to the world at large—and our work and loved ones—is easy and, unlike most things in France, practically bureaucracy-free.

France is definitely a nation of mediaphiles, boasting one of the highest magazine readerships in the world. There are more than 100 local and national newspapers to choose from, so Sunday mornings at the corner café will never be idle. Television also figures prominently in the French leisure sphere, with the average person watching 3.5 hours per day. Expect access to the outside world in unexpected places—wireless hotspots at campgrounds, for instance—and, thanks to government subsidies, count on the cost of getting connected to be within reach.

© AURELIA D'ANDREA

Telephone Service

It's true that there are still a couple of places left in France where you're more likely to get reception using two cans and a piece of string than you are with your mobile phone, but it's not likely that you'll be stranded without access in the Île-de-France region. There's one thing most of us in Paris and abroad have come to rely on, and that's the telephone. To meet the needs—and budgets—of a diverse population, there are numerous options: pay-as-you-go mobile phones, private pay-by-the-unit *cabines* at cybercafés, the aforementioned corner telephone booths, and numerous telecommunications companies willing to sell you all manner of packages for chatting and texting your heart out.

Before you can start making phone calls, you need to know how to do it. When you're placing a call to another French phone within France, the 10-digit number will always begin with a zero. Cell phones begin with 06 or 07, and landline prefixes differ depending on the region. In Paris/Île de France, the prefix is 01; in Brest, Cherbourg, Le Havre, Nantes, Orléans, Rouen, and other cities and towns in northwest France, the prefix is 02; in the north and northeast, it's 03; in the southeast, 04; and in the southwest, 05.

When making a call to France from the U.S. or Canada, you must follow a slightly different protocol, beginning with the international access code, 011, followed by the country code, 33. But wait, there's more: Before you dial the rest of the number, remember to leave *off* the zero at the beginning; it's necessary to include the extra digit only when you're dialing *within* France. So if you're calling Versailles from Vancouver, you'll dial 011 33 1 55 55 55 55. When you want to call the States or Canada from France, dial the international access code followed by the country code, the area code, and the seven-digit number. To call San Francisco from Sceaux, dial 00 1 415/555-5555.

When you need to find the telephone number of an individual or business, use the French version of the yellow and white pages, called *pages jaunes* and *pages blanches,* respectively. They operate the same way as back home, including online access. Hard copies are distributed by the nice people at La Poste once a year.

LAND LINES

In 2009, France Telecom ended its telecommunications monopoly, breathing new life—and new deals—into every corner of the market. Where there used to be just one long-distance carrier for landlines, now there are many, each of them offering great bargains on bundled Internet-phone-cable TV packages. They nearly all work the same way: You order your service online, receive confirmation for your order, then wait for your "box" to arrive. The box is your modem/cable/fiber optic hub, and once you have it—it can take between two days and two weeks to arrive—plug it in and start calling, viewing, and surfing. For around €30 per month for high-speed fiber optic and ADSL Internet, dozens of television channels, and no-cost calls to landlines throughout the world, it's pretty much worth the wait.

The top companies offering this bundled service are the same one providing cell phone service, and sometimes you can add mobile calling service onto your three-in-one "bouquet," making it a four-in-one. France Telecom owns the ubiquitous telecom

© AURELIA D'ANDREA

The public telephone is fast becoming a thing of the past, but you can find them at bus stands and some busy intersections.

company Orange (www.orange.fr), which seems to be leading the telecommunications race; for €36.99 a month, Orange offers a four-in-one Open Mini service that includes an hour of free mobile phone time in addition to cable TV, Internet, and landline service. Bouygues (www.bouyguestelecom.fr) offers a similar package, only with four hours of unlimited cell phone calls each month for €63. If you want something simpler, SFR (www.sfr.com) provides a mobile phone-Internet packages starting at €29.98 per month. Students age 26 and younger get a 10 percent discount. Numericable (www.numericable.fr) is one of the newer companies to join the all-in-one game, with similar plans and less expensive monthly fees—but there's a one-time setup fee, so it makes sense only if you're looking for a long-term deal.

MOBILE PHONES

Getting set up with a "mobile" can be a tricky enterprise for Luddites and techno-wizards alike. The best solution is to carefully consider how often you'll use your phone and what you're willing to spend per month for those privileges. Quad-band smartphones, including Samsung and iPhone models, can be great for the newbie in France, especially if you make use of the scads of apps designed to help you find food, maps, train times, and more. But don't make the mistake of underestimating your American or Canadian carrier's roaming fees, which may be exorbitant. Review your contract or call your carrier to avoid becoming another telecom "victim" saddled with a bill shockingly heavy on zeros.

If you know you're going to be here for at least 12-18 months—the average length of time for most cell-phone contracts—you might choose to start from scratch and purchase a phone and calling plan here. At many telecom boutiques, including Phone House and FNAC, you can get an iPhone or Android for "free" if you don't mind getting locked into a 12- to 24-month contract at around €50-100 per month. Not sure you'll use your phone enough to warrant that kind of expenditure? Then a €25 pay-as-you-go phone might be the best possibility. These cheapies are a good way to try out a service and see how much you use it. Phone House (www.phonehouse.fr) and FNAC (www.fnac.fr) both have big selections, and you can also find phones at *hypermarchés* like Auchan and Carrefour.

Another way to go is to invest in a second phone: Keep your U.S. mobile phone for when you return stateside, and purchase another cheap one to use exclusively in France. This option makes the most economic sense if you're not a phone addict or you don't rely heavily on phones for work. At special phone shops and other electronics stores throughout France, you can buy a bundled phone-and-SIM-card combo for €15-30. When the time you've purchased runs out, you can buy additional minutes in increments of €5-10, starting at €5. The time is purchased in the form of a *carte prépayée* (prepaid card), or, if you purchase it from a *tabac,* you'll be handed a small printed receipt with an access code for you to punch into your phone.

This pay-as-you-go method is a little pricey when it comes to outgoing calls, but incoming calls and SMSs (texts or *textos*) are free and unlimited. You can also purchase minutes exclusively reserved for texts, which are a lot more economical and just as far-reaching. Half-and-half time allotments are also available to those who want to keep their options open. The minutes you buy, whether for texting or calling or both, have an expiration date that's usually two weeks from the date of purchase. Keep in mind that if you don't purchase new minutes at least once every six months, you'll get a text from the SIM service provider alerting you that your account will be shut down if there's not some outgoing-call activity within a certain time frame. (You generally get a two-week warning.)

Another affordable option is to use your "unlocked" phone from home with a new France-compatible SIM card that you buy either before you depart or when you arrive in France (there are shops at the airport and in many cities and towns). In the United States and elsewhere, phones are sold "locked" by the telephone service provider to keep you roped into its service. ("Unlocking" shouldn't be confused with "unblocking" phones that have been reported stolen, which isn't kosher on any continent.) You can use online unlocking companies like Remote Unlocks (www.remoteunlocks.com) and Unlock it Now (www.unlockitnow.com) wherever you happen to be, and while the service isn't free, it's cheapish enough—usually less than US$50.

Long-Distance and International Calls

Even for starving students who don't have an extra €30 per month to pay for high-tech communication packages, it's still possible to make long-distance phone calls on the cheap. Throughout Paris, and particularly in arrondissements with higher immigrant populations, you'll find "cybercafés," which aren't cafés in the traditional sense (you'll be lucky if they have a coffee vending machine) but often little DIY storefronts equipped with computers, printers, fax machines, and *cabines* of varying degrees of funkiness that allow you to make international calls for pennies. The phone's digital display lets you how much you're spending as you make the call, and it's usually more affordable than you'd imagine, especially if you call during off-hours. In France, phone calling-time is sold in units, which cost more during peak calling times (weekdays) and less during off-hours (evenings and weekends). Timing your calls for off-peak periods can save you a bundle over time.

SKYPE

Most people have heard about or are familiar with Skype. It's the traveler's best friend when it comes to staying in touch across oceans and continents, in a very *les* Jetson sort of way. Skype is the next best thing to being there, since you can see the person you're chatting with in real time if your *ordinateur* (computer) or phone is equipped with a camera. If you don't already have this super communications tool at your disposal, get thee to the Internet *tout de suite* and download the free software. The only real drawback is that you need a modicum of privacy to engage this way; talking to your beloved at the *bibliothèque* or cybercafé will make everyone uncomfortable. Skype's long-distance phone calling plans are worth a gander, too. You can purchase credit beginning at US$1 per minute.

Internet and Postal Service

France, like so many other countries, depends on the Internet to connect with the rest of the world. More than 80 percent of the population uses an *ordinateur* at work, and more than 70 percent now use one at home. If you purchase a package deal from one of the big-name telecom companies, you'll get an access code that allows you to tap into your Internet service outside your home, provided your FAI (Fournisseur d'Accès à Internet) service is available in the area. This comes in handy when you're traveling, and out-of-town guests are always happy to use it, too.

You'll find plenty of places out and about, from libraries and cafés to public parks and McDonald's, offering free "wee-fee" (Wi-Fi) access. Tap in using your own code or the one given to you by the service provider. Check in at the local *mairie* or tourist office for a list of local hotspots.

POST OFFICES

La Poste (www.laposte.fr) isn't just a post office: It's a bank, a bill-pay center, an Internet hotspot, and the place where naughty Frenchies hone their line-jumping skills.

The post office is an all-in-one bank, bill-pay center, and communications hub.

Branches are open six days a week (mail is delivered Tuesday-Saturday), and hours are usually 9am-8pm Monday through Friday, with reduced hours on Saturdays and during school holiday periods. Inside, expect to find DIY *vignette* machines with English-language instructions, boxes and padded envelopes for sale, and helpful staff to sell you dozens of different stamps and other services. Outside, you'll find cash *distributeurs* (ATMs) and *boîtes aux lettres* (mailboxes) for depositing your stamped envelopes and packages. A letter weighing less than 20 grams costs €0.66 to mail (it jumps to €1.10 when you hit the 21-gram mark), and overseas postcard stamps will set you back €0.98. A less expensive, but slower option for sending mail within France is choosing the *lettre verte,* which costs €0.61 when mailing an envelope weighing 20 grams or less.

Media

NEWSPAPERS AND MAGAZINES

Want to feel like a true local? The place to begin your assimilation process is at *les kiosques,* aka the tiny green newsstands that exist in every Parisian neighborhood. Each of France's 10 national newspapers appeals to a specific segment of the politically oriented population, and to be able to talk about the 2017 presidential election with a modicum of savoir-faire, you'll need to align yourself with a reliable news source. On the left, there's *Libération;* in the center, *Le Monde;* and to the right, *Le Figaro.* You'll also find more than 100 other weekly or monthly journals to represent your viewpoint—and everyone else's. Don't know if your "left" is the same as your French compatriots?' Check out the online editions of each paper to see which news-delivery style resonates with you, then pick up a copy from the nearest *kiosque* and take it to the café for your afternoon coffee-and-civics lesson.

Popular free papers and journals include *A Nous, Métro, Direct Matin, Stylist,* and *Direct Soir.* Look for them in Métro stations and *gares* (train stations); occasionally you'll find them being distributed by real live humans in busy pedestrian areas.

France is a magazine-loving culture. News agents vend dozens of titles, from the standard fashion fare to a range of subgenres, such as detective tales, boating, video games, and gay culture. Unlike in the United States and Canada, you won't find much of a selection of reading material at most supermarkets or gas stations. But you will often find them at *librairies* (bookstores) in some *tabacs,* and any shop that has a sign reading "La Presse" on the outside. In Paris, English-language bookstore WHSmith (248, rue de Rivoli, www.whsmith.fr) offers an enormous selection of magazines in multiple languages. If you're desperate for a fix, head to the nearest train station, which is always a reliable source of reading material for people on the go and anyone else seeking a little mental stimulation.

TELEVISION

The French consider television their number-one pastime, watching an average of 3.5 hours per day. This may seem a little high when you consider what's on: game shows, game shows, and the occasional game show. (It seems that way, anyway.) The truth is, there's a vast and varied world of television in France, from cooking shows and cartoons (*Les Simpson,* anyone?) to music videos and home-improvement programs.

Expect lots of dubbed-into-French versions of American programs and films, plus a healthy smattering of police dramas. Documentaries are also popular. Basically, anything you'd want to watch at home is available here, only in French, without subtitles.

The major cable television providers will happily offer you English-language channel add-ons for a price, but experience says skip 'em. If you're committed to learning French, relying on Anglophone television channels for your news and amusement will only handicap your efforts in the long run. Instead, use French TV to your educational advantage; tuning in will help you adjust to the colloquialisms and idioms of modern French and keep you in the pop-culture loop. There are several national public television channels to flip through—France 2, 3, 5, and Arte on channel 7, among others—plus dozens of private and pay-TV channels at your disposal.

For small-screen addicts who can't quit *House of Cards* or *Orange is the New Black* there's good news: Netflix is finally coming to France after literally years of negotiations. It's expected to be introduced here before 2015, but if it hasn't arrived by the time your shipping container lands on your doorstep, there are still options.

RADIO

If you're one of the holdouts in the dwindling universe of radio listeners, there's no reason to stop tuning in just because the music is sung in a language other than your own. (At least 40 percent of the songs will be in French—that's a state mandate.) Whether you turn the dial over to hipster channel Le Mouv or überpopular mainstream station RTL, you'll be able to keep up on current events, discover the hot pop act du jour, and, perhaps most importantly, attune your ear to the language. Radio, like television, is great tool for helping you learn local dialects and colloquialisms, and with plenty of public and private options to choose from, all your listening needs will easily be met.

TRAVEL AND TRANSPORTATION

One of the best things about living in the Île-de-France region is the thorough, efficient, far-reaching transportation system. In Paris alone, you can choose between trains, buses, public bicycles, and cars, trams, taxis, funiculars, and even human-powered pedal rickshaws to get you where you need to be. To reach rural destinations, there are even more trains, plus rental cars, public ride-share programs, buses, ferries, and, of course, regional airlines.

If there's one arena the French have perfected, it's rail travel. The world-renowned TGV (*train à grande vitesse,* or high-speed train) is legend for a reason: It propels you to your destination at 300 kilometers per hour, meaning you can leave Paris after breakfast and arrive in sun-drenched Nice in time to enjoy lunch at a terrace café. But the TGV isn't all France has to offer in terms of train travel. There are also normal long-distance trains, affordable regional trains, and—in Lyon, Lille, Marseille, Toulouse, and Paris—the Métro. Using any combination thereof, you could be skiing the Alps, biking along a canal in Amsterdam, or shopping in London within just a few hours of leaving Paris.

Air

Nearly everyone arriving in France from North America lands at Paris's Charles de Gaulle (CDG) airport (known locally as Roissy, or, phonetically, "WAH-see"), 25 kilometers northeast of the city. With nearly 60 million passengers moving through its three terminals each year, CDG is the second-busiest airport in Europe and the seventh-busiest in the world. It primarily handles international flights; most domestic flights run out of Orly, which also serves routes to Africa, the Middle East, the Caribbean (including Cuba), and other points throughout Europe.

Orly to the south and Beauvais-Tillé to the north are the two primary Paris-region airports serviced by smaller, budget air carriers that sell almost-too-good-to-be-true cheap flights—EasyJet, Ryanair, and Wizz Air are the leaders. More often than not, however, you end up paying just as much in transport fees getting to those distant airports as you do for budget flights to Marrakesh and Malaga. (You'll also have to obey strict baggage limits, and it's wise to expect delays.)

For flights within France, Air France (www.airfrance.fr) dominates with the most options, but there are plenty of others worth a look, including newcomer Hop!, a French regional airline company that's a subsidiary of the Air France group. Hop! (www.hop.fr) Offers budget-friendly flights to several points throughout l'Hexagone, plus a few other European destinations, including Amsterdam, Prague, and Rome.

One of the great advantages to living in the heart of Europe is easy access to so many different countries and cultures. To find the best travel bargains, try websites such as Opodo (www.opodo.fr), which offers flights and affordable weekend package deals to destinations all over Europe, North Africa, and the rest of the world. Railway site SNCF (www.sncf.fr) is another good spot to shop for flights, trains, and hotel packages and Promo Vacances (www.promovancances.com) for flights, hotels, and rental cars. Each of these sites allows you to compare prices and choose dates and flights that best suit your schedule and budget.

Train

There's something romantic about train travel. It has a sense of adventure built into it that air travel lacks, and in France, it can even be a relaxing experience: No shoe-removal routines or liquid-toting restrictions apply (though if you're Chunneling over to London on the Eurostar, you'll need to go through a passport check). Between the roomyish bathrooms, generous legroom, and the café car—where a sandwich and a glass of wine are always within reach—train travel feels practically luxurious, even if it's designed for the proletariat.

The national railway line, SNCF (la Société Nationale des Chemins de Fer), links Paris to more than 7,000 stations all over the country. The TGV and other *grande ligne* trains take you on long-haul trips to major cities, and the TER (Train Express Régional) takes you to the smaller stations in between. Long-distance and local trains depart from the same stations, and there are several trains per day for most destinations, so if you miss the first one, you'll likely be able to find a seat on the next.

Train tickets can be purchased up to six months in advance (though most are available only three months in advance) and can be secured in person at the station, at SNCF boutiques throughout Paris and the suburbs, or bought through the SNCF website (www.sncf.fr). Online, you can choose the English-language option if need be, and peruse all the options for the best deals and best amenities. Not all trains are bicycle friendly, for instance, but those that are will display a small bike icon next to the train details. You'll also be able to see which cars have wheelchair access and whether there's a café car. Using your credit card to pay online is a pretty straightforward process, and you can choose to print out your ticket at home, use your credit card to retrieve it from a kiosk at the station (but only with *puce* cards), or, with enough time, have it mailed to you. If you decide to use the phone to make your reservation, you'll be charged a premium rate of €0.34 per minute (as is common with many public services including banking, telecommunications, and electricity/gas.)

Train ticket prices fluctuate according to a number of criteria: time of day, whether or not you'll be traveling during a school holiday period, what age group you fall into, whether you have an SNCF membership card, whether you're traveling in first or second class, whether the ticket is refundable, and how far in advance you're buying. Spur-of-the-moment tickets are more expensive, so buying a week or two (or more) ahead of time will generally result in a price reduction. If you foresee doing a lot of train travel, forking over a few extra euros to get an SNCF "Week-end" membership card will pay for itself over time. The 12-27 age-group membership card costs €50 per year and gives young adults up to 60 percent off ticket prices. Those age 60 and older are eligible for the €60 Senior card, good for reductions of up to 50 percent. Everyone else is eligible for the age 28-and-older €75 card, which gives up to 40 percent discounts. Families with one or two children are eligible for discount train-travel cards valid for three years, but you have to apply for it, and it isn't necessarily a given that you'll be awarded one. To learn whether you qualify for the Carte Enfant Famille, you must first create an online dossier and pay a nonrefundable €19 filing fee. Two outside social services agencies make the ultimate decision, which will be rendered within a week or two after you submit your dossier. Sample one-way, low-end fares for everyday travelers without a discount card include Paris-Lyon: €30; Paris-Nice: €36; Paris-Cologne, Germany: €35. In 2013, the TGV rolled out a new high-speed train direct to Barcelona, Spain. The trip takes about 6.5 hours and ticket prices begin at €59 each way.

Prem's is a discount ticket company that's part of the SNCF system. Tickets don't offer flexibility in terms of cancellation or changing dates, and you won't find nearly as many destinations as you would with a regular-fare ticket, but the prices are dirt-cheap and worth it if you're tight on funds. You can travel from Paris to Aix-en-Provence for as little as €19, or Annecy for €29.90.

On long-distance trains, a conductor will come through each car to stamp passengers' tickets; but on TER trains, you'll need to validate the *billet* (ticket) yourself. Most French train tickets are valid for two months and not just for the date you're scheduled to travel, which is an invitation for some to try and cheat the system by using their tickets twice. To avoid getting slapped with a fee for riding on a nonvalidated *billet,* you'll need to run your ticket through one of the *composteurs* found on the *quai* (platform). If you forget to do it, the onus is on you to seek out the conductor as soon as you board the train, so she can stamp your ticket for you.

French trains are nearly always on schedule, unless there's a *grève* (strike), in which case local, regional, and long-distance trains may be delayed or cancelled altogether. Usually, *some* trains will be cancelled or delayed, but not all of them—for instance, there may be two trains running to Grenoble instead of six. This is uncommon, but when it does happen, you usually have plenty of forewarning from both the news media and the transportation officials. It's also important to remember that France uses a 24-hour clock, so a train that leaves at 3pm will read as 15h00 on your ticket.

Métro

Even at its packed-in-like-sardines worst, the Paris Métro is still a life enhancer for commuters in the City of Light. Extensive, fast, relatively affordable, and generally safe, it gets you where you want to go—and you just feel so *Parisian* getting there. For visitors, the best Métro ticketing option is the €13.70 *carnet* of 10 tickets. They have no expiration date and are also valid for bus travel, so it's good to stock up (prices increase every year). Other options include the Mobilis card, which looks like a standard Métro ticket, but is valid for a day's worth of Métro and RER train journeys. Prices vary according to the travel zones you choose; a single-day ticket in Zones 1 and 2 costs €6.80, and if you want to navigate all five zones, that'll set you back €16.10. The Paris Visit Pass is similar; choose whether you want a one-, two-, three-, or five-day pass for zones one through three or five, and the price varies accordingly. A five-day pass valid in all five zones—which means access to Orly and Charles de Gaulle-Roissy airports, Versailles, and Disneyland—costs €59.50.

For those staying longer than a few weeks who expect to use the system regularly, a Navigo pass is a more cost-effective option. It looks sort of like a credit card, only with your photo on it. Register online (www.navigo.fr), wait for your card to arrive in the mail, then add money to it using automated kiosks inside the station. Cards are also issued on the spot for €5 fee at Le Club RATP offices at some stations, including Gare du Nord and Gare de Lyon. Navigo rates vary depend on whether you want a weekly or monthly service. A week's worth of travel in zones one and two can be had for €20.40, or €67.10 for the month. Always purchase your weekly tickets on a Monday and your monthly tickets on the first of the month to maximize the value of your card.

Navigating the Métro is easy once you've done it a few times. After entering the station by sliding your pass over the sensor or inserting your ticket into the little slot, you follow the signs pointing to the final destination on your line. For instance, if you're traveling from the Louvre to Gare de Lyon, you'll take the train marked "Château de Vincennes," since Château de Vincennes is the last stop in that direction on that line. Hop on a train going the wrong direction? No problem. Disembark at the next station and cross over to the opposite platform to redirect yourself without having to purchase another ticket or exit the station.

When your train pulls up to the platform, stand clear of the doors to allow passengers to exit. You'll often see people exiting the train and standing near the doors; they're just getting out of the way temporarily to make the disembarking process easier for others. Once everyone is off, it's your turn to pile in. A buzzer will sound when the doors are about to close, usually giving you about five seconds to get moving. Once you're on the train, assess the situation. If your car is packed, don't try to sit on the pull-down folding seats near the door. Instead, stand like everyone else. Though it's not mandatory, it's always nice to give up your seat to pregnant women, parents with small children, and the elderly, for which you'll be rewarded with that rare treasure: a smile from a French stranger.

Bus

Traveling in Paris by bus has its merits, though it can be slower and even more crowded than the Métro. For parents traveling with children and those with mobility issues, the bus is definitely the preferred choice. Night owls will be happy to know that the Noctilien bus line offers longer running hours than the Métro, and you get the added benefit of being able to see the sights while you move about town. To access one of the dozens of bus lines zigging and zagging across the city, start by plotting your journey on the RATP website (www.ratp.fr), which has an English-language option. Once you know which bus to take and from exactly where, you'll need a ticket. Your Navigo pass or t+ tickets (the standard Métro-bus-RER train tickets) will work here. You can also buy a ticket directly from the bus driver; as a courtesy, try to use coins (large bills are refused.) To get off at your stop, push the red button to signal the driver. To transfer between buses you must use a second ticket. The night bus (www.noctilien. fr) runs 12:30am-5:30am with stops at big transport hubs, including Montparnasse and Châtelet, as well as suburban destinations. One bus on each Noctilien line departs every hour.

© VALERY VOENNYY/123RF

bus in the Saint-Germain-des-Prés

Long-distance buses also leave from Paris, heading out to points across the country and throughout Europe. UK-based Eurolines (www.eurolines.fr) services most of Europe with uniformly comfortable coaches that run from multiple cities in France to Spain and Portugal. Busabout (www.busabout. com) is one of the newer bus companies geared toward care-free types who want to see the sights and have the flexibility of stopping and staying awhile. For around €500, you can get a six-day Flexi Pass that allows you to get off and on buses traversing the European continent. Unlike Eurail passes, they aren't limited to non-European residents. To travel long distances within France, you're better off making use of the efficient train system.

COMMUTING ON THE SEINE

If the plane, train, bike, Métro, and bus options don't meet your needs, you'll be relieved to know that Paris even offers a boat option for commuters. Batobus (www.batobus. com) glides up and down the Seine, stopping at eight popular tourist areas, including the Jardin des Plants upriver to the east, Notre-Dame right in the center, and downriver to the west at la Tour Eiffel. An annual pass costs €60. Hours are from 10am to either 7pm or 8:30pm, depending on the time of year. Buses come and go every 20-25 minutes.

Bicycle

When then-Paris mayor Bertrand Delanoë rolled out the Vélib' bike-share program in 2007, the global media went gaga. What novelty! How very modern and innovative! What had gone overlooked, apparently, was that bike-share programs had already been established in other cities throughout France for years. Maverick transport system or not, Vélib' has spawned copycat programs throughout the world, and with good reason: It's a convenient way to get around, get your exercise, and help relieve automobile congestion on busy city streets. Your Navigo card gives instant access, or you can purchase short and long-term memberships online or at one of the outdoor station kiosks for between €1.70 (day membership) and €39 (yearly membership with 45 free minutes of travel time per journey). Neither helmets nor those bright-yellow safety vests that are de rigueur now are included in your community bike rental (though they are recommended), but baskets and locks are part of the nominal fee.

Car

COVOITURAGE (CAR-SHARING)

One well-kept secret among locals who want to get from here to there on the cheap is *covoiturage* (www.covoiturage.fr), which translates to "car-sharing." Once you've register online for free, you can plug in your trip starting point and desired end point, hit the *"rechercher"* button, and see if you'll be matched up with someone who has a car who's also making that trip and wants passengers to help pay for gas. If you get a match (or two or three or more), you can read the driver reviews from other passengers, find out whether they allow dogs, music, or smoking in their cars, and see how much they're charging per passenger for the trip. Between Paris and Lille, prices range €10-20 each way; from Paris to Nice, expect to pay around €55-75.

The newest public transportation system to be unveiled in the City of Light is the car-share program called Autolib'. Subscribing online (www.autolib.eu) for periods of a day, week, month, or year gives you access to a fleet of four-seat electric "Bluecars" stationed throughout Paris and the Île-de-France region. A valid driver's license and international permit are required for non-EU drivers, and charges average €10-14 per hour. They are best for short, one-way trips.

© 123RF.COM

Cycling culture has picked up since the Velib' bikeshare program was launched.

DRIVER'S LICENSES

By now, you should know that nothing comes particularly easy in France. They really make you work for it, whether it's getting your *carte de séjour* or opening a bank account. Expect more of the same when seeking a French driver's license. It's definitely possible to acquire one, but not necessarily simple and easy. The first confusing hurdle you'll have to jump over to get closer to your *permis de conduire* (driver's license) is determining whether your state (or province, for Canadians) is one of the dozens with a reciprocal driver's license agreement with France—British Columbia and California do not, but Pennsylvania and Prince Edward Island do. If your state is on the list, just make for the *préfecture,* show your U.S. driver's license, fill out a form, and wait two weeks for your valid-forever French license to arrive. If your home state is not on the lucky list, then you'll have to take the figurative long route to be able to take the literal long route by *voiture* (car). That means finding a school, or *auto-école.* They're everywhere: Type in *"auto-école"* and the name of your city into your favorite search engine and see what comes up. Prices vary somewhat, but you can expect to pay between €700 and €1,500 for an extensive driver's education course that includes classes in theory and driving codes, plus 20 hours of actual driving time. Don't expect to be immediately accepted into the first school you approach; there is generally a waiting time of up to several months for these in-demand academies. You can see how popular they are by looking around the streets of your town and counting the cars with the illuminated *"école"* sign on top. Classes, as you might expect, are taught in French. Don't think your language skills are up to snuff? English-language classes do exist, but you'll pay a premium for that privilege or enlist the services of a translator for the written test.

PEDALING PARIS

Name: Anna Brones
Profession: Writer
Age: 30
Hometown: Vaughn, Washington
City: Paris, 17th

A Portlander turned Parisian in 2013, Anna Brones is a writer and author of *The Culinary Cyclist: A Cookbook and Companion for the Good Life*. She is the founder of the food blog Foodie Underground (www.foodieunderground.com), and most days she can be found cycling, drinking strong coffee, and cooking in her small Parisian kitchen. Here, she offers her two-wheeled wisdom to adventures types in the City of Light.

"Cycling in Paris" sounds romantic. What could be more wonderful than exploring the City of Light on two wheels? It can, of course, be romantic and wonderful, but it can also be nerve wracking. Every time you make it from point A to B without getting into an accident is a cause for celebration.

Before coming to Paris, I spent 10 years in Portland, Oregon, aka Bike Mecca, USA. My trusty Peugeot and I took to the familiar streets every day. When I moved here, I was determined to continue making cycling a part of my everyday lifestyle. I signed up for a one-year Velib' bike-share subscription and launched myself into Paris bike culture.

What's it like cycling in Paris? Hard—but also wonderful. If you pedal across the Seine just as the afternoon sun sets, you find yourself in a moment of pure joy when you wouldn't want to be anywhere else. But navigating the streets here can be harrowing. There are scooters, ruthless taxis, tremendous tourist buses, and cars to deal with. Not to mention pedestrians.

Paris is a city full of people who walk, and unlike countries with strong cycling cultures like the Netherlands or Scandinavia, you often have the feeling that people just don't care that you're on a bike. They walk blindly across bike lanes—sometimes even refusing to move as you ring your bell more times than seems humanly possible. Here, you simply learn to be as aggressive as the four-wheeled drivers.

Fortunately, things are evolving. Several stores around town sell city-friendly commuter bikes, and it's not uncommon to see locals of all ages commuting to and from work. With the launch of Velib' in 2007 (which 9 times out of 10 works very well) that bike culture has continued to grow, and the city has made a big effort to make living a two-wheeled Parisian lifestyle a reality that anyone can achieve.

The thing about bike culture is this: It only evolves if more people ride—one reason I am committed to getting on a bicycle every day. Yes, you have to pay attention much more than you would in other cities, you have to be ready to bike on big streets with lots of traffic, and many times, you simply have to accept that you will get lost navigating Paris's complex web of streets and intersections. But you also get to ride a bicycle in Paris, and at the end of the day, when you're cycling down a quiet street and the sun shines through the trees at just the right angle, you remember how lucky you are.

Driving indefinitely on your valid U.S. driver's license—which is only valid in France for the first year you're here—might be a gamble worth taking if the thought of dealing with another layer of bureaucracy is just too much to bear. Some drivers interviewed for this book claim to never have had a problem related to driving with their non-French licenses, even after racking up countless speeding tickets. (Tickets are generally issued by mail, after a radar trap catches you exceeding the speed limit.) Still, there's nothing like the peace of mind that comes with living life above board, so drive safely, with caution.

© AURELIA D'ANDREA

Need to make a trip to Ikea? Autolib' might be just the thing you need.

BUYING A CAR

Cars can be purchased in France at used-car lots and new-car lots, and through private parties on websites like ParuVendu (www.paruvendu.fr) and La Centrale (www.lacentrale.fr). You'll also see handwritten *"à vendre"* signs tacked to car windows. But you'll not likely see much in the way of junker *voitures* since the government offers financial incentives to people to trade in their environmentally hostile gas guzzlers for more modern, fuel-efficient Renaults, Peugeots, and Citroëns. Even then, the old, gross polluters tend to retain their value, which makes purchasing a new car in France look pretty wise from a fiscal perspective. Whatever path you take to buy a car, you'll need to get it registered immediately afterward.

How you secure your *carte grise,* or automobile registration card, depends on whether you bought a new or used vehicle. If you bought your car new from a dealer, the dealer will submit the paperwork to the *préfecture* on your behalf. When you buy a second-hand car, you can choose to fill out the registration forms in person at the *préfecture* and sometimes at the *mairie's office,* or you can register online (www.cartegriseminute.fr) to get your *plaques d'immatriculation* (license plates) and *carte grise.*

Like the annual smog checks that are mandatory in some U.S. states, all cars in France are subject to a *contrôle technique* every two years. You bring your car to an authorized service station, where everything from your shock absorbers to your seatbelts will be tested for wear and functionality. Expect to pay around €40 for the service, plus any necessary fix-it fees that result from the diagnostic testing. Cars older than five years are also subjected to annual smog checks.

© AURELIA D'ANDREA

If you want to commute by car, you may need to attend driving school.

RULES OF THE ROAD

When traveling by car in Paris, you'll notice a distinct peculiarity: There are no stop signs. Navigating the streets by car, bicycle, or even on foot without those familiar red octagons can be tricky, and it helps to know some basics before getting behind the wheel. In general, the car(s) to your right have the right-of-way—except in round-abouts, where the cars inside the roundabout to your left take priority. Right turns on red lights are strictly prohibited. If you're on a bike, you may be exempt from this rule if you see a small red triangle with a yellow arrow. Pedestrians walk blindly into the streets both in and outside of crosswalks with disarming regularity, so be forewarned.

Parking in Paris can be exhausting work, both finding a spot to squeeze into and then actually squeezing into it. Parking spaces are generally of the *payant* variety, costing €1.20-3.60 per hour, depending on what part of the city you're in. Most of these pay-to-park spots morph into free-to-park spots on weekends, holidays, and the month of August. Purchase your ticket from the green kiosks marked with a bright blue "P," and put the little receipt face-up on the driver's side of your dashboard. (It's also possible to buy pre-paid cards at tabacs and some newspaper stands.) Parking garages are also scattered throughout Paris, and vary in price. Visit www.parkingsdeparis.com to learn more.

Outside Paris, roads vary from fast-moving toll highways to smaller, slower highways and snail-strength surface roads. They'll all get you to your destination, but it's the toll (*péage*) roads that are most efficient and therefore worth the extra cost. Toll roads, or *autoroutes,* usually begin with an A (A1 through A89) but may begin with an E. Tolls vary depending on the road and the distance traveled, so expect to pay anywhere from €1.10 to €35.60. Payments can be made in cash or using a credit card, and some toll booths are staffed by humans who can make change and direct you on what to do if

MÉTRO BOULOT DODO

It started out as a patchwork of words borrowed from the 1951 poem "Couleurs d'Usine," by Pierre Béarn: *Métro, boulot, dodo.* Today, it has evolved into a 21st-century mantra for the overworked masses: commute, work, sleep; same-old, same-old; another day, another dollar. If you want to sound like a real Parisian—and echo the sentiments of the poem's author—sprinkle this expression into the conversation at your next end-of-the-week decompression gathering. Try something like: "This week has been rough—nothing but *Métro, boulot, dodo.* I'm ready for a vacay." (Now try it again, only this time in French!)

you don't have cash or cards. One thing you'll learn pretty quickly after driving on French highways is that the left lane is reserved exclusively for passing; it isn't meant to be a high-speed cruising lane. Use it to pass slower cars, then move back into the right lane until you exit the highway or need to pass another car.

Routes nationales ("N" roads) and *routes départementales* ("D" roads) will also get you where you need to go, albeit much more slowly. One feature of the smaller roads that hinders speed and efficiency is the roundabout. For the uninitiated, France's ubiquitous *ronds-points* can be dizzying. Drivers to the left always have the right-of-way, which means you may have to stop and wait for several cars to pass before you can enter. Only enter the roundabout when there are no cars to your left.

To avoid the radar-enforced speed traps, it's helpful to know the speed limits. On toll roads, the maximum speed is 130 kilometers per hour (km/h). In wet conditions, you must slow down to either 90 km/h or 110 km/h, depending on the road. On main roads, the limit is 90 km/h; when driving through towns, reduce your speed to 50 km/h.

Back in 2008, it became mandatory to carry a reflective warning triangle and neon safety vest (*gilet*) for each passenger. Failing to do so could cost you €137—or worse, your life, if no one can see you changing the tire on the side of the road. You can buy the safety duo for about €20 at auto body shops, some gas stations, and the French equivalent of AAA, called Automobile Club (www.automobileclub.org). The Day-Glo reflective vests are also a common sight on the racks at French thrift stores.

In recent years, the government has launched a series of anti-drinking-and-driving campaigns to curb a growing problem in France. The legal blood alcohol limit is 0.5 grams per liter, or 0.25 milligrams in a breathalyzer, which is how you'll be tested. This is equivalent to two standard glasses of wine (10 cl) or beer (25 cl). If you're pulled over on suspicion of driving under the influence, you could receive a fine and lose six points off your 12-point driving record, lose your license for as many as three years, or end up in prison for up to two years, depending upon your level of intoxication. More information about driving laws can be found on the government's road-safety website, www.securite-routiere.gouv.fr.

Car insurance is mandatory and generally more affordable than in the United States or Canada, since personal health insurance is also mandatory and therefore an unnecessary component of your auto insurance. How much you pay depends on many factors, including the type of vehicle you're driving (motorcycle, caravan), how long you've been driving, and your driving record. Automobile Club offers free quotes, but you can also walk into any storefront offering *"assurances automobile"* and ask for a *devis* (quote).

DRIVING ME CRAZY

Circulation: Do you know what it means? In France, it has less to do with your cardiovascular system and more to do with driving. (It means "traffic.") Before you get behind the wheel of your *voiture* and become part of the *circulation*, you'd best brush up on your roadway lingo.

accident - accident
autoroute - highway
bande d'arrêt d'urgence - emergency lane
chaîs - snow chains
conducteur/conductrice) - driver

dépasser - to pass
embouteillage - traffic jam
feu de signalisation - traffic light
limitation de vitesse - speed limit
passage piétons - crosswalk
péage - toll road/booth
piéton(ne) - pedestrian
pont - bridge
ralentir - slow down
rond-point - roundabout
route - road
sens interdit - no entry
sens unique - one way
tomber en panne - break down

PRIME LIVING LOCATIONS

© AURELIA D'ANDREA

OVERVIEW

There's a lot to love about the City of Light. Postage-stamp size squares mark every neighborhood. Endless dining options will take your taste buds on a journey from Alsace to Sri Lanka. In corner *boulangeries,* still-warm *viennoiseries* call out to you from inside a gleaming glass case. And dozens of museums offer up centuries of world-class art to overwhelm the senses. Paris is beautiful beyond belief, and even in the grittiest neighborhoods in the northern section of the city, you need only look up at a building's facade to revel in a moment of aesthetic pleasure.

Paris is carved into 20 distinct regions called arrondissements, each an administrative unit with its own mayor and town hall. These districts spiral out clockwise from the geographic center of the city, ending in the northeastern quadrant. In each of the 20 arrondissements, you'll notice distinct differences: Some are more congested, others more verdant; some, like the 16th, have a quiet and residential air, while the 18th hums with a more active, lively vibe.

Each quartier in the city's 20 arrondissements is a self-contained village, with all the amenities you'd find in a big city compressed into a single neighborhood. Wherever you settle, you'll be within 45 minutes of anywhere else in the city. The thorough and efficient Métro system makes the distances less daunting, though one of the benefits of Paris life is the bounty that your quartier offers (making it unnecessary to leave if you

© AURELIA D'ANDREA

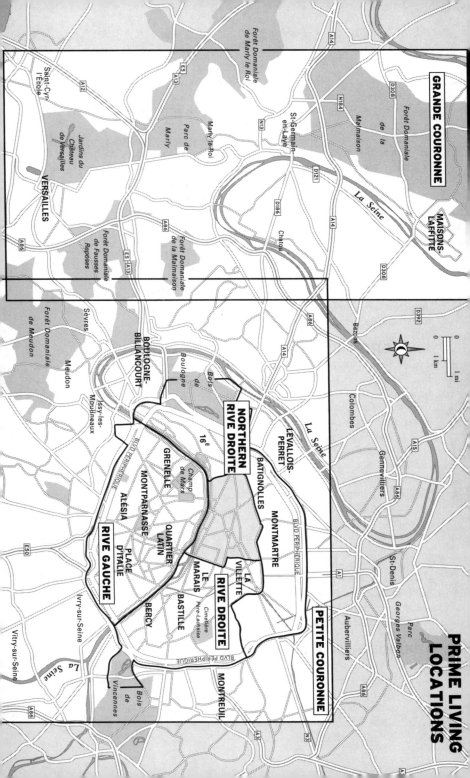

don't want to). With the exception of the 16th arrondissement, every neighborhood in Paris has, within a two-block radius of your apartment, a *boulangerie,* a butcher shop, an *épicerie* for buying vegetables and fruit, and a Métro or bus stop.

Paris boasts more foreigners than any other city in France. Anything you want—even a burrito, which makes some of us Californians extremely happy—can be sussed out here, and employment and housing opportunities trump those anywhere else. Wherever you are in Paris, expect French to be spoken (along with Arabic, Swahili, English, Hebrew, Italian, Portuguese, and Spanish), polite formality to reign, and non-stop opportunities for cultural diversion, educational opportunity, and macerating in a history-rich marinade while you're here.

From chic penthouse apartments with views over Luxembourg Gardens to smart little cottages with a distinctly rural outlook onto vast expanses of forest, Paris and the surrounding Île-de-France suburbs have idyllic housing options for whatever the foreign heart fancies. The best places for expats to settle aren't just those neighborhoods where jobs can be found (or created), but those with a solid social infrastructure that ensures you'll never feel alienated or isolated. Regional idiosyncrasies abound, as do attitudes, and the life you carve out in Maisons-Laffitte will not be the same as the one you make for yourself in the Marais.

RIVE DROITE

On the Right Bank of the Seine, you'll find the Champs-Élysées, the Marais, the Bastille, and the Hôtel de Ville. *La Rive Droite* feels hipper, younger, and edgier, particularly so in the Canal Saint-Martin (10th). Paris's gay hub is centered on the Right Bank, in the old streets of the Marais (4th). Just north of the Bastille (11th), on rue de la Roquette, is where you'll find the highest concentration of pierced and tattooed locals as well as many popular watering holes.

In the perpetually alluring Marais and trendy Bastille—you'll find that the hipsters have hogged up all the affordable places and sent the rental prices on what's left sky-high. Still, you may want to try your luck in the Canal Saint-Martin neighborhood and the northern Marais (3rd) near the newly revamped Place de la République, where a youthful vibe dominates and there's always a cheerful café for kicking back and people-watching.

Hugging the Seine on the Right Bank's far southeastern edge, the Bercy (12th) neighborhood stands out like a beacon of modernity amid the vintage Haussmannian architecture. Formerly a wine warehouse district for the city of Paris, Bercy has been transformed into a verdant and very livable quarter with a mixed population of young university students, families, and retirees. A bit out of the way (though very self-contained), Bercy boasts museums, an enormous dog-friendly park, cinemas, and restaurants—all within easy reach via the super-speedy Métro line 14.

NORTHERN RIVE DROITE

The entire city is in gentrification mode, but you can really feel that transition happening in Paris's deep north. This is still the place to look for the best real estate values in Paris. Around the picturesque La Villette (19th) neighborhood, contemporary urbanism collides with an almost-bucolic, Paris-of-yore feel. Parks, waterways, crowded public markets, multiculturalism, and breathtaking vistas are some of the special

© AURELIA D'ANDREA

The Batignolles neighborhood is still affordable, but it won't be for long.

characteristics of the northeast reaches of the Right Bank. Moving west, past the snow-white Sacré-Coeur Basilica and its tourist throngs, and beyond the fabled Moulin Rouge and camera-toting crowds (18th), the charming Batignolles (17th) neighborhood beckons with its village-like atmosphere. The Saturday morning organic market attracts a loyal crowd and gives newcomers a chance to taste—literally and figuratively—the local's life.

For those who prefer a sedate atmosphere with a distinct aura of security and calm, the 16th arrondissement calls out—albeit quietly. Top-of-the-line Peugots and Renaults glide down manicured streets, past the stately apartment buildings and chic restaurants, exuding a homogenous ambience with a dash of Americana thrown in. Don't be surprised if your neighbors, like you, are expats from an English-speaking corner of the world. They're here for the same reasons so many others choose to settle on the bourgeois west end: access to the expansive Bois de Boulogne, a high degree of safety, and room to stretch out and breathe.

RIVE GAUCHE

The Left Bank, or *la Rive Gauche,* is where you'll find the Sorbonne, the Eiffel Tower, the Catacombs, and those cafés and brasseries made famous over the centuries by writers and philosophers: Brasserie Lipp, Les Deux Magots, Café de Flore. Today, more tourists than locals pull up a chair on their sidewalk terraces, but if you move just south of Saint-Germain-des-Prés, you'll discover homey neighborhoods and a safe, child-friendly atmosphere. The Left Bank feels more sedate, more residential, and slightly less *populaire,* or working-class crowded. Wandering the quieter corners of la Rive Gauche, you might think you were lost in a small provincial town.

Paris's fabled Quartier Latin (5th) rises up and away from the Seine, stretching out to encompass several celebrated landmarks, including the Panthéon, the Sorbonne, and the *jolie* Luxembourg Gardens, hemmed in by some of the city's most coveted real estate. Moving west, it's impossible to miss Paris's tallest landmark—Tour Montparnasse. At its base sits one of the city's busiest train stations and a shopping mall popular with the student set. The area boasts dozens of cinemas and theaters, making it a popular rainy-day destination for city dwellers from every arrondissement. The pace slows as you migrate toward the Grenelle (15th) neighborhood—especially if wander around (rather than through) the Champs-de-Mars and the perennially popular Tour Eiffel. In spite of its proximity to Paris's most iconic monument, Grenelle retains an unassuming, low-key profile, and offers residents an unrivaled sense of safety and security.

PARIS: *FLÂNEUR'S* PARADISE

Nineteenth-century poet Charles Baudelaire brought the term *flâneur* to life, and there's little question that his hometown, Paris, was the inspiration. The *flâneur*–walkabout, stroller, urban explorer–thrives on the sensory experience of the city, absorbing its sights, smells, and sounds, synthesizing the disparate elements into a meaningful whole.

"For the perfect *flâneur*, for the passionate spectator, it is an immense joy to set up house in the heart of the multitude, amid the ebb and flow of movement, in the midst of the fugitive and the infinite," wrote Baudelaire in 1863. For modern-day *flâneurs*, Paris is the winning lotto ticket–the mother lode of *flâneurial* fodder.

Each of the city's 20 arrondissements is its own universe, with a unique breed of inhabitants and dynamic character. In the 1st arrondissement, you could sit for hours at the fountains in the courtyard of the Louvre, inhaling the cacophony of foreign languages until the sun sets over the Seine. In the 4th, men in black hats frame the doorways of the Jewish *boulangeries*, a Jerusalem street scene recreated in the City of Light. In the 16th, women of a certain age, dressed in fur and designer shoes, promenade their pooches in the bourgeois safety of this tidy neighborhood. What do they know of the *banlieue*, just over the *périphérique*, where cars sometimes burn and the police wear riot gear?

There's no such thing as a boring day in Paris; the visual stimulation and inspiration are endless. Whether or not you identify with the *flâneur's* philosophical perspective, you will not be able to help–as Baudelaire suggests–but experience the streets as you roam them, from Porte de Clignancourt to Porte d'Orléans.

Farther south in Alésia (14th) and Place d'Italie (13th), the city becomes practically suburban, though you're never far from transportation, markets, and restaurants. If you can't imagine apartment living and don't want to give it a whirl, consider a move to these Parisian 'burbs, where your options will run the gamut from apartments and lofts to single-family homes with roomy gardens.

PETITE COURONNE

Paris's ring of nearby suburbs, dubbed la Petite Couronne (the Little Crown), came into being during the Industrial revolution, when it mushroomed with factories and housing for factory workers. In the intervening two centuries, those factories have been razed and replaced by smart communities offering more square meters for your euro, links to fast and efficient transportation, and easy access to forests and green spaces. Made up of three *départements* (92, 93, and 94), the Petite Couronne circles the City of Light, encompassing dozens of exciting possibilities for expats who desire city access without living in the city itself.

Sceaux

If quiet, sleepy, and friendly are your idea of home, you're going to love Sceaux. This is a close-knit community of welcoming people who aren't afraid to crack a smile. Quiet, well-kept streets and a perfectly appointed, pedestrian-friendly downtown gives Sceaux a pleasant provincial vibe. An enormous park with jogging paths, fountains, and topiary gardens feels like a trip to the country, yet Paris is just a few kilometers away.

Move to Levallois-Perret and this could be your local fruit stand.

Boulogne-Billancourt

Dream of living in the 16th arrondissement, but can't afford the sky-high rents? Shift your gaze a little to the west and you might find exactly what you want in Boulogne-Billancourt. Safe and loaded with amenities and good schools, Boulogne-Billancourt is a great spot for families (especially families with two cars). This is a place you can stretch out, feel a strong sense of security, and enjoy suburban life with all the perks of Paris at your doorstep.

Levallois-Perret

There's a lot to like about this unassuming suburb just northwest of Paris. Tiny, neat, and tidy, Levallois-Perret has everything you need within a short walk of your front door—the Métro, outdoor markets, lively cafés, and restaurants with a wealth of cuisine options. All this, with Eiffel Tower views too!

Montreuil

A little gritty and rough around the edges, the eastern suburb of Montreuil is an unlikely candidate at first glance, but scratch beneath the surface and what you'll find is a dynamic, multicultural oasis with a thriving arts scene and unbeatable real-estate prices. The *bobos* (bourgeois bohemians) have caught on, so you won't be alone in your discovery. A massive urban overhaul is under way and the future looks bright for new families to move in. In coming years, more schools will be built, more parks will be developed, and more eco-friendly and affordable housing will become available.

© AURELIA D'ANDREA

If you crave a country feel, Maisons-Laffitte might be right for you.

GRANDE COURONNE

Beyond the Petite Couronne and the twinkling lights of la Tour Eiffel, lies the Grand Couronne, a ring of four départements dotted with rivers, forests, and livable communities within an hour's journey of Paris. Why choose to settle in the outer limits of the Île-de France-region? The fresh air, the bucolic rural vibe, and the chance to have a house with a big yard—all without sacrificing the all-important transport links to Paris. The only thing you give up in the suburbs are the tourist crowds—unless, of course, you move to Versailles—but even then, the out-of-towners tend to restrict their visits to the gilded confines of the famous château's gates.

Versailles

A tourist town in its own right, Versailles offers the perfect blend of big city amenities (museums, shopping) and small town values. Good schools, easy access to nature, and a short commute to Paris make this a good choice for families, and a thriving senior scene make it great for retirees, too. The famous château is Versailles's star attraction, so expect lots of out-of-town house guests if you move here.

Maisons-Lafitte

This is horse country, with a town that attracts the kind of people who can afford them—in other words, those with money. There are beautiful yet understated old houses and plentiful green spaces, and the cute main street feels like something out of the American Midwest. The English-speaking community is strong, which can be a real comfort for newcomers who've yet to master the language.

RIVE DROITE

The right bank of the Seine, known as the Rive Droite, might not possess the legendary cachet of its left bank counterpart, but just because it lacks a monument of Tour Eiffel proportions doesn't mean there's no glamour and sparkle to found in its cobblestone streets.

Historically, the Rive Droite claims multiple bragging rights (just not the Lost Generation kind of bragging rights). After all, this *is* the home of both the most visited museum in the world and of scooter-riding French President François Hollande. Planted on a hill overlooking the mansard-roofed landscape is the Sacré-Coeur Basilica, one of Paris's most recognizable landmarks. And perhaps you've heard of a little event known as the storming of the Bastille? Or that little revolutionary spectacle called the Paris Commune? That's the *real* spirit of the right bank: a bit rebellious, a smidge brazen, with a bit of outside-the-box rabble-rousing thrown in for good measure.

People are drawn to the right bank for multiple reasons, including its cool factor. The perpetually popular Marais is more than just the gay Ground Zero; it's also home to dozens of art galleries showing the work of Paris's up and coming Monets, Manets, and Man Rays. Paris's hippest pop music venues are clustered here, including La Maroquinerie, the Flèche d'Or, and the Nouveau Casino. There's something unique about the right bank that allows new ideas to flourish in ways that aren't possible

© DENNIS DOLKENS | DREAMSTIME.COM

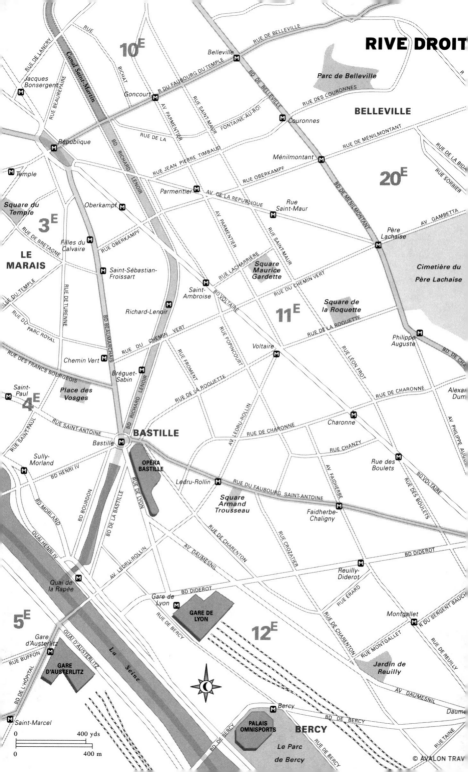

anywhere else in the city, and for many—both newcomers and longtime residents—that freedom is what gives the area its allure. Tell people you live in the Rive Droite, and they'll instantly size you up as someone who is less traditional, more of a risk-taker, and someone who might even like living life on the edge.

Paris's slow lean toward architectural modernity is most palpable on the right bank. You won't necessarily feel that in the Marais, where the city's oldest dwellings—their walls bowed with the weight of centuries and dampness from the Seine—lean into one another and invite you take a step back into the heady past. For a distinctly 21st-century feel, follow the Seine upstream to Bercy, where gleaming glass-and-metal skyscrapers tower over its expansive park and wide-open pedestrian promenades. Further downstream, the bourgeois 16th arrondissement offers Parisians a prim and pretty ambiance with family-friendly vibe—and *rue* after tidy *rue* of Haussmann-era apartment blocks with ornate iron balconies bedecked with colorful geraniums. Dynamic, diverse, and delightful, *la belle* Rive Droite is yours for the taking if you dare to *dit oui* (say yes).

THE LAY OF THE LAND

The neighborhoods lapping at the shore of the right bank offer million-euro views of quintessential Paris. From the 16th on the west side all the way to Bercy in the furthest eastern reaches, this giant swath of central Paris gives residents glimpses of la Tour Eiffel, Notre-Dame and the Bastille. Rue de Rivoli, a kinetic thoroughfare clogged with buses, bikes, and automobiles, connects the Champs-Elysées with the busy Bastille roundabout, though many prefer to skip the sights (and the traffic) and stay underground on Métro Line 1. The canary-yellow line follows Rivoli's same Seine-side trajectory and extends even further, to La Défense on one end and the Bois de Vincennes on the other. No matter which mode you choose to navigate the inner Rive Droite, you'll find that, like most of Paris, it's easy enough getting from here to there on public transport, by foot, or pedal power. (Cars? Not so much.)

Because of its centrality and proximity to so many tourist hotspots, this part of Paris can feel crowded at times—almost to the point of wanting to shout "Tourists be gone!" from the rooftops. If you want to settle here, you'll need to make the necessary attitude adjustments. (Because really, isn't an 18th-century townhouse with beamed ceilings and views over the river worth it?) For more breathing room, Belleville and Bercy are better bets.

Le Marais

The Marais neighborhood encompasses most of the 3rd and 4th arrondissements. Its border stretches from the Seine on the south to the Place de la République on the north. To the west is the shopper's paradise of Les Halles; to the east, the Place de la Bastille and its gold-statue-topped Colonne de Juillet rise above the traffic of the frenetic *rond-point*.

As the oldest neighborhood in Paris, the Marais is, not surprisingly, one of the most stereotypically French in character, with crooked cobbled streets, half-timbered buildings, charming squares, and loads and loads of tourists. If you want to live in the heart of the city, with direct access to bars, restaurants, museums, and shopping, the

© 123RF.COM

L'As du Fallafel on rue des Rosiers

Marais is your place. It helps if you're OK with crowds (narrow streets coupled with a never-ending tourist stream can make the claustrophobic feel edgy), and don't plan on driving a car. Access to parking is not a selling point in the Marais, which is best navigated on foot or by bicycle.

Though not as ethnically diverse as some other Parisian quartiers, the Marais does offer more than just croissants and coffee as its metaphorical neighborhood composition. This is the old Jewish quarter, with nearby synagogues, Holocaust memorials and museums, and Jewish delicatessens galore where you can have your rugelach and eat it, too. Every day except the Saturday sabbath, tourists and locals in droves queue up for the famous Israeli falafel at L'As du Fallafel (32-34 rue des Rosiers), considered by many (including famous patron Lenny Kravitz) to be the best in town. But wander the skinny streets within spitting distance of L'As and you'll discover dozens of copycats eager for your business.

The hub of Parisian gay life is in the Marais, which is the equivalent of San Francisco's Castro or Montreal's le Village. To immerse yourself in this aspect of Marais culture, attend the next Gay Pride parade, held each June, which starts on rue des Archives.

HOUSING

The Marais's housing opportunities vary wildly. Tucked into unassuming alleyways (and protected by enormous and imposing wood doors) are magnificent *maisons particulières* that fetch small fortunes on the real estate market, and equally, there are oodles of ancient walk-ups with beamed ceilings and bucketfuls of more accessible Medieval charm. The most expensive areas (surprise!) sidle up to the area's prettiest green spaces, so if you want to live near the stately Place des Vosges (and who doesn't?), expect to pay upwards of €13,000 per square meter if you're buying. The best deals for homebuyers can be had in the area north and west of the Georges Pompidou center known as Les Halles. Once the site of the city's main wholesale food market and then a haven for all manner of illicit activities is Les Halles, just west of the Marais. This area is now undergoing a major revamp, and part of that overhaul includes creating more livable spaces and cutting down crime.

In other words, get in while the getting is good and affordable! It won't be cheap for long. As of 2014, it was still possible to buy something deep in the heart of the Marais for the reasonable price of €7,500-8,500 per square meter. You might get lucky and find a 55-square-meter, one-bedroom flat on rue de Temple, constructed in 1700, with a spic-and-span courtyard and friendly *gardienne* for €650,000. For the slightly more affordable price of €390,000 you could land yourself a smaller version a block from Place des Vosges with beamed ceilings and an entirely refinished and modernized interior.

Renting is another ball of wax. Prices per square meter average around €36, which translates to a one-bedroom apartment with those high-in-demand beamed ceilings and views over a pedestrian promenade for €1,300 per month. With a bigger budget, you could find a two-bedroom corner apartment for €1,450 in the Saint-Paul neighborhood (in the southern Marais), known for its plethora of antiques shops and Old World ambiance. Hopefully you like exposed-beam ceilings, because most every apartment in this area is equipped with them.

DAILY LIFE
Schools and Community Centers

The Marais isn't Paris's most family-friendly neighborhood (some sidewalks are barely big enough for two feet, let alone a stroller), but kid-oriented amenities including nurseries and playgrounds, and elementary, and middle-, and high-schools are scattered throughout its narrow streets. If you settle in the 3rd, it would behoove you to visit the Relais Informations Familles on the ground floor of the *mairie* (RIF, 2, rue Eugène Spuller, tel. 01/53 01 75 90). Here, friendly staff people will answer all of your questions about enrolling your child in local educational institutions and childcare centers. The 4th arrondissement is home to three different university campuses, including the Sorbonne's Malher center for historical and legal research (www.univ-paris1.fr). To learn more about the educational opportunities available to you in the 4th, no matter your age, pay an actual or virtual visit to the *mairie* and investigate the *vie scolaire* section (2, place Baudoyer, www.mairie.04.paris.fr).

Shopping

The Marais offers something many Parisian neighborhoods cannot claim: open-on-Sunday business hours. Commerce is queen in this neck of the woods—especially so on rue des Francs Bourgeois, rue des Archives, and rue de la Verrerie. (The big shopping mall at Les Halles and the vintage BHV department store keep with the old school closed-on-Sundays tradition.) You won't find huge grocery stores here, but there are plenty of Carrefour City and Franprix markets, plus a smattering of little family-run *épiceries* where you can stock up on fresh fruit, canned foods, and wine.

© AURELIA D'ANDREA

The Marais is more than just a popular tourist area; it's also a great place to live.

Rue de Rivoli is one of Paris's most renowned shopping streets, and its wares were designed for the proletariat. H&M, Zara, Mango, and other retail giants line the thoroughfare, which cuts right through the Marais before leading you down to the Golden Triangle and its higher-priced goods built for big wallets.

Not all shopping is done in stores here in the Marais. Each autumn, the *mairie* of the 3rd arrondissement in the trendy northern Marais hosts the popular Bourse aux Vélos. The public is invited to roam among the rows and rows of old and new bicycles and potentially snap up a pair of wheels at an affordable price.

Leisure

One area that the Marais does not skimp on is recreation. The Piscine Suzanne Berlioux inside the shopping center at Les Halles is fun for both actual swimmers and the armchair variety, who can watch the Speedo-clad activities through the pool's giant floor-to-ceiling windows facing out into the shopping area. Entry is €4 and a bathing cap is required. If you're the sporty type or have one living with you, check in with the Office du Mouvement Sportif du 4e at the *mairie* (www.om4paris.org). They'll help you find an association that meets your needs, whether that's a tennis club, runner's group, or martial arts association.

The Marais also earns high marks in the area of theater. Small productions in interesting spaces abound here, including fringe theater at the Café de la Gare (41, rue de Temple, www.cdlg.org), absurdist humor at the Théâtre des Blancs Manteaux (15, rue des Blancs Manteaux, www.blancsmanteaux.fr), and stand-up comedy at Le Point Virgule (7, rue Sainte-Croix de la Brettonerie, www.lepointvirgule.com). Living in a lively nightlife hub like the Marais means making use of all its cultural amenities, and diving right into the theater scene is a fun and entertaining way to get acquainted with the local cultural idiosyncrasies.

Getting Around

The perennial question "why drive when you've got the Métro?" takes on heightened significance when filtered through the prism of parking in the Marais. Finding secure parking here takes serious effort—even with a Smart Car—but it's not impossible. However, car ownership will limit the fun you can have on your Parisian adventure. Better to invest in a Navigo pass or buy a *carnet* of public transport tickets and leave the driving to someone else. The Marais is well served by an efficient network of underground trains (especially lines 1, 8, and 11) and above-ground buses. Bus line 69, which is almost as good as a sightseeing bus, is a stellar option. You can hop on the bus on rue de Rivoli and hop off at the Louvre, la Tour Eiffel, and even Père-Lachaise Cemetery.

For trips further afield, Marais locals head to the Châtelet-Les Halles station, where regional trains whisk travelers to destinations throughout the Île-de-France region.

Hundreds of Velib' stations pepper the Marais, and are the ideal way to navigate the tiny back streets, most of which are outfitted with bike lanes. On clear days during *apéro* hour, there can be traffic jams around Velib' stations positioned in popular café areas, so plan accordingly. You may end up having to race another rider to the next open parking space a few blocks away. (It happens to all of us at least once!)

Bastille

The Place de la Bastille roundabout is so much more than just the site of an historic event that kicked off the French Revolution; it's also the gateway to one of the most dynamic and lively neighborhoods in Paris. The 11th arrondissement resembles a giant pie wedge, sliced on the west by the boulevard Richard-Lenoir, on the north by boulevard Voltaire, and to the southeast by rue du Faubourg Saint-Antoine. This giant triangle feels central, even if it's a tad off the main tourist path, and accessible without being utterly in the thick of things.

Butted up against the 4th and 12th arrondissements, the Bastille was once a forlorn, neglected area full of working-class immigrant families and grungy youth hostels. In the past 20 years, new parks have been installed, boutiques have sprung up, cafés have blossomed on virtually every corner, and the neighborhood has become both more appealing and more expensive. If you can snag a place in your price range here, you'll find great outdoor markets, renowned restaurants, plenty of corner parks, excellent transportation, a well-respected public hospital, and plenty of shops to meet your daily needs.

HOUSING

The market has shifted considerably in recent years. Gone are the days of €100,000 one-bedrooms with parquet floors and fireplaces. Bargains can still be had, but you have to really dig for them. With a modest budget of €200,000, you might be lucky enough to score a pretty studio overlooking a quiet courtyard near the Lédru-Rollin Métro and its ideal access to the giant Monoprix, daily markets, and *épiceries*. Double

THE GOLDEN TRIANGLE

In the 2006 film, *Avenue Montaigne*, a neurotic cast of characters try to pull their fraying lives together on the beautifully cinematic 8th arrondissement street of the same name. The backdrop, consisting of theaters, haute couture boutiques, and elite hotels, becomes an imposing character in its own right. When you visit the Golden Triangle, you'll feel it: A quiet, moneyed hush that floats overhead, which, depending on how you approach it, can feel cozy and cocooning or a tad oppressive. The apartments here are a mix of old and new, but always well-manicured and scrubbed to the point of sparkling. For families with kids who attend the local Montessori school or parents who work at La Défense, this neighborhood makes a lot of sense.

HOUSING

That man walking down avenue Montaigne that looks like film director Roman Polanski? That is Roman Polanski. He and his wife, the French actress Emmanuelle Seigner, live here, as do many famous athletes, politicians, and artists. The Golden Triangle attracts bourgeois types with lots of money who are willing to pay for a prestigious address and access to high-society privileges that include walking distance to exclusive restaurants, theater, and shopping. You can find *maisons particulières* here, but apartment living is the norm. The average real estate price per square meter here is double the Paris average, with million-euro apartments selling every week. Expect to shell out €800,000 for a one-bedroom apartment in a 1930s building one block from the Champs-Élysées. Other options include a third-floor apartment in a Haussmannian building on rue Francois 1er. Inside, you'll find marble staircases and a doorman. The price for 90 square meters of living space: €1,430,000, which includes a fabulous remodeled kitchen. Renters have it a bit easier, but not much. A furnished one-bedroom in a 1930s building with 60 square meters of space costs €3,200 per month, and includes an enormous clawfoot bathtub—a true rarity in Paris.

SCHOOLS AND COMMUNITY CENTERS

Anglophone expats often enroll their children in the local bilingual Montessori school (65, quai d'Orsay). Other private schools include the Catholic primary school Saint-Pierre de Chaillot (10, rue Christoph Colomb), where the four-course lunch options for five-year-olds include roast beef with mushroom sauce and seafood paella. (The third course is always, of course, a cheese plate.)

The Petit Palais and the Grand Palais (belle époque landmarks) host not only revolving art exhibits and swanky society events, but do triple duty as atelier spaces for children on Wednesdays and Saturdays. The *mairie* of the 8th arrondissement (3, rue de Lisbonne, www.mairie08.paris.fr) can point you toward these and other activities for your children. The Maison des Associations du 8ème (23, rue Vernet) can hook you up with a broad range of activities that meet your budget, interests, and schedule.

SHOPPING

Shopping is one of this area's big draws. Whether you're looking for a luxury car on the Champs-Elysées or a luxury handbag (hello, Louis Vuitton!), your big-ticket item is right outside your door in le Triangle d'Or. Though grocery stores exist in this area, most savvy residents make good use of the markets' free delivery service.

Several celebrity dining establishments have their homes here, including Alain Ducasse's three-star Michelin-rated restaurant at the Plaza Athénée. If you can afford to drop a grand on dinner, this might be your local dining spot. More down-to-earth options include a mix of Lebanese restaurants, juice bars, and sushi spots on rue Marbeuf, and traditional French brasseries and cafés, including le Bar des Théâtres (44, rue Jean Goujon, www.bardestheatres.fr).

The Bastille neighborhood is where you'll find the highest concentration of Parisian hipsters.

your budget to make a spacious 19th-century one-bedroom on rue Paul Bert, with its chic restaurants and pleasant neighborhood park, your east Paris home. For renters, the possibilities vary depending on whether you've got the goods (aka a fat dossier full of paperwork) to arrange your rental through a local real estate agent or not. If you're looking at the latter situation, you'll pay a premium for apartments on Craigslist and agencies like Halldis (www.halldis.com), which market specifically to foreigners who aren't eligible for the "locals" deals. For a one-bedroom flat, you should clear at least €1,200 from your monthly budget to direct toward housing costs. The 12th arrondissement, which borders on the Bastille and encompasses the pleasant area around the Marché d'Aligre, ensures that 20 percent of its available housing is subsidized, so if you have your heart set on this area but can't afford the going rates, check in with the *mairie* to see what your options are.

DAILY LIFE
Schools and Community Centers
The city has risen up to meet the influx of families arriving in the Bastille area, building new public schools for all age levels. If you have children and want to enroll them in a public school, visit the local *mairie* (in the 11th or 12th, depending on which part of the Bastille you've settled in) to learn when the next enrollment period begins and what all of your options are.

For university-level students, the options are limited but do include a couple of private institutions, one of which is IFOPI, otherwise known as the École Supérieure

Technique Privée (21, bvd Richard-Lenoir, www.FEDE.org) offering two-year degrees in computer science, business management, and related subjects.

Depending on which side of the Bastille you settle in, you could have access to five or six neighborhood *centres d'animation* bursting with amenities for young and old. In the 12th, the Centre d'Animation Maurice Ravel (www.animravel.fr) offers courses in Arabic, capoeira, and guitar (among others) for kids, and adults can take French classes, piano, and tai chi. Over in the 11th, the Piscine de la Cours de Lions (9, rue Alphonse Baudin) offers swimming lessons for adults and children, and is accessible to people with restricted mobility.

At the annual springtime event called Fête des Voisins, neighbors meet up at the Jardin Nomade (48, rue Trousseau) to share food made from the on-site community garden. This is an ideal opportunity for Bastille-area newcomers to meet people from the neighborhood and get acquainted with a pleasant Parisian tradition.

Shopping

One of the Bastille neighborhood's greatest draws is its outdoor markets. The Thursday and Sunday Marché de la Bastille on boulevard Richard-Lenoir is one of the city's biggest and most boisterous—which is code for "fun." In addition to more than 100 fruit and vegetable vendors, you'll also find prepared foods ranging from croissants to paella. On Saturday, the same plein air venue morphs into an art-and-clothing market, featuring the wares of local craftspeople.

Moving south and west across rue du Faubourg Saint-Antoine, you'll eventually bump into the popular Marché d'Aligre, where locals have been shopping for food and other treasures for more than a century. Tuesday-Sunday the market offers an

Discovering your local outdoor market is a rite of passage for every new Parisian.

© AURELIA D'ANDREA

authentic food-shopping experience with a side of *marché aux puces* (which is another way of saying there's a fabulous little flea market smack in the middle of the square).

Leisure

The Bastille area's open spaces aren't all built the same. There are the usual corner squares with their *potagers* (kitchen gardens) and kids' play equipment, and there are also open plazas like the one on boulevard Richard-Lenoir that stretches from the Bastille all the up to avenue Voltaire and beyond. Some of these open spaces have been overrun with boozed-up men drinking the hard stuff out of cans, but there are also fountains and recreation areas and room for skateboarding, skipping rope, or even a game of badminton. Visit the Square de l'Impasse des Jardiniers if you want to sample a bit of everything: ping pong, manicured gardens, and free Wi-Fi.

Getting Around

Access is one of the Bastille's main selling points. The Bastille Métro station is served by three lines, including Line 1 with direct access all the way to La Défense. If you have to make the daily commute to one of Paris's main business zones (including the Champs-Élysées), it's easy to do from here. Velib' is a popular form of local transport, and the neighborhood is well served with the public bicycling kiosks on nearly every block.

Bercy

Follow the Seine upstream toward the eastern périphérique, and there, between the imposing clock tower of the Gare de Lyon and the cluster of modern high-rise office complexes, sits one of the city's most interesting neighborhoods. The 12th arrondissement lies at an important crossroads, hemmed in on one side by a railroad superhighway and by the Seine on the other and within spitting distance of the A4 motorway, which continues all the way to the German border in eastern France. It may be far from central Paris, but Bercy is well connected by local transport links, and within walking distance of the Bois de Vincennes and Chinatown.

The Bercy neighborhood has undergone a major facelift in recent years, morphing from an industrial wasteland to a spic-and-span district gleaming with modernity and packed with amenities galore. But it isn't just the leisure opportunities that attract people to Bercy; the area is also an important business and economic zone with banking and telecommunications headquarters for several well-known institutions. For would-be Parisians who prefer modernity over Old-World charm, and those who demand easy access to transportation, Bercy holds a lot of appeal.

HOUSING

Bercy's housing options are limited mostly to new construction, much of it eco-friendly and built with big budgets in mind. Prices are higher here because of its proximity to transport, services, and those towering office buildings that shade the streets below. Renters fare better here than buyers; it's possible to find a two-bedroom flat for less than €1,500 per month, but you'll have a hard time finding a two-bedroom apartment for

© AURELIA D'ANDREA

The Bois de Vincennes is one of the great
pleasures of Paris.

sale that rings in at less than €500,000.
A local real-estate agency with English-
speaking staff is FAI Immobilier (www.
fai-immo.com). Schedule a rendezvous
with a helpful realtor who can point you
toward rentals and for-sale spaces in your
price range, from affordable(ish) to lux-
ury-level properties.

DAILY LIFE
Schools and Community Centers

Bercy has its own primary and secondary schools for children, and in 2018, it
will also have a college campus for kids
in an older age bracket. The Sorbonne
Nouvelle Paris 3 campus will move here
from its current location in the Quartier
Latin after its completion (construction
commences in 2015), which will inject
another dose of youth culture into this
already young and vibrant part of Paris.

Shopping

Locals shop for produce at the small Wednesday afternoon/Sunday morning marché
on Place Lachambeaudie, and have come to depend on the local Monoprix (60-62,
cour Saint-Emilion) for everything from toilet paper to cat food. Smaller *épiceries* fill
the fresh vegetable and wine gap for after-hours shopping. Tip: Do like your neighbors
and get to know the markets in adjacent quartiers, including Picpus and Nation, both
of which are in the 12th just north of Bercy.

Leisure

This is a work-hard, play-hard community, and the preferred play area among locals
is, without question, Parc de Bercy. This 14-hectare urban green-zone was built on
the plot of earth that once housed the world's largest wine-trading arena. In the 19th
century, before it became incorporated into the city of Paris, Bercy was a tax-free haven
packed with taverns where people could drink on the cheap after a long work week.
Today, locals still enjoy their tipple, but Bercy is better known for its healthy recreation
opportunities than anything else (though the city has planted a small vineyard here in
memory of the area's wine-soaked past).

Inside the park is a little something for everyone. The sheltered skateboard park attracts daredevil teens on bikes and boards, and the open walking paths lure dog walkers
and small children on *trotinettes* (kick scooters). Green spaces have long been attractive to picnickers and wine enthusiasts all too happy to keep Bercy's drinking culture
alive. Nearby Bercy Village offers shopping and dining opportunities that border on
the Disneylandesque with their English-style pubs and Tex-Mex restaurants targeting

an English-speaking crowd, but don't let that lack of authentic vintage appeal keep you from exploring and enjoying. A giant UGC cinema offers new-release films and discount ticket prices that lure university students from the college campuses just across the Seine in the 13th.

Directly across the Seine sits one of Paris's most revered recreation spots: the Piscine Josephine Baker on quai François Mauriac. This outdoor pool built right alongside the Seine is one of the most picturesque places to get your swim on in the city of Light, and to get your tan on while you're at it. Inside is a sauna and hammam, and the price is right at just €3 for access to the pool, or €10 for the full shebang.

The Bercy stadium hosts concerts (Beyoncé and Justin Timberlake both played here recently) and sporting events including a recent international ping-pong championship competition, and the Cinémathèque draws movie-lovers from all over France to its film-oriented exhibitions and themed events.

Getting Around
Both the Gare de Lyon and Gare d'Austerlitz are here, as is the speedy Métro Line 14.

Belleville

Just north and slightly west of the Bastille, wedged between Père-Lachaise Cemetery and Parc des Buttes-Chaumont, you'll find the Belleville. If you listen carefully in the 20th arrondissement, you can practically hear the voice of famous resident Edith Piaf echoing through the streets. Bounded by boulevard de Belleville, rue de Belleville, rue de Menilmontant, and the inner ring road of boulevard Mortier, this hilly rectangle offers an interesting landscape punctuated by Chinese markets, funky thrift stores, and mom-and-pop stores of every stripe. At the neighborhood's core is the Parc de Belleville, home to one of Paris's few wine-producing vineyards. Wander the crooked streets around this public green space, and you might think you somehow ended up in the country. It's these quiet corners of the neighborhood that give it a unique appeal.

Belleville is also home to one of Paris's Chinatown districts and is an interesting place to spend an afternoon while you debate its livability factor. This neighborhood hasn't gentrified, and for some people, that's a good thing. For others, the *populaire* masses can just be overwhelming. If you like Asian food, mingling with people from Arab-speaking countries, and don't mind a hilly landscape, you'll appreciate what Belleville has to offer.

This part of Paris has a couple of tourist attractions at its core, including the celebrated Père-Lachaise Cemetery, where so many revered French and international icons are buried, including Edith Piaf, who was born and raised in this neighborhood. (A small, private museum created in her honor is open to the public by appointment. Call 01/43 55 52 72 to schedule a visit.) Every day, swarms of people from around the globe make the pilgrimage to the pretty, park-like graveyard to plant kisses on the tomb of Oscar Wilde, leave bouquets for married-and-buried-together couple Yves Montand and Simone Signoret, and bottles of booze for Jim Morrison. Locals use the cemetery as a park of sorts, and you might like to too, if you move here.

Belleville is also a haven for artists, and creative expression is part of the visual landscape.

© AURELIA D'ANDREA

Belleville is home to affordable rents and urban ambiance.

Take a walk down nearly any Belleville street to see interesting graffiti, murals, and colorful art installations that add a dash of vibrancy to the neighborhood.

HOUSING

Belleville offers lower-than-average housing costs. The average price per square meter is €6,500 for buyers, with prices creeping higher once you cross boulevard de Belleville south toward Bastille and République. Seloger.com is a good starting place on your housing quest in Belleville. Recent searches pulled up such diverse offerings as a 50-square-meter modern-built one-bedroom with a huge balcony and south-facing views for €375,000, and a three-bedroom unit in a 1960s apartment complex on rue de Belleville for €475,000. Renters can expect to pay similar prices to those in La Villette (about €24 per square meter).

DAILY LIFE

Belleville brims with young residents, who flock here for the affordable rents and art-splashed urban ambiance. Local government and nonprofit organizations have risen up to meet this population's needs. One cultural hotspot beloved by Parisians from every corner of the city is La Bellevilloise (www.labellevilloise.com). Founded in 1877, this multi-purpose event space was created with the idea that people from every socioeconomic level should have access to the arts. In that spirit, La Bellevilloise hosts concerts, Sunday brunch events at the on-site café, art exhibitions, and interesting conferences and multi-day conventions. An upcoming event dedicated to the theme of *écologie* will give participants the chance to meet regional Green Party elected officials and candidates, and learn what steps the local government is taking to make Belleville greener. La Bellevilloise also hosts a weekly organic market and CSA-type (Community Supported Agriculture) system called AMAP (Association pour le Maintien d'une Agriculture Paysanne) that allows consumers to buy locally grown organic vegetables directly from the farmers. To learn more about the AMAP movement in Belleville, visit www.amap-idf.org.

An online magazine called *Belleville Village* (www.belleville-village.com) will keep you up-to-date on all the events happening in the area, and covers events as varied as yoga classes and pledge drives for local nonprofits to addresses for all the local schools and resources for job-seekers.

Schools and Community Centers

Nearly a dozen public and private *maternelles* and *élémentaires* serve the youngest student sets, while two *collèges* educate the middle school community. Belleville is home to Lycée Étienne Dolet (7-9, rue d'Eupatoria, www.ac-paris.fr), a vocational school for teens that offers courses in a variety of disciplines. Among its nearby academic institutions is the École Nationale Supérieure d'Architecture (60, bld de la Villette, www.paris-belleville.archi.fr), a respected school of architecture where up-and-coming Gustave Eiffels and Le Corbusiers graduate into polished professionals.

Shopping

Belleville's primary commercial activity is clustered on boulevard de Belleville and rue de Belleville, which run perpendicular to each other, but share a similar shopping experience: Asian grocery stores and boutiques chock-a-block with trendy, affordable clothing and shoes imported from China. In between are the standard amenities, such as small grocery stores, pharmacies, natural-food markets, and cafés galore.

Because it's off the beaten tourist path, Belleville is a good place to experience authentic Paris with an Asian flair. The Marché Belleville (Tuesday and Friday) is a popular neighborhood fixture, and the best local spot to stock up on olives.

Leisure

The lovely Parc de Belleville, whose claim to fame is that it's the highest park in Paris, is home to one of Paris's few vineyards. The residential area around the park is a fascinating blend of private houses and public apartment complexes, and a fun place to explore on foot as you get acquainted with northern Paris. A free on-site museum inside the park called the Maison de l'Air (47, rue des Couronnes) offers an all-ages education on the subject of pollution and ecology and is definitely worth the price of admission.

Getting Around

Métro Lines 2 and 11 intersect at the Belleville station, but you needn't limit yourself to underground travel to get to this Paris neighborhood. Bus line 26 offers another option, but savvy commuters know that Velib' is the best choice here, thanks both to the number of bike-rental stations and the many separate bike lanes. The nearest Grand Ligne station is Gare du Nord, easily accessible on Métro Line 2. While many Bellevilloises choose car ownership, the steep hills can make parking a challenge for less experienced drivers.

PRIME LIVING LOCATIONS

NORTHERN RIVE DROITE

Try raising the Rive-Gauche-versus-Rive-Droite topic at your next dinner party and listen as the vociferous arguments unfurl. "We've got the Moulin Rouge, Sacré-Coeur, and a dynamic arts culture" might say denizens of the Northern Rive Droite. And they'd be right. The arrondissements to the far north of the Seine are Paris's new frontier, where classic Paris and its beloved landmarks meet the 21st century. Vegetarian restaurants—once considered a quirky passing trend—flourish in the north in a way you never see on the south side of the river, and art openings known as *vernissages* are a testament to the youth-driven creative scene that continues to expand throughout the more affordable areas of the 18th, 19th, and 20th arrondissements. The once seedy Pigalle neighborhood at the foot of Montmartre has recently morphed into a mecca for trendy tiki bars and American-owned burger joints, and some might say the Canal Saint-Martin area has already reached its hipster peak (though the continued colonization by Australian-owned coffee bars selling filtered cups of Joe would suggest otherwise), and that its once-affordable live-work spaces are now the exclusive domain of moneyed *bobos*.

Whatever the current thinking on the northern neighborhoods is, there's no denying that there is an evolution taking place, and—for better or worse—a gentrification process that's shifting the North- and West-African neighborhoods that have existed

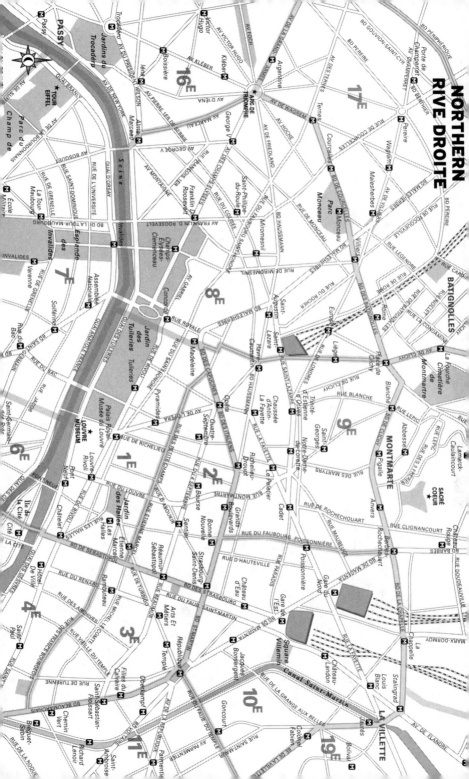

here for decades over to make room for artists, young families, and immigrants from other parts of the world.

THE LAY OF THE LAND

In mid-2013, after more than a year of reconstructive work, Paris unveiled its latest public beautification project—Place de la République. Once a messy, traffic-clogged artery, République (as it's called locally) has morphed into an all-ages magnet for outdoor fun, replete with cafés, fountains, and room to dance (and skate, and stroll, and cycle). This inviting space has transformed into a more welcoming gateway to the evolving neighborhoods of northern Paris, including Belleville, Montmartre, La Villette, and even Batignolles.

What becomes immediately evident to Paris newcomers (but is less clear to tourists) is that Paris is not an enormous city; reaching the Northern Rive Droite arrondissements is straightforward and relatively quick, especially if you skip the car and opt for the Métro. From the heart of the Marais (Métro stop: Hôtel de Ville) to the thick of Montmartre (Métro stop: Abbesses) is a mere 20-minute trip. Short commute times are just one of the many appealing reasons newcomers are drawn to the north side. This is also a multicultural melting pot and filled with good food.

On the downside, northern Paris can at times feel extremely "urban." Traffic jams, noise, and pollution can be overwhelming on the worst days. But on the best days, the beauty of the landscape and the stories it tells make living here worth it.

The Northern Rive Droite has industrial roots. Throughout the 19th century, factories mushroomed along the banks of the Canal Saint-Martin—built at the behest of Napoléon I—and further up on the Canal de l'Ourcq. The remnants of many of these structures are still visible today, and sometimes still function as workplaces. More often than not, however, these old factories and workshops have been transformed into new

© AURELIA D'ANDREA

Old factories along the Canal de l'Ourcq are being transformed into new creative and commercial spaces.

enterprises, including movie theaters, night clubs, and yes, even housing. Though it's difficult to generalize, it wouldn't be too big of a stretch to say that these unique live-work spaces attract similarly unique genre of Parisian; risk-takers, perhaps—or at least those with open minds who are willing to see the potential that resides in the unconventional.

These new frontiers are goldmines of affordable housing, and bastions of quirky culture in a city that loves convention and conformity. If you're not afraid to tread new ground and appreciate diversity with a bit of urban grit, northern Paris will likely be a good fit for you.

16th Arrondissement

The only bad thing you'll ever hear about the 16th arrondissement is that it's "too nice." What does that mean? Well, the implication is that the streets are so tidy, the crime rates so low, and the parking so manageable that it borders on, well, boring. But if that is its only detriment, you'd have to call that a win for this upscale district on Paris's west end.

To reach the 16th, simply follow the Seine downstream until the Pont de l'Alma. On the left bank, you'll spot a familiar landmark—la Tour Eiffel—and to the right, the splashy Trocadéro esplanade. Getting here by boat is just one of the many ways you can reach the 16th, but most people choose the Métro, the bus, or, as is more common in this neck of the woods, a car. The 16th is roomy and expansive, and far enough from central Paris to allow you to exhale and leave the sound of honking horns and police sirens behind you.

© JOHNYPAN/DREAMSTIME.COM

The Trocadéro esplanade acts as a gateway to the 16th arrondissement.

EXPAT EXPERIENCE: LIVING IN THE 16TH

Name: Christopher Horton
Age: 36
Profession: Software developer

Where are you from originally?
Los Angeles, California.

When and why did you move to Paris?
I moved to Toulouse in September 2010. I wanted a change of scenery from living in the U.S. I enjoy living and traveling in Europe and so I wanted to make France my permanent base because of its amazing history, culture, landscape, and beautiful language. I consider France my home, thanks to the wonderful people I've met and the things I've learned.

In which arrondissement do you currently reside?
I live in the 16th.

How did you find your current home?
We found our apartment via the well-known site Particulier à Particulier (www.pap.fr). We tried www.Century21.fr, but the requirements for people just starting their jobs in the trial period were a bit much.

Are you a homeowner or do you rent?
I rent a large studio with my girlfriend.

What are some of the factors you considered before moving to this location?

Well, my girlfriend and I didn't have a lot of choices when we moved to this location. The owners were looking for a responsible couple and we fit the bill. Our strong references helped a great deal as well. The agencies that we visited required that we have a *garant* to ensure rent payments. We find that the cost of having an apartment is about what you would expect. The area is quite safe and getting into the center is relatively easy via the Métro or by walking. I can get to my job in about 20 minutes door to door.

Describe your quartier to someone who's never been there before.
We live in the lower part of the 16th near the Porte de Saint-Cloud Métro station. We feel that our quartier is extremely diverse. You will find people from all walks of life here thanks to various restaurants, a large and diverse street market, bars, bistros, le Parc des Princes, at least two schools, the wonderful Métro system, and la Seine. The proximity of la Tour Eiffel is also a nice aspect of living here. I personally thought I'd find the people rather reserved given the posh history of the 16th. Perhaps that is still the case in the northern parts of the 16th, like in Passy. We've only been living here since November 2013 so we guess we'll need a little time to really get to know some of the people in my neighborhood. As for the neighborhood's character and vibe,

The 16th arrondissement has long been a magnet for moneyed expatriates and wealthy French families attracted by the proximity to the forest, the deluxe housing opportunities, and the open, airy feel of the oh-so-safe streets. Diplomats and NGO leaders feel right at home here amid the many embassies and international think-tanks, and the dozen or so private schools makes it convenient for parents who want their kids educated nearby.

English is spoken more widely here than in most other arrondissements, which can make the transition process a lot smoother for native Anglophones. Enter the popular Starbucks on pretty shopping street rue de Passy, close your eyes, and tune in to the background noise. You could be in New York or San Francisco, based on the accents of the teenage clientele.

I guess it can be described as typically French. The large street market, which begins every morning until midday, allows everyone to get together and talk about everything under the sun. I think it really does help to allow people from all walks of life to connect.

Is the quality of life in your arrondissement what you expected it to be?

We didn't think much about moving to the 16th at first due to the average cost of rents here, along with the famous posh reputation of the people. Living here for just a few months changed our view for at least part of the 16th.

Describe your experience making friends with neighbors or others in your community.

We haven't really made any friends yet in our neighborhood. We've mostly been discovering Paris. There is so much to see and do here.

What do you like least about living where you live?

I find that l'Administration Français is still the main hindrance to any sort of progress. For example, simply changing the address on your identity card will take months via their registration system, a system put into place to make things *easier*. It shouldn't be that difficult. Administrative tasks seem to take more time here in Paris than in Toulouse. I guess that is due to the larger population.

What do you like most?

The transportation system, the supermarkets, and the many restaurants are really top notch.

PHOTO COURTESY OF CHRIS HORTON

Chris Horton loves his new digs in the 16th arrondissement.

The Trocadéro and La Muette neighborhoods are popular choices for expats, and are especially favored by single women who can afford the serenity and sense of security that the areas offer. The 16th is also a hospitable place for the senior set; expect to see lots of ladies in fur coats roaming the *rues,* shopping bags and fluffy dogs in tow. Mostly though, the 16th is known as a bourgeois family district, and it becomes clear after a few hours spent roaming the tidy neighborhoods that there are a lot of children here. If you want easy access to beautiful parks and gardens, great schools (many of them private), and room to park your his-and-hers Citroëns or your family-style French minivan, the 16th is a really good bet.

HOUSING

The 16th is Paris's largest arrondissement, and while it is well-served by public transportation, there aren't Métro stations on every other block the way there are in other parts of the city. The areas around the main transport hubs such as RER station Henri Martin and the busy Trocadéro center command higher real-estate prices in part because of their proximity to trains, buses, and taxi stands. If you're shopping for deals, you might want to choose a different arrondissement, or at least focus your search on the far southern fringes near the Métro Exelmans. Foncia Real Estate (www. fr.foncia.com) offers a broad selection of housing options, including a 44-square-meter Trocadéro studio built in 1930 going for €390,000 (it's on the ground floor, which might help explain its "cheap" price), and a 100-square-meter Passy area flat with ornate moldings and a decorative fireplace for €1.2 million.

Renting affords some slightly more accessible options. For €1,700, you could curl up every night in a Passy apartment and watch the Eiffel Tower lights twinkling right outside your living room window. Spending €3,000 per month will land you a two-bedroom apartment in a 1930s Trocadéro unit equipped with a dishwasher (*mon dieu!*) and private deck. Paris Stay (www.paristay.com) offers a slew of options and takes the fuss out of the rental process—for a price.

DAILY LIFE
Schools and Community Centers

The *mairie* of the 16th (71, avenue Henri Martin, www.mairie16.paris.fr) offers a free booklet listing all of the neighborhood associations, making it easier for newcomers of all ages to get involved in civic life. Seniors will find plenty to keep them busy here, but because of the family-friendly nature of the area, activities geared toward children dominate. The 20-page *Guide Jeunes 16ème* lists every public and private school in the area, job-search resources, and student-housing contacts. The 16th might very well be the only arrondissement where private schools outnumber public institutions; for every public *collège,* there are two private schools to choose from. Among them is the International School of Paris (www.isparis.edu), which counts Princess Caroline of Monaco's son, Andrea, as one if its alumni. A popular choice among expats with younger children is l'École Bilingue les Moineaux (www.ecolebilinguelesmoineaux. com), a bilingual elementary school that accepts children as young as two years old.

The little-known Mona Bismarck American Center for the Arts (34, avenue de New York, www.monabismarck.org) was founded in 2011 and is dedicated to expanding the American art influence in Parisian circles. Volunteering at this museum and education institution is one creative way to make contacts within the formidable expat American community in west Paris.

Shopping

Given the upper-crust reputation of this arrondissement, one might assume that the average denizen shops exclusively at the designer boutiques along rue du Faubourg Saint-Honoré and avenue Montaigne. While the odds are high that they head there to load up on chic Chanel and Louboutin, everyday needs for food, drink, and other pedestrian necessities are easily met in every 16th quartier. Beyond the neighborhood *fromageries, cavistes,* and *boulangeries,* the 16th is home to several popular commercial zones, including avenue Victor Hugo, rue de la Pompe, and rue de Passy. Passy Plaza (53, rue de Passy) has the look and feel of a typical American shopping mall, complete with Starbucks and Gap. For a more "French" experience, wander the streets around the mall to discover the *épiceries,* boutiques, and mom-and-pop shops give the neighborhood its west-side Parisian flair.

Leisure

The Bois de Boulogne is often referred to as Paris's left lung. (The Bois de Vincennes is its right.) This expansive forest clings to the west side of the 16th arrondissement and gives those who live at its borders the sense that they can easily commune with nature. In this enormous green space that's more than double the size of New York's Central Park, everyone has the right to picnic, jog, bicycle, or row a boat across one of its two lakes. Deeper inside the park sits the popular Jardin d'Acclimation. This 150-year-old children's amusement park was modeled after Victorian-era English parks, and has welcomed such dignitaries as Malia and Sasha Obama, who visited not long after their father was first elected president of the United States. The park swarms with designer-coat-clad children and their nannies every day of the week (though traffic increases significantly on Wednesdays), and costs €3 to enter.

Being the cultured and refined arrondissement that it is, the 16th is *plein de* (full of) museums to fit every interest, from Asian art and architecture to fashion.

Getting Around

Car enthusiasts, gather round. Here's a news flash with your personal interests in mind: The 16th arrondissement is practically parking paradise. In addition to street parking, you'll be happy to know there are several secure short- and long-term parking garages scattered throughout the district. What's more, if you register with the city and apply for a parking permit, you'll be eligible for a discount of up to 40 percent off the proletariat price for both garage *and* street parking. For more information, visit the city of Paris website (www.paris.fr) and enter "*stationnement*" into the keyword box.

For those who prefer to leave the driving to others, there are myriad transportation possibilities. The 16th is served by Métro lines 6, 9, and 10, and by the RER line C. Between these four options, you'll be able to reach most of the arrondissement's neighborhoods with a minimum of walking. The RER is a comfortable option, with stops at the sleepy Henri Martin station and the avenue du President Kennedy station, just before the train crosses the bridge over to Rive Gauche. Another speedy option is the PC1, which plies the inner ring road from Porte de Champerret all the way down to the deep southwest of Paris, stopping at rue de Longchamp, Porte de la Muette, and Porte de Saint-Cloud along the way.

Batignolles

In the 17th arrondissement—just north of the Saint-Lazare railway station and its trains choo-chooing off to points westward—rests the once-sleepy Batignolles neighborhood. Until the late-19th century, the dynamic quartier sat just beyond the Parisian *périphérique*. It wasn't incorporated into the city until 1860, but even then, it was still thought of as the hinterlands of the French capital. Today, the neighborhood is considered at once livable, chic, and laced with an edgy vibrancy. Behind the office of the *mairie*, the tidy streets are filling up with new art galleries and interesting boutiques. Rue de Batignolles has a small-town feel to it, with *boulangeries*, antiques shops, and hardware stores tucked amid the banks and little groceries. A few blocks north, on avenue de Clichy, traffic roars past a dozen or so funky Chinese-owned clothing stores selling trendy designer knockoffs at ridiculously low prices. Two parks give added value to the neighborhood, including the classic Square des Batignolles and the newer Parc Martin Luther King, each with their own children's play areas, water gardens, and no-dogs-allowed policies.

HOUSING

Housing options in Batignolles are a mixed bag. On the south side of avenue de Clichy, real estate prices are steadily increasing, whereas on the north side, they remain some of the lowest in the city. This is all about to change with the completion of the Clichy-Batignolles redevelopment project. Along with 3,400 new apartments—500 units of which are reserved specifically for students—this massive urban overhaul will inject a new vitality into a once-depressed area, and make it more inviting to families of all income levels.

In 2014, it's still possible to find two-bedroom apartments for sale for less than €300,000, but that's shifting. Safety isn't a major concern here, but the construction of the new Palais de Justice at Porte de Clichy will bring an added sense of security to the neighborhood that won't help but to increase the value of local real estate. On the north side of avenue de Clichy, a one-bedroom apartment with a balcony and remodeled interior sells for €220,000. There's a *boulangerie* downstairs and an elementary school across the street, and the nearest bus stop is a half-block away. Renters might be interested in a bright and roomy two-bedroom apartment across the street from Parc Martin Luther King currently on the market for €1,500 per month. Browse the window displays at the many local real estate offices to get a good idea of current availability and pricing in this changing neighborhood.

DAILY LIFE
Schools and Community Centers

Elementary and middle schools are bountiful in the Batignolles area, and a few blocks north, on boulevard Bessières, you'll find Lycée-Collège Honoré de Balzac (118, bvd Bessières, www.ac-paris.fr) an enormous international middle/high school that welcomes students from all around the globe. The office of the *mairie* offers a free booklet with detailed information on this school and all the other Batignolles-area educational institutions.

One of the best neighborhood resources is the local library. Tucked away on the third

© WITTAYAMU/123RF

Gare Saint-Lazare

floor of the *mairie*'s headquarters, this wonderful space overlooking a café-lined square offers author readings, children's workshops, and, of course, books. At the doorway is a rack loaded with flyers for neighborhood cultural events, from theater and concerts to dance performances. If you see a flyer here for the association AGF 17 (www.agf17. fr), pick one up. If you don't see one there, visit the nonprofit organization's website to learn about the low-cost French immersion courses for adults they offer.

Shopping

The local commercial hotspot is the covered market a block away from the Brochant Métro stop. Inside, vegetable vendors, butchers, and cheesemongers hock their wares, and several independent restaurants vie for hungry visitors' business. There's also a G20 supermarket for everyday necessities like laundry soap and coffee filters. Just outside the market on rue des Moines, shoppers will find bookstores, natural-foods markets, pharmacies, and plenty of *cavistes* to keep that irrepressible thirst for a fine Bordeaux at bay. Batignolles's small-village atmosphere sucks you in and makes you want to stay, to which, judging by the families with small children in tow, many have succumbed.

Leisure

The two main parks in this neighborhood, Square des Batignolles and Parc Martin Luther King, are two of its biggest draws. They are extremely different in terms of aesthetics and amenities; the old-school Square des Batignolles has ducks bobbing in an artificial stream, old men playing *pétanque* out in the park's expansive *boulodrome*, and a vintage carrousel to amuse the little ones. Down the road, Parc Martin Luther King offers a skateboard ramp, community garden, well-groomed areas for lounging on the grass, and an endless parade of joggers who come here to work off all those delicious baguettes they've been indulging in.

The nearest recreation center sits a few blocks north on rue de la Jonquière, where two swimming pools lure locals all year round for aqua gym and children's swimming lessons. The price of a three-month membership at Piscine Bernard Lafay is €37. Around the corner at the *Centre Sportif Fragonard*, kids and adults can take fencing lessons or study martial arts.

Getting Around

Most of Batignolles is within a 15-minute walk of Gare Saint-Lazare. From the station, you can board trains for Normandy (hello, Monet's garden!) or for suburbs within the Petite Couronne and the Grande Couronne, including Maisons-Laffitte. Métro line 2 is a popular public transport option, with stops at both Rome and Place de Clichy. But it's the dedicated bike lanes and dozen or so Velib' stations that make the neighborhood popular with cyclists and fresh-air enthusiasts. And because this district is small, it's possible to *faire les courses* (run errands) without any other transport other than your own two legs. This is a pedestrian-friendly neighborhood—make the most of it!

Montmartre

Some of the earliest photographs of the 18th arrondissement depict a hilly, green landscape punctuated by windmills, horses, and tiny wooden houses. In some ways, not much has changed; a few vintage windmills still stand, police on horseback patrol the winding cobblestone streets, and the peak that bears the famous Sacre Coeur basilica is indeed a verdant spot. Gone, however, are the little wood cabins, replaced by blond-stone apartment buildings, and any empty spaces you happen upon are certainly brimming with tourists. Bounded on the west side by the cemetery de Montmartre, tree-lined rue Coulaincourt to the north, rapidly gentrifying rue de Clignancourt to the east, and boulevards de Clichy and de Rochechouart to the south, Montmartre is near enough to feel thoroughly connected to Paris, yet it retains an old-timey, village-like atmosphere that tourists and locals alike find so perpetually alluring.

In many ways, Montmartre feels like the unofficial amusement park of the city of Paris. This is especially true at the top of the hill, around the picturesque place du Tertre, where portrait-painters and roaming accordionists compete for your attention before a backdrop of packed sidewalk cafés. The big white basilica and its egg-shaped domes standing sentinel over the city welcome worshippers every day, but even this house of God has taken on a faintly Disneyland-ish air, with a constant line of camera-wielding men, women, and children moving in and out of its front doors. This is "real" Montmartre, but it gets even more real the further down the hill and away from the trinket shops and jaw-dropping views you venture.

Montmartre's homiest, most village-like neighborhood is known as Abbesses ("ah-BESS"). The Square des Abbesses for which it is named is hemmed with cafés and buzzes with life all year long. The art nouveau Métro station that sits in the middle of it all is one of the most photographed in the city, and with good reason: It's delightful to look at. The square is also a fine place to wander and soak in the Old World

© AURELIA D'ANDREA

The views from atop Montmartre are legendary.

ambiance, especially during the autumn months when chestnut vendors fill the square and the smell of burnt praline perfumes the air.

The rue des Abbesses stretches from the picturesque square nearly all the way to the Montmartre cemetery on rue Caulaincourt. In between are all the amenities you want or need in a place you call home: *boulangeries*, vegetable stands, Italian delicatessens, ice-cream shops, and cafés in droves. Getting to know the local vendors is one way to get a sense of the neighborhood and whether you'll fit in. Be bold, and ask shopkeepers for ideas and recommendations to help you better understand the hood.

HOUSING

Montmartre's rough edges have been in a constant smoothing-out state since *bobos* "discovered" it a couple of decades ago, and it's those French yuppies you have to thank for making the streets safer—and for raising the cost of living here. The housing market is nowhere near as out-of-reach for average Joes and Josephines as, say, the Golden Triangle, but keeping expectations realistic will help you avoid disappointment when you launch your house-hunt. The most expensive areas in Montmartre sit around rue Lepic and avenue Junot, where it's a bit quieter and more residential in feel. If you want to rent an apartment here, consider setting aside about €2,000 for a 60-square-meter apartment dripping with 19th-century charm. On the more economical end of the spectrum, you could land yourself an apartment of similar size and amenities in the more *populaire* Marcadet-Poissonnières quarter for about half the price. If you're really lucky, you might find a newly remodeled space somewhere in between with its own private courtyard where Fifi or Fido (or you and your significant other) can lounge in the sun on warm summer days. The real estate website Nestoria (www.nestoria.fr)

has dozens of listings in all areas of Montmartre, but you'll need to have a high-level dossier with all the paperwork in order to grab the best deals. Perfectly Paris (www. perfectlyparis.com) is a great option for renters looking for their ideal Montmartre digs. The English-speaking staff can help you find something in your budget and without the over-the-top challenges you often encounter with French agencies.

For folks looking to buy, expect to fork over between €8,000 and €9,000 per square meter. Big budgets can translate into big bargains here, meaning a five-bedroom, 125-square-meter apartment that would set you back a couple of million in a more exclusive arrondissement can be had in Montmartre for €800,000, with a parking spot included in the price. Check www.pap.fr to find great deals offered directly from the sellers to would-be buyers.

DAILY LIFE
Schools and Community Centers

There are no university campuses in this corner of the city, but plenty of opportunities exist for younger students. Besides the standard public *maternelles* and *écoles primaires*, there are private Catholic schools including Saint-Jean de Montmartre (www. enseignement-prive.fr), where tuition runs about €1,000 per year. This same parochial school system includes a vocational high school that prepares its students for post-grad working life (www.lycee-stjeandemontmartre.com) in professional kitchens, sales careers, and health-related fields.

Shopping

People come from all over Paris to shop at the vintage stores here (Chine Machine on rue des Martyrs is a known favorite), and to browse the diverse, well-appointed boutiques. Australian skincare company Aesop has one of its sleek shops on rue des Abbesses, as does upscale French clothing line BA&SH. Yet it's the small, independent stores that are the big draw. Get to know the neighborhood by dedicating a day to roving the *rues* and participating in that Parisian pastime known as *faire du lèche-vitrine* (literally "window licking," known in less creative corners of the world as simply "window shopping").

For more than a century, professional and amateur tailors have flocked to the dozens of shops at the foot of Sacré-Coeur that sell fabrics, buttons, tassels, and other necessary goodies for producing something beautiful with a needle and thread. For a truly old-fashioned shopping experience, visit the Marché Saint-Pierre (2, rue Charles Nodier, www.marchesaintpierre.com). The archaic system of selecting and paying for your fabulous fabrics has to be experienced to be believed.

The area around Métro station Château Rouge has the feeling of an African bazaar. This is the place to bring your sense of adventure and allow yourself to be transported to Côte d'Ivoire or Mali for a moment. Plaintains, yams, cassava, and more exotic fufu and garry are just some of the edibles you'll discover here. For more familiar fare, head to one of the nearby outdoor markets. A local favorite is the Friday Marché d'Anvers (at Place d'Anvers) where you can fill your wicker basket with everything from organic fruit to *fruits de mer* (seafood).

EXPAT EXPERIENCE: LIVING IN MONTMARTRE

Name: Emily Dilling
Age: 31
Occupation: Founder, Paris Paysanne
Hometown: San Jose, California
Current City: Paris, 18th

Emily moved to Paris in 2005 and found her niche in the wonderful world of organic markets. Her popular website, Paris Paysanne (www.parispaysanne.com), has been guiding foodies to the freshest organic produce in the city and beyond since 2010. Besides being well acquainted with Parisian markets, Emily is also intimate with Paris's many urban green spaces, including her neighborhood community garden. Here, Emily shares one of her fun strategies to help green thumbs and others integrate into the local way of life.

How did you first discover your local community garden?

I was just strolling through my neighborhood one day and it caught my eye! I was living on the outskirts of Paris and noticed patches of green and bright flags on the abandoned platforms of the railroad tracks that encircle the city. I was immediately intrigued so I did some research to find out how to become a member.

Were there any challenges or unforeseen obstacles you experienced while becoming a member?

Unlike most things in France, the process of becoming a member was incredibly easy! I got in touch through the garden's Facebook page, paid a small fee online, and was sent my membership card and instructions on how to access the garden. I also put my name on a wait list to be able to garden, and a year later I had my own plot of land to cultivate.

How often do you visit, and what kinds of things do you do while there?

I visit frequently, at least once a week, in the spring and summer. I typically stop by to take care of my plants (usually tomatoes, kale, and courgette), picnic, or just find a sunny spot to read. In the winter I go less often, but do stop by to drop off compost or say hi to the chickens.

What kinds of people might you find in a community garden like yours?

All kinds! The members are of all different ages and backgrounds. It's a really refreshing mix of people, demonstrative of the diversity of Parisians today.

How, if at all, has joining a community garden helped you develop relationships within your neighborhood or made you feel more integrated?

Being part of the community garden makes me feel more involved in the effort to make Paris a greener and more enjoyable city.

Would you recommend joining a community garden to a newcomer in Paris?

Definitely! Even if you don't get a space to garden right away (there are often long wait lists), I would say it's an overwhelmingly positive experience and provides a unique way to enjoy the city and meet new people.

What are some other ways you have found to deepen your roots in your community or that have made you feel more "Parisian"?

I think deepening roots in a community happens when we work towards positive change in our environment that will have a lasting effect. Working with associations or individuals that are anchored in, and inspired by, Paris is a great way to learn about community organizing and making a home in France.

Leisure

© IVAN BASTIEN /123RF

a typical street in Montmartre

Montmartre's parks and squares tend to be heavily populated with tourists, but when they're roomy and attractive, like the Jardin des Arènes de Montmartre, you tend not to mind so much. The much-photographed park at the foot of the *mont* has been a fixture in many cinematic productions, including the classic 2001 film *Amélie*. Here you can catch the funicular to the top of the hill and picnic with a bottle of wine. When the crowds get thick, you have to get creative, and move on to places like the cemetery and the hilltop vineyard to get your nature fix. But this is Montmartre, so it's (really) all good.

Montmartre has a long history of attracting artists to its twisty cobblestone streets, Toulouse-Lautrec and Van Gogh among them. It is also the original home of the French can-can and cabaret scene, so it should come as no surprise that the Montmartre of today still serves as a haven for the artistic community and those who appreciate the arts. Nightlife-wise, in lower-Montmartre you can't really miss the saucy X-rated theaters nor the legendary Moulin Rouge (and crowds of snap-happy tourists outside), but it's the independent arts venues hidden in those tight Abbesses alleyways that offer the most authentic entertainment experiences in northern Paris. Theaters like Manufacture des Abbesses (www.manufacturedesabbesses.com) and the hyper-charming le Théâtre de l'Atelier (www.theatre-atelier.com) offer cutting-edge, independent, and sometimes off-beat entertainment that's usually worth the price of admission. It helps if you speak French, but if you don't, it can be a good introduction to the language of the arts.

Getting Around

Unlike other Parisian neighborhoods, Montmartre offers one extra-special form of transport: the *funiculaire*. Sometimes the prospect of walking up hundreds of vertiginous steps—even if they lead to breathtaking views over Paris—can wear you out before you even begin the ascent. From Square Louise Michel, the train takes a vertical, 90-second ride to the top of the hill, letting you save your breath for all the oohs and aahs you'll be making. If you want to make like a local, take the Métro line 12, which hits all of Montmartre's prime destinations, including hyper-trendy Pigalle, Porte de Clignancourt and its sprawling flea market, and Place des Abbesses, with its lovely, oft-photographed art nouveau Métro entrance.

A dedicated off-road bike lane on boulevard de Rochechouart gives cyclists an extra sense of security . . . which is often thwarted by pedestrians who prefer a promenade along the *piste cyclable* to the roomy sidewalk. Another possibility for getting around

Montmartre's twisty streets is the Montmartobus (www.ratp.fr), an electric minibus that stops at many popular sites and some not-so-popular ones too. It is used mostly by locals, and travels between Pigalle and the *mairie* of the 18th at Métro Jules Joffrin daily.

La Villette

A skip and a jump away from Montmartre is La Villette. The 19th arrondissement is a former factory zone that's been transformed into a hip, expansive neighborhood with a vast green oasis—the Parc de la Villette—at its core. To get here, follow the canal from Bastille by foot, boat, or bike until you reach the Place de Stalingrad and the Bassin de la Villette (or take Métro line 2, 5, or 7 to the Jaurès stop). If you get distracted along the way, that's understandable; the neighborhoods around La Villette are kind of exciting, including the hipster hood of Canal Saint-Martin (named for the waterway that leads you here) and dog-friendly Buttes Chaumont. Take time to appreciate the special beauty of the area and allow yourself to get lost. If you hit the *périphérique*, you know you've gone too far!

Like many other northern Paris neighborhoods, this one is culturally diverse; you'll find kebab stands next to natural food stores next to trendy canal-side bars, plus family- and dog-friendly public spaces that are almost nice enough to make you forget that you don't have a real backyard of your own. Until relatively recently, this neighborhood was a cultural dead-zone, but today, a thriving art and music scene attracts people from all over the Île-de-France region, who migrate here for cutting-edge theater and dance. When you throw in a bourgeoning café culture and oodles of affordable housing, you can see the allure. Watch out, Canal Saint-Martin, because La Villette is poised to steal your place in the hipster spotlight.

HOUSING

One of the reasons the community here is so dynamic is because the city of Paris has allocated a sizeable chunk of subsidized housing to students and artists. This population has injected a youthful vibrancy into the area, and definitely upped its cool quotient. Residence Quai de le Loire (www.ciup.fr/residence-quai-de-la-loire) is one of these subsidized-housing experiments that has worked really well. The international program allows people from all over the world to apply for a dwelling, and is a good option for Americans coming to Paris specifically for studies.

The usual housing options exist here, too, of course. Investing in real estate is a smart option for those who can afford it, because this area is only becoming more *bobo* and more connected in terms of amenities offered. There may not be a cool café on every corner yet, but there will be soon. The prices here are below the Parisian average, so you can expect to find properties in the €6,500-per-square-meter region. In simplified terms, that could look like a two-bedroom apartment in a modern (1980s) building a block away from the Crimée Métro station for just a bit more than €200,000, or an 18-square-meter studio overlooking a quiet courtyard for €130,000. To rent something here, it's helpful to have an agent to help you score a good deal. RV Immobilier (17 bis, avenue Jean Juarès, www.r-v.fr) has English-speaking staff who can help you navigate the process, but ground your expectations in reality. You'll pay around €24 per square meter to rent here, which could mean a bright studio with balcony and wood floors for €650 per month, or a roomy one-bedroom with a coveted gas stove (a rental rarity in Paris) for €1,000 per month.

DAILY LIFE
Schools and Community Centers

La Villette is loaded with green spaces and it's also packed with social amenities. Finding "your people" here is easy, with a little excursion to the *mairie* (which sits directly across the street from the gorgeous, historic Parc des Buttes-Chaumont). They can point you toward the nearest mosque or synagogue (the 19th is home to one of Paris's largest Orthodox Jewish communities and counts more than a dozen Jewish community centers), or tell you the dates of the next jazz festival, or even give you directions to the nearest kids' café serving vegetarian meals (Café Zoïd, www.cafezoide.asso.fr).

Everyone who lives in this neck of the 19th eventually discovers le Cent-Quatre (www.104.fr), which used to be the city morgue but now serves the community in a more lively way, with theater, alterative commerce opportunities (food trucks, cafés, a farmer's market, and thrift stores are housed inside the vast space). If you're interested in dance classes, this is your place. Come any day of the week to watch dozens of hip-hop dancers practicing their popping, locking, and other grooves in the indoor courtyard, and let them inspire you to flex your movement muscles, too.

La Villette is a family-friendly neighborhood, and where there are families, there are often children. The neighborhood boasts a dozen *écoles élémentaires* and *maternelles* to serve the wee ones' scholastic needs. Middle school students attend Collège Sonia Delaunay (14, rue Euryale Dehaynin), but high school students will need to venture to adjacent neighborhoods to expand their education.

Shopping

The main commercial districts in the La Villette neighborhood can be found on avenue Secrétan and avenue Jean Jaurès. The former boasts a Monoprix, several pharmacies, clothing stores, eyewear boutiques, and several fruit-and-veg markets brimming with colorful produce, no matter the season. The latter offers more of the same, only on a broader street with more sidewalk room for wheeling around your *chariot*.

On Thursday and Sunday mornings, locals in droves descend upon the Marché Joinville (1, rue de Joinville), a crowded, lively marketplace where it's easy to stretch your euro a long way. Another destination for maximizing your euro is at Emmaüs. This nonprofit thrift store chain, which benefits homeless and unemployed people throughout Europe, has its big warehouse here, where you can procure dishware, furniture, and vintage clothing on the cheap. It's also a great place to donate unwanted goods after a spring cleaning frenzy or before you ship off to your next destination.

Leisure

Besides the Parc de la Villette and its museums, exposition halls, and music venues, the canal itself is a big draw. Throughout the year, people flock to the banks of the old waterway to picnic, play *boules*, and attend cultural events. Paris Plages, the novel month-long summer festival that transforms parts of the Seine into a mini Riviera, has its second location along the Quai de la Seine, though you might also stumble upon a regional organic farmers' convention or a lively *vide-grenier* (community yard sale). Locals have made this attractive outdoor area an extension of their own homes, and a place where every member of the family—young, old, and four-footed alike—is welcomed.

Getting Around

To get to La Villette, you can take Métro line 2, which stops at Jaurès at the bassin de la Villette, the line 5 on the canal's right bank or the line 7 on the left bank. Other options include bus line 75, which runs between la Villette and Pont Neuf, with stops at Hôtel de Ville and République and the new(ish) Line 3 tramway that opened in 2012 and will soon circle the entire circumference of Paris. (The local transit authority is still working on the links between Porte de La Chapelle and Porte d'Asnières.) Another option is to board one of the Canauxrama (www.canauxrama.com) boats that ply the canal from the Bastille all the way to the bassin de la Villette. Bikes are yet another possibility, and a rather a good one when you consider that dedicated bike paths can you get you all the way here from several areas in the city, including the Bastille and Montmartre.

RIVE GAUCHE

Paris's Left Bank, known as Rive Gauche, staked its claim in the hearts and minds of expats more than a century ago, when creative types from America, Europe, and North Africa migrated here to explore and refine their crafts in a supportive, booze-fueled atmosphere. Hemingway, Baldwin, Stein, and Wilde need no further introduction; on the Left Bank, their spirits can still be felt in the very same Saint-Germain cafés where they and other Lost Generation legends scribbled their poems, laughed and fought, and likely drank too many *verres de vin rouge*.

Today, Rive Gauche doesn't exude the same artistic free-for-all of a century ago, but it is still a magnet for philosophers, thinkers, and provocateurs. This city's south side is home to the Sorbonne and UNESCO, the French National Assembly, and countless *café-philos* clubs that debate the hot topics of the day. It's also where many Parisian luminaries rest their heads at night, including former president Jacques Chirac, who is known to frequent a certain Saint-Germain bar where he can sip his rum-based elixir without being bothered by the public. More than anything, the Left Bank represents the intellectual spirit of yore. Bookstores and cinemas, lecture halls and think tanks are the motors propelling Rive Gauche into the 21st century, and a big part of the mystique that continues to draw newcomers into the south-of-the-Seine fold.

Left Bank neighborhoods can and do vary greatly in terms of the energy they emit.

© SOPHIA PAGAN/WWW.SOPHIAPAGAN.COM

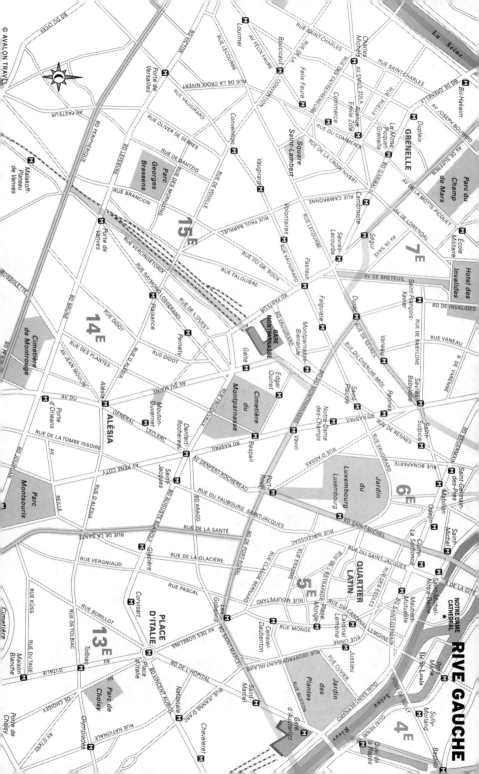

The nearer the Seine, the more intense the ambiance, but that goes with the territory; the Musée d'Orsay, Quartier Latin, and Tour Eiffel—three major tourist attractions—cozy right up to the river. Saint-Germain-des-Prés, with its cafés and churches, draws political luminaries and celebrities who cling to the notion of Old Paris and its moneyed exclusivity. More accessible to expats are the areas a tad further out from the *quais de la* Seine. Alésia, Montparnasse, and Grenelle are a few of the best down-to-earth choices, especially for families with children. The wild card here might Place d'Italie—it isn't on too many newcomers' radars, save the university student population and Asian immigrants with built-in family ties to the area. Its slightly off-the-beaten-path flavor gives it its understated allure.

If you're thinking of moving to Paris and care less about cachet and hipster cred than you do about safety and ease of transport, the Left Bank offers the chance to discover the hidden attractions of Paris's calm and cool south side and decide for yourself if this is a place to call home.

THE LAY OF THE LAND

The Rive Gauche is, as its moniker implies, the left bank of the River Seine. If you've ever wondered how it was determined which side would be right and which would be left, the mystery can be unraveled with a simple explanation: It's all about the direction of the flow. As the river rushes downstream toward the English Channel, you—the pilot of your very own Seine cruiser—will have at your right Rive Droite, and to your left, Rive Gauche. *Donc, voilà!* Makes sense, right?

The Left Bank is *un peu plus* (a little more) compact than its north-of-the-Seine neighbor, and a little trickier to navigate by private automobile. The tight, narrow

the Panthéon in the Quartier Latin

streets of the Quartier Latin spill out into confusing one-way thoroughfares clogged with taxis and *motos,* and occasionally transform into pedestrian-only roadways when you least expect it. Best leave the driving to others and get to know the area on foot or by bicycle.

Montparnasse tower, Paris's tallest building, rises up from the heart of the Left Bank, acting as a beacon to direct you to the *gare* Montparnasse-Bienvenue and its local and long-distance trains. Face the station straight: to the right of the tower sits the safe and sedate Grenelle neighborhood; to the left, the equally staid and calm Alésia quarter. Allow your eyes to continue their migration toward the southeastern *périphérique* and eventually they'll settle on Place d'Italie. Whatever Left Bank neighborhood you settle on, it won't be long before you, like the philosophers and artists before you, wax poetic about your new hood's inspiring idiosyncrasies.

Quartier Latin

If you stand in the sprawling courtyard before the majestic Notre Dame cathedral and then turn to stare south across the Seine, you're staring into the thick of the 5th arrondissement. Squint and you can make out the crowds of students and tourists converging at a popular landmark, the Saint-Michel fountain. Luxembourg Gardens are just a little further up the road, beyond the student bookstores and independent cinemas that call out to creative intellectuals. From boulevard Saint-Michel to Gare d'Austerlitz, the Quartier Latin can sometimes feel like one giant college campus—and in a sense, an education in art and history is what you get every day you choose to wander this ancient corner of the city.

The vibe in the Quartier Latin is a little less gay, and a lot more student-oriented than its parallel neighborhood on the other side of the river. This part of the Rive Gauche is the cradle of Paris's educational civilization, and it's got the university campuses to prove it. The Sorbonne is here, as is the prestigious Paris School of Public Works. Where there are students, there are student bars, lots of student housing, cheap lunches to be had, and affordable entertainment opportunities. It's a good place to live if you want that Lost Generation Left Bank ambiance at a more affordable price than in the neighboring 6e arrondissement. Bibliophiles, especially, will appreciate this neighborhood, which is practically bursting at the seams with bookstores, including the revered English-language treasure trove, Shakespeare and Co. (37, rue de la Bûcherie, www.shakespeareandcompany.com). Literary history runs thick on the streets and in the Quartier Latin cafés. Ernest Hemingway lived nearby, and scribbled notes for what would later become *A Moveable Feast* in local watering holes.

The Quartier Latin is also a favorite haunt for citizens with cinematic leanings; art house theaters abound, and some host fun events like all-night movie screenings with breakfast included in the price of admission. It's a bit more family-friendly than the Marais, and boasts the magnificent Jardin du Luxembourg, with its puppet theater, playground, art-filled grassy spaces, and well-worn tennis courts.

Notre-Dame on the Île de la Cité

HOUSING

Some of Paris's most interesting real estate deals can be had in the Quartier Latin. The sheer volume of students here means it's easy to score a minuscule studio apartment in the €600-per-month range, but that kind of tight-space living is only doable for a couple of semesters. For a place you can really stretch out and relax in, you'll need to budget a bit more. Finding rentals in the €25-per-square-meter zone is a distinct possibility. That might look like an open, modern studio apartment with views over the Panthéon for €1,000, or a vintage 1930s one-bedroom with wood floors and a fireplace for €1,100. If you're working with a bigger budget and want to purchase a little plot of the Quartier Latin to call your own, the prices range from affordable to seriously spendy, but that's to be expected when your neighbors are Scarlett Johansson and Sophia Coppola. Near the Jardin du Luxembourg, the prices skyrocket, but in more unassuming quartiers near Métro Jussieu and Maubert-Mutualité, you might find a *rez-de-chaussée* (ground floor) studio apartment in the back of a cobblestone courtyard surrounded by greenery for €285,000, or a two-bedroom flat with parquet floors and its very own *cave* (basement) for €420,000.

DAILY LIFE
Schools and Community Centers

Anyone who comes to Paris to study will probably spend a good deal of time in the Quartier Latin, where more than a dozen university campuses welcome students from all over the world who come to learn about the decorative arts, language, philosophy, medicine, and other subjects. The *mairie* of the 5th (21, place du Panthéon, www.mairie05.paris.fr) offers a free booklet on student life and learning opportunities throughout Paris and the Left Bank. For unabashedly curious types, simply step onto one the ubiquitous campuses and have a look around. Some, like the École des Beaux Arts in the 6th, open their doors to the public every day for art exhibits and other cultural events.

The Left Bank is crammed with historical relics including the old Roman arena called les Arènes de Lutèce (59, rue Monge). One of Paris's most popular museums is the Musée Cluny, dedicated to artifacts from the Middle Ages. These and other institutions melding art and history serve as community beacons, and are popular with school groups and tourists alike. As a local, you'll want to get acquainted with all the mentally stimulating destinations this part of Paris offers. At the Institut du Monde Arabe (1, rue des Fossés-Saint-Bernard, www.imarabe.org), you can take in art exhibits and music performances, spend hours in their ground-floor bookshop, and continue the Arab-themed fun with a visit to the Grand Mosque just around the corner. Here, you can sip mint tea and, if you're a woman, take a relaxing steam bath at the mosque's hammam/spa.

Shopping

The Quartier Latin isn't known as a major shopping destination, but Boulevard Saint-Michel is good for procuring books and trendy clothing. Fashionistas with more sophisticated tastes will want to roam the narrow streets that inch toward the 6th arrondissement, and along Boulevard Saint-Germain, where more upscale spending opportunities await.

One of the Left Bank's greatest treasures are its outdoor markets, including the organic Raspail market and the adorable, *très* French rue Mouffetard market. On market days, these shopping zones pulsate with life and give locals a chance to socialize with their neighbors over mounds of ripe cherries and stinky country cheeses. There's nothing that makes a person feel more Parisian than schlepping your little plaid shopping cart to the market and filling it up with locally grown goods.

Leisure

From traditional French brasseries to the more eclectic dining options favored by students—Vietnamese, Tibetan, Mexican, Ethiopian—the Quartier Latin has it all. A couple of Monoprix department/grocery stores and dozens of smaller supermarkets open the food-procuring options and make it easy to enjoy one of Paris's greatest pleasures: its food and wine. Student bars, jazz clubs, and more low-key wine bars sit cheek-by-jowl on the hilly streets, inviting those who dare to enter, experience, and enjoy the diverse drinks-and-entertainment scene. Especially popular among the younger Anglophone set are the Highlander English pub and the Moose Bar, a Canadian watering hole selling greasy snacks to remind you of home.

There are a fair number of tourist-trap hot zones in the Quartier Latin, but they're not all to be avoided. Some of the best falafels in town can be found at the two Maoz (www.maozusa.com) locations, both of which sit smack in the busiest tourist zones. Brave the throngs and get some of this addictive fast food that actually isn't bad for you.

Getting Around

The compact Quartier Latin was made for walking—or taking a bus, or riding a bike.

Anything that isn't a car will do here. Public transportation options include two RER lines—B and C—which intersect in the heart of the district, as do Métro lines 4 and 10. Vélib' is a fast, convenient option and the Quartier Latin has the highest concentration of bike stations in the city of Paris.

Grenelle

The family-friendly Grenelle neighborhood is in the 15th arrondissement, south of la Tour Eiffel. The Pont de Bir-Hakeim acts as the gateway from the Right Bank to this quartier and the Métro tracks overhead are your tour guide. Follow them past *boulangeries*, corner cafés, and shops and into the pleasant neighborhoods that comprise the area.

This neighborhood isn't as polished and scrubbed on the outside as the nearby 16th, but it holds a lot of the same appeal, with community safety at the top of the list. Because of its proximity to various American institutions including the American Library, American Cathedral, and American University, the Grenelle neighborhood is popular with (yep, you guessed it) Americans and other English-speakers. If you've landed a job or are pursuing academics at one of the Anglophone institutions, this Grenelle neighborhood makes a lot of sense. Plus, it's one of a few neighborhoods where you'll find a celebrated Poilâne bakery (49, bvd de Grenelle), known for its delicate sourdough loaves. Buying and devouring fresh-from-the-oven croissants is a neighborhood tradition.

HOUSING

You'll have stiff competition while out combing the cobblestone streets for your ideal Grenelle-area home. Networking your way into a river-view apartment is a smart idea and it would behoove you to enlist the aid of an agency if you are set on living in this desirable neighborhood.

Vingt Paris (www.vingtparis.com) specializes in executive housing and offers a nice selection of homes for sale and for rent in the Grenelle area. How about a modern, penthouse apartment with its own celebrity-designed rooftop garden overflowing with jungle-like greenery? All 130 square meters can be yours—sweeping views included—for a cool €1.9 million. Working with a more modest budget? The same agency just sold a darling studio apartment for the more-down-to-earth price of €145,000, and with luck, there could be something else like it with your name on it when you're ready to take the real estate plunge.

For students at the American University, there's an entire housing division dedicated to helping you find a place to lay your head for the duration of your study-abroad experience. The university has partnered with a local real estate agency to get you settled in an apartment that meets your needs, whether that's a solo situation or *co-location* arrangement. And, of course, every living space on offer is equipped with that all-important high-speed Internet service. Send your queries to the English speaking staff at housing@AUP.edu, or call 01/40 62 05 99 to speak directly to someone armed and ready with resources to assist you.

SOPHIA PAGAN/WWW.SOPHIAPAGAN.COM

Grenelle offers constant views of the Tour Eiffel.

DAILY LIFE
Schools and Community Centers

This corner of Paris brims with American academics, political analysts, and even librarians who serve both the Francophone and Anglophone communities at various American-based institutions, including the American University of Paris (31, avenue Bosquet, www.aup.edu) with its nine campus outposts scattered throughout the area, and the American Library (10, rue du Général Camou, www.americanlibraryinparis. org). The American Library is noteworthy for its fun, informative, and free monthly events where wine and snacks are always part of the program. The library's old-school bulletin board is a good place to look for leads on housing and jobs, and the speaker events offer some of the best networking opportunities this side of the Seine.

Another networking hotspot is WICE (10, rue Tiphaine, www.www.wice-paris. org), an American-run nonprofit organization offering classes, workshops, and friendly community. At their teeny-tiny headquarters a few paces away from the La Motte-Picquet-Grenelle Métro stop, you can attend art openings, volunteer your time, or just pop in to learn more about the programs and services offered by the dynamic group of expat women and men.

UNESCO, known as the intellectual arm of the United Nations, has its headquarters here, and is a major employer in the Grenelle area. The UNESCO website (www. en.unesco.org) should be one of the first stops for job-seekers with global nonprofit experience, and the site also lists leads and resources for apartment seekers.

Shopping

Between Grenelle's brasseries and cafés are all the services you expect in a perfect Paris neighborhood, including dry cleaners, hair salons, bakeries redolent of butter and yeast, well-stocked grocery stores, and post offices. The area boasts several pedestrian shopping streets, including rue de Commerce (at bvd de Grenelle), with its quaint cheese shops, wine boutiques, and *traiteurs* vending piquant olives and other savory delicacies. On the other side of the Champ-de-Mars sits a treasure trove of treats that more than a few American expats have been excited to discover: The Real McCoy (164, rue de Grenelle). This is the place to load up on junk food that will carry you back to your childhood with every sweet, greasy, bad-for-you bite. To be fair, you'll also find goods like canned refried beans, peanut butter, and other difficult-to-source comestibles that aren't necessarily detrimental to your health.

Leisure

No conversation about the Grenelle neighborhood would be complete without spending at least a few minutes waxing poetic about its most revered public space, the Champ-de-Mars. This long swath of grassy space leading straight up to the Eiffel Tower is the outdoor equivalent of a front-row-center seat at the opera. Any place you spread out your blanket and set down your picnic basket guarantees unobstructed views of the world's most celebrated monument. Bastille Day (July 14) is the most exhilarating day of the year to experience this park-like setting. Free concerts, fireworks, and rousing renditions of *La Marseillaise* are practically guaranteed to make you fall under Paris's magical spell, and fall in love with this charming neighborhood beside the Seine.

Getting Around

Public transportation is a big plus, with RER line C passing through at the Champ-de-Mars station, as well as Métro Lines 6, 8, and 10. The Métro is easy to spot; it's that noisy thing clanging as it charges through on the elevated platforms looming over boulevards de Grenelle and Garibaldi. A dedicated bike lane studded with Vélib' stations following the path of the Métro tracks encourages the local populous to get out of their cars and turn-of-the-century sardine cans and enjoy a pleasant commute to the local Monoprix, university campus, or UNESCO office job.

Montparnasse

In Paris, it seems, all roads lead to Montparnasse station, which is one good reason to take the Métro or RER train here before setting off and exploring broad boulevards of the 14th arrondissment. Bounded by ave de la Maine to the south and west, by boulevard Montparnasse to the north, and rue de la Santé to the east, this compact neighborhood packs a lot of interesting features into its tiny quarters, including the Catacombs and the Paris Observatory.

Most visitors to Paris know at least one little fact or two about Montparnasse: The skyscraper rising above the train station is the tallest building in the capital and offers the best bird's-eye views of the Île-de-France region, perhaps; or that its eponymous cemetery is the final resting place of two of France's most revered wordsmiths, Baudelaire and Serge Gainsbourg. Montparnasse boasts even more impressive claims to fame, but to really let the history and ambiance of this pretty neighborhood soak into your skin, it helps to pay a visit and stay for a while. How else will you be able to explore its under-recognized museums and dine at its fabled brasseries once frequented by the likes of Modigliani and Jean-Paul Sartre?

Expat families tend to be drawn more to Paris's southern arrondissements more so than the northerly ones, and when roaming Montparnasse's wide boulevards, you can understand why. There's room to breathe here, and it feels secure and, dare we say it, *normal*. Sure, it has its share of impressive architecture and points of interest (the modern art installations at the Fondation Cartier pour l'Art Contemporain on boulevard Raspail shouldn't be missed), yet at its heart, Montparnasse is sort of an average neighborhood with average amenities, and that's not too shabby.

HOUSING

In real estate, it's all about location, location, location. In terms of proximity to transportation, Montparnasse has location in spades. Every hour of every day *Grande Ligne* trains leave the station for points south and west, including Bordeaux and Toulouse, and regional trains ferry passengers back and forth from the suburbs and outlying departments for work and pleasure. Four Métro lines pass through this busy station, too, and sometimes, it almost feels as if it would be faster to walk from one side of Paris to the next rather than navigate the epic underground tunnels bridging the various Montparnasse transport systems. It's those connections, though, that make this part of Paris so appealing. You have options! You can leave the city when you want, and take direct connections by both bus and train Orly and Roissy-Charles de Gaulle airports. If you work as a flight attendant or a pilot, this could be worth noting.

Housing options lean toward 19th-century construction, and the average price per square meter hovers around €10,000. That slightly elevated price point buys you

© SOPHIA PAGAN/WWW.SOPHIAPAGAN.COM

Broad boulevards define Montparnasse.

access to not only great transportation, but a dynamic commercial zone where restaurants, theaters, and shopping malls sit right outside your door. A two-bedroom apartment with a fireplace and wood floors bordering on the chichi 6th arrondissement will run you €600,000. A slightly larger apartment in a 1980s building with a balcony and bathtub is on the market for €795,000. Recent dwellings available for rent in Montparnasse include a 36-square-meter studio with vaulted beam ceilings, skylights, and a modern bathroom for €1,300 per month all inclusive, and a furnished one-bedroom on Edgar Quinet with across-the-street access to a children's play area fetched €1,700. An interesting cross section of Montparnasse apartment listings is available through the agency Paris Stay (www.paristay.com).

DAILY LIFE
Schools and Community Centers

More than 400 nonprofit associations have been created to serve citizens of the 14th arrondissement that encompasses Montparnasse, and anyone who moves here is invited to investigate and join as many groups as hold their interest. To learn about all the activities and cultural events available to you here, contact Maison des Associations (22, rue Deparcieux, www.mairie14.paris.fr).

It's not all grown-up fun in this neighborhood, though. Kids are encouraged to participate in civic life in the 14th, and the office of the *mairie* has developed a youth council open to locals aged 13-25 who want to have a voice in the public arena on issues as varied as the environment, politics, and education. The Conseil de la Jeunesse meets every two weeks at l'Antenne Jeunes Didot (40, rue Didot) and occasionally at the office of the *mairie* (2, place Ferdinand Brunot).

Living in Montparnasse means access to educational opportunities for kids of all ages. *Maternelle*-aged *enfants* attend École Delambre (24, rue Delambre), while expat tweens and teens tend to enroll in Lycée Paul Bert (7-9, rue Huyghens, www.scola.ac-paris.fr), a nonreligious private school with an emphasis on bilingual learning. Adults who wish to expand their academic horizons might do well to consider the École Spéciale d'Architecture (www.esa-paris.fr), where students from around the world have been tutored in the art of design for more than 140 years.

Shopping

Montparnasse's shopping opportunities are legend. The area around the train station is not unlike one giant, open-air mall (especially rue de Rennes); an actual mall attached to the station makes it all-to-easy to part with your euros. You can't buy groceries at Galeries Lafayette, though, can you? For everyday shopping needs, locals head to the twice-weekly organic Marché Raspail (Tuesday and Friday, between rue du Cherches-Midi and rue de Rennes) where piles of pretty produce encourage healthy eating, stall after stall after stall. Shopping here is a true event, and first-timers often spend hours combing through the comestibles and talking to *producteurs*. A Simply supermarket, a few Franprix groceries, and a couple of long-established natural-food stores round out the food- and household-goods possibilities.

Because of the transient nature of the train station, local vendors are used to seeing people come and then go. If you stay—and return to the same store or market stall more than twice—the person behind the counter will be sure to remember you, and might hand you your warm baguette or morning paper before you even ask for it. This friendly community building is just one of many perks that await in Montparnasse.

Leisure

Historically, Montparnasse's rich café culture has been a major neighborhood draw, and jazz lovers from around the world flocked here during its 20th century heyday to see the late greats perform. Today, diners still enjoy oysters, champagne, and white-tablecloth service at La Rotonde (105, bvd Montparnasse), and music enthusiasts sidle up to the Swan Bar (165, bvd Montparnasse) to hear updated versions of classic jazz tunes.

Getting Around

The *gare* is the frontrunner when it comes to public transport providers. Inside, or just outside the station, you can take airport shuttles, taxis, more than a dozen local buses (including the late-night Noctilien line), four different Métro lines (4, 6, 12, and 13), and the relatively new RER N line. All that, plus long-distance and regional trains for destinations south and west. Kind of makes you want to get moving! Adding to the mix is Vélib's strong presence here (the station on rue Montparnasse has more than 40 bikes available for use), as is Autolib', with a half-dozen car-rental kiosks skirting the station.

Alésia and Place d'Italie

Students—and those who appreciate peace and quiet—discovered Alésia (in the 13th arrondissement) and neighboring Place d'Italie (in the 14th arrondissement) long ago, but these two Left Bank neighborhoods are still mostly unknown to tourists and Parisian outsiders. This is good news for anyone considering settling here, because when the competition is low, the odds of scoring the perfect apartment increase.

You'll find these neighborhoods tucked behind—but still within easy proximity of—some of Paris's best features, including Luxembourg Gardens, Parc Montsouris, and the Jardin des Plantes. This so-close, yet-so-far-away feel is what makes these areas so appealing. Alésia sits between Porte d'Orléans on the southern *périphérique* and the Montparnasse Cemetery to the north. To the east is Place d'Italie, the portal to Paris's Chinatown, and beyond, the Porte de Choisy and the A6 motorway leading to the famous forest and château at Fountainebleau.

Walking distance from Montparnasse are the pleasant, family-friendly Alésia and Place d'Italie neighborhoods. Slightly off the beaten path, their out-of-the-way distinction contributes to each district's "authentic" Paris vibe. In both quartiers, you'll find independent butcher shops, *boulangeries*, and stinky cheese stores that further propel that old-timey ambiance, yet each neighborhood is outfitted with all the modern conventions you'd expect in a world-class city like Paris, including department stores, supermarkets, transport links, and tidy, user-friendly green spaces.

The Place d'Italie roundabout in the 13th arrondissement gets its name from the road that originates here and stretches all the way to the land of pizza and linguini. For decades, immigrants from China and other Asian countries have settled here, subsequently building infrastructure to meet the needs of their community. It's a slightly unexpected, yet recommended location for expats; look past the tall office complexes and thundering roundabout traffic and give this neighborhood a chance to work its charms on you.

HOUSING

Alésia, like Montparnasse, is a quartier rich with housing possibilities *à la ancienne*—in other words, vintage construction to match the pace of the neighborhood's demographic, which leans a little older than the population you'll find in Bercy or the Bastille. Subsidized student housing, in particular, abounds here, partly due to spillover from the nearby 5th arrondissement and its many university campuses. If you're a student looking for roommate situations, check the listings at www.parisetudiant.com.

Graduates will find housing opportunities aplenty on Alésia's staid streets. Stop in and visit a local realtor (there are several to choose from on the main commercial drag, avenue du Général LeClerc), or call the numbers listed on the À Louer and À Vendre signs affixed to the windows of available dwellings. The price per square meter for buyers is less expensive than in the nearby Quartier Latin, and it's not entirely out of the realm of possibility to find a stand-alone house to call your own here.

The average price per square meter in this neck of the woods is €8,800. Prices creep slightly higher on either side of the adorable rue Châtillon, where old and new construction sits side by side, giving the neighborhood a contemporary flavor. A two-bedroom, 70-square-meter flat built in 1990 and overlooking a public garden will set you back €490,000. Better deals can be found nearer boulevard Brune, otherwise known as the inner ring road. Here, it's possible to find a spacious one-bedroom dating back to the belle époque and oozing period charm (fireplace, wrought-iron balcony) for as little as €275,000. Renting something similar would ring in at the more affordable price of around €800 per month, while something a bit larger and more modern—like a brand-spanking-new 100-square-meter flat currently on the market overlooking Parc Montsouris—will cost you closer to three times as much.

Place d'Italie doesn't have the same name-recognition or cachet that Alésia claims, but renters and buyers alike will find similar quality in accommodation as they would one neighborhood over, but at lower price points. One of Place d'Italie's most distinct features is its high-rise tower blocks. What they don't offer in aesthetic appeal they make up for in affordability. These sky-high apartment complexes are often all-in-one communities with kids' play areas, supermarkets, and little shops on the ground floors.

High-rise living not your thing? There are other options, but most of them tend toward more modern construction. The benefit of newer construction means more efficient heating and cooling systems, and often bigger kitchens and bathrooms.

The average per-square-meter price here is just €8,000, with prices tilting higher on either side of main drag, avenue des Gobelins. Near hospital Salpêtrière, a two-bedroom apartment built in the '70s is on the market for €678,000, which sounds like a lot until you read the fine print and realize it includes its own parking space, an enormous terrace, and a *cave* for storing all your bikes and camping gear. In the average price range, you could find a 45-square-meter one-bedroom brimming with 1930s charm for €360,000. A rental in the same building, with wood floors, fireplace, and views over the building's quiet courtyard, is on the market for €1,200 per month.

DAILY LIFE
Schools and Community Centers

Throughout the 13th, there are roughly 75 public and private schools open to children ages two and older; a nice cross section of those institutions fall within the Place d'Italie neighborhood. The combination Collège-Lycée Claude Monet (1, rue Docteur Magnan) promises a solid education on traditional subjects, only with an extra emphasis on the arts, including music, theater, and classic languages. The private Group Scholaire de Saint-Vincent-de-Paul (49, rue Bobillot, www.gs-svp.com) provides a Catholic education to children from elementary school through high school. The *mairie* of the 13th (1, place d'Italie) is the best resource for detailed information on the full buffet of academic choices in this part of Paris.

Another major draw to the Place d'Italie is its *bibliothèques* (libraries), some of which are connected to local universities and others that are open to the general public. At the modern, welcoming *bibliothèque* Marguerite Durand (named in honor of the French feminist), you can browse an impressive collection of manuscripts, postcards, and works by celebrated women writers and artists, including Colette, Sarah Bernhardt, and George Sand.

Between Alésia and Place d'Italie sit a half-dozen public hospitals and private clinics. The 14th is not a bad place to be if you're in need of medical attention.

Shopping

One of Alésia's primary attractions to both outsiders and locals is its "stock" boutiques, which sell upscale brand-name clothing and accessories at discount prices. The pretty Sonia Rykiel dress you had your heart on last season

The elevated Métro line 6 slices through Place d'Italie.

or the Tara Jarmon coat that you drooled over in a high-end window display the previous winter can be yours for a song if you've got the shopper's stamina gene in your DNA. Carry a bag big enough to fit a reusable water bottle (you can refill it at the public fountains found throughout the area) and pack one of those tasty baguette sandwiches on offer at every neighborhood *boulangerie* if you want to fully exploit the fashionable advantages of this shopper's treasure trove. Look for these and other shops on rue d'Alésia between Métro stop Plaisance and Métro Alésia.

Pedestrian shopping street rue Daguerre has lured locals for centuries, and was even featured in the 1976 documentary by filmmaker Agnès Varda titled *Daguerréotypes*. Stopping by to see how much—or really, how little—the street has changed over the decades is recommended.

Leisure

One of the most pleasant parks in all Paris resides in this neighborhood, and whether you're coming to scope out the hinterlands of the 14th as a tourist or a would-be resident, you should make a point to enjoy all that Parc Montsouris has to offer. A lake (and lakeside café) adds a dash of Impressionistic "Déjeuner sur l'Herbe" to any promenade, and the Ping-Pong tables, carrousel, and *Guignol* puppet theater virtually ensure your wee ones will never have to experience a dull moment.

Place d'Italie is a generous cross section of leisure-time activities for adults and children alike. At the 14-screen MK2 cineplex on rue de France, you can take in a movie and have a drink at the cinema's bar afterward, surrounded by students from the nearby Université Paris Diderot, then dance till dawn at Wanderlust or catch

EXPAT EXPERIENCE: LIVING IN THE 14TH

Name: Dan Smith
Age: 62
Profession: Currently a bon vivant, but previously worked in the pharmaceutical industry.

Where are you from originally?
I was born in Idaho and lived in New York State and the Philadelphia suburbs for many years.

When and why did you move to Paris?
I moved to Paris in 2004 as a temporary expatriate for my global pharmaceutical company. We are supposed to say "global" but it is really a French company.

In which arrondissement do you currently reside?
In the 14th between Alésia and Pernety.

How did you find your current home?
I found my current apartment on SeLoger (www.seloger.com). I made the application myself with the many required documents.

Are you a homeowner or do you rent?
I rent.

What are some of the factors you considered before moving to this location?
I originally selected this area because of the proximity to my company's shuttle bus to my place of work in the southern Paris suburbs. Since moving here, I have grown to know and love this area.

Describe your quartier to someone who's never been there before.
The 14th arrondissement is what I would call a French middle-class area, not as diversified as other Paris areas but not as "prosperous" as others. It's a working-class area even though the apartments are fairly expensive. The area around Alésia has a wide range of services: *boulangeries, bouchers, fromageries,* supermarkets, cinemas, boutiques and more. [It's] more diverse than my former

---

a musical performance at the Batobar, a floating nightlife spot right on the Seine. Among the local museums is the small but interesting Museum of Sports, where you ogle wooden bicycles, watch short films, and purchase beautiful vintage-reproduction posters at reasonable prices.

If you appreciate Asian cuisine, a bounty of edible opportunity is to be discovered in the Place d'Italie. On nearby avenue Ivry, Asian supermarkets emitting strong aromas lure curious shoppers and encourage them to take home a few bundles of bok choy, tubs of tofu, and canned goods from across the spectrum. These surrounding streets are chock-a-block with Vietnamese noodle restaurants, dim sum houses, and bubble tea stands. In summertime, you might think you're in Beijing or Ho Chi Minh City.

Getting Around

Metro lines 4, 5, 6, and 7 serve the Alésia and Place d'Italie neighborhoods. The RER line B also whizzes through the area, stopping at Denfort-Rochereau before continuing toward Sceaux and other southern suburbs. The closest long-haul train stations are Montparnasse (closer to Alésia), and Gare d'Austerlitz (closer to Place d'Italie).

If you really want to own a car, you could do so here without too much trouble. Public parking lots are easy to find, and street parking opportunities are generous.

residence on rue de Vaugirard in the 6th. Everyone establishes relationships and often goes to the same store for daily needs. There is a market Wednesdays and Sundays that I attend. The vendors recognize me and know what I bought before.

Is the quality of life in your arrondissement what you expected it to be?

The quality of life is very good here. I know vendors in the area and have discovered many special boutiques and restaurants that are out of the mainstream of tourists in Paris. There is only one touristic place in the 14th, the Catacombs, where I take guests to view a special macabre experience of ancient Paris.

Describe your experience making friends with neighbors or others in your community.

Living in my area I have met many people and experienced many one-on-one relationships with vendors, my *gardienne*,

and people on the streets. The closeness of living in a city requires a certain level of closeness and mutual understanding. Interaction with others, even strangers, makes life special here. At the same time, proximity with others brings conflicts as well. I am often frustrated walking along the streets when tourists, casual shoppers, and those families who walk hand-in-hand with toddlers blocking us fast walkers who know exactly where we are going. Even these negatives seem trivial compared with the benefits.

Have you made any unexpected discoveries in your neighborhood?

Some of the streets and buildings in the 14th have not changed in the last 100 years. I feel like a piece of history living in an apartment where people have lived for 120 years, walking the streets where people have walked for centuries. All I see now will exist a century after I leave. I will become like the others before me, a ghost of the past, a habitant of this quartier forever.

Of course, the smaller your car, the better your chances of finding an on-street parking space. Online portal Neoparking (www.neoparking.com) can help find a place to park and even offers the opportunity of pre-booking your spot. Better still, subscribe to Autolib' (www.autolib.eu) for a reasonable annual fee and minus all the parking hassles.

PRIME LIVING LOCATIONS

PETITE COURONNE

Not every Parisian dream was built upon a cobblestone cliché of the Champs-Élysées penthouse with Eiffel Tower views. Plenty of Paris transplants arrive in the City of Light with no preconceived ideas—except perhaps that of a daily croissant washed down with a café crème. For all the open minds out there, here's an interesting proposition: *la banlieue.* The word simply means "suburb," but in the last decade, it's taken on a negative connotation due in part to a couple of notorious episodes involving disenfranchised youth in the northern Paris regions. Those isolated incidents shouldn't color your perception of suburban habitation, which can actually be much safer, calmer, and far more affordable than life within Paris's city limits.

The suburban ring around Paris, known as la Petite Couronne (or "the Little Crown"), consists of dozens of connecting small-to-medium-size towns within the three departments immediately surrounding the Paris periphery. The majority of these towns are serviced by the Métro system or RER—and if they're not, the bus service rolls in to fill the void. Practically within walking distance of Paris proper, these suburban towns are thriving communities in themselves, with cinemas, restaurants, public swimming pools, schools, and parks, which virtually eliminate the need to venture into Paris for anything more than a museum exhibit or concert.

Paris is famously expensive, and on the flipside, the suburbs are notoriously

© AURELIA D'ANDREA

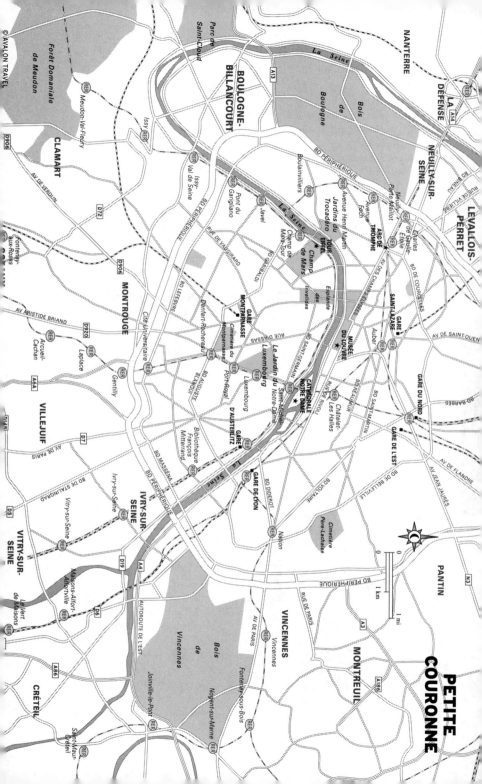

affordable, which is appealing to those who crave home ownership but can't afford the sky-high euro-per-meter prices in Paris's best neighborhoods. Another perk of outside-the-circle living is the space. Every day, Paris swells with tens of thousands of nonresidents who commute into work, then head home again at day's end to their suburban abodes. That sometimes-suffocating sense of congestion you can feel in the city center is a non-issue in the suburbs, which benefit from the reverse commute. This can also lend a sleepy feel to suburban town centers—but for many of us, that's not a bad thing.

The recommended *banlieues* were selected based on specific criteria: safety, housing opportunities, transport links, and quality-of-life perks like restaurants and green spaces. From artsy, multicultural Montreuil to tidy, practically prim Levallois-Perret, there's a suburb to fit every type of expat. Some towns, like Sceaux, offer a village vibe that feels a million miles away from Paris. Boulogne-Billancourt, on the other hand, is practically an extension of the 16th arrondissement neighborhood it borders—only with more modern architecture and a less homogenous population of locals.

Sceaux

If one had to describe Sceaux (pronounced "So") in a single word, it would be "pleasant." Just 10 kilometers and a 20-minute RER train ride from the center of Paris, Sceaux feels like a provincial town somewhere in the French heartland, and that's one of many compelling reasons people are drawn here. Retirees especially love this corner of the Île-de-France. The stately, well-groomed Parc de Sceaux with its 18th-century château is a popular rendezvous spot for the town's senior set, but they don't get all 200 hectares to themselves. *Beaucoup de* joggers, cyclists, and weekend ramblers have made this an extension of their backyards, too.

On the other half of the Sceaux age divide, there is a sizeable population of students, due to its proximity to the area's many university campuses and other institutes of higher learning. Academics are a long-standing Sceaux tradition; during the French Revolution, the château and the property surrounding it was confiscated and converted into an agricultural school. (Today, it's a museum and public park.)

If the town's spirit seems soaked in centuries-old historical pomp and revelry, that's because this small city of 20,000 was established nearly a millennia ago. In the intervening years, it's played the part of royal weekend getaway destination, served as a regional center of

© AURELIA D'ANDREA

A pretty, old church sits in the heart of Sceaux.

learning for horticulturists, and blossomed as a tourist destination for lovers of history and the great outdoors.

WHERE TO LIVE

Sceaux is positioned in an undulating patch of former agricultural land just south of Paris in the department of Hauts-de-Seine. On the south side of the city is the prim and proper Parc de Sceaux, with its museums, fountains, and pretty multi-purpose paths. To the east is the neighborhood of Quatre-Chemins, which is bisected by a verdant path called the Coulée Verte. A former railway line transformed into a walking, cycling, and skating path, the Coulée Verte becomes a hotbed of activity in the warm months, and turns this formerly tranquil part of town into an outdoor-lovers thoroughfare. The proximity to Faculté Jean Monnet, a law school connected to the University of Paris, translates to students, students, and more students, who give the neighborhood a vibrant, youthful vibe.

Even the least desirable area in Sceaux, Blagis, still isn't all that bad. The neighborhood holds the unpopular title of having the highest number of unemployed residents and is also where you'll find the most public housing. The area is in the midst of an urban renewal project, and there are some gems to be discovered here, in terms of places to live and things to do. The feeling in Blagis is more suburban, meaning fewer amenities directly out your doorstep and great distances between those amenities, but take advantage of the wood-and-glass Piscine de Blagis (5, rue de l'Yser, tel. 01/55 59 67 90) with its three pools, tennis courts, and the Théâtre les Gemeaux (49, avenue Georges Clemenceau, www.lesgemeaux.com) and you'll see the how the neighborhood is building its allure.

© AURELIA D'ANDREA

Sceaux offers a pleasant blend of old and new dwellings.

HOUSING

If you have your heart set on a house, you may find yourself waiting a long time to land the home of your dreams. The inventory on single-family dwellings is low in Sceaux, and houses that do come on the market get snapped up quickly, often selling at lofty, practically Parisian prices. You'll pay somewhere around €5,100 per square meter for an apartment versus €6,500 per square meter for a house.

If you're okay with apartment living, you'll definitely be able to find a place to call home without an epic wait. It will likely be modern construction—meaning built in the latter half of the 20th century—and come with a balcony and views over some manner of green space. Have your heart set on a pre-war gem, with manicured trees in the front and period features inside? There's a

PRIME LIVING LOCATIONS

55-square-meter, two-bedroom rendered in beautiful 1930s brick, with green shutters and a tidy front yard shared with your neighbors. The monthly cost for this little slice of vintage living is €1,100; as with most dwellings secured via a real estate agency, you'll have to pay a non-refundable *honoraire* (finder's fee) equivalent to one month's rent. A modern version of the same apartment—only with a balcony and better closet space—will cost exactly the same, only with slightly lower move-in fees.

If you want to be near the elementary schools so your kids can walk to school, you'll want to settle in the *centre-ville*. A one-bedroom apartment in a 19th-century building right on the charming pedestrian street rue Houdan can be yours for a monthly rent of €842, plus charges, which is standard throughout France and usually encompasses water, heat, garbage, and gardien(ne) services. If you have a more generous budget, a spacious three-bedroom apartment across the street from the Coulée Verte on rue des Pépinières could be yours for €2,000. Apartments come with a private garden, basement storage space, and parking. A new-construction home with a huge garden and American-style garage sells for €790,000.

The neighborhoods of Parc de Sceaux and Musiciens are the most family-friendly and the places you'll find the most strollers being pushed down the sidewalks *and* the most single family dwellings. A beautiful 1930s house with a gated garden, three bedrooms, and a remodeled kitchen in the quartier des Musiciens is on the market for €930,000.

If you're determined to live in Sceaux and want to stretch your euro further, Blagis is the place to look. Keep in mind that improvements are being made throughout the community to improve safety and well-being of all its inhabitants. Blagis is the focus of a lot of civic attention. The average price per square meter is approximately €300 less here for renters who choose this part of Sceaux rather than the more coveted *centre-ville*, and a whopping €500 less per square meter for buyers. That might look like a sweet 1920s house with a yard twice the size of the house itself. Inside are hardwood floors, a marble fireplace, and some really bad bathroom tile that could easily be replaced. The price: €540,000, including a garage with room for a car and a few bicycles. Better bargains can be had, but it's also easy to fork over a million euros (or even two) for a place to call home in Sceaux—even in the least-desirable neighborhoods.

Renting has its advantages and allows you to try on the area without a long-term commitment. The going price for a small (25-square-meter), contemporary one-bedroom flat within a three-minute walk of the RER station and five minutes from the local pool is €700 per month. For an interesting look at Sceaux from a real estate perspective, visit the website www.carte.changerdeville.fr. Here you'll find all kinds of fascinating demographic information, including the number of doctors and restaurants in any given neighborhood, average housing costs, and other points of interest.

DAILY LIFE

Life in Sceaux is centered on academics, but the town is not immune to the daily exodus to Paris. When the Paris city limits are just 10 minutes away by train, you start to believe in the commuter lifestyle. Those who work inside the city tend to be small-business owners who give Sceaux its commercial anchor and provide the locals with the services they need to maximize the pleasure of living here.

A visit to the *mairie* is a must for anyone considering a move here. Vintage 19th century on the outside, sleek and modern on the inside, this is where you'll load up on

EXPAT EXPERIENCE: LIVING IN SCEAUX

Name: Barbara Joly
Age: 51
Profession: English teacher

Where are you from originally?
I was born in California and grew up in Hawaii.

When and why did you move to Paris?
I moved in February 1990 to marry my fiancé, who is now my husband of 23 years.

Describe Sceaux to someone who's never been there before.
Sceaux is a charming and quiet suburb town. It has wonderful amenities, excellent schools, a magnificent park and is within easy reach of Paris by road and RER. The center city is less ethnically diverse than the surrounding quarters; [it] has small stores and a large supermarket along its pedestrian street, rue Houdan. The people in Sceaux are generally pleasant.

Is the quality of life what you expected it to be?
When I was still living in the U.S., I had no expectations of what life could be here. Fortunately, I have a good life in Sceaux.

Describe your experience making friends with neighbors or others in your community.
It took me a long time to [get to] know people in the neighborhood. People were slow to befriend. I did become close to a few neighbors and also made acquaintances in the quarter.

What do you like most about living in the suburbs?
The tranquillity, green spaces, and a slower pace of life than in Paris. I come to Paris twice a week to work and perhaps three to five times per month outside of workdays. I see friends, go to expositions or museums, or go shopping.

What do you like least?
A lack of cleanliness in some areas.

Have you made any unexpected discoveries in your neighborhood?
Good surprises: A small and friendly shopping center where regular clients are greeted warmly.

PHOTO COURTESY OF BARBARA JOLY

American Barbara Joly loves her life in Sceaux.

information about daily life in Sceaux. Pick up a copy of *SceauxMag,* the monthly color magazine detailing local news and events. Regular features include snapshot profiles of Scéens (residents of Sceaux), which give a visual sense of who your neighbors will be. Nearly every month, Sceaux hosts a festival of some sort, and these happenings help bind the community together and make it stronger. Some of the most interesting are the annual film festival (March), the Vélo en Ville celebration that promotes bicycling in the community (May), and the Salon des Artistes that spotlights the work of local artists each spring and autumn.

© AURELIA D'ANDREA

Crêpes are just one of many delicious offerings in Sceaux.

Integrating into the flow of daily life is easy with a bit of effort. A good starting place is Bienvenue à Sceaux (Welcome to Sceaux), a nonprofit organization that helps newcomers adjust to life here through community activities and a monthly get-to-know-you potluck. Pick up their newsletter at the tourist office, library, or *mairie*, or give them a call (tel. 01/43 50 45 05) or pop into their offices (14, rue des Imbergères) and put those French lessons into practice.

On the spiritual end of the spectrum, Sceaux expresses plenty of diversity. Near the RER station is the SOKA Buddhist center (4, rue Raymond Gachelion, www.soka-boud-dhisme.fr), whose primary mission is philanthropy. In the center of town, the Mouvement Juif Libéral de France welcomes reformists to Shabbat services (www.mjlf.org), and Catholics can worship at the old, dusty-pink Saint-Jean-Baptiste church (www.paroisse-sceaux.fr) right across from the central marketplace.

Centre-Ville

Sceaux's town center is conveniently located between the main thoroughfare, rue Houdan, and the sprawling Parc de Sceaux. Within these narrow borders, are a big supermarket, post office, library, and a stretch of rue Houdan that was pedestrianized in 1976. The foot-friendly shopping promenade is lined with cheesemongers, vegetable vendors, banks, and more. The Wednesday and Saturday outdoor market sets up outside the municipal Marché du Centre, which got a big revamp in 2003 that didn't change its belle époque look, but just brought it up to modern standards. Right around the corner you'll discover the Jardin de la Ménagerie, with its updated children's play areas, tennis courts, and well-manicured gardens. This is also where the tiny, welcoming tourist office sits. Here, friendly staff can help you find activities to keep you busy for the day, week, or year.

The center of town is self-contained, easily navigable by foot, and fully equipped with nearly everything you need. The Trianon cinema (3, rue Marguerite Renaudin, www.sceaux.fr/films-au-trianon), which first opened in 1921, is the oldest independent art-house movie theater. The single-screen cinema shows an interesting mix of old, new, foreign, and locally produced films. A couple of blocks away is the town library (7, rue Honoré de Balzac, www.bibliotheque.sceaux.fr), a hub of social and cultural activity with art, film, and author readings. The bibliothèque also hosts events for younger children and adolescents on a regular basis.

The *centre-ville* truly is a village center, and you feel that sense of community when you stroll the streets. People are friendly, welcoming, and prone to that elusive act known in Anglophone circles as "smiling." Maybe it's the ease of life here, or something in the water, but Sceaux's welcoming attitude is definitely part of its appeal.

Schools and Community Centers

Sceaux is a good place to be if you're a student. There are no fewer than three university campuses in town, including the Université Paris-Sud XI. In total, there are 10,000 students, which means that more than half the population attends school on a regular basis. It also means that there are a lot of teachers here—and a potential for teaching jobs.

For school-age children, there are a total of eight *maternelles* and *écoles élémentaires*, including the private Sainte-Jeanne-d'Arc school network. For middle- and high-school-age children, there are three possibilities. La Cité Scolaire Publique Lakanal is a combination *collège/lycée*, as is La Cité Scolaire Publique Marie-Curie. The Lycée des Métiers and a private Catholic high school are two other options. For more information on educational opportunities, pick up a copy of the *Guide de la famille et de l'écolier* at the office of the *mairie*.

For university-age students, there are three campuses in Sceaux: the school of economics (www.jm.u-psud.fr), the technology institute (www.iut-sceaux.u-psud.fr), and the school of engineers (www.epf.fr). All three offer study-abroad programs for international students, and might be worth considering if you're looking for a program that happens to be offered by one of the schools.

For more mature minds that want to stay flexible, the *Sorties du Jeudi* program targets the 70-and-older crowd with guided visits to museums and *macaron* factories, memory workshops, and even senior gymnastics. Fees are nominal and spaces are limited. To reserve a spot, contact the Services for Seniors department at the *mairie* (tel. 01/31 13 32 89).

Leisure

An impressive 56 percent of the Sceaux's cityscape is dedicated green space, so you are never far from a park or greenbelt. The area's most impressive park is the famous Parc de Sceaux. Open year-round, this 200-acre oasis looks like something out of a children's fairytale book, with its pretty château, enormous cone-shaped topiary trees, and green fields punctuated by spitting fountains. People come from all around the Île-de-France region to visit the park's painting-and-sculpture-filled museums and roam its many groomed paths. At one end of the park sits a sports complex with a swimming pool, track for running, and tennis courts; on another end is a *parcours* trail dotted with fitness equipment for those who prefer to get their exercise needs met en plein air. There are three cafés within the park grounds where you can relax with a refreshing drink and a bite to eat.

Because of the easy access to nature and the outdoors, dogs are a prominent feature in the local scene. Thanks to waste dispensers conveniently positioned throughout town, the streets are delightfully poo free, as are the multi-use paths that form the Coulée Verte.

Getting Around

To reach Sceaux by car, take the D920 from Porte d'Orléans in southern Paris; the trip will take all of 10 minutes. Better still, buy a €2.45 ticket and hop on the RER from one of the several Paris stations serving Sceaux (including Châtelet-Les Halles

© AURELIA D'ANDREA

Trains can shuttle you into Paris in 15 minutes.

and Saint-Michel). In less than 20 minutes you'll be at the quiet little Sceaux station, and from there, it's an easy five-minute walk to the town center. Two bus lines serve the town—Line 6, which stops at the *gare,* and makes a big figure-eight loop through town, and Line 16, which is the school-goers route, stopping at Lycée Lakanal and the EPF school of engineering, among others. Tickets for either line are the same ones you use for the Paris Métro. You can purchase them at the train station from automated machines, or directly from the conductor on the bus. If you have your Navigo pass, you can use it on the bus as well as the RER. For more information on Sceaux's bus network, visit the Transdev website at www.transdev-idf.com.

Many local residents choose to walk or bicycle around town, and students can take advantage of a subsidized bicycle rental system that charges just €5 per month. Information is available at each of Sceaux's three university campuses.

One alternative for getting around town is Autolib', the public car-share system first launched in Paris in 2011. The little "bluecars" are 100-percent electric, and require a simple membership subscription to use, on top of which you pay an hourly fee. Autolib' is ideal for short jaunts to Ikea or picking up friends at Orly.

Boulogne-Billancourt

Parisians are loath to admit it, but they are not immune to address envy. Certain arrondissements hold more sex appeal than others, and for folks who fancy themselves elegant with a dash of conservative chic, the 16th is the obvious neighborhood match. But if you want an actual driveway in which to park your luxury sedan or have your heart set on either a giant terrace or grassy back yard to frolic in, Boulogne-Billancourt has it.

Boulogne-Billancourt—called simply "Boulogne" (boo-LOHN-yuh) by locals—sits just over the south-westernmost edge of Paris, hugging the Seine on one side, and the Bois de Boulogne on the other. You might call it the gateway to the kings' country, since it borders on the celebrated forestland where the French royals once cavorted, and Versailles is just a 10-minute car ride away. Regardless, Boulogne is a very nice place loaded with attractive qualities and a high standard of living.

Boulogne's streets are sedate and clean, and peppered with amenities, including supermarkets, clothing stores, and even car dealerships. It also holds the distinction of having more city residents with post-baccalaureate degrees than anywhere else in the country. Forty-three percent of the population holds jobs in the cadre of "intellectuelles supérieures," which is just another way of saying there some really smart people here. That might not be palpable when walking the streets, but the sense of safety and security definitely is noticeable. Boulogne spent a nice chunk of change totaling nearly one million euros on a video surveillance program, which may or may not actually deserve credit for making the city safer. Whatever the reason, crime rates are lower here than the national average for cities of comparable size.

Exciting plans for urban development are under way. L'Île Seguin is getting a major makeover to transform from a derelict industrial area into an eco-friendly live-work-play destination. Approval for a huge arts complex, pedestrianized commercial strip, landscaped gardens, and a 16-screen movie theater are already in the works. One of the most exciting projects set to break ground in 2014 is the Cité Musicale, a flagship cultural institution that will host concerts, and dance and theater performances.

WHERE TO LIVE

Boulogne offers a bit of everything: an interesting waterfront area that's currently being developed, a famous forest with acre upon acre of room to roam, a vibrant town center with every imaginable commercial opportunity at your disposal, and quiet residential streets lined with grand houses and smart apartment complexes.

There are six primary neighborhoods in Boulogne, most of which follow the town's tradition of hyphenation: Parchamp-Albert Kahn, Silly-Gallieni, Billancourt-Rives de Seine, République-Point-du-Jour, les Princes-Marmottan, and the *centre-ville*. The most desirable neighborhood is les Princes-Marmottan, but not because of its proximity to Parc des Princes, otherwise known as the home of Paris's Paris-Saint-Germain football (soccer) team. During the football season, game nights can make getting in and out of the neighborhood a real hassle, but the rest of the time the area is extremely pleasant. The feeling is safe, residential, and skewed slightly older. Lots of dogs live in this neighborhood, judging by the look of the sidewalks, but some good citizens actually use the dog-poo-bag dispensers installed on nearly every corner in this hood. Stade Rolande Garros, the famous tennis-tournament stadium, is here, too. During the French Open the neighborhood population swells by many hundreds. Local residents have been known to leave town during the tournament and rent their places at exorbitant prices, with plenty of eager renters waiting to lay down cash for easy access to the matches. Another neighborhood plus: the Bois de Boulogne is within walking distance.

The *centre-ville* neighborhood isn't a bad place to expand your home search. The

© AURELIA D'ANDREA

French children love carousels, including those in Boulogne.

access to transport, shops, and restaurants makes it more attractive for young suburbanites who want a Paris vibe at a slightly scaled-down pace. Northwest of the *mairie* you'll find enormous 1960s and '70s apartment complexes with large terraces and good views that offer easy access to Boulogne's best bits.

HOUSING

Boulogne has an interesting housing supply. The most fascinating architecture is from the city's industrial heyday—the 1930s. Influenced and designed by the great architects of the time, these private houses and multi-family complexes created in sleek, modern style take up block after block in the northern neighborhood of les Princes-Marmottan. You can also find some of these chic *immeubles* clustered further south near Place Marcel Sembat. The city's architectural pride and joy are the buildings designed by celebrated architect Le Corbusier, known for his avant-garde approach to urban design. (His atelier on the Boulogne-Paris border is open to the public for visits, www.fondationlecorbusier.fr.) Today, those designer dwellings are highly sought after, with prices that reflect their desirability, but that's not to say you can't have a piece of the real-estate pie.

The price of housing here is less expensive than Paris, and considerably less expensive than the 16th arrondissement. You'll be looking at around €6,800 per square meter if you're eyeing apartments, and around €8,600 per square meter if it's a house you're after. Translated into real-life examples, for slightly more than €1 million, you could have a three-story, single-family townhouse built in 1930, tucked into a quiet courtyard and surrounded by greenery. A two-car garage and updated kitchen are selling points. A more modest budget of €350,000 could afford you a one-bedroom flat with

Fancy living in your own gated mansion? Anything is possible with a big enough bank account.

a spacious balcony in a modern complex complete with on-site *gardien(ne)*. You'll find a nice selection of houses for sale at Boulogne-based Kalitea Immobilier (99, bvd Jean Jaurès, www.kalitea-immobilier.com).

If it's rental housing you seek, the options are good, from teeny-tiny studios to grand *maisons particuliers*. In mid-2014, a sampling of rental properties turned up a good-size 1970s-era studio apartment with a balcony and views over a tree-shaded garden for €750 per month. A gorgeous little garden cottage with an airy loft-like feel went for €1,000 per month.

DAILY LIFE

If you want to start a business, Boulogne is good place to settle. The city-sponsored, nonprofit Boulogne Business Club (BBC) was launched in 2009 to support local entrepreneurs in their quests to create new business enterprises—and, hopefully, local jobs. Members meet regularly to welcome new businesses, host guest-speaker events, and provide community to start-ups. Join the group's LinkedIn network or call event manager Florence Louette (florence.louette@agglo-gpso.fr) to learn when the next meeting will be held. Similarly, Seine Ouest Entreprise et Emploi (SOEE) supports small-business owners with tools and resources designed to help their ideas flourish. Visit the organization's website (www.seineouest-entreprise.com) to learn more about the free workshops, speaker events, and training offered by the organization. Making use of these and many other resources that exist specifically to help you launch a business venture is a great way to get connected with your neighbors and really feel part of the community.

Daily life isn't all *Métro, boulot, dodo* in Boulogne. People make time for leisure activities and the veritable buffet of "life-enhancement" opportunities here. The 100-page *Guide des Activités* available for free at the *mairie* lists classes available through Boulogne's extensive network of nonprofit associations. Taking advantage of the half-dozen French-language classes is a great idea for newcomers. Annual fees vary from around €35 to about €150. The number of English-language courses available hint at opportunities for teaching jobs for expats too, which is definitely worth exploring.

Another great resource for newcomers is the magazine *Culture(s)*. This bi-monthly publication keeps you up to date on local theater and music productions, gallery openings, and more. Feature articles on local celebrities or celebrated authorities can also be found within its pages.

Centre-Ville

The *centre-ville* is one of Boulogne's six neighborhoods, and in this approximation of a "downtown," you'll find the tourist office, *mairie*, main post office, library, and local mall or *centre commercial* known as Les Passages. Inside this tidy, compact shopping center you'll discover a Starbucks, Monoprix, SNCF boutique for purchasing train travel tickets, and an interesting selection of clothes and housewares boutiques. The mall also houses a novel lending library called Les Livres de Passage. The way it works is simple: Take a book, leave a book. Comfy club chairs and a friendly "librarian" make it an inviting place to come and hang out for a while. Learn more about it and the pleasant shopping center on its dedicated Facebook page: www.facebook.com/centrecommercial.lespassages.

Outside is a giant square with amenities for children, including a colorful carrousel, permanent cotton-candy vendor, and a generous swath of space to kick a ball around. A movie theater and interesting cross section of restaurants abound, from Tex-Mex to Japanese and Lebanese. Avenue Jean Juarès is a major commercial hub, with more of everything shopping- and eating-oriented. Banks and real estate offices are also well represented here. Looping back around the corner in the direction of the *mairie*, you'll run into the Espace Multimedia Landowski. The small, charming 1930s museum (www.annees30.com) is part of this complex, as is a pleasant café, cinema, and multi-media library.

Schools and Community Centers

Boulogne's reputation for offering higher-than-average academic training is warranted; three of the city's *lycées* are top-ranking schools with a nearly 100-percent success rate passing the tough *baccalauréat* examination. With more than 30 *maternelles* and *écoles élémentaires*, plus four *collèges* and two *lycées* to choose from, your child is guaranteed a spot in the right academic environment. If private school is a priority, Open Sky International School (www.open-sky-intl.com) accepts children as young as two years old into its bilingual classes, which are based on the Montessori method. For older kids, there are two nearby options, including the Sections Internationales de Sèvres (SIS), located just over the river in the town of Sèvres (www.sis-sevres.net). SIS is unique in that it acts as an academic supplement to your child's French public school education. Kids from preschool age through high school attend classes, take trips, and participate in theater and other cultural events outside of regular school hours, to develop and maintain their English-language skills. Employment tip: SIS regularly recruits English-speaking teachers and other staff. The exclusive American School in Paris (www.asparis.org) is actually located in Saint-Cloud, also situated across the river from Boulogne. For close to €30,000 per year, your child will receive a bilingual education on a homey, four-hectare campus with a supportive staff. Limited scholarships are available.

The Wednesday afternoon tradition of extracurricular fun runs particularly strong in this community, with sports and artistic activities among the most popular. For kids aged 3-16, the École Municipale des Sports (tel. 01/55 18 53 00) is among the most interesting possibilities, with classes and workshops in fencing, climbing, and judo, among others.

Houses of worship are plentiful in Boulogne. Catholic churches dominate the scene, though Muslims and Jews also have options. There's a mosque and a synagogue in town and even a Russian Orthodox church. You'll find all the religious possibilities in the annual *guide pratique* available free at the *hôtel de ville*. The guide also includes a comprehensive list of community services, including schools, museums, social clubs, athletic associations, and local doctors.

Leisure

A huge part of Boulogne's allure is its proximity to green space. With the Bois de Boulogne as your backyard, there's no need for a gym membership. This is a jogger's paradise and a recreational hotspot for cyclists, skaters, and row-boaters. Directly southwest across the river is the Parc de Saint-Cloud: the former royal hunting grounds are now host to a number of annual festivals, including the three-day Rock en Seine music festival. More than two dozen well-equipped squares, parks, and gardens dot the city, with amenities that vary from Ping-Pong tables to jungle gyms. With the development of l'Île Seguin, several more acres of outdoor recreation space will be available in this generously proportioned *ville fleurie*.

Getting Around

One welcome perk for residents of Boulogne-Billancourt is the free SUBB bus. This electric bus line does a circuit through town every 15 to 20 minutes, from approximately 7:30am until 6:30pm Monday through Saturday. SUBB North runs a loop from the *hôtel de ville* up past the Parc des Princes, to the Porte de Boulogne, past the hospital Amboise Paré, and back to the *mairie*. The southern route starts at the *mairie*, then heads east and south to the Pont de Billancourt, to Place Bir-Hakeim, Pont de Sèvres, and back to the *mairie*. Buses are wheelchair accessible. Métro Line 9 begins here (or ends here, from the point of view of Montreuillois), and works the same way the Métro works throughout Paris: with individual tickets or a Navigo card.

The fancy new T2 tramline stops every four minutes at the nearby Parc de Saint-Cloud and Musée de Sèvres stops. This is a convenient route to take to get to La Défense or the convention center at Porte de Versailles. The nearest SNCF *gares* with connections to destinations throughout France are located in Saint-Cloud and Issy-les-Moulineaux, both of which are easily reachable by bus.

Levallois-Perret

Sandwiched between posh Neuilly-sur-Seine and the humble suburb of Clichy-la-Garenne, Levallois-Perret delivers charm and an unbeatable quality of life within skipping distance of west Paris. Though the population hovers at around 65,000, Levallois (luh-vahl-WAH), as it is known locally, exudes a homey, small-town feeling that only hints at its location next to the French capital. The square-shaped suburb in the department of Hauts-de-Seine (92) spans 241 hectares, which is a fraction of the size of the nearby Bois de Boulogne. And within those tidy 241 hectares sit countless reasons why you should consider calling Levallois home.

Levallois's strongest selling points are its small-town community feel coupled with big-city amenities. The main commercial area is compact and easily navigable on foot, and the entire town center can be experienced in an hour. Levallois is full of schools—more than 20 public and private institutions altogether—and enough recreation centers to keep the town's entire population of under-16s occupied and out of trouble on Wednesdays and other non-school days. There are three weekly markets spread over five days, offering convenient access to fresh fruit, vegetables, and other goodies from friendly vendors in quintessential outdoor-market settings. The welcoming, orderly town center boasts a variety of chic boutiques that eliminate the need for trips to Paris or La Défense. But hardware supply stores and shops selling kitchen accoutrements are also part of the commercial landscape. And no French city could function without a *caviste* (wine vendor), cheese shop, and, of course, a *boulangerie*—or five.

Its weakest point is its traffic, which wouldn't be so bad at times were the streets not so narrow. (One double-parked car can cause a remarkable traffic jam.) The city gets high marks for security; women report feeling safe here when coming home late—something that cannot be said of all towns constituting the Petite Couronne. Housing is varied and much more affordable than in Paris, and transportation is equally diversified and dependable.

If you appreciate the serenity that comes with living in a town that's sleepy after dark and feels a bit ghost-townish on weekends (you're going to have to make the big, five-minute trip to Paris for nightlife), but still want the option of choosing between sushi or saag aloo for dinner, Levallois could be the perfect blend of quiet and cosmopolitan that's just right for you.

WHERE TO LIVE

Levallois sits in a prime position for commuters; it's within an easy public-transport trip or bike ride to both central Paris and La Défense. The river hugs Levallois's north side, and from a staircase on the Pont de Levallois, you can access Île de la Jatte, an island on the Seine made famous by Impressionist painter Georges Seurat in his work *Un Dimanche Après-Midi à l'Île de la Grande Jatte.* Along the two-kilometer stretch of island, you'll find tennis courts, a couple of small parks, a restaurant, and an aquarium-themed museum. This is also the honey-producing corner of town, with two dozen beehives used as both a pedagogical resource and as a moneymaker for the city, which harvests the honey and sells 2,000 jars of it to the public each year.

To the east is Paris, and more specifically, the bourgeois neighborhoods of the 17th

The square in front of the *mairie* offers a fine vantage point of the local architecture.

arrondissement. Porte de Maillot—with its RER station, Air France shuttles to Roissy-Charles de Gaulle airport, and big buses to the more distant Beauvais airport—is an easy 15-minute trip, and to reach the Champs-Élysées you'll just need to spend five minutes more on the Métro.

You can't go wrong in Levallois—nearly every corner of this town is what even the most discerning property evaluators would deem "high-standard living." The exceptions would be the farthest southeast section of town, near the SNCF train station and the great ring road known as the *périphérique*. The feeling here is a bit industrial, and the noise levels tend to be higher. If you want guaranteed "pretty" and "calm," confine your search to the areas south and west of cacophonous rue Victor Hugo.

HOUSING

The architecture styles in Levallois range from late-19th century apartment complexes to built-last-week single-family dwellings. What you choose depends on your lifestyle, sense of aesthetics, and most importantly, your budget. The *plus cher* (more expensive) housing is found in the most desirable neighborhoods, which are almost exclusively on the Neuilly side of rue President Wilson, one of the main streets bisecting the city. Houses are in very limited supply and start at around a half a million euros and just climb higher and higher from there. Apartments, on the other hand, are plentiful. A recent search turned up a vintage one-bedroom apartment with two fireplaces and hardwood floors for €350,000, and if you increase your budget by €100,000, you might find a spacious, new apartment on the Neuilly border with a terrace big enough for a small dance party.

a typical corner in Levallois

Renters have good options here. Short-term rental agency Paris Attitude (www.parisattitude.com) offers a decent selection of apartments, beginning at about €800 per month for a studio, not including the agency's finder's fee. Another online destination to apartment scout is ImmoStreet (www.en.immostreet.com), which acts as a one-stop clearinghouse for all the available housing on the local market. The generous inventory covers all manner of dwellings, from luxury apartments to simple studios. Each listing includes the languages spoken by the realtor representing the space, and most list English.

DAILY LIFE

The bee, or *abeille*, is the town's official mascot, and like the horses of Maisons-Laffitte, you see bee iconography splashed all over town. Symbolically, the bees represent the industrious, hard-working nature of the Levalloisiens. In previous epochs, Levallois was, like other cities in the Petite Couronne that encircles Paris, an industrial zone dotted with factories and workshops representing various crafts and trades. Today, many of the old brick and stone buildings from the industrial heyday have been revamped and transformed into attractive office buildings and living spaces.

Finding work won't be hard if you include Paris, which is literally minutes away, in your job search. If you're in the medical profession, the American Hospital in Paris—which is right next door in the upscale town of Neuilly—boasts a staff of 850 and regularly recruits new hires directly from the hospital's website (www.american-hospital.org). You don't have to be a doctor or a nurse to land a job here; the hospital also needs full-time plumbers, administrative assistants, and maintenance workers. Other

The *centre-ville* is where you'll find all of life's necessities.

local employment resources can be found on the Blog Ressources Emploi Formation (www.leblogbref.wordpress.com).

Though the city ethos is family-centric and sedate, daily life always includes downtime over *un verre* or *un café*. Meeting people and developing a social life in Levallois is easier if you speak French, and easier still if your personality is outgoing. Attending local events, such as the lectures and art exhibits offered by the three municipal *médiathèques* (www.mediatheque.ville-levallois.fr), is the best way to integrate and have fun while you do it.

Centre-Ville

Levallois's commercial center is clustered around the *mairie*, which sits tall in a sprawling plaza kitted out with fountains and eye-catching sculptures. Three blocks away is the pedestrian quarter and covered marketplace, plus a Monoprix, and a Carrefour supermarket. This is also where you'll find some of Levallois's nicest cafés and restaurants. The Maurice Ravel music conservatory (33, rue Gabriel Péri) is here. The school, named for the French composer who is buried in the local cemetery, hosts many music, dance, and theater performances throughout the year, and opens its doors to the music-making public interested in using the recording studio and rehearsal spaces.

Schools and Community Centers

Levallois is fully equipped for families with school-age children. Depending on where you live and your child's education level, he or she might be placed in one of 11 *maternelles*, 10 *écoles élémentaires*, or 4 *collèges*. The only local high school, Lycée Polyvalent Léonard de Vinci, sits a few blocks west between the Palais des Sports and the Seine.

Local lycéens can also attend the Lycée Montalembert in Courbevoie, on the other side of the river near La Défense. Registration begins as early as a year in advance depending on the school, so the minute you know you're going to settle in Levallois, visit the *mairie* and ask for help with *pre-inscriptions,* or download the registration forms from the *mairie*'s website at www.pi.ville-levallois.fr.

There is also the option of enrolling your kid(s) in two private combo *maternelles/ écoles élémentaires*: Emilie Brandt (www.emiliebrandt.fr), which is based on the teachings of Maria Montessori, and Sainte-Marie—Saint-Justin (www.stemarie-stjustin.fr), a Catholic school also open to middle-school students. If interested, make an appointment to visit the schools and talk to bilingual administrative staff.

While there aren't any university campuses in Levallois-Perret, adults still have a nice selection of educational opportunities. Two local associations offer French-language classes for non-native speakers. Association Pluriel (www.associationpluriel.free.fr, tel. 01/47 56 92 28) is a women's organization that offers two-hour classes four days a week at a nominal fee. Association Apprendre (www.apprendre-levallois-perret.org) is a little more expensive, but is open to everyone.

Acceuil des Villes Françaises (AVF, www.avf.asso.fr/fr/levallois) is a national Welcome Wagon of sorts. The group in Levallois will help you acclimate to local life and volunteers speak multiple languages, including English.

The center for the arts known as L'Escale is a great resource. Besides arts courses like life-drawing, pottery, and jewelry making, l'Escale also offers floral arranging and free digital arts training. Early registration begins in May for classes beginning in September. Register early to ensure you get the classes you want.

French communities love their public swimming pools, and the folks in Levallois are no different in their love of a watery workout. The indoor pool at the Centre Aquatique (15, rue Raspail, tel. 01/47 15 74 50) is just one of the draws; the hammam, sauna, and Jacuzzi are others. Classes for all age levels include diving and aquagym.

Leisure

Nearly 20 percent of Levallois's real estate is dedicated green space, yet another reason this place is so livable. Of the dozens of parks and squares scattered throughout the city, the largest, Parc de la Planchette, is the most pleasant. Inside the stately gated park two blocks from the *mairie*, a sea of green grass bordered by bright clusters of flowers awaits you. There's a children's play area, a pleasant pond with fountain, and benches galore.

Getting Around

It's worth repeating that Levallois is small. You can easily get by here without a car, and you probably should, since streets are narrow and parking comes at a premium price.

Two of the town's three Métro stations are within a four-block radius of the *mairie*, which gives easy access into Paris. Levallois is well served by public transport—specifically, Métro Line 3 and its three stops in the city that ensure you're never more than a 15-minute walk away from a quick ride into Paris. There are also 11 different public buses departing Levallois for destinations throughout the west side of the Île de France that accept Navigo and standard t+ transport tickets, plus a free local bus service called Les Abeilles. Les Abbeilles's two lines (A and B, or "Bee" if you like to have fun with words) cover the entire town, and run seven days a week (with limited hours on Sunday).

A smart way to travel around town is by Velib'; there are 14 stations throughout Levallois, and you can also take the bicycles into Paris and park them at any Velib' station there without penalty. Another great option is walking. This is the best method for discovering all the town's hidden treasures, and getting a sense of the community's vibe.

Montreuil

The suburb of Montreuil sits in the department of Seine-Saint-Denis (93), sits just over the eastern edge of Paris's city limits, sandwiched between the suburb of Bagnolet to the north and Saint-Mandé to the south. This diverse city has one of the area's highest populations of immigrants from Mali, and a whopping 40 percent of the total population is younger than 30. You can expect to see small clusters of teenagers hanging out on corners around the city, interspersed with families out pushing strollers and walking dogs.

In Paris, everything east of the Bastille has a palpable cool factor. There's a vaguely rough-around-the-edges vibe on the east side that's distinct from the more grown-up ambiance oozing out from the west-side arrondissements. With the east side's hipster quotient as a starting point, you can leap over the *périphérique* and into Montreuil (pronounced "mon-TROY"), which some cultural analysts call the new frontier for creative types in the Île-de-France region, based in large part on its cheap housing. That's one of Montreuil's huge draws.

Since 2008, the city has transformed under mayor Dominique Voynet into an eco-friendly, modern, and urban community. The *centre-ville* has undergone a massive makeover, and student housing developments, a shopping and commercial center, theater, and subsidized daycare center for children have increased Montreuil's overall value and made it more attractive to newcomers. More public works projects are scheduled, including community gardens and green housing developments.

Artists, attracted by the cheap rent and access to creative space, began moving into Montreuil, sometimes renovating rough and raw spaces. Today, a flourishing independent art scene is gaining more attention from communities outside the Montreuil city limits. Autumn open-house events in the artists' ateliers are a big draw for Parisians eager to see the works of the next Jean-Michel Basquiat or Toulouse-Lautrec. These and other art-world events get support from the city government, which rolls out the welcome mat to new residents employed in creative fields. Today, Montreuil is second only to Paris for the number of artists per capita.

If you work in a liberal profession, appreciate a diverse community with a strong immigrant population, are working with a modest housing budget (or want to get a lot of room for your euro), and aren't afraid to tread new ground in an area that many consider a little too edgy, Montreuil could definitely be for you.

WHERE TO LIVE

Besides the *centre-ville*, there are five primary neighborhoods: Bas Montreuil, Bel Air, La Noue, Ramenas, and Ruffins; each has its own character and flavor. The neighborhoods bordering the *centre-ville*—Bas Montreuil and La Noue, in particular—are

one of Montreuil's pedestrianized commercial strip

considered the most attractive to newcomers, based on their proximity to commercial services and transportation. In the city's far southeastern corner you'll find a few unattractive housing projects that aren't as bad as they look, though this quartier could definitely use a bit of spiffing up. The further north and east you are, the more suburban Montreuil feels, but you're never more than a few blocks from a hub of commercial activity.

Montreuillois are passionate about their city, describing it as having a village-like atmosphere with a dash of "It's a Small World After All." But with the influx of *bobos* who've raised real estate prices, the working-class populations have been pushed to the periphery—especially out toward Haut Montreuil, in the northeast section of town. The most desirable areas are still those nearest transportation and to Paris—Bas Montreuil being particularly attractive. The neighborhoods that border on upscale Vincennes offer a great value for the money; people looking for a bit of cachet will want to seek out housing opportunities in the Croix de Chavaux neighborhood, which offers some of Montreuil's best shopping and dining. If you're looking for dirt-cheap options that require work and a bit of a schlep to get to the nearest transport hub, try the area around Parc Montreau known as Le Morillon.

HOUSING

Considering its proximity to Paris, Montreuil is an incredibly affordable place to live, especially if you want to invest in real estate. Where else can in the area can you buy a house for less than €200,000 (or an apartment for half that) that's within walking

© AURELIA D'ANDREA

Montreuil's *hôtel de ville* evokes a modern sensibility that's reflected throughout the city.

distance of a Métro station where trains will whizz you into central Paris in just 15 minutes? Be forewarned: The news is spreading! With luck, there'll still be a solid supply of safe, affordable accommodations when you arrive in arty, eclectic Montreuil.

Subsidized housing is available to those most in need, in generous quantities. But even those with modest budgets can get a grasp onto Montreuil's housing prices, which tend to be lower than other Parisian suburbs. Throughout the city you'll find single-family houses, row-house bungalows, multi-story apartment complexes, and vintage belle époque apartments with quiet courtyards and wrought-iron balconies. Finding the right place for you is best done with the help of an expert, and there are many *immobiliers* at your disposal throughout Montreuil.

If you're a family of three earning less than €45,000 per year, you're eligible for Habitations Bon Marché (HBM) in Montreuil. The options vary, but if you're lucky, you might land a lovely eco-friendly apartment in the newly revamped town center. Discover your options at www.adil93.org.

If budget isn't such a big concern, you'll find options galore. Expect to spend about €800 for a new-construction one-bedroom apartment that includes a parking space, or slightly less for something similar, sans parking, built in the 1930s and rendered in brick. With a slightly bigger budget, you'll be able to acquire a lot more room, including outdoor space. For around €1,100, you could have a cute *maisonette* with a back-yard that's double the size of your inside living space. With a budget closer to €1,500, you could find a two-bedroom, eco-friendly apartment with a parking space and a balcony overlooking a quiet square.

With a buyer's budget, the options continue to expand. From cozy studios ringing in at less than €100,000 to three-bedroom houses built on tree-studded parcels of land next to Parc Montreau for triple that price, options abound. Inventory is still copious in Montreuil, but that will surely change in the next five years, as more and more people discover this gem.

Students have good housing options. Scouting the possibilities online is easy at the Office de Tourisme's student housing portal (www.montreuiltourisme.fr/logements-etudiants.html). Submit your requirements via a secure online form, or take the initiative and call the numbers listed beneath the ads for the housing options that look the most interesting.

DAILY LIFE

The evolution of Montreuil is a favorite topic in Paris media circles (pundits have compared it to post-Wall Berlin, based on Montreuil's eclectic, graffiti-splashed façade and youthful, artsy spirit). Each quartier has its own twice- or thrice-weekly public market that brings the locals out as much for the fresh vegetables as for the social component. The Thursday-Friday-Sunday Marché Croix de Chavaux at la Place du Marché is the most frequented, and is conveniently located next to the Métro around the corner from the Office of Tourism. Here you'll find fresh fruit and vegetables, clothing, food stalls, household goods, and thick crowds.

While it sometimes feels as though life in France revolves around food, there is definitely more to Montreuil than its markets and restaurants. One fun way to get your hands dirty is by becoming a member of a community garden. Montreuil's history is steeped in horticultural tradition, and that legacy lives on in the nine *jardins partagés* positioned throughout the city. For a small fee, you get access to a small plot of earth *and* a new community of green-thumbed friends. To find the community garden nearest you, contact the city's department of the environment (tel. 01/48 70 67 94) and ask for a list.

Another way to attune to the rhythms of daily life here is to volunteer. The website www.francebenevolat.org can connect you to opportunities; if you're outgoing, consider becoming an official Montreuil "greeter." Greeters welcome newcomers and take them on walking tours of the city's most interesting corners, sharing history and local lore, and offering practical information. To become a greeter, visit the department's website at www.tourisme93.com. To test out a tour, contact the wonderfully helpful, friendly, bilingual staff at the Office de Tourism (1, rue Kléber, tel. 01/41 58 14 09). They're eager to help and are much more accessible than the public information staff at the *mairie*.

Centre-Ville

Montreuil's *centre-ville* is built around the *mairie*, also called the *hôtel de ville*. This is not only the municipal hub, but a place where citizens gather to shop, socialize, and relax. This quartier is undergoing an exciting transformation, with the intent of making Montreuil's center an even more livable, enjoyable environment for all. A cinema, environmentally friendly affordable housing, a neighborhood nursery, and pedestrian shopping promenade designed by some of France's best and brightest architects are just some of the projects already completed or currently under way, with an estimated completion date for the entire project scheduled for 2015. The city's webpage (www.montreuil.fr) offers an exciting glimpse into the Montreuil of the very near future.

Schools and Community Centers

City developers anticipate continued growth in Montreuil and are building an infrastructure plan to support the arrival of more families (with school-age children, in particular) into the area. Several new schools are in the works, which will beef up Montreuil's already hefty number of educational institutions. More than 25 *maternelles* are scattered throughout Montreuil, as well as more than 20 *écoles élémentaires*. Of the four lycées, one is a trade school (www.lyceehorticulture93.fr) dedicated to preparing horticulturists for jobs as fruit and vegetable farmers, florists, or landscape designers.

Between the pleasant Parc des Beaumonts and the smaller, more charming Parc Montreau, you'll find the university campus for IUT Montreuil, an institute of technology that's part of the University of Paris system. The school offers two-year degrees in information technology and computer science. International students are welcome. To apply, visit the Campus France website (www.campusfrance.org).

Those who want to expand their skill sets and learn new crafts have a bounty of options. At La Maison de Quartier Espéranto (14, allée Roland-Martin, tel. 01/41 58 50 92), adult classes include a weekly dressmaking atelier and four-days-a-week French immersion class that's a bargain at just €20 for the academic year. Children's classes and events geared toward seniors are also on the menu.

In alignment with its artistic nature, Montreuil is home to a professional school of music and dance called Le Conservatoire (www.conservatoire-montreuil.fr). Housed in a funky, futuristic building designed and constructed in the 1970s, Le Conservatoire welcomes students of all ages and offers public performances in its Maurice Ravel auditorium.

Leisure

Nature lovers will appreciate Montreuil's proximity to one of Paris's "lungs," otherwise known as the Bois de Vincennes. The forest (*bois*) sits just south of the city in neighboring Vincennes and is one of the few places in the area where you can escape the sound of traffic. Within Montreuil's city limits, there are parks aplenty, including the 22-hectare Parc des Beaumonts, the hilly Parc Jean Moulin, and the exceptionally pleasant Parc Montreau. It's here that you'll discover the Musée de l'Histoire Vivante (www.museehistoirevivante.com) and its marvelous collection of historical photos and documents. No one should miss the town's most celebrated *espace vert* called Les Murs à Pêches. The area around this 30-acre garden a few blocks east of the *mairie* has been a peach-growing region since the time of Louis XIV. Today, the walled gardens serve as an outdoor education center and horticultural museum that makes a great excursion for people of all ages.

© AURELIA D'ANDREA

Three Métro stops offer plenty of access to Paris.

Montreuil doesn't have the same gastronomic reputation as Paris, but you definitely won't go hungry. In addition to restaurants serving tapas, Asian cuisine, and traditional fare, the city boasts no fewer than a dozen food trucks, most clustered around the central market at Croix de Chavaux.

Getting Around

Montreuil's two-lane main road, rue de Paris, stretches a few kilometers from Porte de Montreuil past the Robespierre Métro stop to the city's second Métro stop at Croix de Chavaux, where traffic twists and flows and bends. The street changes names a few times before bringing you to the office of the *mairie* at Place Jean Juarès, the site of many major urban-renewal plans slated for the coming years.

You'll find nearly 20 Velib' stations scattered throughout Montreuil, as well Métro line 9, with its three stops including Robespierre, Croix de Chavaux, and Mairie de Montreuil. Either option is good for getting you into Paris in a jiffy. Nine bus lines serve the city, with routes that tend to run between suburban transport hubs. You'll find the nearest RER station over the *périphérique* in Paris, at Nation, where trains will transport you throughout the Île-de-France region.

GRANDE COURONNE

The Grand Couronne's gently rolling landscape looks as if it were pulled from the pages of a children's fairy-tale book. Between forests and châteaux sit scenic villages, their church steeples piercing the skyline in the town center. At midday, the church bells sound off, harking back to an era before mobile phones or even wristwatches. It seems almost unfathomable that this bucolic terrain is less than a 45-minute train ride from one of the world's busiest tourist destinations.

The Grand Couronne forms the outer ring of the Île-de-France region and comprises four administrative departments that include Seine-et-Marne (77), Yvelines (78), Essonne (91), and Val d'Oise (95). Versailles and Maisons-Laffitte are located within the département of Yvelines, but other livable cities and towns are scattered through the "Big Crown" and are worth exploring for newcomers who want a *Green Acres* lifestyle, but crave big-city access.

Versailles sits roughly 20 kilometers southwest of Paris. To get here by train or car, you'll pass through national forest land that echoes with the history and legends of the great monarchs, including the Sun King, Louis XIV, who lived and died at the Versailles headquarters where he reigned over France for more than 70 years. The town's regal bearing hasn't tarnished over the years; it's still a city worthy of royalty—or anyone who likes to live like a king or a queen. Full of world-class amenities yet

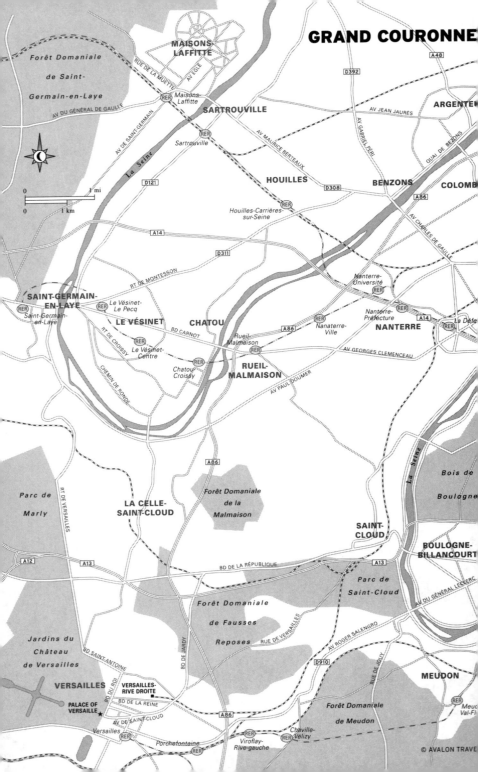

small enough to navigate without a car, Versailles is the perfect place to call home if you find Paris overwhelming but still want a slice of city life.

Though Maisons-Laffitte isn't a household name outside of France the way Versailles is, the town of 23,000 has cultivated a local reputation over the years as a green and pleasant place to lay down roots. Maisons-Laffitte exudes an equestrian vibe thanks to the hippodrome, a plethora of stables where locals and out-of-towners keep their horses (some stables have even been revamped as short-term rental units for tourists). Bridle paths zig-zag from the town center out to the nearby forest of Saint-Germain-en-Laye. Local residents will tell you this is a great place to raise kids and to experience a country-like lifestyle with the great advantage of being able to escape to the city in just 20 minutes.

Versailles

If you didn't know any better, you might think that the only thing Versailles has going for it is its famous château. While it's true that the sprawling, gilded royal palace pumps an endless stream of tourist dollars into the local economy, Versailles is a fully functioning town in its own right. Local industry includes museums, several institutions of higher learning and dozens of elementary and high schools, and five railway stations. And there are also restaurants, hotels, and shops by the dozens that serve both the year-round tourist population and the permanent local community.

Twenty-first century Versailles is not what it was when young Marie Antoinette and her husband Louis XVI occupied that giant swath of land that makes up the western

© AURELIA D'ANDREA

Can't find the castle gates? Follow the crowds.

quadrant of the city. While French everywhere, including Versailles, might say they still feel the pinch of over-taxation, it's easy to see that a good chunk of those hard-earned euros have been invested into the community for the betterment of all who trod the cobbled streets. Sidewalks are tidy and nearly dog-poo free, the transportation system is efficient and well-organized, and social services for residents are plentiful. Music, theater, and art are important facets of local culture, and the city government makes events and activities accessible to all throughout the year.

The average age of a Versailles resident is 39 years old, though there is a thriving senior population and a host of social services to support this segment of the population. The sheer numbers of both private and public schools translates to an evolving population of young people who inject a youthful vibe into the city, and keep the entertainment options interesting and varied.

Versailles is a good location if you want big-city amenities in a sedate, safe, and pretty community. It helps to be okay with apartment living—or have a sizeable budget to be able to afford a house here, which doesn't come cheap—and to be forgiving of tourists, who flood the city day in and day out. Locals describe this as a good place to raise children, and outdoorsy types appreciate the immediate access to nature. Come visit, step off the tourist trail, and decide for yourself whether this historic city is a place you can call home.

WHERE TO LIVE

Versailles sits 19 kilometers, or roughly 12 miles, southwest of Paris in the department of Yvelines (78). The city is carved into seven distinct neighborhoods: Bernard-de-Jussieu (often called simply "Jussieu"), Chantiers, Clagny-Glatigny, Montreuil, Notre-Dame, Porchefontaine, and Saint-Louis. The two neighborhoods expats will want to consider for their convenient proximity to shops, transportation, nightlife, and entertainment are Saint-Louis and Notre-Dame. (If you face the palace head on, the former sits to the right, and the latter to the left.) Saint-Louis is the quieter neighborhood, with a beautiful 18th-century cathedral at its center, and on Saturdays an adorable organic market springs up in the square in front of the cathedral. The neighborhood has a sort of antiquated charm, but suffers from the occasional tourist overflow—especially on the restaurant-lined rue de Satory. Generally, the neighborhood is calm and pleasant, and close to several green spaces. Heading the other direction, you'll find yourself in a more vibrant and dynamic Notre-Dame neighborhood—Versailles's commercial center. Besides the thrice-weekly market, this is where you'll discover the city's café life. The further away from these two quartiers you move, the more suburban it feels. Wherever you end up in Versailles, it's practically guaranteed to be safe, pleasant, and not too far from shops and transportation.

HOUSING

Versailles is a *ville* consisting primarily of apartment dwellers. When searching for a place to call home, you'll find more 19th-century options than you will modern construction, but there are definitely plenty of post-war options offering more space for your euro. Depending on your budget, you might find yourself in a teeny-tiny *chambre de bonne* (maid's room) the size of a typical American walk-in closet, or a belle époque house tucked into tidy gardens. It's a case of you get what you pay for,

Housing options include pretty 19th-century townhouses.

and on the lower end of the spectrum, you can fork over less than €100,000 for a minuscule bachelor pad or more than €1 million for your dream home. There's a little something for most everyone here—"little" being the operative word, unless your budget is generous. The price per square meter is less here than in Paris, but it doesn't always feel that way when you explore the real estate market. Keep a positive attitude and meet with local realtors regularly to broaden your possibilities. Recent real estate searches turned up an eighth-floor studio apartment with a *jolie* terrace overlooking the verdant countryside for €260,000—parking and *cave* (basement space) included. For just a bit more, you could buy a brand-spanking new villa—with a pool!—near the Gare des Chantiers, with three bedrooms and lots of space for kids to run around.

Renters won't feel the real estate sting quite as acutely; you can find a roomy studio apartment built in 1970 that overlooks a pleasant garden for €500 per month in the Montreuil neighborhood, for example. For €100 more, you could have yourself a lovely one-bedroom built in 1800 with parquet floors and a bathtub (a rarity in French apartments) in the heart of the desirable Saint-Louis neighborhood. In the same neighborhood, with a monthly budget of €1,350, you could even have your own two-bedroom house with beamed ceilings and a *boulangerie* and restaurants right out your doorstep.

When conducting your exploratory visit of Versailles, pick up a copy of the Logic-Immo booklet available outside most real estate offices. Inside you'll find a fabulous cross section of local for-sale and rental options. Seloger.com is another site to bookmark and visit regularly. You'll find both rentals and for-sale options here, too.

DAILY LIFE

Because of its proximity to Paris, Versailles is considered a bedroom community of the French capital. Train delays aside, the RER trip into Paris is shorter than a Métro ride from the Louvre to Porte de Saint-Cloud. And the train ride to the Val de Seine, an important business district just over the Parisian *périphérique,* where many high-tech and communications companies have their headquarters, is just 20 minutes away. That's not to say that work can't be found within walking distance of your Versailles home. There are many ways to land meaningful work in Versailles, but finding it requires an investment of time and energy. For college students, au pair work affords many opportunities, and American-owned companies including the swank, Hilton-owned Trianon Palace Hotel regularly hire expats with the right qualifications. Academia is another good place to launch your professional search. Teaching English—or another subject at which you excel—is a perennial favorite career choice for expats.

With your money-making concerns out of the way, you can focus on enjoying the relaxed way of life that Versailles offers. Weekend retreats to the forest are a favorite local activity, and offer great bird-watching, hiking, and biking opportunities. The Bibliothèque Centrale (5, rue de l'Indépendance, tel. 01/39 07 13 20) is one popular hub of cultural activity, and getting your library card is a rite of passage that gives you access not just to reading material, but lectures, kids' events, art openings, and film screenings. Families with more than three children are also eligible for a *familles nombreuses* card that gives discounts on local services including transportation and cultural events.

Centre-Ville

An estimated 10 million tourists flock to the château every year, but only a fraction of those folks venture a few blocks over to experience the charming *centre-ville* and its cafés, pedestrian passageways, and historical corners. *C'est dommage* because there's really so much to do and see for a compact city of 90,000, and much of what's interesting sits smack in the middle, including picturesque daily and weekly markets, museums, cinemas, and theaters.

The local commercial center is clustered around the Halles Notre-Dame, which you might refer to as "vintage Versailles." At the behest of the Sun King himself, the town was expanded beginning in 1681 and retains its old world glamour with a few modern updates. Inside the covered marketplaces are wine merchants, fish mongers, butchers, cheese vendors, vegetable sellers. If it's Tuesday, Friday, or Sunday, the food offerings outside double, with dozens of vendors erecting their temporary stalls overflowing with seasonal fruits and vegetables. On Saturdays, the same outdoor market space morphs into a clothing and knick-knacks market bursting with kitchen utensils and other household goods, shoes, and body care products.

There is no shortage of *boulangeries* here; in fact, there seems to be more bread being baked in Versailles than the city population could possibly consume! Part of the fun in getting to know Versailles is doing some exploratory tasting. Scattered around the *centre-ville* are a Monoprix, Super U, and Franprix, each offering additional possibilities for food shopping. You'll also discover clothing stores for every variety of stylista, hardware stores, and hair salons. The terrace cafés that seem sedate in winter, fill when the sun is shining and inject a dose of vitality into the public sphere.

Terrace cafés appear sedate in winter.

Schools and Community Centers

Versailles is a community that values academics; there are a dozen lycées, 10 university-level public and private institutions, and a highly developed infrastructure to support local and foreign students who come here to further their educations. For a comprehensive list of schools, short- and long-term courses, and other educational programs, pick up a free copy of the *Guide des Lycéens et Étudiants de Versailles* at the *mairie*. Twice a year, in September and January, schools host open-house events called *journées ouvertes portes* that give parents and prospective students the chance to investigate the schools, meet the academic staff, and learn more about each school's philosophy and curriculum. Versailles also hosts an annual student salon that serves as a one-stop shop for all academic inquiries. The weekly news magazine *L'Express* publishes an online magazine for students called *L'Étudiant*. The site is comprehensive and includes dates of all upcoming salons and events in Versailles and throughout France.

Teenagers and young adults will benefit from familiarizing themselves with *Jeunes à Versailles* (www.jversailles.fr), a web portal offering access to issues of interest to that demographic, including student housing, cultural opportunities, employment, and other goings on about town.

Outside of academia, Piscine Montbauron (7, rue Léon Gatin, www.vert-marine.com/piscine-montbauron-versailles-78) is a hotspot for seniors—especially the Tuesday and Thursday morning "aquastretching" classes. Entry to the pool alone is €4.60, though you get a good discount when you buy a 10-entries card (€37). Children, depending on their ages, can enter either free or for €3.60 per visit. Prices for classes vary, but it's worth looking into an annual or monthly membership, which gives access to the pool, sauna, steam room, and gym equipment.

Each of Versailles' eight neighborhoods has its own *maison de quartier* that can help you discover activities and events. These volunteer-run associations are helpful when it comes to finding French-language courses; enrolling in one is one of the best ways to integrate into the community.

Every year during the first week of September, the town hosts a *portes ouvertes* event for locals to get acquainted with the more than 100 community *associations* (nonprofit and often volunteer-run organizations) where you can join others with an interest in tennis or hip-hop or swing dance or knitting. Can't make it to the open house event? Visit the *mairie* and ask for a free copy of the latest *Guide des associations de Versailles*.

The staff of the *mairie* (4, avenue de Paris, www.versailles.fr) are extremely friendly, and you'll likely be given more welcome-to-Versailles brochures than you could have ever hoped for. For a guaranteed English-language experience, you're better off making a beeline for the Office de Tourism (2 bis, avenue de Paris, www.versailles-tourisme.com). Open seven days a week, this busy spot two minutes from the château offers a lot of the same information you'll find at the *mairie,* though with a less personal and more informal delivery (this is where tourists come seeking information). Be sure to pick up a copy of the hefty bilingual *Guide du Tourisme à Versailles.* Inside are maps, restaurant listings, a calendar of events, and hotel recommendations.

If you're planning to settle in Versailles, you must visit the Préfecture des Yvelines (1, rue Jean Houdon, tel. 01/39 49 78 00), where you'll register as an *étranger* (foreigner) and apply for your *titre de séjour* (and hopefully retrieve your *carte* once your dossier has been submitted and paperwork approved). The building is conveniently located across from the *mairie.*

© AURELIA D'ANDREA

The covered market is a foodie's paradise.

Leisure

Beyond the 800-hectare green space that encompasses the château, Versailles is hemmed in by forest land, which the royals called their backyard. In 2013, a greenbelt circling the city was completed. This multi-use path offers walkers, runners, equestrians, and cyclists 18 kilometers of bucolic tree-lined pathway. To find it, head to the Parc Balbi (12, rue Maréchal Joffre). The path skirts the southern edge of this pretty park, where you'll also find traces of the original *potager* (kitchen garden) planted for a royal mistress. The well-manicured green space gives off a proper English garden vibe, with its ponds, statues, gazebo, and grotto. Herons and other birds like to visit its waterways, and so do locals, who picnic here in fair weather.

Outside of the palace gardens and forest area, the most impressive green space in the area is the 2,000-hectare Forêt de Marly le Roi, just northwest of the château. This is the former hunting grounds of the bloodthirsty royals, and today there are still a few creatures to be found in the woods, including deer, pheasants, and foxes. Roaming the groomed trails of this verdant paradise is the ideal antidote to a stressful day at the office.

Getting Around

From Paris, you can get to Versailles by train, car, bus, or bicycle (it's really not that far), and once you've arrived at your destination, the terrain is mostly flat and easy to navigate on foot. Versailles boasts five railway stations, spread out across the city from north to south and east and west. The station closest to the château, Gare Rive Gauche, is also the closest to the *centre-ville*. Walking out the front doors of this station puts you out onto avenue Charles de Gaulle.

Versailles's public transportation system is known as Phébus, and includes a network of buses, public bicycles, and local train. Tickets for single ride on the bus or regional train are €2, or you can buy a *carnet* of 10 tickets—the same ones you use in Paris for the Métro and buses—for €13.70. On buses, you can buy tickets from the driver. Children 4 years old and younger ride free, and kids between the ages of 4 and 10 are entitled to a half-price discount.

Bicycles can be hired by the hour (€2), day (€12), or year (€300). Reserve your bike online (www.velo-versailles.fr) or make the transaction in person at Place Raymond Poincaré, just in front of the Versailles-Chantier train station. If you have a Navigo pass, there's good news: The local transportation network is linked to the Navigo system, meaning you can use your pass on local buses and trains. For more information on using Navigo, see the *Travel and Transportation* chapter.

Maisons-Laffitte

A 20-minute train ride northwest of Paris brings you to the little town of Maisons-Laffitte (population 23,000). Horse culture dominates this two-by-four-kilometer rectangle of land along the Seine; enthusiasts from around the world flock to the town's celebrated hippodrome for horse-jumping and dressage, races, and other events. Reminders are everywhere: statues of horses, horse silhouettes on commercial signs, horse paths literally carved right next to pedestrian walking paths throughout town. You don't have to love horses or know how to ride them to live here, but it definitely doesn't hurt and it's one of the reasons so many expats are attracted to the area. Because where there are horses, there are also places to ride them, and this region is full of beautiful forest paths and wide-open green spaces for trotting and galloping your way to a good life.

A major lure for newcomers is the room you have here to stretch out, to breathe, and to feel like you've got a little slice of provincial France (trees, gardens, backyards), while still keeping Paris and all its amenities within close reach. If you want a beautiful vintage house with an expansive green lawn for the dogs and kids to run amok in, you can find that here—at a price. Good schools and an almost old-fashioned community feeling are other reasons out-of-towners come to lay down roots.

Besides the horse theme running through Maisons-Laffitte, one thing you're sure to

© AURELIA D'ANDREA

Maisons-Laffitte is a welcoming city with a small-town feel.

notice right away is that English is spoken throughout town. That's due in large part to l'Ermitage, the American-owned international school on avenue Eglé, which attracts a worldly crowd of kids, many of whom are expats from North America and England. Further evidence of a strong Anglophone presence here are restaurant menus, which are often written in both French and English. Waiters tend to be multilingual, as are local shopkeepers, making the transition process for English-speaking newcomers that much smoother. Maisons-Laffitte gives a small-town vibe with many big city amenities—yet another reason it's so attractive to expats and others.

WHERE TO LIVE

Maisons-Laffitte sits on the *rive gauche* bend of the Seine as it winds west and north of Paris, on its way to the coast where it empties out into the harbor at Le Havre. To the west sits the forest of Saint-Germain-en-Laye, a haven of chestnut, beech, and oak trees that supports a diverse ecosystem of flora and fauna.

The town is bisected by the RER railway line. On one side lies a manageable tangle of narrow, suburban streets, lined with shops, sedate apartment housing, and the usual businesses and services. On the other side, the view is much greener, with vast swaths of grassy field and park space, carved into quintessentially French starbursts, and lined with stately houses surrounded by wrought-iron gates. Those who live on the verdant side of Maisons-Laffitte pay for the privilege by way of higher taxes, but you don't have to reside on this side of town to appreciate its wide-open spaces.

Wherever you settle, you'll be close to amenities and within walking distance of a pleasant green space, but if you want immediate proximity to the train station and amenities at your doorstep, concentrate your search on the area south and west of the train station. This is also the most affordable part of town; you'll pay less in taxes on this side of rue de la Passerelle, and find more choices here than in the über-coveted quarters to the north and east.

HOUSING

Moving to the suburbs usually means cheaper housing, but that's not true of Maisons-Laffitte. This is a town in high demand and housing prices reflect the quality of life coupled with proximity to Paris. To increase your chances, make sure your dossier is in order if you're a renter, or that your mortgage has been secured if you're ready to buy. Several real estate agents have their offices on ave

Shops along Maisons-Laffitte's main commercial strip have a definite French flair.

de Longueuil, but it's a good idea to peruse the possibilities online before you arrive to get a sense of what's available and to budget for the housing component of your living-abroad expenses. Local *immobiliers* online include Agence LeCocq (www.agencelecocq.com) and Alexendrie Immobilier (www.immobilier-maisons-laffitte.com). These agencies can help you locate potential new homes, whether you're looking for one of the coveted single-family homes or prefer the simplicity of apartment living.

The bulk of housing options here are apartment-style dwellings. Inventory ranges from vintage 19th-century walk-ups with parquet floors and wrought-iron balconies to late-20th-century-style apartments with a boxy flavor and more wiggle room, both inside and out. What you choose is a matter of aesthetics, budget, and availability, but you will have options—more so with a bigger budget. Inventory is slim, which is why the starting prices are so high. Expect to spend no less than €250,000 for a one-bedroom, one-bath house. The good news is that the value is usually good; if your budget can inch into the higher price brackets, you'll get more square meters for your euro than your apartment-dwelling counterparts.

Rental prices average roughly €20 per square meter for both houses and apartments. That translates to a 40-square-meter studio with parking and a *cave* (cellar storage area) in a contemporary building for €835 per month, or a spacious, 70-square-meter converted stable with two bedrooms and a shared yard for €1,125 per month. Houses are a little tougher to come by, but you might get lucky and land yourself a three-bedroom bungalow built in 2001 with a terrace and room enough to park two cars for €2,400 per month.

Real estate is snapped up quickly in this pretty part of the Île-de-France region.

DAILY LIFE

Like many Parisian suburbs, Maisons-Laffitte is a commuter town, with most of the local citizenry carpooling or training it into Paris every day. From rue Croix Castel, you can see the cluster of buildings that comprises La Défense, and the direct trains that depart the station throughout the day and evening, shuttling workers and day-trippers back and forth with ease. The town isn't completely without its own industry; a few high-tech companies have set up base here, including Altasys, Altersis, and ReadSoft. Other major employers include SNCF railway lines, and more than one dozen public and private elementary schools. Lunchtime means men and women in business attire filing in and out of the most popular restaurants, including Caffè e Cucina and Le Cosy, both of which attract a faithful clientele. Weekends, especially in warm weather, families are out enjoying the benefits of suburban living, both in town and in the neighboring forest of Saint-Germain-en-Laye.

The town's monthly magazine, *Vivre Maisons-Laffitte* (www.maisonslaffitte.fr), is available for free at both the *mairie* and the office of tourism across the street. Each issue details the month's cultural events and municipal news, and it is an excellent resource for anyone living in town. Directly across from the *mairie* is the town's cultural center, another important destination for the latest arts-related events. Expect an impressive offering of community activities that help make the place an interesting, vibrant, utterly un-dull place to live. Dance, theater, and musical events in a variety of genres are an important part of the local entertainment scene, and the cinema, l'Atalante, shows a varied selection of international films in their original languages (VO, or *version originale*) with subtitles, which is a real pleasure if you've ever sat through one of those dreadful dubbed films still playing at some French movie theaters.

You'll find plenty of wide-open spaces in Maisons-Laffitte.

On Wednesday and Saturday mornings, *la halle du marché* behind the railway station erupts into a lively shoppers mecca and gives neighbors another excuse for socializing. Fresh flower vendors, fish mongers, butchers, and vegetable sellers set up shop here, and can help you plan your evening meal (complete with cooking instructions) if you dare to solicit their advice *en français.*

Centre-Ville

Maisons-Laffitte's main commercial strip, avenue Longueuil, slices through the busiest few blocks of town, and anchors the commercial activity in the *centre-ville.* On both sides of the street, from the train station down to the rue de la Muette and the gates of the more verdant quarter of town three blocks east, are all the amenities you could hope for: butchers, bakers, and maybe candlestick makers—but definitely grocers, hair salons, restaurants, and doctor's offices. The street life here is a bit like an extension of one's living room; expect to meet up with friends or neighbors on the street, and to stop and chat for a while and catch up on the latest news.

Schools and Community Centers

Tax dollars in Maisons-Laffitte support not just the well-groomed green spaces, but a quality school system comprising both public and private institutions. The international school accepts high-school students, but it is the only *lycée* in town. Public options require a trip to neighboring Satrouville. For younger children, there are options aplenty, including eight *maternelles*, six *écoles élémentaires*, and three *collèges.* For more detailed information on the town's educational opportunities and how to enroll your child in school here, contact the Service des Affaires Scolaires (3, rue du

EXPAT EXPERIENCE: LIVING IN MAISONS-LAFITTE

Names: Mark and Cynthia Tronco
Age: 61 (Mark) and 48 (Cynthia)
Profession: Mark is a *garçon de cour* at a local racing stable; Cynthia is an IT professional

Where are you from originally?
New Jersey.

When and why did you move to Paris?
We originally moved to Paris when Cynthia was offered a three-year assignment at her firm's Paris office; Cynthia was working in the New York office at the time. We lived in Paris for four and a half years and have now been in Maisons-Lafitte for two and a half years.

Are you a homeowner or do you rent?
We are apartment owners.

What are some of the factors you considered before moving to the suburbs?
We do not have children so any related subject was not an issue. We wanted to find a place that was easily accessible for travel to and from Paris and La Défense, where Cynthia works, and the major airports, and where we would not need to own a car. Being within walking distance of train stations and shops was a necessity. The Paris real estate market was quite hot and high priced, and the search for a Paris apartment became too stressful to manage. Luckily, through Mark's interest in horses, we had made a few friends here and liked the town, so it became a natural alternative to Paris for us, in terms of price, availability of apartments to see, and indeed in terms of lifestyle and convenience.

Describe Maisons-Lafitte to someone who's never been there before.
Maisons-Lafitte is known as *Cité du Cheval*, which is how we wound up here. Mark has a strong interest in horses and the town is known for its training facilities. People are outgoing and friendly and the acclaimed international school here makes it popular with expats. We

Fossé, tel. 01/34 93 12 38). Depending on your child's age and school-year level, enrollment will take place either in March or April for the following academic year, so it's wise to plan ahead.

There's a lot for children to do to fight off the boredom that sometimes comes with living in a small town. At the Espace Jeunesse (6, rue du Fossé, www.espace-jeunesse. com), workshops and classes designed just for young minds are on offer and many are free of charge. A few blocks away, a revamped public swimming pool (107, rue de la Muette, tel. 01/39 62 44 41) offers a refreshing indoor-outdoor space for recreation and relaxation. International kids in town also get a lot out of the Scouts program (www. maisons-laffitte-scouts.fr), which is structured a lot like Boy Scouts or Girls Scouts of America, with a "be prepared" motto and group activities that challenge children to work together and make a positive impact in their communities.

Many Maisons-Lafitte parents allow their teenagers to make the 12-minute train ride to La Défense to catch films at the giant multi-screen cineplex there, or simply to wander the enormous expanse of shopping malls.

Anglophones who want to become fluent in French should get in touch with the nonprofit organization A.S.T.I. (www.asti-maisons-laffitte.com), which offers annual would not describe the town as ethnically diverse—a lot of expats, mostly British and American, who embrace the same culture as the French residents here. The amenities are quite adequate: theatre, athletics, great transportation, commerce, and of course a lovely French market twice weekly. Just walking from our apartment less than 10 minutes to the RER, we pass four bakeries. One point worth noting: Paris restaurants spoiled us for their innovative and varied cuisine, which can be somewhat lacking here.

Is the quality of life what you expected it to be?
We were familiar with the lifestyle here, so we would have to say that it met our expectations, and we are quite happy here. We have not owned a car since we moved. We use public transportation except for occasional rentals when we are vacationing in other areas of France, where public transportation might not be quite as handy.

Describe your experience making friends with neighbors or others in your community.

We had friends here before our arrival, so the network of friends grew quite organically. As for making new friends, it is not as easy to integrate into the community here in France as it is in the U.S., but certainly making friends here was simpler than it was in Paris. Our immediate neighbors have been very welcoming.

What do you like most about living in the suburbs?
The abundant green spaces and the sound of horse hooves in the morning.

What do you like least?
It is not as dynamic as city life at times. (We lived in Newark, New Jersey, for 15 years before moving to France.) We visit Paris and have dinner with friends, go for walks, visit museums, or do some shopping once per week at minimum. We are mostly city people by nature, but we believe here we have found a good balance between city life (20 minutes from Paris by train) and country life (loads of greenery and we are 1.5 kilometers from the Forêt de Saint-Germain-en-Laye). All of our needs are easily satisfied.

subscriptions at a nominal fee and access to the many services the volunteer-run organization offers. Private courses are also available.

If you're religious, you might be interested in the sense of community offered through Holy Trinity Church (15, avenue Carnot, www.htcml.com), which has become something of a hub for expats. Beyond the usual services, the church has a strong social component that includes barbecues, picnics, and other after-hours gatherings.

Leisure

Maisons-Laffitte is an ideal village in which to set up house. While the town's primary housing is apartments, most buildings are set in a garden and the few that don't offer their own green spaces are never more than a few yards from the nearest grassy knoll. The 3,500-hectare forest of Saint-Germain-en-Laye is a major area attraction, with its well-marked walking paths stretching out for kilometers, cycling and horse paths, and fabulous picnic spots. This is the place to bring your dog and the rest of the family for serious outdoor fun.

Every summer, the park hosts an event called the Fête des Loges, which gives off a distinct county-fair feel with its whirling, spinning rides and stalls selling *barbe-à-papa* (cotton candy). If you're in town in July and you have children, this event is practically obligatory.

Getting Around

Getting around is easy by foot, bike, or even by horse. You can get by without a car, which can't be said of all suburban towns. One thing is certain: If you do have a car, you'll find parking a breeze. Make sure to lock your car and never leave valuables in plain sight. Even though Maisons-Laffitte is a safe place to live and crime is practically non-existent, the occasional car break-in does happen here.

Everyone in Maisons-Laffitte benefits from having a bicycle, if only to get to and from the train station, where dozens of sheltered bike-parking spaces are waiting. You'll also find plenty of parking for your two-wheeled vehicle outside the public pool, the *mairie*, the library, and other public spaces.

For those without other means of transport, there are three local bus lines within the regional transportation network. Line 12 services the town of Maisons-Laffitte, Line 2 will get you to the neighboring towns of Saint-Germain-en-Laye and Le Mesnil-le-Roi, and Line 6 also services Le Mesnil-le-Roi. Tickets are €1.70 each and can be purchased from the driver. Paris Métro tickets (t+) also work on the bus, as do Navigo passes. For hours and itineraries, visit www.transdev-idf.com or www.vianavigo.com.

RESOURCES

Consulates and Embassies

UNITED STATES AND CANADA

There are 11 French consulate bureaus in the United States and 6 in Canada, each presiding over a consular region. Where you go for your in-person appointment depends on which state or province you live in; to figure out which one is your regional HQ, begin your search at the French embassy in Washington, DC, or Ottawa, Canada.

French Embassy in the United States

FRENCH EMBASSY
4101 Reservoir Rd. NW
Washington, DC 20007
tel. 202/944-6000
www.ambafrance-us.org

French Consulates in the United States

ATLANTA
The Lenox Building
3399 Peachtree Rd. NE, Ste. 500
Atlanta, GA 30326
tel. 404/495-1660
www.consulfrance-atlanta.org
Jurisdiction Alabama, Georgia, Mississippi, North Carolina, South Carolina, Tennessee

BOSTON
Park Square Building
31 Saint James Ave., Ste. 750
Boston, MA 02116
tel. 617/435-0418
www.consulfrance-boston.org
Jurisdiction Maine, Massachusetts, New Hampshire, Rhode Island, Vermont

CHICAGO
205 North Michigan Ave., Ste. 3700
Chicago, IL 60601
tel. 312/327-5200
www.consulfrance-chicago.org
Jurisdiction Illinois, Indiana, Iowa, Kansas, Kentucky, Michigan, Minnesota, Missouri, Nebraska, North Dakota, Ohio, South Dakota, Wisconsin

HONOLULU
Alii Place, Ste. 1800
1099 Alakea St.
Honolulu, HI 96813|
tel. 808/547-5852
Jurisdiction Hawaii and the U.S. Pacific Islands

HOUSTON
777 Post Oak Blvd., Ste. 600,
Houston, TX 77056
tel. 713/572-2799
www.consulfrance-houston.org
Jurisdiction Arkansas, Oklahoma, Texas

LOS ANGELES
10390 Santa Monica Blvd., Ste. 410
Los Angeles, CA 90025
tel. 310/235-3200
www.consulfrance-losangeles.org
Jurisdiction Arizona, Colorado, New Mexico, Southern California, Southern Nevada

MIAMI
Espirito Santo Plaza, Ste. 1050
1395 Brickell Ave.
Miami, FL 33131
tel. 305/403-4150
www.consulfrance-miami.org
Jurisdiction Florida, Puerto Rico, U.S. Virgin Islands

NEW ORLEANS
1340 Poydras St., Ste. 1710
New Orleans, LA 70112
tel. 504/569-2870
www.consulfrance-nouvelleorleans.org
Jurisdiction Louisiana

NEW YORK
934 5th Ave.
New York, NY 10021
tel. 212/606-3600
www.consulfrance-newyork.org
Jurisdiction Connecticut, New Jersey, New York

SAN FRANCISCO
40 Bush St.
San Francisco, CA 94108
tel. 415/397-4330
www.consulfrance-sanfrancisco.org
Jurisdiction Alaska, Idaho, Montana, Northern California, Northern Nevada, Oregon, Utah, Washington, Wyoming

WASHINGTON, DC
101 Reservoir Rd. NW
Washington DC 20007-2185
tel. 202/944-6195
www.consulfrance-washington.org
Jurisdiction Delaware, Maryland, Pennsylvania, Virginia, Washington, DC, West Virginia

French Consulates in Canada
CALGARY
525 11th Ave. SW, Ste. 500
Calgary, AB T2R 0C9
tel. 403/264-1777
www.ambafrance-ca.org
Jurisdiction Alberta, Saskatchewan. Embassy services are available here.

MONCTON
77 Rue Main, Ste. 800
Moncton, New Brunswick E1C 1E9
tel. 506/857-4191
Jurisdiction New Brunswick, Nova Scotia, Prince Edward Island, Newfoundland. Visa applications are processed at the Consulate General in Montréal.

MONTRÉAL
1501 McGill College, Bureau 1000
Montréal, QC, H3A 3M8
tel. 514/878-4385
www.consulfrance-montreal.org
Jurisdiction Québec, Nunavut

QUÉBEC CITY
25 Rue Saint-Louis
Québec City, QC G1R 3Y8
tel. 418/266-2500
www.consulfrance-quebec.org
Jurisdiction Québec City. Visa applications are processed at the Consulate General in Montréal.

TORONTO
2 Bloor St. E, Ste. 2200
Toronto ON M4W 1A8
tel. 416/847-1900
www.consulfrance-toronto.org
Jurisdiction Manitoba, Ontario

VANCOUVER
1130 West Pender St., Ste. #1100
Vancouver, BC, V6E 4A4
tel. 604/637-5300
www.consulfrance-vancouver.org
Jurisdiction Alberta, British Columbia, Saskatchewan, Yukon, and Northwest Territories

North American Embassies in France
Both the American and Canadian embassies in France are good sources of information for new residents in France, offering

referrals, services, and information on such topics as how to avoid pickpockets and how to report a lost or stolen passport.

AMERICAN EMBASSY
2, avenue Gabriel
75008 Paris
tel. 01/43 12 22 22
www.France.usembassy.gov

CANADIAN EMBASSY
37, avenue Montaigne
75008 Paris
tel. 01/44 43 29 00
www.canadainternational.gc.ca

Planning Your Fact-Finding Trip

ANGLOINFO
www.paris.angloinfo.com
News and current information for expats and would-be Parisians in the Île-de-France region.

FRENCH ENTRÉE
www.frenchentree.com
An online guide to living, working, and vacationing in France.

FRENCH GOVERNMENT TOURIST OFFICE
www.us.franceguide.com.
A useful site with current information on all things related to tourism in France.

FUSAC (FRANCE USA CONTACTS)
www.fusac.org

An excellent resource for finding a short-term rental during your stay in Paris and beyond.

LE FOODING
www.lefooding.com
Digital dining guide for foodies headed to the City of Light.

SNCF
www.sncf.fr
The French national railway website, where you can purchase train and airplane tickets, book rental cars, and more.

TIMEOUT PARIS
www.timeout.com/paris/en
Current events guide with ideas for sightseeing and eating.

Making the Move

IMMIGRATION AND VISAS
THE CALCULUS GROUP
www.calculusgroup.org
An agency that will file your visa paperwork on your behalf.

CRÉDIT AGRICOLE
www.credit-agricole.fr
This popular French bank's website has a thorough section on moving to France, including immigration and visas.

FRENCH LAW
www.frenchlaw.com
A basic site explaining French immigration law.

GLOBAL VISAS
www.globalvisas.com
Immigration specialists who will handle all your paperwork for a fee.

OFII (OFFICE FRANÇAIS DE L'IMMIGRATION ET DE L'INTÉGRATION)

www.ofii.fr

New arrivals in France will need to register with this office to complete the temporary residency process.

WORK AND STUDY PERMITS
Working in France
ASSOCIATION FOR INTERNATIONAL PRACTICAL TRAINING

www.aipt.org

The Americans Abroad program helps U.S. citizens who have found jobs in France acquire work permits.

COUNCIL ON INTERNATIONAL EDUCATIONAL EXCHANGE (CIEE)

www.ciee.org

Offers information for students on working in France.

EUROPEAN-AMERICAN CHAMBER OF COMMERCE (EACC)

www.eaccfrance.com

Provides would-be investors and entrepreneurs with advice and resources for launching a business in France.

JUST LANDED

www.justlanded.com

A useful website that extensively explains the work permit process.

TRANSITIONS ABROAD

www.transitionsabroad.com

This established publication is an excellent resource for job seekers in France.

Studying in France
FRENCH MINISTRY OF FOREIGN AFFAIRS

www.diplomatie.gouv.fr

This government website offers an English-language guide to studying in France.

IES ABROAD

www.iesabroad.com

An informative study-abroad site.

STUDY ABROAD

www.studyabroad.com

A handy, thorough site for anyone thinking of studying in France.

CUSTOMS AND SHIPPING COMPANIES
ERC (EMPLOYEE RELOCATION COUNCIL)

www.erc.org

EURA (EUROPEAN RELOCATION ASSOCIATION)

www.eura-relocation.com

FIDI (INTERNATIONAL FEDERATION OF INTERNATIONAL FURNITURE REMOVALS)

www.fidi.com

GROSPIRON

www.grospiron.com/fr/lien

OMNI (OVERSEAS MOVING NETWORK INTERNATIONAL)

www.omnimoving.com

BLOGS
DAVID LEBOVITZ

www.davidlebovitz.com

Possibly the most popular food blog in all of France, penned by a California transplant who worked in the fabled Chez Panisse kitchen before moving to Paris.

THE KALE PROJECT

www.thekaleproject.com

Kristen Beddard deserves all the credit she's been getting for reintroducing this

RESOURCES

ancient green to the French public. Her blog documents kale's domination in every corner of Paris and beyond.

LOST IN CHEESELAND
www.lostincheeseland.com
This popular blog's Franco File Fridays series spotlights expats doing cool things in Paris.

PARIS (IM)PERFECT
www.parisimperfect.wordpress.com
American writer Sion Dayson shares her honest and witty observations about life in the City of Light.

PARIS MISSIVES
www.parismissives.blogspot.com
Randy Diaz moved to France from San Francisco in 2008, but don't you dare call him a Francophile. This blog details his food-oriented experiences in Paris and beyond, always with a dose of humor and insight.

PARIS PAYSANNE
www.parispaysanne.com
California transplant Emily Dilling explores Paris's organic markets and shares tips for buying the best local, in-season produce.

POLLY-VOUS FRANÇAIS?
www.pollyvousfrancais.blogspot.fr
Funny, insightful posts on French pop-culture topics and expat follies written by a smart American cookie who may or may not actually be named "Polly."

GETTING SETTLED
ANGLO INFO
www.france.angloinfo.com
A comprehensive site for expats, including information on jobs, housing, buying a car, having a baby, and finding a builder who speaks English.

THE ESCAPE ARTIST
www.escapeartist.com
Plenty of good, basic information on retiring or otherwise settling abroad can be found here. The site also has a job-search section with employment listings in France.

EXPATICA
www.expatica.com
Detailed job listings, plus useful forums to answer all your move-to-France questions.

FRENCH ENTRÉE
www.frenchentree.com
This site will become your move-abroad bible. It covers everything you'd want to know about life in France, from buying a home to putting your kids in school to dealing with local bureaucracy.

JUST LANDED
www.justlanded.com
As its title suggests, this website offers practical information related to every facet of your move, as well as links to other sites.

TRANSITIONS ABROAD
www.transitionsabroad.com
This established magazine has a thorough, well-organized website loaded with resources for those who want to live, work, or study in France.

Housing Considerations

RENTING

COLOCATION
www.colocation.fr
This is France's top roommate-finding database for renters. Includes detailed information about roommates, such as whether they smoke, keep late hours, or have pets.

CRAIGSLIST
www.paris.fr.craigslist.org
Craigslist is the number-one source for finding almost-no-hassle rental housing. Other cities around France don't have as strong a Craigslist community as Paris does, but it's worth investigating their outposts of the site anyway.

FUSAC
www.fusac.fr
The go-to resource for the Paris Anglophone community for more than 20 years has advertisements for housing, jobs, and other services, plus household items and other things for sale.

PARTICULIER À PARTICULIER
www.pap.fr
This source of for-rent ads is extremely popular, so start making those calls on Thursday morning as soon as the new issue comes out.

RENT A PLACE IN FRANCE
www.rentaplaceinfrance.com
Small but excellent selection of long-term housing for English-speaking renters through English-speaking proprietors.

BUYING

CENTURY 21
www.century21.fr
This well-known name in real estate has a strong presence in France. In addition to buying and selling, the company also lists rentals.

FRANCE THIS WAY
www.property.francethisway.com
A thorough, easy-to-navigate, real-estate database targeting the English-speaking community and encompassing every region of France.

FRENCH ENTRÉE
www.frenchentree.com
This English-language site offers regional listings and detailed articles on buying or renting a home or apartment.

FRENCH PROPERTY
www.french-property.com
This website, which has been providing extensive information for years, offers an excellent database of houses for sale, usually by the Anglophone community for the Anglophone community.

SELOGER
www.seloger.fr
A popular online real-estate service that gives home seekers access to nationwide listings of studios apartments, villas, and even châteaux, along with rental listings.

RESOURCES

Language and Education

GENERAL RESOURCES
APPRENDRE LE FRANÇAIS EN FRANCE
www.fle.fr
A comprehensive list of all the public and private French language-learning institutions in France.

FRENCH UNIVERSITIES DATABASE
www.dr.education.fr/Serveurs_Etab/Univ_alpha.html
A complete listing of all the French universities that accept international students.

INTERNATIONAL GRADUATE
www.internationalgraduate.net/eurofrance.htm
Helpful information for students planning to enroll in graduate school in France.

LANGUAGE SCHOOLS
Paris
ALLIANCE FRANÇAISE
www.alliancefr.org
Nonprofit language school and cultural center offers classes at every level, plus events and expositions.

ATELIER 9
www.latelier9.com
A stellar reputation and small classes (no more than nine students per class) are the hallmarks of Atelier 9.

MAIRIE DE PARIS
www.cours-municipal-d-adultes-cma.cma-paris.org
The affordable French language courses offered through the Mairie are in high demand. Plan ahead to snag a seat.

THE SORBONNE
www.english.paris-sorbonne.fr
If you learn by doing, enroll in a program at the Sorbonne. Classes are in French, so it's sink or swim.

Brittany
INSA RENNES (INSTITUT NATIONAL DES SCIENCES APPLIQUÉES DE RENNES)
www.insa-rennes.fr
This *grande école* offers intensive French-language courses in the summer for incoming students.

Paris
AMERICAN GRADUATE SCHOOL IN PARIS
www.ags.edu

AMERICAN UNIVERSITY OF PARIS
www.aup.edu

ÉCOLE SUPÉRIEUR DE CUISINE FRANCAISE
www.egf.ccip.fr

INSTITUT CATHOLIC DE PARIS
www.icp.fr

LE CORDON BLEU PARIS
www.lcbparis.com

SCIENCES PO
www.sciencespo.fr/en

THE SORBONNE
www.english.paris-sorbonne.fr

Health

ASSOCIATION DENTAIRE FRANÇAISE
7, rue Mariotte
75017 Paris
tel. 01/58 22 17 10
www.adf.asso.fr

ASSURANCE MALADIE
www.ameli.fr

FÉDÉRATION HOSPITALIÈRE DE FRANCE
1 bis, rue Cabanis
75014 Paris
tel. 01/44 06 84 44
www.fhf.fr

FRENCH HOSPITAL GUIDE
www.hopital.fr

SANTÉCLAIR
www.santeclair.fr

EMERGENCY CONTACTS
AMBULANCE
Dial 15

EUROPE-WIDE EMERGENCY NUMBER
Dial 112

FIRE
Dial 18

POLICE
Dial 17

HOSPITALS AND PHARMACIES
Paris
AMERICAN HOSPITAL OF PARIS
63, boulevard Victor Hugo
92200 Neuilly-sur-Seine
tel. 01/46 41 25 25
www.american-hospital.org

ASSISTANCE PUBLIQUE HÔPITAUX DE PARIS
Hôpital St. Antoine
184, rue du Faubourg Saint-Antoine
75012 Paris
tel. 01/49 28 20 00

BRITISH AND AMERICAN PHARMACY
1, rue Auber
75009 Paris
tel. 01/42 65 88 29

CENTRE HOSPITALIER DES COURSES DE MAISONS-LAFFITTE
19 bis, avenue Eglé
tel. 01/30 86 36 22

CENTRE HOSPITALIER INTERCOMMUNAL ANDRÉ GRÉGOIRE (MONTREUIL)
56, boulevard de la Boissière
tel. 01/49 20 30 40

CLINIQUE MÉDICALE ET PÉDAGOGIQUE DUPRÉ (SCEAUX)
30, avenue Franklin Roosevelt
tel. 01/40 91 50 50

GRANDE PHARMACIE INTERNATIONALE DE PARIS
17 bis, boulevard de Rochechouart
75009 Paris
tel. 01/48 78 03 01

HÔPITAL AMBROISE PARÉ (BOULOGNE-BILLANCOURT)
9, ave Charles de Gaulle
tel. 01/49 09 55 18

HÔPITAL PRIVÉ DE VERSAILLES
7b, rue de la Porte de Bac
tel. 08/26 30 33 33

HÔPITAL ST. LOUIS
1, avenue Claude-Vellefaux
75010 Paris
tel. 01/42 49 49 49

PHARMACIE DU DRUGSTORE DES CHAMPS-ÉLYSÉES
133, avenue des Champs-Élysées
tel. 01/47 20 39 25

DR. NINA ROOS
26, rue Vavin
75006 Paris
tel. 01/30 84 75 97
www.docteurninaroos.fr
Cosmetic dermatologist

DISABLED ACCESS
ASSOCIATION DES PARALYSÉS DE FRANCE
www.apf.asso.fr
Advocacy organization for people living with paralysis.

AUTISME FRANCE
www.autisme.france.free.fr
Support and resource organizations for families living with autism.

CAISSE NATIONAL DE SOLIDARITÉ POUR AUTONOMIE
www.cnsa.fr
Government-run association promoting independent living for the elderly and disabled.

PERSONNES HANDICAPPÉES
www.fondationdefrance.org
Organization working to support and uphold French disability laws and better the lives of the disabled public.

Employment

STARTING A BUSINESS
THE AMERICAN CHAMBER OF COMMERCE IN FRANCE
www.amchamfrance.org

APCE (ASSOCIATION POUR LA CRÉATION D'ENTERPRISES)
www.apce.com

BOUTIQUES DE GESTION
www.boutiques-de-gestion.com

CHAMBRE DE COMMERCE ET D'INDUSTRIE DE PARIS
www.ccip.fr

INVEST IN FRANCE
www.invest-in-france.org

NACRE (NOUVEL ACCOMPAGNEMENT POUR LA CRÉATION ET LA REPRISE D'ENTERPRISE)
www.emploi.gouv.fr/nacre

JOB SEARCHES
APEC
www.apec.fr
French-language job-seeking website with listings in multiple industries.

BERLITZ
www.berlitz.fr

An established English-language institute that's always looking for new recruits.

CRAIGSLIST

www.paris.en.craigslist.org

The Paris-focused Craigslist site offers the most employment-related ads of all the French regional sites.

EUROJOBS

www.eurojobs.com

Search engine for job seekers throughout France and the rest of Europe. Emphasis on high-tech industry opportunities.

FAT TIRE BIKE TOURS

www.fattirebiketours.com

A local, American-owned employer that's always on the lookout for qualified staff.

FUSAC (FRANCE USA CONTACTS)

www.fusac.org

Job listings for English teachers, hotel and restaurant workers, and tourism-related industries.

PÔLE EMPLOI

www.pole-emploi.fr

French portal for job seekers in France.

WALL STREET INSTITUTE

www.wallstreetinstitute.fr

Each of the institutes 70 centers throughout France accepts résumés year-round.

VOLUNTEERING

CADIP (CANADIAN ALLIANCE FOR DEVELOPMENT INITIATIVES AND PROJECTS)

www.cadip.org

This Vancouver-based nonprofit aims to support volunteering abroad with humanitarian projects.

CARE FRANCE

www.carefrance.org

Nonprofit French volunteer organization with projects all over the world.

GO ABROAD

www.goabroad.com

This U.S.-based database of volunteer programs includes an extensive selection of possibilities in France.

WWOOF (WORLD WIDE OPPORTUNITIES ON ORGANIC FARMS)

www.wwoof.com

Free food and lodging in exchange for your work on organic farms throughout France. Always welcoming new members.

Finance

BNP PARIBAS
www.bnpparibas.com

CAISSE D'ÉPARGNE
www.caisse-epargne.fr

CRÉDIT AGRICOLE
www.credit-agricole.fr

LA BANQUE POSTAL
www.labanquepostale.fr

PHILIPPE JEDAR
Financial Planner
tel. 06/01 78 35 55

Communications

PHONE AND INTERNET SERVICE
BOUYGUES TELECOM
www.bouyguestelecom.fr
Internet, television, and telephone service.

FNAC
www.fnac.fr
This chain sells a wide variety of mobile phones and other communication devices.

ORANGE
www.orange.fr
Internet, television, and telephone service.

PHONEHOUSE
www.phonehouse.fr
The leading mobile-phone store in France, where you can also buy your *puces*.

SFR
www.SFR.fr
Internet, television, and telephone service.

NEWSPAPERS
LE CANARD ENCHAÎNÉ
www.lecanardenchaine.fr

THE CONNEXION
www.connexionfrance.com

LE FIGARO
www.lefigaro.fr

FRANCE SOIR
www.francesoir.fr

LIBÉRATION
www.liberation.fr

MÉTRO
www.metrofrance.com

LE MONDE
www.lemonde.fr

NOUVEL OBSERVATEUR
www.tempsreel.nouvelobs.com

LE PARISIEN
www.leparisien.com

MAGAZINES
A NOUS
www.anous.fr

L'EXPRESS
www.lexpress.fr

MARIANNE
www.marianne2.fr

PARISCOPE
http://spectacles.premiere.fr

PARIS MATCH
www.parismatch.com

LE POINT
www.lepoint.fr

Travel and Transportation

GENERAL RESOURCES

AIR FRANCE
www.airfrance.fr
France's national airline.

COVOITURAGE
www.covoiturage.fr
National public ride-share program.

EUROLINES
www.eurolines.fr
Long-distance bus company.

EUROPECAR
www.europecar.fr
Nationwide car-rental agency.

OPODO
www.opodo.fr
Popular online travel agency.

SNCF
www.sncf.fr
French national railway lines.

REGIONAL TRANSPORTATION
Paris and the Île-de-France

PHÉBUS
www.phebus.tm.fr
Local transport services for the city of Versailles.

RATP (RÉGIE AUTONOME DES TRANSPORTS PARISIENS)
www.ratp.fr
Information in English for the bus, Métro, regional trains, and transport passes.

TRANSILIEN
www.transilien.com
Routes and pricing information in French and English for the bus, Métro, regional trains, and transport passes.

VÉLIB'
www.velib.paris.fr
Paris's public bike-sharing system.

VEOLIA TRANSPORT
www.idf.veolia-transport.fr
Local transport services for Maisons-Laffitte.

RESOURCES

Prime Living Locations

PARIS
General
PARIS CONVENTION AND VISITORS BUREAU
www.en.parisinfo.com

PARIS MAIRIE DIRECTORY
www.paris.fr

PARIS TOURIST BOARD
www.parisinfo.com

Schools
AMERICAN SCHOOL OF PARIS
www.asparis.org

BILINGUAL INTERNATIONAL SCHOOL OF PARIS
www.bilingualschoolparis.com

LYCÉE HONORÉ DE BALZAC
www.balzac-apesa.org

PARIS.FR
www.equipements.paris.fr
City of Paris's official list of primary schools and list of *lycées*.

Boulogne-Billancourt Schools (registration)
ESPACE ACCUEIL FAMILLES
Hôtel de Ville
26, avenue André Morizet
tel. 01/55 18 53 00

Levallois-Perret Schools (registration)
PLACE DE LA RÉPUBLIQUE
Robert Forget, Directeur de la Vie Scolaire
tel. 01/49 68 31 20

Maisons-Laffitte Schools (information)
SERVICE DES AFFAIRES SCOLAIRES
Mairie Annexe
3, rue du Fossé
tel. 01/34 93 12 38

Montreuil Schools (information)
SERVICE ÉDUCATION
Municipal Opale
3, rue de Rosny
tel. 01/48 70 62 95

Sceaux Schools (information)
www.sceaux.fr

Versailles Schools (registration and information)
Hôtel de Ville
4, avenue de Paris
tel. 01/30 97 84 78

Glossary

l'addition: restaurant check, bill
aller-rétour: round trip
apéro: snack eaten with a drink before dinner
ascenseur: elevator
assurance: insurance
attestation: written and signed statement or testimonial
auberge: inn
banlieue: suburbs
billet: ticket
bisou: kiss
bobo: *b*ourgeois *b*ohemian, yuppie
boulangerie: bread shop where pastries and other baked goods are often sold
bricolage: DIY, do-it-yourself
brocante: antiques and collectibles sale
café: cup of coffee; establishment where you drink coffee
carte bleue: debit card
carte de séjour: residency card
caviste: wine seller
chariot: personal shopping cart on wheels
chien(ne): male/female dog
cinema: movie theater
clic-clac: foldout couch-bed
clinique: private hospital
college: middle school
composteur: ticket stamping machine at train stations, on buses, and at Métro stations
crèmerie: shop that sells dairy products
déménager: to move house
demi: half-pint of beer
distributeur: ATM
dossier: file (n)
école élémentaire: elementary school
encore: again
enfant: child
épicerie: grocery shop
étranger/étrangère: foreigner
étudiant(e): male/female student
facture: bill (n)
garant(e): financial guarantor
gare: train station
gratuit(e): free/no cost
grève: strike (n)
hôtel de ville: town hall, city hall (see also *mairie*)
ici: here
immobilière: real-estate agent

impermeable: raincoat
libre: open/available
lycée: high school
maire: mayor
mairie: mayor's office, town hall (see also *hôtel de ville*)
maison particulier: independent house, usually of grand standing
manifestation: demonstration
marché aux puces: flea market
maternelle: preschool
maternité: maternity hospital
mutuelle: supplemental insurance
notaire: notary
ordinateur: computer
panier: shopping basket
parapluie: umbrella
patisserie: pastry shop
périphérique: ring road
permis de conduire: driver's license
petit(e) ami(e): boyfriend/girlfriend
populaire: working-class/crowded
prefecture: regional headquarters for the Ministry of the Interior
préfecture de police: police headquarters
presque: almost
La Presse: newsstand
quartier: neighborhood
rendezvous: appointment
rentrée: the start of a new school year
rosé: pink wine
rue: street
sac: plastic shopping bag
salariée: employee
sans papiers: undocumented workers
SDF: "sans domicile fixe," homeless
SVP: "s'il vous plaît," please
Syndicat: union or association
tabac: tobacco shop that also sells bus tickets, lottery tickets, and sometimes magazines and beverages
tartine: slice of bread
travail: work
verre: a glass (usually of wine or beer)
vide-grenier: community rummage sale
viennoiserie: breakfast pastry
voiture: car

French Phrasebook

French is an intimidating language. It isn't so much the rolling *R*s and figuring out how the accents work that makes it so—it's the fear of sounding silly, saying things "wrong," and ultimately not being understood. But rest assured that the French will always meet you halfway if you at least *try*, even if your response to *"merci"* ends up as *"beaucoup."* Set those feelings of vulnerability aside and let 'er rip. You'll be rewarded for your efforts! Remember to begin all requests and queries with *"Excusez-moi, s'il vous plaît"* (ex-cue-zay MWAH, see voo play) and end them with *"Merci, madame/monsieur"* (mair-SEE mah-DAHM/muh-SYUH).

PRONUNCIATION

Before you start practicing your French, relax. This isn't rocket science, though it does take a bit of diligent practice. Getting a grip on French accents will help you read the language—as will pronouncing the consonants and vowels—and let you avoid ordering a cold meat terrine (*pâté*, pah-TAY) when you really want pasta (*pâte*, PAHT).

Vowels

Accents do not always change the sound of the vowel. French is tricky like that.

é accent *aigu*
à, è, ù accent *grave*
â, ê, î, ô, û accent *circonflexe*
ë, ï, ü accent *le tréma*
a as the "a" in "also" *place* PLAHSS (plaza, place, space)
ai as "ai" in "rain"; *maison* may-ZOHn (house)
ail as "ai" in "aisle"; *ail* EYE (garlic)
ais, ait as "e" in "bed"; *voudrais, voudrait* voo-DREH (would like)
au as "au" in "au pair"; *auberge* oh-BAIRZH (inn)

e as "e" in "bed" or "e" in "hamlet"; *mec* MECK (guy), *retour* ruh-TOOR (return)
é as "ay" in "bay"; *café* cah-FAY (coffee, café)
eau as "o" in "oh"; *bâteau* bah-TOH (boat)
er, ez as "ay" in "stay"; *regarder* ruh-gar-DAY (to look), *rez-de-chaussée* raid-shoh-SAY (ground floor)
et as "e" in "bed"; *complet* cohm-PLEH (full)
I as "i" in "police"; *minute* mee-NEWT (minute); exception: in closed syllables ending in "-in" the "i" is pronounced as a nasal "an"; *vin* vAn (wine)
o as "o" in "pope"; *stop* STOHP (stop)
oi as "wa" in "water"; *oiseau* wah-ZOH (bird)
ou as "oo" in "moon"; *bouche* BOOSH (mouth)
u as "ew" in "stew"; *prune* PREWN (plum)
ui pronounced "ew-ee"; *fruit* frew-EE (fruit)

Consonants

With a few exceptions, French consonants are pronounced as they are in English. Exceptions: The letters **d, n, p, r, s, t,** and **x** are generally not pronounced at the end of a word. When a consonant is followed by an e, the consonant is pronounced.

c as "c" in "cut"; when followed by e, i, or y, it is pronounced like "s" as in "salad"; *cadeau* kah-DOH (gift), *céréale* say-ray-AHL (cereal), *cycle* SEE-kluh (cycle)
ç *la cédille*; when followed by a or o, is pronounced like "s" as in "salad"; *ça* SAH (that), *façon* fah-SOHn (way, manner)
ch as "sh" in "shower"; *chat* SHAH (cat), *champignon* shahm-peen-NYOHn (mushroom)
g as "g" in "game"; when followed by e, i or y, it is pronounced like the "s" in "leisure"; *gare* GAHR (train station), *guide* GEED (guide) *géant* zhay-AHn (giant, gigantic)
gn as "ny" in "canyon"; *mignon* meen-NYOHn (cute)
j as the "s" in "leisure"; *jus* ZHEW (juice)
h silent when it's the first letter in a word; *hôpital* oh-pee-TAHL (hospital), *horloge* or-LUHZH (clock)
ph as "f" in "film"; *pharmacie* farm-ah-

SEE (pharmacy), *philosophe* fee-loh-SOFF (philosopher)

qu as "k" in "kick"; *qui* KEE (who)

s not pronounced at the end of a plural word; *lettres* LETT-ruh (letters)

th as "t" in "tuna" (note that there is no "th" sound in French); *thé* TAY (tea), *théâtre* tay-AH-truh (theater)

NUMBERS

0 *zéro*
1 *un*
2 *deux*
3 *trois*
4 *quatre*
5 *cinq*
6 *six*
7 *sept*
8 *huit*
9 *neuf*
10 *dix*
11 *onze*
12 *douze*
13 *treize*
14 *quatorze*
15 *quinze*
16 *seize*
17 *dix-sept*
18 *dix-huit*
19 *dix-neuf*
20 *vingt*
21 *vingt-et-un*
22 *vingt-deux*
23 *vingt-trois*
30 *trente*
31 *trente-et-un*
32 *trente-deux*
40 *quarante*
41 *quarante-et-un*
50 *cinquante*
51 *cinquante-et-un*
60 *soixante*
61 *soixante-et-un*
62 *soixante-deux*
63 *soixante-trois*
64 *soixante-quatre*
65 *soixante-cinq*
66 *soixante-six*
67 *soixante-sept*
68 *soixante-huit*
69 *soixante-neuf*
70 *soixante-dix*
71 *soixante-et-onze*
72 *soixante-douze*
73 *soixante-treize*
74 *soixante-quatorze*
75 *soixante-quinze*
76 *soixante-seize*
77 *soixante-dix-sept*
78 *soixante-dix-huit*
79 *soixante-dix-neuf*
80 *quatre-vingts*
81 *quatre-vingt-un*
82 *quatre-vingt-deux*
83 *quatre-vingt-trois*
84 *quatre-vingt-quatre*
85 *quatre-vingt-cinq*
86 *quatre-vingt-six*
87 *quatre-vingt-sept*
88 *quatre-vingt-huit*
89 *quatre-vingt-neuf*
90 *quatre-vingt-dix*
91 *quatre-vingt-onze*
92 *quatre-vingt-douze*
93 *quatre-vingt-treize*
94 *quatre-vingt-quatorze*
95 *quatre-vingt-quinze*
96 *quatre-vingt-seize*
97 *quatre-vingt-dix-sept*
98 *quatre-vingt-dix-huit*
99 *quatre-vingt-dix-neuf*
100 *cent*
101 *cent un*
125 *cent vingt-cinq*
200 *deux cents*
300 *trois cents*
1,000 *mille*
2,000 *deux mille*
1,000,000 *un million*
2,000,000 *deux millions*
one billion *un milliard*
one quarter *un quart*
one third *un tiers*
one half *un demi*
three-fourths *trois-quatre*

DAYS AND MONTHS

Neither the days of the week nor the months of the year are capitalized in French.

Monday *lundi*
Tuesday *mardi*

NATIONAL HOLIDAYS

The French celebrate a handful of national holidays, or *jours fériés*, throughout the year (and despite the country's claim to be utterly secular, many are religious holidays). They include:

- New Year's Day *(Jour de l'an)* January 1
- Easter and Easter Monday *(Pâques and lundi de Pâques)* March/April, date varies
- Labor Day *(Fête du Travail)* May 1
- WWII Victory Day *(Fête de la Victoire/Commémoration de la Victoire)* May 8
- Pentecost and Pentecost Monday *(la Pentecôte and lundi de Pentecôte)* May/June, date varies
- Bastille Day *(Fête nationale)* July 14
- All Saints' Day *(La Toussaint)* November 1
- Armistice Day *(l'Armistice)* November 11
- Christmas Day *(Noël)* December 25

Wednesday *mercredi*
Thursday *jeudi*
Friday *vendredi*
Saturday *samedi*
Sunday *dimanche*
today *aujourd'hui*
yesterday *hier*
tomorrow *demain*
January *janvier*
February *février*
March *mars*
April *avril*
May *mai*
June *juin*
July *juillet*
August *août*
September *septembre*
October *octobre*
November *novembre*
December *décembre*
spring *printemps*
summer *été*
autumn *automne*
winter *hiver*

TIME

France uses the 24-hour clock. Instead of a colon, an "h" is used; so 1:00am appears as 1h00 and 11:30pm appears as 23h30.

1am *une heure*
2am *deux heures*
3am *trois heures*
4am *quatre heures*
5am *cinq heures*
6am *six heures*
7am *sept heures*
8am *huit heures*
9am *neuf heures*
10am *dix heures*
11am *onze heures*
noon *midi*
1pm *treize heures*
2pm *quatorze heures*
3pm *quinze heures*
4pm *seize heures*
5pm *dix-sept heures*
6pm *dix-huit heures*
7pm *dix-neuf heures*
8pm *vingt heures*
9pm *vingt-et-une heures*
10pm *vingt-deux heures*
11pm *vingt-trois heures*
midnight *minuit*
morning *le matin*
afternoon *l'après-midi*
evening *le soir*
night *la nuit*
What time is it? *Quelle heure est-il?*
one minute *une minute*

two minutes *deux minutes*
early *tôt*
late *tard, en retard*
10 minutes late *dix minutes de retard*

THE BASICS

"Please" and "thank you" are the first steps toward making yourself welcome in France. Once you've mastered those niceties, expand your vocabulary with these quotidian basics.

yes *oui*
no *non*
OK *d'accord*
maybe *peut-être*
I *je*
me *moi*
my *mon, ma, mes*
you *vous (formal)*
your *votre/vos*
he *il*
him *lui*
his *son/sa/ses*
she/her *elle*
her (possessive) *son/sa/ses*
we/us *nous*
our *notre/nos*
they *ils/elles*
them *eux/elles*
their *leur/leurs*
who *qui*
what *quoi*
when *quand*
why *pourquoi*
where *où*
how many *combien*
because *parce que*
thank you *merci*
thank you very much *merci beaucoup*
you're welcome (formal) *je vous en prie*
you're welcome (informal) *de rien*
I'm sorry *je suis desolé(e)*
I don't understand *je ne comprends pas*
open *ouvert*
closed *fermé*
closed on Sundays *fermé le dimanche*
push *poussez*
pull *tirez*
stop *errêt*
post office *la poste*

bank *la banque*
empty *vide*
full *plein(e)*
happy *heureux/heureuse*
sad *triste*

GREETINGS

Greetings are an important formality and a many-times-a-day ritual. It's imperative that you master these common salutations for successful living in France.

Hello. *Bonjour.*
Hi! *Salut!*
Good evening. *Bonsoir.*
Good day. *Bonne journée.*
Good night. *Bonne soirée.*
Good weekend. *Bon weekend.*
My name is ... *Je m'appelle...*
What's your name? *Comment-vous appelez-vous?*
I'd like to introduce you to ... *Je vous présente...*
Nice to meet you. *Enchanté(e).*
Goodbye. *Au revoir.*
See you later. *À tout à l'heure.*
See you soon. *À bientôt.*
How are you? *Comment allez-vous?*
How's it going? *Comment ça va?*
It's going well, thanks. *Ça va bien, merci.*
It's going well, and you? *Ça va bien, et vous? (et toi, if informal)*
Enjoy your meal *Bon appétit*

GETTING AROUND

Where is ...? *Où est...?*
a hotel *un hôtel*
the airport *l'aéroport*
the train station *la gare*
the bus station *la gare routière*
the Métro (subway) *le Métro*
the bus stop *arrêt de bus*
right *à droite*
left *à gauche*
straight ahead *tout droit*
on the corner *au coin*
here *ici*
there *là*
nearby *près d'ici*
for rent *à louer*

for sale *à vendre*
deposit *caution, acompte, consigné*
available *disponible*

ACCOMMODATIONS

Do you have a room available? *Avez-vous une chambre libre?*
We're full. *Nous sommes complets.*
I have a reservation. *J'ai une réservation.*
How many nights? *Combien de nuits?*
I'd like to stay three nights. *Je voudrais rester trois nuits.*
double room *avec un grand lit*
bed *lit*
key *clé*
the price *le prix*
cheap *pas cher*

FOOD

to eat *manger*
to drink *boire*
breakfast *petit-déjeuner*
lunch *déjeuner*
dinner *dîner*
snack *casse-croûte*
water *l'eau or une carafe d'eau*
wine *vin*
beer *bière*
menu *la carte*
first course *entrée*
main course *plat or plat principal*
I'd like . . . *Je voudrais . . .*
I'm vegetarian/vegan. *Je suis végétarien(ne)/végétalien(ne).*
without . . . *sans*
with . . . *avec*
the check *l'addition*
supermarket *supermarché/hypermarché*
fruit *fruit*
vegetables *légumes*
cheese *fromage*
butter *beurre*
milk *lait*
soy milk *lait de soja*
coffee *café*
tea *thé*
hot water *eau chaud*
jam *confiture*
egg *oeuf*

meat *viande*
bread *pain*
noodles *nouilles*
pasta *pâte*
rice *riz*
salt *sel*
pepper *poivre*
ketchup *sauce tomate or ketchup*

SHOPPING

Fruits and vegetables are sold by the kilo at French outdoor *marchés* and supermarkets. If you want less than a kilo, ask for *cinq cents grammes* (a half-kilo) or *un quart* (a quarter-kilo).

to go shopping *faire les courses*
How much does this cost? *C'est combien?*
I'm looking for . . . *Je cherche . . .*
I'd like to buy . . . *Je voudrais acheter . . .*
I'd like a half-kilo, please. *Je voudrais cinq cents grammes, s'il vous plait.*
That's too much. *C'est trop.*
It's too small/big. *C'est trop petit/grand.*
Do you have any others? *Vous en avez d'autres?*
Do you accept bank cards/credit cards? *Est-ce que je peux payer avec une carte bancaire/carte de crédit?*

SHOE SIZES

M, W	European
3.5, 5	35
4.5, 6	36
5.5, 7	37 1/2
6.5, 8	38 1/2
7.5, 9	40
8.5, 10	42
10.5, 12	44

BANKING

bank card *carte bancaire (CB)*
savings account *compte d'épargne*
checkbook *carnet de chèque/chèquier*
account *compte*
checking account *compte chèque*
overdraft *découvert*
withdrawal *prélèvement*
bank statement *relevé bancaire*

HEALTH

an emergency un urgence
pain douleur
I'm sick. Je suis malade.
sharp pain douleur vive
swelling des oedèmes
flu grippe
stomach flu gastro
prescription un ordonnance
to refill a prescription renouveler un ordonnance
diagnosis diagnostic
X-ray une radio

ultrasound/sonogram une échographie
examination of heart, lungs, ears l'auscultation du cœur, des poumons, des oreilles
pap smear un frottis
pregnancy/pregnant grossesse/enceinte
midwife sage-femme
ophthalmologist ophthalmologiste
cardiologist cardiologue
physiotherapist kinésithérapeute
dentist dentiste
homeopathy homéopathie

Suggested Reading

Ernest Hemingway did it best write about the French experience from an American's perspective, albeit with a candid pen fueled by copious amounts of alcohol. Honest yet romantic, he made legions of dreamers yearn for their own Lost Generation era in Paris's Left Bank. Hemingway left big shoes for others to fill—and boy, have they tried. These tomes, written by scholars, cultural and social critics, cooks, and other France aficionados, will get you revved up (and duly warned) in anticipation of your move.

HISTORY AND CULTURE

These will help prep you for the culture shock you're likely to experience after you move, even if you've visited France a hundred times before.

Lebovitz, David. *The Sweet Life in Paris.* New York Broadway Books, 2009. A delicious introduction to France from a top blogger, cookbook author, and Paris expat.

Nadeaux, Jean-Benoît and Julie Barlow. *Sixty Million Frenchmen Can't Be Wrong.* Chicago Sourcebooks, Inc., 2003. An insightful look at French history and contemporary French society.

Druckerman, Pamela. *Bringing up Bébé.* New York Penguin Press, 2012. The first book to examine French childrearing tactics has spawned a slew of copycats. The original is smart and humorous.

Timoney, Charles. *Pardon My French.* New York Gotham, 2008. A funny look at all the French-language errors you'll probably make during your stay in France.

MEMOIRS

First-person memoirs written by Anglophones who've up and moved to France are officially a genre unto themselves. Some of the most popular are:

Baldwin, James. *Notes of a Native Son.* Boston Beacon Press, 1984. Among these essays by the revered American writer are tales of his years in France.

Beach, Sylvia. *Shakespeare and Company.* New York Harcourt, 1959. The owner of the famous Paris bookstore reminisces about her exciting literary life in Paris's Left Bank and beyond.

Corbett, Bryce. *A Town Called Paris.* New York Broadway Books, 2008. A

RESOURCES

saucy Australian finds true love—with a showgirl—in the City of Light.

Gershman, Suzy. *C'est La Vie.* New York Viking, 2004. A woman of a certain age moves to France and begins anew after her husband's death.

Gopnik, Adam. *Paris to the Moon.* New York Random House, 2001. A New Yorker writer spent several years in Paris with his family; these are his memories.

Hemingway, Ernest. *A Moveable Feast.* New York Scribner, 1964. Classic Hemingway about writing, writers, drinking, and adventure in France.

Mayle, Peter. *A Year in Provence.* New York Knopf, 1990. The quintessential move-to-rural-France tale, full of humor and insight.

Rochefort, Harriet Welty. *French Toast.* New York St. Martin's Press, 1997. An American moves to France, marries a Frenchman, and pens the delicious details.

Sedaris, David. *Me Talk Pretty One Day.* Boston Back Bay Books, 2001. Humorous essays detailing Sedaris's language foibles and other funny disasters in France.

Stein, Gertrude. *Paris, France.* New York Liveright, 1970. The famous 20th-century author's homage to life in France.

Turnbull, Sarah. *Almost French.* New York Gotham Books, 2002. Another Australian moves to France, settles in Paris, and shares the witty details.

FICTION

Clarke, Stephen. *A Year in the Merde.* New York Bloomsbury, 2005. The goofy tale of a middle-aged Englishman's adventures in the City of Light.

Guene, Faiza. *Kiffe Kiffe Tomorrow.* Orlando Harcourt, 2006. The story of a young North African immigrant girl's life in the Paris suburbs.

Hugo, Victor. *The Hunchback of Notre Dame.* A dramatic, sorrowful tale of lives intertwined in the heart of medieval Paris.

Hugo, Victor. *Les Misérables.* A riveting story of perseverance, revenge, and survival by one of France's most revered writers.

McClain, Paula. *The Paris Wife.* New York Ballantine Books, 2011. A fictionalized "memoir" in the voice of Hadley Richardson, Ernest Hemingway's wife.

Nemirovsky, Irene. *Suite Française.* An edge-of-your-seat story set in Paris and the French countryside during World War II.

Suggested Films

The Lumière brothers are credited with inventing the final link in cinema technology, bringing the art form to life in France at the turn of the 19th century. (The Institut Lumière, dedicated to the work of the Lyon-born siblings, should not be missed.) Since then, French filmmaking has evolved into an honored and honorable tradition, and France boasts a long list of directors whose films are consistently compelling Jacques Demy, Jean-Luc Godard, François Ozon, Jacques Chabral,

IF YOUR FRENCH IS UP TO SNUFF . . .

You should really try reading some of these authors' works in their own language—but if you can't tell your *voilà* from your viola, you can still find semi-decent translations of some of France's most revered writers.

Albert Camus

Colette

Simone de Beauvoir

Guy de Maupassant

Jean de La Varende

Alexandre Dumas

Victor Hugo

Anaïs Nin

Marcel Proust

Jean-Paul Sartre

Voltaire

Marcel Pagnol, Jean Renoir, François Truffaut, Ousman Sembène, Louis Malle, Agnès Varda, and many more. A (very) short list of must-sees includes:

DRAMAS AND COMEDIES

Amélie. Directed by Jean-Pierre Jeunet, 2001. Burbank, CA Buena Vista Home Entertainment, 2002.

Amour. Directed by Michael Haneke, 2012. Paris, France TFI Video, 2013.

Betty Blue. Directed by Jean-Jacques Beineix, 1986. United States Cinema Libre Studio, 2009.

Breathless. Directed by Jean-Luc Godard, 1960. Livingston, NY Criterion Collection, 2007.

Le Cercle Rouge. Directed by Jean-Pierre Melville, 1970. New York Criterion Collection, 2004.

City of Lost Children. Directed by Marc Caro and Jean-Pierre Jeunet. Culver City, CA Columbia Tri-Star Home Video, 1995.

Delicatessen. Directed by Marc Caro and Jean-Pierre Jeunet, 1991. Hollywood, CA Paramount Home Video, 1992.

Elevator to the Gallows. Directed by Louis Malle, 1958. New York Criterion Collection, 2006.

The Grand Illusion. Directed by Jean Renoir, 1937. Chicago, IL Home Vision Cinema, 1999.

La Haine. Directed by Mathieu Kossovits, 1995. Irvington, NY Criterion Collection, 2007.

l'Intouchables. Directed by Olivier Nakache and Eric Toledano, 2011. Paris, France Gaumont, 2011.

Hollywoo. Directed by Frédéric Berthe and Pascal Serieis, 2011. Paris, France StudioCanal, 2011.

Paris, je t'aime. Directed by Olivier Assayas et al, 2006. Los Angeles First Look Home Entertainment, 2007.

Pauline at the Beach. Directed by Eric Rohmer, 1983. Santa Monica, CA MGM Home Entertainment, 2003.

The Red Balloon. Directed by Albert Lamorisse, 1956. New York Janus Films, 2008.

The Triplets of Belleville. Directed by Sylvain Chomet, 2003. New York Sony Picture Classics, 2004.

RESOURCES

SUGGESTED MUSIC

There's nothing like the sound of Edith Piaf's warbling to put you in the mood for France. Here are other musical "arteests" who croon *en français* that are worth getting to know:

Air
Arielle Dombasle
Ben l'Oncle Soul
Georges Brassens
Camille
Lou Doillon
Daft Punk
Yaya Herman Dune
Françoise Hardy
Laurent Garnier
Gojira
Serge Gainsbourg
Kamini
Keren Ann
Les Innocents
Louise Attack

Mano Negra
Miss Kitten
Noir Désir
Nouvelle Vague
Les Nubians
Paris Combo
Phoenix
Rhinôçérôse
Sabina Sciubba
MC Solaar
Superbus
Sebastien Tellier
Telephone
Velvet Condoms
Yelle

The Town Is Quiet. Directed by Robert Guédiguian, 2002. Agat Films & Cie/Canal+, 2000.

Umbrellas of Cherbourg. Directed by Jacques Demy, 1964. Port Washington, NY Koch Vision, 2004.

DOCUMENTARIES

The Gleaners and I. Directed by Agnès Varda, 2000. New York Zeitgeist Video, 2002.

Kings of Pastry. Directed by Frazer Pennebaker and Flora Lazar, 2009. New York First Run Features, 2011.

Man on Wire. Directed by James Marsh, 2008. United States Magnolia Home Entertainment, 2008.

Index

Acknowledgments

I'm so grateful to the many generous and patient people who supported this project in so many wonderful ways: Jeff Rogers, Mark and Cynthia Tronco, Steve Kocheran-Letrouit, Chris Horton, Emily Dilling, Kristen Beddard, Bryan Pirolli, Terresa Murphy, Jennifer Eric, Philippe Jedar, Bryan Pirolli, Anna Brones, Dr. Nina Roos, Dr. Cindy Davis, Elisabeth Lyman, Barbara Joly, Chris Charman, Andrew Dinh, Melissa Feineman, Claire Price, Catherine Plato, Louise Westmoreland, Isabelle Valentin, Mark Hulbert, Regis Vidal, and Fanny, my beloved dog. If I missed anyone, let me make it up to you over a glass of bubbly—my treat!

MOON LIVING ABROAD PARIS

Avalon Travel
a member of the Perseus Books Group
1700 Fourth Street
Berkeley, CA 94710, USA
www.moon.com

Editor: Sabrina Young
Copy Editor: Mary Calvez
Production and Graphics Coordinator:
  Lucie Ericksen
Cover Designer: Lucie Ericksen
Map Editor: Kat Bennett
Cartographers: Brian Shotwell, Stephanie
  Poulain, Kat Bennett
Indexer: Greg Jewett

ISBN-13: 978-1-61238-916-5
ISSN: 2373-3330

Printing History
1st Edition – December 2014
5 4 3 2 1

Front cover photo: Montmartre © Jon Arnold
Images Ltd/Alamy
Title page photo: Eiffel Tower © Iakov
Kalinin/123RF
Front matter photos: pg. 8: Notre Dame
cathedral and the Seine River © Ivan Bastien/
123RF; pg. 9: view from balcony of Notre
Dame cathedral © Sergey Krasikov/123RF; pg.
10 inset: Sacre-Coeur basilica in Montmartre
© nightman1965/123RF; bottom: detail of
the Alexandre III bridge © scaliger/123RF;
pg 11 top-left: booksellers on the left bank
© Kathryn Osgood; top-right: Luxembourg
gardens © Kathryn Osgood; bottom left:
street wine seller © Aurelia d'Andrea;
bottom-right: Grand Palais © Fat Tire Bike
Tours

Printed in Canada by Friesens

KEEPING CURRENT

Although we strive to produce the most up-to-date guidebook that we possibly can, change
is unavoidable. Between the time this book goes to print and the time you read it, the
cost of goods and services may have increased, and a handful of the businesses noted
in these pages will undoubtedly move, alter their prices, or close their doors forever.
Exchange rates fluctuate—sometimes dramatically—on a daily basis. Federal and local
legal requirements and restrictions are also subject to change, so be sure to check with
the appropriate authorities before making the move. If you see anything in this book that
needs updating, clarification, or correction, please drop us a line. Send your comments via
email to feedback@moon.com, or use the address above.